The Blackwell Guide to

Ancient Philosophy

——— Blackwell Philosophy Guides ———

Series Editor: Steven M. Cahn, City University of New York Graduate School

Written by an international assembly of distinguished philosophers, the *Blackwell Philosophy Guides* create a groundbreaking student resource – a complete critical survey of the central themes and issues of philosophy today. Focusing and advancing key arguments throughout, each essay incorporates essential background material serving to clarify the history and logic of the relevant topic. Accordingly, these volumes will be a valuable resource for a broad range of students and readers, including professional philosophers.

The Blackwell Guide to
Ancient Philosophy

Edited by

Christopher Shields

BLACKWELL PUBLISHING
350 Main Street, Malden, MA 02148-5020, USA
9600 Garsington Road, Oxford OX4 2DQ, UK
550 Swanston Street, Carlton, Victoria 3053, Australia

First published 2003 by Blackwell Publishing Ltd

4   2008

Library of Congress Cataloging-in-Publication Data

The Blackwell guide to ancient philosophy / edited by Christopher Shields.
        p. cm. — (Blackwell philosophy guides ; 13)
Includes bibliographical references and index.
        ISBN 978-0-631-22214-9 (alk. paper) — ISBN 978-0-631-22215-6 (pbk. : alk. paper)
        1. Philosophy, Ancient. I. Shields, Christopher. II. Series.
        B171 .B65 2003
        180—dc21

                                                                    2002006209

A catalogue record for this title is available from the British Library.

Set in 10/12.5pt Galliard
by Graphicraft Ltd, Hong Kong

The publisher's policy is to use permanent paper from mills that operate a sustainable forestry policy, and which has been manufactured from pulp processed using acid-free and elementary chlorine-free practices. Furthermore, the publisher ensures that the text paper and cover board used have met acceptable environmental accreditation standards.

For further information on
Blackwell Publishing, visit our website:
www.blackwellpublishing.com

Contents

Contents

Notes on Contributors

Robert Bolton is Professor of Philosophy at Rutgers University and author of numerous articles on Aristotle and other ancient authors. His most recent work explores the topic of Aristotle on the varieties of human understanding.

Thomas C. Brickhouse is Professor of Philosophy at Lynchburg College. He is the co-author (with Nicholas D. Smith) of the following: *Socrates on Trial* (Princeton and Oxford), *Plato's Socrates* (Oxford), *The Philosophy of Socrates* (Westview). He is also co-editor (with Nicholas D. Smith) of *The Trial and Execution of Socrates: Issues and Controversies* (Oxford).

Daniel Devereux is Professor of Philosophy at the University of Virginia. He is the author of many articles on Plato and Aristotle.

Lloyd P. Gerson is Professor of Philosophy at the University of Toronto. He is the author of many articles and books in Ancient Philosophy, including: *God and Greek Philosophy* (Routledge), *Plotinus* (Routledge), and *Knowing Persons: A Study in Plato* (Clarendon).

John Gibert is Associate Professor of Classics, University of Colorado at Boulder. He is the author of *Change of Mind in Greek Tragedy* (Vandenhoeck & Ruprecht), *Euripides: Ion* (Cambridge), and (with C. Collard and M. J. Cropp) *Euripides: Selected Fragmentary Plays II* (Aris & Phillips).

R. J. Hankinson is Professor of Philosophy, University of Texas at Austin. He is the author of many articles and books in Ancient Philosophy, including: *Cause and Explanation in Ancient Greek Thought* (Oxford) and *The Sceptics* (Routledge).

David Konstan is the John Rowe Workman Distinguished Professor of Classics and the Humanistic Tradition and Professor of Comparative Literature at Brown University. His many books include: *Some Aspects of Epicurean Psychology* (Brill), *Greek Comedy and Ideology* (Oxford), *Friendship in the Classical World* (Cambridge), and *Pity Transformed* (Duckworth).

Michael Loux is George Schuster Professor of Philosophy, University of Notre Dame. He is the author of *Substance and Attribute* (Reidel), *Primary Ousia* (Cornell), and *Metaphysics* (Routledge).

Gareth Matthews is Professor of Philosophy at the University of Massachusetts, Amherst. In addition to many articles in Ancient Philosophy, he is the author of *Socratic Perplexity and the Nature of Philosophy* (Oxford) and the editor of *Augustine, On the Trinity* (Cambridge).

Richard McKirahan is Edwin Clarence Norton Professor of Classics and Professor of Philosophy at Pomona College. He is the author of *Principles and Proofs: Aristotle's Theory of Demonstrative Science* and *Philosophy Before Socrates* (Hackett).

Fred D. Miller, Jr. is Professor of Philosophy and Executive Director of the Social Philosophy and Policy Center at Bowling Green State University. He has written many articles in Ancient Philosophy and is the author of *Nature, Justice and Rights in Aristotle's Politics* (Oxford).

Phillip Mitsis is A. S. Onassis Professor of Hellenic Culture and Civilization at New York University. He is author of *The Pleasures of Invulnerability: Epicurus' Ethical Theory* (Cornell).

Gerasimos Santas is Professor of Philosophy, University of California at Irvine. He has written on a wide range of topics in Ancient Philosophy. His books include: *Socrates: Philosophy in Plato's Early Dialogues* (Routledge), *Plato and Freud: Two Theories of Love* (Blackwell), and *Theories of Good: Plato, Aristotle, and the Moderns* (Blackwell).

Christopher Shields is Professor of Philosophy and Classics, University of Colorado at Boulder. He is the author of *Order in Multiplicity: Homonymy in the Philosophy of Aristotle* (Oxford), *Aristotle's De Anima: Translation and Commentary* (Oxford), *Classical Philosophy: A Contemporary Introduction* (Routledge), and (with Robert Pasnau) *The Philosophy of Thomas Aquinas* (Westview).

Allan Silverman is Professor of Philosophy at the Ohio State University. He is the author of *The Dialectic of Essence: A Study of Plato's Metaphysics* (Princeton).

Nicholas D. Smith is James F. Miller Professor of Humanities at Lewis & Clark College. He is co-author (with Thomas C. Brickhouse) of *Socrates on Trial* (Princeton and Oxford), *Plato's Socrates* (Oxford), *The Philosophy of Socrates* (Westview), and *Plato and the Trial of Socrates* (Routledge). He has also co-edited (with Thomas C. Brickhouse) *The Trial and Execution of Socrates: Issues and Controversies* (Oxford) and (with Paul Woodruff) *Reason and Religion in Socratic Philosophy* (Oxford).

Nicholas White is Professor of Philosophy, University of California at Irvine. He is the author of *Plato on Knowledge and Reality* (Hackett), and *Individual and Conflict in Greek Ethics* (Oxford).

Editor's Introduction

General Purpose and Intended Audience

This book guides students through more than a millennium of Western Philosophy, beginning with its earliest period in the sixth century BC and extending down what is conventionally regarded as the end of the ancient period, in the sixth century AD. As a guide, this volume contains authoritative yet accessible introductions to all of the principal figures and movements of this period. It begins with philosophy as it existed before the transformations wrought by Socrates and Plato, by reviewing the contributions of the Presocratics, the first philosophers, and the Sophists, a loosely knit group of intellectuals and teachers who did much to challenge what were until their arrival conventional patterns of thought and comfortable modes of moral decision making. It then turns to Socrates, Plato, and Aristotle, all towering figures active during Greece's Classical Period. Thereafter, it treats the primary Hellenistic Schools, whose works have received a welcome renaissance of interest over the last half-century: the Epicureans, Stoics, and Skeptics, both Academic and Pyrrhonist. It concludes, finally, in the Late Antique period with an overview of the difficult and sorely neglected philosophy of Neoplatonism.

Although intersecting in various ways, each chapter is free-standing and self-contained. This guide is not, therefore, a continuous intellectual history, conceived and executed from a single point of view. It is, instead, a presentation of the main developments and accomplishments of Ancient Philosophy, intended to serve both as an introduction to the novice and as a stimulus to further research and reflection for those already possessing some familiarity with the period. Throughout, the authors offer clear expositions of the positions advanced by the principal figures treated, together with varying amounts of critical assessment and evaluation. In different ways, each chapter invites the student first to understand the views it expounds and then to form an independent appraisal of their merits. Our ultimate hope is that this volume will serve as a springboard to advanced research in Ancient Philosophy, an activity the individual authors have all themselves found richly rewarding.

How to Use This Book

This book contains six main sections, divided, where appropriate, into subsections of more specialized natures. Students wishing to investigate a particular topic in Ancient Philosophy may therefore turn directly to the relevant chapter, though they are encouraged, if they have no experience at all of the period or figure in question, first to read the introduction at the head of the section in which their chosen chapter appears. These introductions aim to orient the novice by providing brief biographical and general background information. Students who do not yet have a particular topic in view are advised simply to begin by familiarizing themselves with the main periods and figures of Ancient Philosophy by reading this general introduction, together with section introductions, before turning to a specific topic of inquiry.

Scholars conventionally divide Ancient Philosophy into discrete periods. This volume employs the following main divisions:

1. Philosophy before Socrates
2. Socrates
3. Plato
4. Aristotle
5. Hellenistic Philosophy
6. Late Antique Philosophy

These divisions are intended to reflect pivotal moments of philosophical progress; the relative importance of individual contributors; the emergence of coordinated fields of inquiry and investigation; and, to some extent, broader historical trends and events. For the most part, though, these sections correspond to the sorts of divisions a student might well encounter in an undergraduate or early graduate curriculum. Such curricula are not arbitrary. On the contrary, they reflect settled patterns of presentation which in turn draw on a broad scholarly consensus regarding the central accomplishments of Ancient Philosophy.

Because our sources of evidence vary from period to period, we have in some cases considerable data in the form of continuous treatises, but in others only fragmentary material, often preserved in the form of direct quotations and paraphrases by early chroniclers and historians of philosophy. Where it is appropriate, individual authors focus on scholarly questions pertaining to matters of source and evidence; in other cases, because our sources are relatively full and secure, they pass over such matters in silence. In general, we have a wealth of material for Plato and Aristotle, fragmentary evidence for the Presocratics, Sophists, and Hellenistic Schools (where the evidence, though fragmentary, is extensive nonetheless), mixed sources for Late Antiquity, and disputed data for Socrates, who wrote little but engendered an entire genre of composition, the Socratic dialogue. In view of these facts, it has been possible to subdivide some of the main six sections into specialized subsections, in order to pursue well-supported topics of interest in greater depth. Thus, in particular, the sections on Plato and Aristotle each have four subsections dealing with central facets of their work. The divisions employed carve up their works in ways in which Plato and Aristotle themselves did not. This does no violence to their philosophy, which should, in any case, be experienced first hand by reading their own output. Instead, these divisions help direct their readers to salient substantive issues which continue to concern philosophers and other reflective thinkers today. Our view is that their views matter, and that we are likely to improve and refine our own thinking by taking their works seriously, as live philosophy, and not as exhibits in a museum of intellectual history.

At any rate, the bibliography contains recommendations for additional reading. For each section, there are first, and most importantly, primary texts in translation. Thereafter, there are included additional secondary sources for further study. The bibliographies do not aim at comprehensiveness. Rather, each recommends only those works to which a reader of this book might usefully turn after having exhausted what this guide has to offer. A general bibliography at the end of the volume contains additional works especially suited for student research. Again, though, our first impulse is to direct you to the primary sources themselves. These may be read and reread with profit many times over.

Part I

Philosophy before Socrates: Introduction

Philosophy before Socrates is piecemeal. We are left to discern the philosophical accomplishments of the earliest philosophers mainly from the reports of those who followed them, including, most notably, Aristotle, who was the first systematic historian of philosophy. So, we face formidable problems of interpretation. In the first instance, this means that we read today only fragments of what they actually wrote – snippets of works now long lost, wrenched from their original contexts and often quoted for plainly polemical purposes. Still, all is not lost. In some cases, we possess reasonably lengthy quotations; in others, it is possible to conjecture the likely positions of the earliest thinkers on the basis of paraphrases and reports whose primary purpose was the transmission of the views of the ancients to posterity, so that we can see directly, without inference, what they intended to maintain.

On the basis of the surviving evidence, it is reasonable to focus on two distinct groups of thinkers who are, if in very different ways, important for our understanding of the course taken by philosophy through the Classical and Hellenistic periods, and so, eventually, even into the Late Antique period. These are the *Presocratics* and the *Sophists*. The earliest philosophers included among the canonical Presocratics are those whom Aristotle called the natural philosophers (*physiologoi*) because of their tendency to identify the principles and causes of things in naturalistic terms (*Metaphysics* 983b6–984a4).[1] According to Aristotle, these thinkers differ in important ways from some of their own predecessors and contemporaries who propagated mythological explanations, which tended to be framed in terms of the often whimsical and utterly unpredictable activities of supernatural gods.

Others among the Presocratics engage in recognizably epistemological argumentation. From very early in its history, philosophy has been an intensely self-critical discipline. No sooner did the earliest natural philosophers ridicule the forms and standards of explanation implicit in mythology than they faced challenges to their own preferred idiom of naturalistic explanation, including challenges put by skeptics who sought to undercut *all* claims to human knowledge of any form. In the wake of such skeptical challenges came ever more sophisticated rejoinders, engendering a dialectic of skeptical challenge and response which persisted through the Hellenistic period and beyond.

McKirahan recounts the story of the earliest philosophers, emphasizing the ways in which their thought is at once philosophical and scientific. He not only describes their views, but suggests how they influenced subsequent generations of thinkers. For this reason, those altogether unfamiliar with the history of Ancient Philosophy will find his chapter an indispensable point of departure.

As McKirahan notes, the Presocratics were less concerned with social-political philosophy and ethics than were Socrates, Plato, and Aristotle. These later philosophers were not the first, however, to introduce speculation into these matters. On the contrary, they often found themselves in the position of responding to the views put forward by the Sophists, a loosely knit group of professional intellectuals and teachers active in Greece in the mid-fifth through the first quarter of the fourth centuries, a time of broad political and cultural upheaval. During this period, matters regarding which there had hitherto been broad forms of cultural consensus came in for intense questioning and scrutiny: the objectivity of value; the force and validity of custom, tradition, and law, both natural and conventional; the worth of higher education; the legitimacy of rhetorical persuasion within a democratic context; and, indeed, the legitimacy of Sophistry itself, especially insofar as it was conducted as a commercial enterprise. That is, the Sophists asked for – and received – handsome sums for the instruction they offered, mainly to the sons of socially prominent families with aspirations for political ascendancy.

As Gibert observes, attitudes regarding the Sophists divide rather sharply, today as in antiquity. Some view them as having had a liberating effect: their unapologetic refusal to defer to traditional mores helped usher in new forms of social awareness. Others, including to some extent both Plato and Aristotle, saw them as having a destabilizing, even pernicious effect: however right they may have been to question traditional modes of moral thinking (a critical activity embraced, after all, by both Plato and Aristotle), the Sophists seem self-serving in their easy and expedient refusal to provide grounded alternatives for the views they rejected. In particular, both Plato and Aristotle fault them for embracing naïve forms of relativism, thereby initiating a debate about the foundations of morality and science which remain with us even today.

That said, as Gibert rightly argues, it would be a mistake to adopt a monolithic attitude towards the Sophists, to treat them, that is, as if they themselves reached consensus about core philosophical concepts or rallied themselves around any sort of unifying credo. To begin, the problem of sources for them, as for the Presocratics, is especially acute. It is not always easy to ascribe determinate views with confidence to an individual Sophist. Moreover, insofar as it is possible to judge with confidence what a particular Sophist actually believed, it also becomes necessary to distinguish distinct and often incompatible positions among the strains generally understood as constituting "the Sophistic Movement." Gibert surveys both the question of sources and the broad range of positions falling under that general designation.

As McKirahan and Gibert both point out, an understanding of all of Ancient Philosophy begins with an appreciation of philosophy as it existed before Socrates.

They posed questions and challenges which the philosophers who followed them could not escape addressing.

Note

1 On using this form of citation to Aristotle's works, see Part IV, "Aristotle," n. 1.

Chapter 1

Presocratic Philosophy

Richard McKirahan

Preface

Greek philosophy began in the early sixth century BC in the Ionian city of Miletus, on the Aegean coast of Asia Minor. By the end of the fifth century it had made astonishing leaps in sophistication and had framed many of the issues that have remained central to philosophical investigation until today. This period is known, not altogether appropriately (since some of the most important "Presocratics" were contemporaries of Socrates), as the Presocratic era. The Presocratics stand at the beginning of the Greek and therefore of the entire Western philosophical tradition. In an important sense they were also the first scientists the Western world produced and their accomplishments in the study of nature are the direct ancestors of science as we know it. Since none of the writings of the Presocratics survives, our knowledge of the men and their ideas comes from other ancient sources which quote their actual words or summarize and sometimes criticize their theories, a situation which leaves room for differing interpretations. The thinkers discussed in this chapter were selected partly for their importance, partly because of the wide range of interests and the differing approaches they display, and partly because of the fascination they continue to have for people living two and a half millennia after their time.

Ionian Beginnings

Thales

Thales, we are told, predicted an eclipse of the sun that took place May 28, 585 BC. In addition to this astronomical feat, the ancients regarded him as the earliest Greek mathematician and attributed to him certain specific results in geometry. His declaration that water is the primary kind of material made him the founder of what was later called "natural philosophy." He is also said to have declared that all things are full of gods and that magnets have souls because they move iron. He gave military and engineering advice to King Croesus of Lydia, and political counsel to the Greek cities in Ionia. Later tradition also made him the first absent-minded professor, alleging that once he was so absorbed in looking at the heavens that he fell into a well.

How much of this is true we cannot be sure, because Thales was already a legendary figure by the time our information about him was being written and he would be just the person to attach discoveries to in order to establish a venerable pedigree for a discipline such as geometry. In fact, Thales is a shadowy figure many or all of whose claims to fame can be disputed, but who must have been a figure of great importance nevertheless, since there is no better way to account for the fact that so many different things are attributed to him. It is worth mentioning that Thales is said to have learned geometry in Egypt and that it is from Egypt too that he imported his doctrine that the earth floats on water; and if he actually did predict an eclipse of the sun, it can only have been on the basis of the astronomical records that had been kept in Babylon since 747 BC. It is possible, then, that the beginnings of Greek mathematical and scientific speculation owe a heavy debt to the older civilizations of Mesopotamia and the Nile, even though the Greeks developed these and other ideas in novel ways.

Thales' view that water is the primary kind of material has been interpreted as meaning that all things are somehow composed of water and, alternatively and perhaps more plausibly, that in the beginning (although no longer) there was only water, and that from the primeval moisture there developed the diversity of things present in the world today. His reasons for proposing this view are unknown (Aristotle, writing in the fourth century BC, was reduced to guesswork). It is also unknown whether he was following Egyptian mythology here or introducing a new way of thinking about the world, a way that is characteristic of later Presocratics and already prominent in Thales' immediate successors, according to which it is no longer the actions of anthropomorphic gods but the behavior of natural substances that account for the things and events in the world around us.

Anaximander

Thales was followed by two other Milesian thinkers, Anaximander and Anaximenes. Anaximander was regarded as Thales' successor in investigating nature, and Anaximenes as Anaximander's student and associate. Biographical information is practically nonexistent for these men, although we are told that Anaximander was sixty-four in the year 546 and that he travelled to Sparta, where he constructed some kind of sundial and predicted an earthquake. He is also said to be the first Greek to draw a map of the world and to have been the leader of a colony of Miletus on the Black Sea. Anaximander's range of interests was narrower than that of Thales, more closely confined to what we would call the scientific. He sketched an account of the origin and structure of the world and accounted for such phenomena as eclipses, thunder and lightning, and other meteorological events, as well as the origin of life. In connection with this last topic, he identified and offered a solution to a problem that arises in accounting for the origin of humans. Babies cannot fend for themselves, but need parents; but parents grew from babies. How did this cycle begin? Anaximander "declares that in the beginning humans were born from other kinds of animals, since other animals quickly manage on their own, and humans alone require lengthy nursing. For this reason, in the beginning they would not have been preserved if they had been like this." He "believed that there arose from heated water and earth either fish or animals very like fish. In these humans grew and were kept inside as embryos up to puberty. Then finally they burst and men and women came forth already able to nourish themselves."

Anaximander is best known for his view that the origin of the world is the *apeiron*, an eternal substance, boundlessly large and without any definite characteristics: neither hot nor cold, neither wet nor dry, neither white, black, nor any other color. Again, his reason for introducing such an unfamiliar origin for our world, in contrast to Thales' view that the origin of all things was water, can be reconstructed with some probability. The world around us is marked by contrasts: some parts of it are wet, others are dry, and so on. But if the origin of the world were wet, it is hard to account for the existence of anything that is not wet. The originating material must therefore not be either wet or dry, neither hot nor cold, and so on. It must, in fact, be indefinite (one English meaning of *apeiron*). Also, if it is the origin of everything, it cannot have a beginning itself: hence it is eternal. (The Greek philosophers are unanimous in supposing that anything that is without a beginning is also without an end.) And it must be boundlessly large ("boundless" is another meaning of *apeiron*) in order to be able to generate not only our world but also an indefinitely large number of other worlds that according to Anaximander come into existence and perish at different times and in different places.

What survives of Anaximander's account of how our world was formed goes as follows: "what arose from the eternal [i.e., the *apeiron*] and produces hot and cold was separated off at the coming to be of this world, and a kind of sphere of flame from this grew around the dark mist about the earth like bark about a tree. When it was broken off and enclosed in certain circles, the sun, moon and stars came to be." Anaximander gave the dimensions of our world: "the earth is cylindrical in shape, and its depth is one-third its breadth." "The sun is equal to the earth and the circle [on which] it is carried is twenty-seven times the size of the earth." "The circle of the sun is twenty-seven times [that of the earth] and that of the moon [eighteen times]." Particularly noteworthy here are the assumptions that the world has a simple geometrical structure and that the sizes and distances of the earth and the heavenly bodies are related by simple proportions, as well as the lack of any conceivable empirical basis for making these claims.

Anaximander also wrote the first surviving fragment of any Greek philosopher, an incomplete sentence that seems to describe how a variety of phenomena in our world, such as day and night, and the seasons, take place. "[The things that are perish into the things out of which they come to be,] according to necessity, for they pay penalty and retribution to each other for their injustice in accordance with the ordering of time." The bracketed words are most likely not to be Anaximander's, but the remainder, with its images of necessity, justice, and punishment, is apparently original, some of the very earliest surviving Greek prose. The picture is that of not just a world but an ordered world, a *kosmos*, in fact, which is characterized by regular processes of change and alternation (say, between hot and cold weather, or between daylight and darkness) that are governed by an impersonal judge, namely time, who guarantees that each contender holds sway to the right degree and for the appropriate duration. In fact, the talk of justice and punishment is unlikely to be a mere metaphor, but rather an expression of the widespread early view that there is no clear dividing line between humans and the rest of the world, that the same forces and processes that we experience in our human life are found elsewhere in the world as well, that man is a part of nature.

Anaximenes

Anaximenes too concerned himself with matters scientific. A less original thinker than Anaximander his best-known contribution is the view that the origin of all things and the fundamental form of matter is air. He was able to justify this divergence from Anaximander's compelling argument for an indefinite originative material by explaining how air (which is already a fairly indefinite material with few clear properties) changes form. "It differs in rarity and density according to the substances [it becomes]. Becoming finer it comes to be fire; being condensed it comes to be wind, then cloud, and when still further condensed it becomes water, then earth, then stones, and the rest come to be out of these." By means of becoming more dense and more rare, air changes into different forms just as water changes into ice and steam, "and the rest come out of these" – the remaining substances are formed through combinations of the different forms of air. Anaximenes held that other qualities depend on rarity and density, hot and cold for example: "a person releases both hot and cold from his mouth, for the breath becomes cold when compressed and condensed by the lips, and when the mouth is relaxed, the escaping breath becomes warm through the rareness." In addition, air, which constitutes our soul or principle of life, "holds us together and controls us" and it plays a similar role in the context of the *kosmos* as well, surrounding it, pervading it and keeping everything in its right place and functioning in the appropriate way. Bearing in mind the remarks made above concerning justice and punishment in Anaximander's fragment, we are able to infer that for Anaximenes not only humans and animals, but the *kosmos* as a whole is a living thing.

Xenophanes

One of the most unexpected features of early Greek philosophy is the way it accounts for the origin and functioning of the world in naturalistic terms. No more are the gods of Greek mythology responsible for events in the world; rather it is substances like water, air, and the *apeiron*, and processes and events like separation, condensation, and rarefaction that make things happen. Moreover, the world is seen as a place of order rather than chaos, where natural laws, not the capricious desires and rivalries of personified gods hold sway. The implicit criticism of the Olympians and the ways of accounting for phenomena in the world that are based on belief in such gods became explicit in the poetry of Xenophanes (c. 570 to after 478 BC). Xenophanes was born in Colophon, another Ionian city of Asia Minor, and spent much of his life as a bard, travelling from city to city and singing the poems of Homer and others, including himself, for his supper. Two of his most famous fragments (about forty survive) challenge the anthropomorphic view which the Greeks had of their gods:

> Ethiopians say that their gods are flat-nosed and dark,
> Thracians that theirs are blue-eyed and red-haired. (frag. 16)

> If oxen and horses and lions had hands
> and were able to draw with their hands and do the same things as men,
> horses would draw the shapes of gods to look like horses
> and oxen to look like oxen, and each would make the
> gods' bodies have the same shape as they themselves had. (frag. 15)

There is no good reason other than vanity or limited imagination to suppose that the gods look like Greeks, or the larger than life and more beautiful Greeks that we see in the artwork that survives from ancient Greece. Not that Xenophanes or his Milesian forebears were atheists. Anaximander's *apeiron* was divine, as was Anaximenes' air. And Xenophanes sketches his own view about the divine:

> God is one, greatest among gods and men,
> not at all like mortals in body or thought. (frag. 23)

> He always remains in the same place, moving not at all,
> nor is it fitting for him to go to different places at different times. (frag. 26)

> All of him sees, all of him thinks, all of him hears. (frag. 24)

> But without effort he shakes all things by the thought of his mind. (frag. 25)

It is disputed whether fragment 23 means that Xenophanes believed in a single god, or a god supreme among others, but it is clear that there is only one god who controls the events of the world, and he does so not through physical means but by his thought or will. It is also clear what Xenophanes' criterion was for determining the nature of god: what "is fitting," that is to say, what he, a mere human thinking for himself, judged appropriate for the ruler of the universe to be like. For instance, the activities of the Olympian gods are not fitting for a true divinity, as the following fragment indicates:

> Homer and Hesiod have ascribed to the gods all deeds
> which among men are a reproach and a disgrace:
> thieving, adultery, and deceiving one another. (frag. 11)

Rejecting the Olympians in this way was a revolutionary move in more than one way. It meant changing beliefs, but more profoundly it meant changing attitude as well. No longer is cultural tradition (embodied preeminently in the poetry of Homer and Hesiod) seen as an unquestionable source of truth. Rational criteria replace tradition as a way of justifying beliefs, and the world becomes different. There is a rational order to it, and knowledge of it can be attained: a rational god rules it and as rational beings we can for the first time hope to understand how it works.

To Xenophanes too we owe the beginnings of reflection on the difficulty of finding out the truth and of the skeptical tradition that knowledge cannot be attained, as the following fragments show:

By no means did the gods reveal all things to mortals from the beginning,
but in time, by searching, they discover better (frag. 18)

No man has seen nor will anyone know
the truth about the gods and all the things I speak of.
For even if a person should in fact say what is absolutely the case,
nevertheless, he himself does not know, but fashions belief over all things (frag. 34)

The first of these fragments is a statement of the possibility of discovery through research, whereas the latter, while distinguishing between truth, knowledge, and belief, denies the possibility of absolute knowledge, at least about the kinds of difficult and remote topics that were the concern of Xenophanes and the other Ionian philosophers of the sixth century.

Conclusions

Most of the subjects treated by the earliest philosophers would nowadays be considered scientific, not philosophical. The origin of the world, its composition and present structure, how it functions, how life arose – these are topics in astronomy, physics, meteorology, biology. And discussions of the nature of the divine are more at home in theology than philosophy. On the other hand, Xenophanes, who is clearly a member of the Ionian tradition of thought, first raised questions that are still with us in epistemology, and these were questions that would naturally arise for a thoughtful person engaged in the critical work that is characteristic of the early thinkers.

One of philosophy's historical roles has been to serve as the source of other disciplines. For example, psychology was considered a part of philosophy until the late nineteenth century, and only when it developed its own distinctive methods was it acknowledged as a separate subject. Science too was commonly called natural philosophy until the eighteenth century. From this perspective, it is not surprising that no distinction was made in theory or in practice between science and philosophy in the very beginning, and it is an artificial and anachronistic project to distinguish the philosophical from the scientific side of the Presocratics.

Aside from their particular views, though, many of which from our point of view may have little or no relevance to philosophy, there is a common feature of their approach that is evidently original with them and which is still very much characteristic of philosophy. I call this feature rational criticism. Each of the thinkers we have considered reflected on current ideas and the views of his predecessors. They identified objections and produced new theories immune to those objections. They rejected theories because they failed to fit observed facts or because they did not satisfy rational criteria. Theories were not accepted or rejected through mysterious processes controlled by a few privileged individuals, but were accessible to all and the grounds for accepting and rejecting them were publicly stated – because the standard for acceptance was "what is fitting" rather than what tradition says or what the gods approve. The practice of rational criticism led in the initial stages to rapid advance, with each successive theory improving in certain respects on its predecessor. Traditional mythological accounts were speedily eliminated from this kind of discourse since mythology and authority based simply on the familiarity of long tradition are not in position to withstand critical scrutiny or to mount a rational defense.

Another feature the speculations of these early thinkers have in common with philosophy as we know it today is that many of the theories that were proposed are not easily open to refutation on empirical grounds. It would be hard to imagine what kind of data could be brought to refute the view (possibly Thales') that water was the origin of all things, or (Anaximander's) that the world had its beginning in some *apeiron* substance, or (Anaximenes') that all kinds of things are compounds of fire, air, wind, and so forth, or (Xenophanes') that all events in the world are governed by a divinity that is "not at all like mortals in body or thought." They were accepted or rejected on grounds of rational plausibility, not because they were hypotheses confirmed by evidence, much less the experimental method. In fact, in the entire history of ancient science we find very little use of the experimental method as we understand it, although in some cases, such as Anaximenes' observation that the temperature of our breath is affected by whether we exhale rapidly or slowly, observational evidence is brought to bear, sometimes with imagination and sophistication. And this is only to be expected, since one of the primary goals of these men was to understand important observed features of the world that surrounds us.

The remainder of this chapter will focus on three Presocratic philosophers of very different stripes. All of them share with the first philosophers a serious interest in the nature and structure of the physical world, but their thought ranges more widely, and as we shall see, the elements in it that are recognizably philosophical soon come to the foreground.

Heraclitus

Born a generation later than the thinkers so far considered, Heraclitus (c. 540–480 BC) of Ephesus, a Greek city located not far from Miletus, was an arrogant and enigmatic figure who broadened the scope of enquiry from cosmology, the principal pursuit of the early Ionians, to include matters more properly considered philosophical. Over 120 original fragments survive from his book, most of them short and pithy sayings whose precise meanings are unclear (in antiquity Heraclitus was known as "the obscure") and whose significance and interconnections are left for us to discover. Heraclitus expressed views on many subjects, including the faults of earlier and contemporary writers from Homer to Pythagoras and Xenophanes, and the stupidity of ordinary people. He had positive views on cosmology but also on matters concerned with ethics, politics, and religious practices, and also on the nature of god and of the soul or mind. In addition he had much to say on how and how not to go about inquiring into the true nature of things. But the most striking ideas of Heraclitus are more general and underlie all his work. His fundamental principles are encapsulated in the following words:

> This *logos* holds always, but people always prove unable to understand it, both before they hear it and when they have first heard it. For even though all things happen in accordance with this *logos*, people show their lack of experience when they experience such words and deeds as I set out, distinguishing each one in accordance with its nature and saying how it is. (frag. 1)

> Listening not to me but to the *logos* it is wise to agree that all things are one. (frag. 50)

> Things taken together are whole and not whole, something being brought together and brought apart, in tune and out of tune; out of all things there comes a unity, and out of a unity all things. (frag. 10)

Heraclitus claims to have made a great discovery, one that accounts for no less than absolutely everything that is and that comes to pass in the world. It is a single principle, which he calls *logos*, that holds completely generally and explains all things and all events. Except for Heraclitus and despite his efforts to teach it, no one understands the principle, a (or the) primary implication of which he states at the end of fragment 10: "out of all things there comes a unity and out of a unity all things." The world is a single dynamic whole made up of many things related to one another in various ways. We need to understand both the many and the one: how the one world works and how the many things in it work as well, and to do so involves understanding that the many things are interrelated in many and unexpected ways, and understanding that they work together, not each on its own, and how they do so; likewise it involves understanding how the world is a unity composed of many parts and how each part contributes to the whole. Two case studies of this one–many relation appear in the following fragment:

> They do not understand how, being at variance with itself, it agrees with itself. It is a backwards-turning attunement like that of the bow and lyre. (frag. 51)

In order to function, bows and lyres require their strings to be stretched. Otherwise no arrows will be shot, no music played. Two things happen simultaneously in order for the tension ("being at variance") in the string to occur: the wood must be pulling on the string and the string must be pulling on the wood – and the pulling must be equal, or either the string will snap or the wood will break. Consider the bow as simply a piece of wood and a string, and you cannot understand what makes it work, what makes the wood and string *a bow*. It is their special mutual relationship of balanced tension that accounts for their working together as a functioning bow. On the other hand, the tension by itself does not make up the bow, because the tension cannot exist without the wood and the string. Once we understand how the bow works, we also have a better understanding of its components. The wood and string are no longer just wood and string, but things with properties that enable them to work together in certain specified ways. While the bow and the lyre are typical of how things in the world work, they also represent the world as a whole.

Heraclitus employed other familiar phenomena as well to illustrate his "one and many" doctrine. Several of his examples are based on things that are opposites of one another, presumably because opposites would seem to be obvious counter-examples to the principle of "all things are one." The most elaborated of these examples is the following:

> The sea is the purest and most polluted water; to fishes drinkable and bringing safety,
> to humans undrinkable and destructive. (frag. 61)

Here the opposites are the superlatives "purest" and "most polluted," and Heraclitus' insight is that one and the same thing can have both properties – as long as it has them in relation to different kinds of living things. In fact, the two properties go hand in hand: an environment that is "purest" for fishes must be "most polluted" for humans, and this tells us something important not only about those two opposite properties, but also about seawater and about fishes and humans as well.

It is important to point out that Heraclitus never states simply that any pair of opposites is "the same." He always gives examples, and he states them so as to make clear how to resolve the apparent paradox. Indeed, as soon as we identify any such paradox in the world we must already have solved it. Also, the way Heraclitus states these apparent paradoxes makes it clear that he is using them as teaching devices to illustrate the workings of the *logos* in the world, so that we can gain experience in understanding how the world works and in due course go on to conduct our own investigations. When we fully understand the world (if we ever do), we will also understand everything in the world and how it all fits together and works together to make up the world. And despite the apparent diversity and discord, or rather *because of* it, we will understand how the world is a harmonious whole.

Such a message is open to attack on two fronts. First, it may seem too general to have any concrete content: nothing could possibly count as disproof of the claim, so the claim tells us nothing in particular about the world. Second, it may seem to counsel a kind of blind and fatuous idleness and optimism in the face of the world's disasters: everything fits together to make a harmonious world, so don't try to change how things are and don't be distressed by misfortune because it is all part of a happy bigger picture. As to the first objection, we should begin by recalling that even if it is valid, Heraclitus fares no worse on this count than the other thinkers we have considered, whose theories were, as noted above, not easily open to empirical tests. But more important is that Heraclitus put forward this general principle as something that can be confirmed, and confirmed only with effort, imagination, and dedication:

> Men who are lovers of wisdom must be inquirers into many things indeed. (frag. 35)

> Unless he hopes for the unhoped for, he will not find it, since it is not to be hunted out and is impassible. (frag. 18)

The enquiry needed to discover the workings of the principle in the world is partly empirical, partly introspective:
> All that can be seen, heard, experienced – these are what I prefer. (frag. 55)

> I searched myself. (frag. 101)

and few are able to carry it out:
> Eyes and ears are bad witnesses to people if they have souls that do not understand the language. (frag. 107)

> For many, in fact all that come upon them, do not understand such things, nor when they have noticed them do they know them, but they seem to themselves to do so. (frag. 17)

> They are at odds with the *logos*, with which above all they are in continuous contact, and the things they meet every day appear strange to them. (frag. 72)

He offered many examples of how the *logos* applies in widely differing situations, and made it plain that some phenomena are difficult to explain.
> Nature loves to hide. (frag. 123)

> The Lord whose oracle is at Delphi neither speaks nor conceals, but gives a sign. (frag. 93)

Further, the proper explanations will appear confusing to those who do not understand (frag. 1, quoted above). He even suggests that we should devote our lives to understanding the principle:

> Wisdom is one thing, to be skilled in true judgment, how all things are steered through all things. (frag. 41)

Right thinking is the greatest excellence, and wisdom is to speak the truth and act in accordance with nature, while paying attention to it. (frag. 112)

As to the second objection raised above, we should first notice that the counsel to understand and accept one's place in the world and not fight against destiny need not be shallow and need not be intended as comforting, as the following fragments (which are probably intended to convey symbolic as well as literal meanings) indicate:

It is necessary to know that war is common and justice is strife and that all things happen in accordance with strife and necessity. (frag. 80)

War is the father of all and king of all, and some he shows as gods, others as humans; some he makes slaves, others free. (frag. 53)

And Heraclitus is explicit that some things are worth striving for.
The people must fight for the law as for their city wall. (frag. 44)

It belongs to all people to know themselves and to think rightly. (frag. 116)

The best renounce all for one thing, the eternal fame of mortals, but the many stuff themselves like cattle. (frag. 29)

In concentrating on the one – many principle this brief sketch has omitted many important aspects of Heraclitus' thought. I will mention three very briefly, first the prominence of fire:

The *kosmos*, the same for all, none of the gods nor of humans has made, but it was always and is and shall be: an ever-living fire being kindled in measures and being extinguished in measures. (frag. 30)

All things are an exchange for fire and fire for all things, as goods for gold and gold for goods. (frag. 90)

These and other fragments establish that fire is the basic material of the world in somewhat the same way as air was for Anaximenes. But fire has an active, violent nature absent from the material principles of Heraclitus' predecessors which makes it more suitable for directing and controlling events in a dynamically active world:

For fire will advance and judge and convict all things. (frag. 66)

Thunderbolt steers all things. (frag. 64)

Second, the river fragments:

Upon those who step into the same rivers, different and again different waters flow. (frag. 12)

It is not possible to step twice into the same river. (frag. 91)

As the basis of the doctrine of "Heraclitean flux," that there is no stability in the world but all things are constantly changing in all respects, the second of these statements has enjoyed a great deal of attention from the time of Plato, who discussed it critically in his dialogues *Cratylus* and *Theaetetus*. However, many scholars believe that fragment 91 is unauthentic, a misremembered and misquoted version of fragment 12, which has the appearance of a typical Heraclitean fragment on the unity of opposites (here "same" and "different") and in which there is no difficulty about stepping more than once into the same river.

Third, two puzzling fragments about the soul, which may show that Heraclitus had grasped the paradoxical nature of self-consciousness.

You would not discover the limits of the soul although you travelled every road: it has so deep a *logos*. (frag. 45)

The soul has a self-increasing *logos*. (frag. 115)

Parmenides

Parmenides (c. 515 to after 450 BC) and Zeno (born c.490), both from Elea, a Greek city in southern Italy, together with Melissus (probably a little younger than Zeno), from the Aegean island of Samos, are known as the exponents of a new style of philosophy called Eleatic after the birthplace of its founder. The two principal innovations of Eleatic philosophy are its use of deductive argument and its subject matter. Until this time, as far as we can tell, the Greek philosophers had presented their theories without arguing for them. The Milesians told "likely stories" about how the world came into being and how it functions, and even though we can detect some ways in which one account might be thought more likely than another, and can construct arguments they might have used to show the superiority of their views over others, there is in fact no trace of argument in the source materials. Even Xenophanes' attacks on traditional views of the gods are not stated in the form of arguments, although we can supply the additional premises needed to reach the conclusions he intended, and Heraclitus' brief and frequently cryptic pronouncements are devoid of the logical connective tissue found in philosophy from Parmenides onward.

One reason why the Eleatics may have chosen to employ arguments is that their views needed this kind of support because they go so strongly against what people deeply believe. A basic characteristic of deductive reasoning, in which one or more premises are stated and a conclusion is declared to follow from them, is that if we believe that the premises are true and if we also believe that the conclusion does follow from the premises, then we have no choice but to accept the conclusion as true. Consequently, while referring to an obvious fact of experience will tend to convince people, and while telling a story may be sufficient to recommend it to people who find it likely, when what we want to maintain directly conflicts with our audience's experience and well-established beliefs, simply asserting our view will probably not make them change their minds. They will need to be convinced, and a well-constructed argument, whose premises they cannot fault and whose reasoning they find impeccable or at least irrefutable, is an excellent tool for this purpose.

In what follows I shall consider only Parmenides, the founder of Eleatic philosophy and the most important of its proponents. Melissus used different arguments for mostly the same conclusions as Parmenides, and Zeno constructed arguments, most famously the one known as "Achilles and the Tortoise," that supported Parmenides by showing that the deep-set beliefs which make us hostile to Parmenides' conclusions in fact are riddled with contradictions: If Achilles gives the tortoise a head start in a race, he must first reach the point from which the tortoise started, by which time the tortoise has gone some (smaller) distance ahead, and by the time Achilles has reached that point, the tortoise has again gone ahead some (even smaller) distance. Thus the tortoise must always be some distance ahead, so that Achilles can never catch it.

In a carefully constructed sequence of arguments Parmenides claims to prove the following theses: there is no coming to be or perishing, no change or motion; what is has all possible parts and attributes; it is undivided and continuous; only one thing exists; only one thought or statement is intelligible: "it is"; consequently, our senses are wholly misleading and our ordinary ways of thinking and talking are false, incoherent, and incomprehensible.

Interestingly, Parmenides presents his philosophy as truth revealed to him by a goddess and sets forth his arguments in the epic meter of the Homeric *Iliad* and *Odyssey*, which had connotations of solemnity and authority. While we may regard these features of his writing as mere rhetorical ploys and irrelevant to the philosophical content of the work and to the soundness of the arguments, we will do well to remember that Parmenides' hearers and readers were unfamiliar with the use of argument in philosophy, and Parmenides will have done well to emphasize the seriousness which his arguments were put forth and the almost divine binding power of sound argument.

The poem has three parts: an introduction (frag. 1) which tells of Parmenides' mystical journey to the goddess and her promise to reveal to him "all things – both the unshaken heart of persuasive truth and the opinions of mortals, in which there is no true reliance" (frag. 1, lines 28–30), which is followed by sections on each of these two headings, the Way of Truth (frags. 2–7 and frag. 8, lines 1–49) and the Way of Mortal Opinions (frag. 8, lines 50–61 and frags. 9–18). It is a matter of dispute why Parmenides wrote the Way of Mortal Opinions, which contained an account of the origin and functioning of the world that is along the lines of other Presocratic accounts of these phenomena, since he declares it to be deceitful and fundamentally mistaken (frag. 8, lines 52–3).

The rest of this discussion will concentrate on the Way of Truth, of which many think almost all (we have almost eighty lines) has survived. The goddess begins (frag. 2) by identifying "the only ways of inquiry there are to think." The first is "the path of persuasion (for it attends upon truth)" and it is described as the way "that it is and that it is not possible for it not to be." The second way, "that it is not and that it is necessary for it not to be," is "a path completely unlearnable." In fragment 6 we find that the subject of these clauses is "that which is there to be spoken and thought of." The claim, then, is that anything that is an appropriate subject of thought and speech is and must be, and conversely that it is impossible to conceive of or to express in language that which is not and which cannot be. And this claim is based on the short and difficult argument that goes as follows:

> That which is there to be spoken and thought of must be. For it is possible for it to be, but not possible for nothing to be. I bid you consider this. For I bar your way from this first way of inquiry. (frag. 6, lines 1–3)

Parmenides holds that what is not cannot be coherently thought of. Any account of reality that makes mention of or depends in any way on what is not is thereby proved unacceptable. In deducing his account of the nature of reality, Parmenides applies this principle time and again:

> But the decision about these matters lies in this:
> it is or it is not. But it has been decided, as is necessary,
> to let go the one way as unthinkable and nameless (for it is not
> a true way) and that the other is and is real. (frag. 8, lines 15–18)

This consideration also tells against another way of inquiry, which is the way of thinking we ordinarily employ:

> but next [I bar your way from] the way on which mortals, knowing nothing,
> two-headed, wander. For helplessness
> in their breasts guides their wandering mind. But they are carried on
> equally deaf and blind, amazed, hordes without judgment,
> for whom both to be and not to be are judged the same and
> not the same, and the path of all is backward-turning. (frag. 6, lines 4–9)

We mortals think in a confused way, one that combines the two paths previously identified. In ways we will see below, our normal way of thinking and talking involves reference to what is not, and so by Parmenides' principle it is not a possible way to follow.

In the lengthy fragment 8 we find the arguments that establish the true nature of reality. Parmenides identifies "signs exceedingly many" on the only path that is left to pursue. The "signs," or attributes that any existing thing has, are the following:

being ungenerated it is also imperishable,
whole and of a single kind and unshaken and complete.
Nor was it ever nor will it be, since it is now, all together,
one, continuous. (frag. 8, lines 3–6)

In this way Parmenides asserts that anything we can coherently think of or speak of exists, but also that it did not come to be and will not cease to be (he argues this in lines 6–21). Further, it is undivided, unique, changeless and uniform (lines 22–5), motionless (lines 26–33), and to it belong whatever attributes can be coherently conceived to apply to anything (lines 22–5, 42–9). The lines quoted above, then, set the agenda for most of the remainder of the Way of Truth.

Further, some of the arguments may be systematically related to one another. The argument at lines 22–5 seems to take as its premise the conclusion of lines 6–21, that there is no generation or perishing; motionlessness, argued for in lines 26–33, follows from changelessness, proved in lines 22–5. However, Parmenides' obscure language makes it unclear how far this line of interpretation can be maintained.

To turn to some of the actual arguments, coming to be is eliminated in a series of arguments, one of which runs as follows:

For what birth will you seek for it?
How and from where did it grow? I will not permit you to say
or to think that it grew from what is not; for it is not be said or thought
that it is not. (frag. 8, lines 6–9)

Since perishing can be eliminated by parallel reasoning it follows that what is did not come to be and will not be destroyed. Parmenides likewise argues that what is is undivided, continuous, and complete in the sense that it has all possible parts and attributes:

It is right for what is to be not incomplete;
for it is not lacking; if it were lacking, it would lack everything. (frag. 8, lines 32–3)

If it lacked some part or attribute, a description of it would require mentioning what is not. It follows also that there is only one thing, since if there were more than one, each of them would have some attributes that the others lack (e.g., being here rather than there, or being this thing rather than another). For similar reasons what is cannot change, since change would involve acquiring or losing some part or attribute, or move, since motion would imply moving from where it is to where it is not, and yet since there is only one thing it is identical with its place:

Remaining the same in the same and by itself it lies
and so stays there fixed; for mighty Necessity
holds it in the bonds of a limit, which pens it in all round. (frag. 8, lines 29–31)

Perhaps the most difficult point in this extraordinarily difficult text is the claim that only one thought is possible, "it is."

> Thinking and the thought that it is are the same.
> For not without what is, in which it is expressed,
> will you find thinking; for nothing else either is or will be
> except that which is, since Fate shackled it
> to be whole and unchanging; wherefore it has been named all names
> mortals have established, persuaded that they are true –
> to come to be and to perish, to be and not to be,
> and to change place and alter bright color. (frag. 8, lines 34–41)

This too depends on the principle stated above. Ordinary thinking and language are unreliable, since they contain such illegitimate words and concepts as "change," "coming to be" and "is not." But this is only the beginning. Thinking and talking about ordinary physical objects are eliminated because such things cannot exist since they are thought to undergo change, to have different parts, and the like. And the same holds for the attributes ordinarily ascribed to such things. Contrastive terms such as colors, numbers and shapes cannot be admitted into the proper language, since being yellow involves not being red, being square involves not being round, being three involves not being two, and so on.

The conclusion of Parmenides' reasoning is that there is only one possible thing and only one possible thought, which is expressed in only one word, *esti*, the Greek word translated "it is." Any other thought or expression in language would inevitably involve reference, directly or indirectly, to what is not. Other thoughts we have are illusions; other words we use are nonsense; the world we see about us does not exist as such. Since our belief that it does is founded on the reports of our senses, it follows that our senses are systematically and grossly deceptive, since they tell us that the world contains many things, and that those things are different from one another and change and move and pass into and out of existence. But, Parmenides warns us in words that may reflect the strenuous resistance his arguments evidently encountered, reason should prevail over the senses; since the senses are fallible and can lead us astray, our criterion for truth should be founded not on them but on arguments that stand up to critical examination:

> Do not let habit born from much experience compel you along this way
> to direct your sightless eye and sounding ear and tongue,
> but judge by reason the heavily contested refutation
> spoken by me. (frag. 7, lines 3–6)

Fifth-Century Atomism

The Eleatic legacy to philosophy and science consisted in a "heavily contested refutation" of our ordinary ways of thinking about the world, and the immediate task for philosophy and science was to meet this challenge one way or another. In order to establish the reality of the world we experience and to give an acceptable account of that world, it was necessary either to refute Parmenides' arguments or to find an acceptable way around them. No one challenged his reasoning, but the alternative approach was undertaken in the following generation by Empedocles, by Anaxagoras, and by Leucippus and Democritus, who were the first proponents of the ancient atomic theory. All of these thinkers accepted some Eleatic claims – notably that nothing can be generated out of sheer nonbeing and that something that is cannot perish into sheer nonbeing either. On the other hand, they all denied the Eleatic theses that there is only one thing in existence and that motion cannot exist. They all distinguished between two realms of reality, which we can call the basic realm and the phenomenal realm. The phenomenal realm is the world we see around us, which includes plurality, change, motion, coming to be and perishing, while the basic realm consists of other entities – atoms and void for Democritus, fire, air, water, and earth for Empedocles, an apparently unlimited variety of stuffs and attributes for Anaxagoras. At the basic level we have entities that are not created nor destroyed and that in other ways satisfy to a lesser or greater degree the conditions the Eleatics established for existing things. The phenomenal world is then accounted for in terms of the behavior of the basic entities. The rest of this section will explore fifth-century atomism, which in addition to being the ancestor of modern atomic theory claims our interest for its own sake as a particularly successful reply to the Eleatics and as the first attempt to work out the fine details of a physical system, as opposed to sketching out a theory in broad strokes.

Leucippus is said to be the inventor of the atomic theory. It seems that he expounded it in general terms and used it to account for the origin and present constitution of the world in a typical Presocratic manner. Democritus accepted the theory and used it to explain a wide variety of natural phenomena. He wrote many works (we have the titles of about seventy) which were on topics as diverse as mathematics, meteorology, the mind, and music, and many of which presumably explained their subject matter in terms of the behavior of atoms. More fragments attributed to Democritus survive than do for any other Presocratic philosopher, but most of them have to do with ethics and their genuineness is uncertain as well as what relation they have (if any) to the atomic theory.

The atomic theory is based on the idea that things in the phenomenal world are composed of tiny, indivisible bodies called atoms, which move in the void. In Greek, *atomos* means "uncuttable." There are an infinite number of atoms which differ from one another only in size and shape. Some are spherical, others have rough edges, others hooks, and so on. There are an unlimited number of shapes, on the grounds that there is no more reason for them to have any one shape than any other. They are ungenerated, indestructible, and unchanging. They are too small to see. They are solid but have no color nor other qualities. They are all made of the same stuff. In between atoms is void or emptiness, which allows them to preserve their identity. (If there were no void between atoms, they would unite to form one atom, which would violate the ban on generation and destruction at the atomic level.) The atoms move through the void. As they move they sometimes bump into one another and when this happens they sometimes intertwine: their hooks become entangled or their rough edges interlock. When this happens they form a compound. When enough atoms combine in these ways the compound is big enough to be visible. Unlike their constituent atoms, compounds are generated, and they perish when struck by other compounds or atoms in such a way as to undo the tangling of atoms that holds them together. Also compounds have qualities such as colors and textures, on account of the arrangements of their atoms, and compounds can undergo change, as they take on or lose atoms or as the atoms that make them up are rearranged. In this way the observed features of the phenomenal world are accounted for in terms of the unobserved features of the atoms and void, and this constitutes the basis of the atomists' answer to the Eleatics.

However, even at the atomic level, the theory as stated violates several tenets of Eleatic philosophy. It is fundamental to atomism that there be many atoms and that they move, but the Eleatics had argued that there is no motion and no plurality. Also the atomists held that there are two basically different kinds of entities: atoms and void. Where the Eleatics had argued that anything that exists has all possible attributes, the atomists held that atoms have attributes that void lacks and vice versa. Atoms are "full" or solid, while void is "empty"; atoms are "compact" while void is "rare." And worst of all from the Eleatic point of view, atoms are called "what is" and "being" while void is called "what is not," "not-being" and "nothing." Where Parmenides had asserted that "it is not possible for nothing to be," the atomists said that what is is no more than what is not, because void is no less than atoms are. In fact, this last point of disagreement is the key to the atomists' response to the Eleatics because it is the void that permits the motion and the plurality of atoms, so the disagreement reduces to the single question whether the void (alias what is not) can be. And the interesting point here is that the nonexistence of what is not is no more and no less fundamental to Parmenides' arguments than its existence is to the atomic theory. As we have seen, Parmenides bases much of his argumentation on this principle, but the principle itself is (as is appropriate for a basic principle) undefended, only asserted. In these circumstances the atomists had a free hand to construct a system based on its denial. If they could construct a coherent system that accounts for the phenomenal world, that would constitute a positive reason to accept that system and to reject the implausible rival views of the Eleatics. Moreover, they did offer positive arguments that void (alias nothing) exists, the most interesting of which is simply

> There is no more reason for the thing to be than the nothing. (Democritus, frag. 156)

Among the phenomena the atomists treated were sensory qualities, which they accounted for in ways that may appear crude to us but which show how this theory could be applied to the phenomenal world. "Some bodies come to be hot and fiery – those composed of rather sharp and minute primary bodies situated in a similar position, while others come to be cold and watery – those composed of the opposite kinds of bodies." "He makes sweet that which is round and good-sized; astringent that which is large, rough, polygonal, and not rounded; sharp tasting, as its name indicates, that which is sharp in body, and angular, bent and not rounded." "Iron is hard and lead is heavier, since iron has its atoms arranged unevenly and has large quantities of void in many places, while lead has less void but its atoms are arranged evenly throughout. This is why it is heavier but softer than iron." "We see that the same continuous body is sometimes liquid and sometimes solid – not suffering this change by means of separation and combination or by turning and touching as Democritus says; for it did not become solid from liquid by being transposed or changing its nature." There are four basic colors: white, black, red, and yellow. Black, for example, is produced by atoms that are rough, uneven and irregular, red by the same kinds of atoms that produce heat, but larger.

Democritus declared that a human being is a small world, a *mikros kosmos*, and treated this "microcosm" as just one more compound of atoms and void. The soul, which for the Greeks was above all the principle of life, that whose presence distinguishes the living from the nonliving, was composed of tiny spherical atoms which caused vital motions by their great mobility. Like other compounds, the soul can be destroyed, and this is what occurs upon the death of the animal. Democritus also developed a way to account for sensation and thought by means of the theory. Physical objects constantly emit films of atoms that go in all directions. Those which hit our sense organs may interact with the organs to produce sensation. Atoms of certain sizes and shapes will affect the eye and lead us to see the object; atoms of other sizes and shapes will affect the ear, the nose, and so forth. Likewise thought "takes place when images enter from outside" – presumably films of atoms that are of a different size and shape again. Dreams were explained similarly. Again, the naiveté of these accounts may make us smile, but they are important as the first attempt to explore a materialistic theory of cognition, and in some cases they seem to be on the right track: most of us would have a hard time thinking of a better type of explanation of how we smell than to suppose that the object smelled emits tiny invisible particles that go through the air to our nose and interact with the matter there in such a way as to excite our sense of smell.

Democritus also explored the consequences his theory had for the nature of knowledge:

> There are two kinds of judgment, one legitimate and the other bastard. All the following belong to the bastard: sight, hearing, smell, taste, touch. The other is legitimate and is separated from this. When the bastard one is unable to see or hear or smell or taste or grasp by touch any further in the direction of smallness, but <we need to go still further> towards what is fine, <then the legitimate one enables us to do so.> (Democritus, frag. 11)

> By convention, sweet; by convention, bitter; by convention, hot; by convention, cold; by convention, color; but in reality, atoms and void. (Democritus, frag. 9)

Knowledge of atoms and void is legitimate because it is based in reality and is objective, whereas the senses give rise to merely bastard judgment because the perceptible qualities they reveal are properties not of atoms but of compounds. In addition, they are subjective because they depend on the varying states of the sense organs of individuals. Reflecting on our epistemologically challenged situation Democritus sometimes sounds like a thoroughgoing skeptic:

> In reality we know nothing about anything, but for each person opinion is a reshaping [of the soul atoms by the atoms entering from without]. (Democritus, frag. 7)

> Either nothing is true, or at least to us it is unclear. (Democritus, reported by Aristotle)

But he also held the apparently unskeptical view that truth is in the appearance, what appears to our senses must be true. If these claims can be reconciled it will be by distinguishing as before between "legitimate" and "bastard" judgment, and supposing that whereas the latter is not knowledge, still it comes at least in part from the objective reality of the atoms which strike the sense organs. In any case, Democritus clearly acknowledged the tension between the subjectivity of the senses and the objective truth which he claimed for his theory. In an imagined dialogue between the senses and the mind he has the senses complain:

> Wretched mind, after taking your evidence from us do you throw us down? Throwing us down is a fall for you. (Democritus, frag. 125)

Conclusion

Although it is the scientific views of the Presocratics that sometimes receive more attention than their philosophical thoughts, any attempt to identify two separate sides of their thought is mistaken. Their aim as they conceived it was to understand everything that is, and this included not only the nature of the physical world but also the method for learning about the world, which led to an interest in deep issues in epistemology and metaphysics, which continued to exercise later Greek philosophers. Concern with questions of ethics and political and social philosophy, while not entirely absent, did not have the centrality they would have in the thought of Socrates, Plato, and the Stoics and Epicureans. However, philosophers' interest in the study of nature did not end in the ancient world with the close of the Presocratic era, as the works of Aristotle and also the physical thought of the Stoics and Epicureans would bear out in later generations.

References and Recommended Reading

Bracketed numbers refer to entries in the general bibliography at the end of the volume.

Primary Sources

Diels, H., *Die Fragmente der Vorsokratiker*. 6th ed. revised by Walter Kranz (Weidmann: 1951).

For a selection of Presocratic fragments in Greek with English translations and helpful commentary, the best source is
Kirk, G. S., Raven, J. E., Schofield, M., *The Presocratic Philosophers*, 2nd ed. (Cambridge University Press: 1983).

Secondary Sources

For clear and accessible introductions to the Presocratics:
McKirahan, R., *Philosophy before Socrates: an Introduction with Texts and Commentary* (Hackett: 1994).
Hussey, E., *The Presocratics* (Duckworth: 1972).
Burnet, J., *Early Greek Philosophy* (London: A. & C. Black, 1908, 1963).
Guthrie, W., *A History of Greek Philosophy*, vols. 1–2 (Cambridge University Press: 1962, 1965).

A full and lively though somewhat less accessible treatment:
Barnes, J., *The Presocratic Philosophers* (Routledge: 1982).

Two good collections of articles:
Furley, D., and Allen, R., eds., *Studies in Presocratic Philosophy* (Routledge: 1970, 1975).
Mourelatos, A., *The Presocratics* (Anchor Press: 1974).

Chapter 2

The Sophists

John Gibert

Introduction

The Sophists were active in one of the better documented periods of Greek history, roughly from 450 to 380 BCE. Sources for the cultural and intellectual history of this period include Athenian tragedy (Aeschylus, Sophocles, and Euripides) and Old Comedy (Aristophanes), the earliest surviving orations and political tracts, and narrative history (Thucydides, Xenophon, and Herodotus to the extent that he reflects the time in which he wrote rather than that in which his subject, the Persian Wars, took place). In addition, Plato and Xenophon present an image of the late fifth century in their Socratic writings. The picture of the intellectual, moral, political, and religious climate that emerges from all these sources includes a great deal of questioning and experimentation. The resulting changes, some of which proved to be lasting and important, were perceived by many contemporaries as symptoms of moral decline, while others enjoyed a sense of liberation. Modern scholars have been similarly divided. Some have compared the "Age of Sophists" to the European Age of Enlightenment, while others agree with the negative verdict pronounced, most influentially, by Plato.

The topics that came in for lively discussion in the period just defined are of such fundamental importance that it is easy to see why the positions taken on them by various Greek thinkers have led to such widely divergent reactions and judgments. They include the proper way to educate the young; the validity of laws, customs, and religion, especially in the face of observed differences among ethnic groups as well as among Greeks of different *poleis*; the related question of nature's role in establishing norms of behavior; the individual's obligations to society, family, and self; and the use and abuse of persuasive language. Since teaching (mainly at the level of what we call "higher education," that is, to pupils just entering adulthood) was among the Sophists' most important activities, it is likely enough that many of them had developed views on pedagogy. Our best evidence concerns Protagoras and comes from the dialogue Plato named after him. Questions about the value of higher learning, who ought to have access to it, and how it ought to be used became part of tense political debates. Broad political considerations, in turn, often seem to have determined reactions to sophistic positions on more specialized topics. In fact, the views held by individuals with a claim to the title "Sophist" vary so much that many scholars doubt whether we ought to speak of a "Sophistic Movement." For contemporaries with vested interests, however, it will have been enough that individual Sophists made provocative observations and raised disturbing questions about things that had long been taken for granted: the essential rightness of religious practice, for example, or of moral obligations to one's father or country. That they taught others, especially the young, to raise similar questions and to speak cleverly and persuasively only made things worse.

The ideas of a Gorgias on rhetoric, then, or a Protagoras on relativism, were most often received against a background of wide-ranging cultural unease. This is not yet to say anything of their philosophical quality. Unfortunately, the writings of the Sophists have been almost entirely lost. The little that survives of their work, though certainly not without interest, cannot be compared favorably, for general sophistication, with such complete works as Thucydides' *History of the Peloponnesian War* or Euripides' tragedies. Plato and Aristotle cast a damning verdict on their methods and conclusions, and we are not often in a position to dispute them. There can be no doubt that some Sophists, some of the time, strove for novelty, paradox, and discomfiture of their opponents in ways that will have left little serious philosophical residue. Yet it is also true, as a sympathetic modern scholar has written, that "Many sophistic puzzles have a double identity. They may have arisen in a purely eristic context; but thinkers who did not dismiss them out of hand often came to realize that profound philosophical issues lay at the logical source of such puzzles."[1] Such puzzles arise most notably in connection with rhetoric and relativism, which will be treated in later sections of this chapter. While the evidence, as we shall see, leaves us wondering exactly who – Gorgias, Protagoras, or only Plato – deserves credit for discerning the profound philosophical issues still to be found in them, it is highly significant for the course of Greek and therefore European philosophy that Plato developed his philosophical program through prolonged engagement with individual Sophists and their ideas.

The attitude of Plato, then, is crucial, and it has been much studied. Only a few points need be made here. The first is that while Plato is by far our most important witness to everything having to do with the Sophists, he is generally quite hostile. That is, he is out of sympathy with the moral and political currents to which he believed the Sophists were contributing, he arrives at very different conclusions on matters of substance, and he decries the tendency of the Sophists as a group to value display (*epideixis*) and competitive refutation (*eristic*) over reasoned and disinterested pursuit of the truth. His discussion of a series of definitions of the Sophist in the *Sophist* is full of vitriol. Considered thus in the abstract, the Sophist has no serious claim to be a thinker; he is immoral and a teacher of immorality besides. On the other hand, Plato is less dismissive of certain Sophists of the older generation, notably Protagoras and Gorgias. Moreover, he acknowledges the urgent need for a philosophical rebuttal of the "sophistic" views he gives to Callicles and Thrasymachus, views he in some sense honors by devoting so much space to them in *Gorgias* and *Republic*, respectively. Callicles (if he existed) and Thrasymachus, however, may never have been so eloquent. It is possible that Plato did not find in the actual writings of the Sophists any sufficiently developed statement of the views he attacks. In such cases, he may well have given better arguments for sophistic positions than did the Sophists themselves.[2]

In reaching our own views of the Sophists, we thus face an unusually acute source problem. Until roughly the middle of the nineteenth century, the condemnation resulting from the combined testimony of Aristophanes, Plato, and Aristotle went virtually unchallenged.[3] Since that time, scholars have been more willing to "read against the grain," and opinion has become increasingly varied and nuanced. The present chapter cannot attempt a full appreciation of the Sophists as a cultural phenomenon. Instead, it looks at some philosophical issues in the areas of language and rhetoric, justice and morality, and relativism.[4] We will see how sophistic ideas on these topics are relevant to Socrates (chapter 3) and set the stage for Plato (chapters 4–7). That the Sophists were not only (and perhaps not even primarily) philosophers in the narrow sense, however, must be borne constantly in mind. Towards that end, the next section offers a little more background, as well as a sketch of the source material.

Background and Sources

We begin with the label "sophists." The Greek word *sophistēs* is an agent noun derived from the verb *sophizesthai*, "to practice *sophia*." *Sophia*, commonly translated "wisdom," is a broad term. It can refer to general intellectual ability or spiritual endowment, and it also embraces such specialized skills as building or operating a ship, and composing or performing poetry or music. Thus *sophistēs* could be used neutrally or in praise of poets, statesmen, and experts of all kinds. But because Greeks, like everyone else, were sometimes resentful or suspicious of expertise, the possibility of using *sophos* and related words disparagingly existed long before Plato's concerted attack on those he identified as Sophists. Because of this possibility, and especially because Sophists were influentially involved in training young men to speak both in political debates and in the law courts, we might compare the cultural position of Sophists to that of lawyers in contemporary Europe and especially the United States. Both sophist and lawyer are well-paid professionals whose cleverness may be admired even as it is considered suspect, both intellectually and morally. Their influence is deplored except when one wants it exercised on one's own behalf. We love them, we hate them, we love to hate them. It is hardly surprising that sophists, like lawyers, became irresistible targets of popular jokes.

The first person to use Sophist as a professional designation may have been Protagoras of Abdera (c. 490 to c. 420 BCE). The character by that name in Plato's *Protagoras* claims that earlier poets and teachers avoided the label "Sophist" and concealed their true sophistic vocation behind their respective crafts. He, in contrast, proudly proclaims himself a Sophist and teacher and believes he has not suffered for it (316d–317c). But if "Sophist" was ever a harmless professional title, passages from Athenian Old Comedy and Thucydides suggest that towards the end of the fifth century this was no longer so. In the fourth century, thinkers and teachers preferred to call themselves philosophers or rhetoricians and reserve the label "Sophist" for their opponents.[5]

Despite the ambivalence many people felt towards them, what the Sophists had to offer was in demand. In Thucydides the politician Cleon sneers at the Athenians' fondness for watching and judging contests of words.[6] In Aristophanes' *Clouds*, Strepsiades expects practical legal advantages from having his son taught by Socrates. That son, however, begins the play with nothing but scorn for the pale, impoverished charlatans who inhabit the place Aristophanes calls the Thinkery. By the end of the play, their positions are reversed. Pheidippides has come to revere his teachers, while his father renounces his earlier immoral opportunism and burns the Thinkery to the ground. These dramatic facts neatly reflect the contradictions in Athenian attitudes towards the Sophists. On the level of substance, Strepsiades goes to Socrates because he knows of a rhetorical method involving opposing speeches, one weaker and one stronger (*Clouds* 112–18); that is, he associates with Socrates what we know to be Protagorean (see below). Protagoras is also said to have written the laws for the Athenian-led pan-Hellenic foundation at Thurii (c. 443 BCE), and Gorgias to have come to Athens as an ambassador on behalf of his native Leontini (427 BCE). These examples – involving oratory, teaching, and statecraft – come to us independently of Plato, who for his part paints a vivid picture of certain Athenians' infatuation with the Sophists (above all at the beginning of *Protagoras*, dramatic date c. 433 BCE). We also know from Plato and others that Sophists charged fees, sometimes quite considerable ones, for their services, and that not everyone approved of the practice.[7] Athens, incidentally, was not the only *polis* (city-state) where there was money to be made by Sophists, but it surely offered exceptional opportunities.

Aristophanes, Plato, and others thus give evidence that alleged sophistic influence on Athenian society was a topic of contemporary interest. Modern scholars too are in the habit of detecting such influence in a wide variety of places, but readers should be warned that it is often hard to tell whether what is labeled "sophistic" is a cause or symptom of something else. Many of the provocative ideas we find in drama, oratory, and historical writing cannot be linked in any way with particular Sophists, and the Sophists themselves are hardly united in a "school" with shared philosophical allegiances or doctrines. Indeed, there is much room for debate as to who should and should not count as a Sophist. Under the heading "Ältere Sophistik," the standard collection of the fragments of early Greek philosophy (abbreviation: DK) prints testimonia and very scanty direct quotations for nine named individuals: Protagoras of Abdera, Xeniades of Corinth, Gorgias of Leontini, Lycophron, Prodicus of Ceos, Thrasymachus of Chalcedon, Hippias of Elis, and Antiphon and Critias of Athens.[8] There are no direct quotations at all of the obscure Xeniades and Lycophron. There are a few for Thrasymachus, but he is hardly less obscure – except as he appears in Book 1 of Plato's *Republic*. The claim of Critias to be considered a Sophist is weak; it rests mainly on a doubtfully attributed fragment of a satyr-play entitled *Sisyphus*.[9] A fair amount can be learned about Protagoras, Gorgias, Prodicus, Hippias, and Antiphon.[10]

Meanwhile, there are some others we might consider adding to the list. On the assumption (itself probable enough) that Euthydemus of Chios was a real person, R. K. Sprague edited his "fragments" and included them in her collection of translations of the DK-chapters on the Sophists. The trouble is that these fragments consist almost entirely of passages from Plato's *Euthydemus*. Kerferd takes the next step and includes Callicles, known *exclusively* from Plato's *Gorgias*, on his list. Although Callicles holds both teaching and philosophy in contempt, he is for Kerferd "beyond argument a very important figure in the history of the sophistic movement" because of the ideas Plato puts in his mouth (Kerferd 1981, 52). Kerferd also argues (55–7) that we should think of Socrates as in some ways part of this movement even though Plato obviously works hard to distinguish him sharply from the Sophists.

The setting of a lower chronological boundary of the "sophistic movement" is also problematic. Once one begins to mine Plato's dialogues (with their dates of composition anywhere in the first half of the fourth century) for sophistic ideas, it becomes hard to see why we should exclude someone like Alcidamas, a pupil of Gorgias whose activity appears to belong to the same period. While it is often of interest whether we can point to attestation of a philosophical idea by, say, a particular stage of the Peloponnesian War (431–404 BCE) or the premiere of a Euripidean tragedy, it is less clear what the advantage is in applying a cut-off date of 400 for a "sophistic movement" in general, when most of the topics of the day continue to have their burning relevance for Plato, Isocrates, and others in the first half of the fourth century. The issue of assigning thinkers to periods intersects that of separating them into schools. If Socrates belongs in a discussion of the Sophists, the same would seem to be true of his companion Antisthenes, who began his philosophical activity in the fifth century and lived well into the fourth. But Antisthenes is not usually classed as a Sophist, whether because of his association with Socrates or because a later tradition considered him a proto-Cynic.

Regarding primary texts, the source situation is most unfavorable. Texts that can be attributed to named Sophists and are more than a page long can be counted on the fingers of one hand. For Gorgias, we have the *Encomium of Helen* (DK 82 B 11) and *Defense of Palamedes* (B 11a), both transmitted directly with title and attribution. They are presumably extracts from the *Techne* (*Art* [*of Rhetoric*]) Diogenes Laertius says he wrote (8.58 = DK 82 A 3). There are also two extended paraphrases of a treatise *On Not-Being* or *On Nature*. All of these will be discussed in the next section. Portions of Antiphon's work *Truth* are preserved in papyri that began coming to light in 1915. For Thrasymachus, there is a page-long fragment of a political speech which may or may not have been intended for actual delivery in the circumstances it depicts (DK 85 B 1). So much for the longer fragments. Sometimes a quoted sentence or two provides the starting point for fruitful philosophical investigation, as notably with Protagoras DK 80 B 4, a famous declaration of agnosticism that began a work *On the Gods*, and of course B 1, the statement of Protagoras' relativism (see section V). More often, however, the shorter direct quotations merely attest a striking phrase, which only occasionally coincides with a striking philosophical idea.

Other texts are to be regarded as sophistic only subject to various qualifications. Xenophon relates an allegory of the Choice of Heracles based on a composition by Prodicus, but it is, he admits, only a paraphrase, and much less grand than the original (*Mem.* 2.1.21–34 = DK 84 B 2). In the work known as *Dissoi Logoi* (from its first words, meaning "Twofold Arguments," DK 90), we have something approaching a whole treatise, 15 pages long in Sprague's English translation (in Sprague ed. 1972). But aside from being anonymous, it is derivative and second-rate. Its great virtues are that it is probably datable to around 400 BCE, and it clearly reveals Protagorean influence. This gives it historical value, but we have earlier and more provocative versions of the most interesting ideas, and what *Dissoi Logoi* chiefly preserves is painfully inept eristic argument. From the *Protrepticus* of the Neoplatonist Iamblichus (third–fourth century CE), scholars extract a few pages with a sophistic feel to them and attribute them to another Anonymous (DK 89). As all agree that Iamblichus did engage in wholesale unacknowledged borrowing from classical works, this method of regaining a sophistic text is unobjectionable in theory, but agreement is not to be expected (nor has it been found) as to the precise demarcation of the source text from its surroundings, the date to which Anonymous belongs, and the philosophical influences on him. In any case, the value of this text is again mainly historical, in that it shows "how far the stock ideas and arguments of the age penetrated into rather ordinary minds."[11] The forty-line *Sisyphus* fragment (DK 88 B 25) certainly belongs in a discussion of sophistic texts – but in the same way as many a passage of Euripides, who may indeed be its author.

The sources just surveyed are a pitiful remnant of what we know was the Sophists' vast literary output, and a satisfactory picture of "The Sophists" can hardly be based on them alone. Moreover, we have seen that there are definitional problems with the category "Sophist." To return to a question alluded to earlier, then, is there any point in speaking of a sophistic movement? The question perhaps admits no clear answer. If "sophistic" is more or less equated, as it often is in casual usage, with "typical of a major strand in the moral and intellectual fabric of the times," then the label is unobjectionable but uninformative. A few further points with some bearing on this question will conclude this section. First, it would be an exaggeration to say that the individual Sophists known to us have nothing in common. With the exception of Critias (who was not properly a Sophist), they all had an interest in language and rhetoric, they all accepted payment for teaching, and probably they all put themselves on display as public speakers. Second, the interest of many Sophists in natural philosophy and other preoccupations of earlier thinkers (especially Eleatics) is well attested. To contemporaries, therefore, what they had in common with those we call "Presocratics" will often have been at least as clear as what set them apart. Third, the context and means of disseminating wisdom were the same not only for Presocratics and Sophists, but to a large extent also for those we know mainly as lawgivers, founders of religio-philosophic cults, musical theorists, interpreters of Homer, and individuals in nascent professions such as medicine, engineering and other crafts. This suggests that we ought always to keep in mind what individual Sophists were and did as well as what they thought.[12] Fourth, we must never forget the Athenocentrism of our sources. The various kinds of specialist just mentioned must have been in demand everywhere, and recent scholars have drawn attention to the evidence of sophistic activity outside Athens. Yet Athens retains certain distinctions. Its size and empire contributed to its concentration of financial and eventually cultural capital, while creating a growing need for citizens who could contribute to public life in all kinds of ways. Democracy gave relatively large numbers of people a chance to meet that need, and the Sophists, as teachers of higher learning, are often said to have arisen, or to have been drawn to Athens, to help them prepare for the challenges they faced. In the next section, we turn to sophistic interest in public speaking, a skill needed by Athenian citizens for a wide variety of reasons.

Language and Rhetoric

Greek interest in persuasive speech did not, of course, emerge suddenly in the fifth century BCE; in various forms it goes back as far as our sources (i.e., Homer and other archaic poets).[13] The Sophists did, however, declare themselves ready to meet a need that grew stronger throughout that century. We have some evidence for interest in specialized linguistic topics, such as grammar and semantics. Both Protagoras and Prodicus, for example, placed a high value on "correctness of language" (*orthotēs onomaton* or *orthoepeia*).[14] Protagoras devised a system of classifying sentence types and used it, in one attested instance, to criticize the opening of Homer's *Iliad* (Arist. *Poet.* 19, 1456b15–18 = DK 80 A 29). He also discussed grammatical gender, thereby providing Aristophanes with material for a few jokes in *Clouds*. Our evidence for Prodicus speaks most clearly to an interest in synonyms, amusingly parodied (though not thereby shown to be useless) by Plato in his *Protagoras* (337a–c = DK 84 A 13).

The Sophists were all public speakers, and their interest in topics like these probably arose in the course of their rhetorical teaching and practice, about which we also know something. Hippias, for example, gave prepared speeches and took questions from all comers at Olympia, the most prominent venue he could have chosen (*Hipp. min.* 363c = DK 86 A 8). He claimed to be able to perform prodigious feats of memory, and Plato even mentions an *Art of Memory*, which would have been of immense practical value (*Hipp. min.* 368d = DK 86 A 12). A joke Aristotle tells about the pricing of Prodicus' various lectures implies that he was adept at gauging his audience's attentiveness (*Rhet.* 1415b12 = DK 84 A 12; cf. Pl. *Crat.* 384b = A 11). His *Choice of Heracles* (DK 84 B 2) may strike us as a rather dreary piece of moralizing, but Xenophon assures us that he adorned it with great eloquence. Protagoras was the author of *Antilogiai* (*Contrasting Arguments*). These will have put into practice his belief that it was possible to speak on either side of any dispute (DK 80 A 20). This is reported by some as a claim to be able "to make the weaker argument the stronger" (DK 80 A 21), which was naturally regarded as scandalous. Finally, Gorgias made a famously big splash when he spoke at Athens in 427 BCE as head of a delegation from his native city Leontini in Sicily (Diod. Sic. 12.53 =

DK 82 A 4). He may have known from back home all about whatever Tisias and Corax were doing in nearby Syracuse that earned them the reputation of having invented the art of rhetoric (though ancient tradition, interestingly, makes Gorgias the pupil rather of the natural philosopher Empedocles). Although he was remembered for flowery language and preposterous figures of speech (displayed prominently – and according to critics as early as Aristotle, tastelessly – in the surviving fragments of his Funeral Oration, DK 82 B 6), Gorgias was expected by his fellow citizens to persuade the Athenians, and according to Diodorus, he did. In the dialogue Plato named after him, he readily assents to Socrates' definition of the rhetorical art he professes as "artificer of persuasion" (*Grg.* 453a = DK 82 A 28).

It has been maintained that certain quasi-technical terms for types of rhetorical or philosophical discourse hold the key to understanding the Sophists' involvement with language and truth as Plato saw it. The terms in question are "eristic," "antilogic," and "dialectic."[15] The easiest to define is eristic, which means the application of any and all skill towards success in debate. The eristic speaker exploits ambiguities and fallacies and is willing to wander into lengthy irrelevance if he believes it will serve his cause. We do not find Plato or anyone else praising eristic, but we do have an entire dialogue (*Euthydemus*) devoted to showing it in action. Most find the portrait of the quibbling and insincere Sophists Euthydemus and Dionysodorus deeply unappealing, as Plato doubtless meant it to be.[16]

"Antilogic" literally pits one argument against another on the same topic. It need not aim only at success, but may be propaideutic and may end in *aporia*. As Plato presents it when he is in a sympathetic mood, its characteristic shortcoming is not dishonesty but philosophical inadequacy. He recognizes it as particularly susceptible to abuse by the young (*Rep.* 7.539b2–7), but even Socrates confesses to lapsing into antilogic at times (e.g., *Tht.* 164c8–d2). Indeed, antilogic can appear rather similar to Socrates' characteristic method of *elenchos*, and this surely helps to explain why Plato does not dismiss it as simply bad.

The hardest term to pin down is dialectic. In origin and in much of its usage, *dialegesthai* is no more specific than "to converse." Accordingly, dialectic sometimes refers merely to dialogue form, especially where questions and answers are to be kept short. But in places where Plato means for the term to bear philosophical weight, it has some connection with his theory of Forms. As such, it is a method to which he is wholly committed, even if it is hard to spell out in detail. The insight we can gain from this review of terms is that the inadequacy of antilogic as Plato understands it exactly explains his view of the inadequacy of those Sophists he does not dismiss as charlatans, mere eristic quibblers. Even the best Sophists, he thinks, stopped when they had achieved an insight into the instability and disputability of things. Rather than continue in disinterested pursuit of the truth (as Socrates did), they honed their ability to fabricate opposing *logoi* about all kinds of things and then offered instruction in this ability as though it were truly valuable.[17] An example of antilogic in action is *Dissoi Logoi*, which may be described as sub-Protagorean both in that it is structured according to the Protagorean principle that there are two sides to every issue and in that it represents sophistic method as filtered through an average mind.

We now return to Gorgias, whose *Encomium of Helen* (DK 82 B 11), though it is not antilogical in form (nor does it overtly commit itself to the Protagorean principle), yet seems to breathe the air of antilogic as it argues for a novel and paradoxical view, the innocence of the mythical Helen, who left her Spartan husband Menelaus for the Trojan Paris. In addition to being typically sophistic in its showiness, the speech contains a few interesting arguments and implies a theory of language that has been much discussed.[18] Gorgias' stated purpose is to show that those who blame Helen for going to Troy are wrong, and the heart of the defense is an analysis of four possible explanations of her going. The third raises the most interesting questions: Gorgias claims that even if Helen went with Paris because he *persuaded* her, she is easily exonerated. The ethical implications of this claim are serious: if having been persuaded gets Helen off the hook, then clearly it will be difficult to enforce any kind of conventional morality. Gorgias' argumentative strategy is to assimilate persuasion to force. In a famous phrase, he calls *logos* a "powerful lord [*megas dynastēs*]," which "by means of the finest and most invisible body effects the divinest works: it can stop fear and banish grief and create joy and nurture pity."[19] A little later, he compares the effect of *logos* on the soul to the power of drugs over bodies. Thus some speeches drug the soul and put it at the speaker's mercy. The suggestion seems to be that persuasive speech itself is a morally indifferent means to either good or bad ends (a position taken by Gorgias in the dialogue Plato names after him).

The *Encomium* also contains a rather different treatment of *logos* as deception. This is slipped in without warning at the beginning of §8 and elaborated in §11, where Gorgias claims that persuasion depends on fashioning a false or deceptive argument (*pseude logon*). A related idea is expressed in §35 of the *Palamedes* (B 11a), where Palamedes reasons that "If, by means of words, it were possible for the truth of actions to become free of doubt <and> clear to hearers, judgment would now be easy from what has been said." But, he adds, this is not the case. This passage could be taken as a commonplace insistence that correct judgment depends on knowledge of facts, but its emphasis on the difficulty of making the truth pure and clear, together with the *Helen* passage's characterization of persuasion as deception, may perhaps be understood better against the background of Gorgias' treatise *On Not-Being* or *On Nature*.

In this work, known only from two extended but far from perfect paraphrases, it appears that Gorgias argued for three propositions.[20] First, that nothing exists. Second, that even if it exists, it is incapable of being apprehended (*akatalepton*). And third, that even if it can be apprehended, it cannot be communicated to another. This argument has most often been taken as a response to Eleatic philosophy, perhaps as it was being represented in Gorgias' day by Zeno and Melissus. On this view, Gorgias adopts the Parmenidean preoccupation with "being" and, generally speaking, Eleatic modes of argument, and shows that one can find oneself committed to "it is not" every bit as easily as to "it is." If, in the state of philosophy at that time, this was a worthwhile undertaking, it makes undeniably amusing reading now. It is also amusing that Gorgias' pupil Isocrates went to the trouble of condemning it as frivolous.[21]

If we take Gorgias seriously, we can perhaps see why he chose in his *Helen* and *Palamedes* to emphasize *logos* as deception, but the question then arises how he can teach rhetoric if he disavows knowledge and the communicability of knowledge. While it is true that rhetoric might be uncommitted to "what is" and thus immune to the first thesis of *On Not-Being*, it would seem that the speaker has a better chance of succeeding if he apprehends something about the way things are (but the second thesis denies that this is possible), and can communicate something about it (but the third thesis denies that this is possible). If, however, Gorgias does not connect his practice of rhetoric with any claims about reality, but only with an observable ability to influence the behavior of his audience, that is probably a good enough answer to keep him in business – if not to earn the respect of Plato!

Justice and Morality

Gorgias professed to be interested in the morality of Helen's actions, and teachers of rhetoric needed in general to prepare their pupils to debate any issue of morality or justice that might arise in practical politics. We know that the Sophists were interested in the nature and limits of freedom and equality, social compact theory, and the teachability of *aretē* ("excellence, virtue"). Only a few important passages, where we find relatively full arguments, will be described here.[22] We begin with Protagoras as he is depicted in the dialogue Plato names after him. Asked by Socrates to demonstrate that *aretē* is teachable, Protagoras responds with a long speech (the first part of which is dressed in mythical guise), in which he tells how human communities came to be constituted as they are, and what place morality and justice have in them (*Prt.* 320c–328d). According to Protagoras, human beings were originally endowed with technical skill, which along with fire enabled them to make practical discoveries (shelter, clothing, nourishment from the earth) and so survive. When a need to protect themselves against wild beasts led them to live together, however, they found that their lack of political skill (*politikē technē*, the ability to live in a *polis*) made this impracticable. Scattered once more, they were in danger of extinction, until Zeus told Hermes to give each human being a share of *aidos* (a sense of shame and respect for others) and *dikē* (a sense of what is right). So equipped, people are capable of living together in communities, but still they require teaching. Teaching is done in part by laws; there is also room for teachers like Protagoras, who because they are better able than ordinary people to lead others towards *aretē*, may reasonably charge a fee for this valuable service.

Socrates will soon ask Protagoras to clarify his view of *aretē*, and in particular to say whether he thinks justice, piety, self-control and the like are parts of one thing, "virtue" in general. In other early dialogues, of course, Plato's Socrates searches for definitions of these several "virtues." A preoccupation with *aretē* is one of the most striking features of Greek philosophy at all periods, and there can be no doubt that explicit or implicit redefinitions of it, along with claims to teach it to those who, under the influence of élitist ideologies, had usually been held incapable of attaining it, were high on the list of reasons why Socrates, Plato, and others found it so important to assess the philosophical value of the sophistic enterprise. Moreover, such matters continue to interest serious thinkers; in certain contexts, what Protagoras has to say about them can be as important now as it was then. In this connection, the first thing to notice about his "Great Speech" is its manifestly democratic tendency. Socrates' professed motive for asking Protagoras to demonstrate the teachability of *aretē* has to do with Athenian democratic practice. While the Athenians take the advice of experts on what they consider to be technical matters, he observes, they allow any citizen who wishes to address the Assembly on broader matters of public policy. Socrates had always thought this was because they believed excellence in such general matters did not lie within the province of a craft (*technē*) and hence was not teachable (319b5–d7). While Socrates professes to see wisdom in this aspect of Athenian democracy (319b3–4), his assumption that *aretē* is not teachable leaves room for those who could assert a traditional claim to it (based on noble lineage, for instance) to favor different political arrangements. With its claim that each human being begins with a share of *aidos* and *dikē* that can be increased through learning, Protagoras' speech provides democracy with a foundation secure against such attack.

Nomoi ("laws, customs") come in only towards the end of Protagoras' story, after he has switched from *mythos* to *logos* (324d), but they play a memorable part in it both because of his progressive view on punishment (325a–d) and because of the image of the city placing the laws before its citizens as a pattern, just as teachers give their pupils ruled paper for practicing the shapes of letters (326c–d). At any rate it is clear that obedience to *nomoi* is an important factor preventing a return to the inferior original state of affairs described in the myth. That original state is what many would call a state of nature (*physis*). Just about every writer of the later fifth century opposes *nomos* to *physis* in some way or another, and many of them, for example the dramatists, in several different ways as occasion arises.[23] In the context of his developmental theory of society, Plato's Protagoras emerges as a staunch defender of *nomos*. At the same time, it is in the nature of *nomos* (which also means "convention") that it can be changed. Protagoras' views favoring *nomos* and democracy could combine with the teachability of *aretē* and various kinds of relativism (on which more later) to produce a potent challenge to established political élites.

The fragments of Antiphon's *Truth* appear to take a different view of *nomos*. There are many disputed points of detail, and we cannot be sure that what we have preserves opinions held by Antiphon. The more or less consistent position that emerges from the fragments, however, is one of hostility to *nomos*.[24] Thus Antiphon writes:

> The examination is being conducted for this reason: because the majority of what is just according to law and convention is hostile to nature. For laws have been established over the eyes, as to what they must and must not see; and over the ears, as to what they must and must not hear; and over the tongue, as to what it must and must not say; and over the hands, as to what they must and must not do; and over the feet, as to what they must and must not go after; and over the mind, as to what it must and must not

desire. Now, the things from which the laws try to dissuade people are no more friendly or akin to nature than the things to which they encourage them. Living and dying belong to nature; and living comes to nature from what is advantageous, dying from what is not. As for advantages, those established by the laws are chains on nature, whereas those established by nature are free. Things that cause pain, at any rate, do not, in truth, benefit nature more than things that give pleasure; things that cause pain, then, are not more advantageous, either, than things that give pleasure. For things that are truly advantageous must not harm but help.[25]

Elsewhere Antiphon observes that although all human beings are alike in important respects determined by nature, *nomos* (apparently) causes Greeks to distinguish between themselves and foreigners (DK 87 B 44 fr. B = fr. 44(b) Pendrick, col. 2.7–15). Besides constraining individuals to act against their own natural impulses, *nomos* also paradoxically enjoins behavior that seems unjust, as when a witness must testify against someone who has done him no harm (DK 87 B 44 = fr. 44(c) Pendrick). Here is what Antiphon advises the individual to do in the face of his analysis:

> Now a man would make use of justice in a way most advantageous to himself if he were to regard the laws (*nomoi*) as great in the presence of witnesses, but nature (*physis*) as great when deprived of witnesses. For the laws are imposed, whereas nature is necessary; and the laws are not born but agreed upon, whereas nature is not agreed upon but born. (DK 87 B 44 Fr. A = fr. 44(a) Pendrick, col. 1.12–2.1)

Challenging ideas about *nomos* and *physis*, justice and morality were much in the air in the late fifth century. It is particularly hard in this area to say whether individual Sophists influenced relevant passages of, say, Thucydides (especially 3.82, the famous chapter on the demoralization that followed civil strife on Corcyra, and 5.84–113, the Melian dialogue) or Euripides (of many relevant passages, the speech of Eteocles at *Phoen.* 499–525 may be singled out). The chance survival of Antiphon's views in the fragments just quoted adds to the justification for treating the views of Callicles (Pl. *Grg.*) and Thrasymachus (*Rep.* 1) as sophistic. The exact positions held by each of these figures and the nature and degree of success of the arguments Plato has Socrates deploy against them continue to be debated. Only a brief sketch is possible here.[26]

Before Callicles enters the discussion in Plato's *Gorgias*, Polus has been trying to defend the thesis that "many human beings are happy through being unjust" (470d). His defense fails, as Callicles rightly observes (482c–e), because he concedes that wrongdoing, while beneficial for the wrongdoer, is nevertheless shameful. Callicles objects that Socrates only won the argument because Polus was ashamed to say what he really thought; further, Polus didn't notice that Socrates, who only won a concession from him about what is held shameful in accordance with convention (*kata nomon*), turned it on him as though he had spoken in accordance with nature (*kata physin*). Turning the tables in this way, Callicles says, is a common but illegitimate trick (482e–483a). He next expounds his own position, that what is just by nature is for the better man to get a greater share of whatever he wants than the worse, the more powerful than the less powerful (483c–d). When Socrates tries to argue that it is "by nature" that many weak people join together to make laws constraining those few who are individually stronger, Callicles impatiently rejects the move as a quibble. What he means by a better man is not necessarily one who is physically stronger in all circumstances, but one who is better by nature (490a). It is natural that such a man should be a ruler and have more of whatever he wants than other men.

In the course of the argument that follows, Plato has Socrates exploit Callicles' unwillingness to allow that the naturally superior man ought to practice any self-control at all and expose some unpalatable consequences of unrestrained hedonism. Many feel that some of Socrates' dialectical moves are suspect and that Plato does not allow Callicles to adopt the most defensible positions open to him. That Plato himself did not regard the triumph over Callicles as wholly satisfactory is indicated both by certain features within *Gorgias* and by the fact that similar issues return in Book 1 of the *Republic* and set the stage for the remainder of that work. Like Callicles, Thrasymachus joins a conversation in which two others have failed to stand up to Socrates' questioning. This time the search is for a definition of justice. Thrasymachus, in a fit of pique, leaps into the fray with the view that "justice is nothing other than the advantage of the stronger" (338c). In response to Socrates' first questions, he clarifies that what he means by the stronger is the party in power, whether one is speaking of government by a tyrant, an aristocracy, or a democracy (338d–339a). Some further turns in the argument lead him to reformulate or change his position: justice, he now says, is what is good for someone else but bad for oneself, and injustice is the reverse (343c). As a result, the just man always and everywhere has less than the unjust.

Naturally, Thrasymachus is not disposed to praise this state of affairs. He argues rather that injustice, because it is profitable, should be recognized as *euboulia* ("prudence" or "good counsel" – just the capacity Protagoras professed to instill in his pupils!), and justice as "noble simplicity" (348c–d). His move in revalorizing these terms differs from that made by Callicles. It also makes apparent to Socrates that the gap between himself and Thrasymachus is unbridgeable. For his part, Thrasymachus no longer attempts seriously to defend his position, but lets Socrates proceed through dialectical maneuvering to the conclusion he wants. Interestingly, Plato's awareness that all is not in order here is again signaled both internally, by Thrasymachus' alienation, and externally, by the fact that Glaucon and Adimantus call for a reexamination of the issues at the beginning of Book 2.

Relativism

Something we may loosely call relativism was being widely discussed at the time of the Sophists. Doctors, for example, were fond of noting that what is good for you when you are healthy may be bad for you when you are sick (e.g., Hippoc. *VM* 8), and we find Protagoras making this and related points in the dialogue Plato names after him (*Prt.* 334). When they came into contact with foreigners, Greeks observed laws and customs that differed from their own, and there is a fair amount of overt reflection on this topic in, for example, Herodotus (e.g., 3.38). Like Herodotus, the author of *Dissoi Logoi* lines up examples of customs that differ from place to place, including from one Greek *polis* to the next (2.9–28).[27] This kind of observation was used by some to justify rejecting customs they found oppressive or inconvenient. We find a caricature of such a situation in Aristophanes' *Clouds*, where the newly educated Phidippides justifies beating his father as follows. First, he says, since it was a man who made the law (the Greek also means "established the custom") that sons should not beat their fathers, he, another man, may establish a different *nomos*. Second, father-beating is observed to be the custom among roosters (*Clouds* 1421–9). Similarly, the Nurse in Euripides' *Hippolytus* nudges Phaedra towards adultery by observing that Zeus and other gods have often succumbed to passion (451–8), and a character in a lost play, apparently in reference to incest with his sister, asks, "What is shameful if it does not seem so to those who practice it?" (Eur. fr. 19, from *Aeolus*). The context in Aristophanes, at least, clearly lays such perversions at the door of the Sophists. It is easy to imagine the appeal they held for some of the Sophists' pupils, for example a young man trying to expand his political opportunities, or escape the authority of a domineering father. Naturally, any philosophical development of such ideas would be seen as liberating by some, as threatening and corrupt by others. A visceral reaction against relativism of this sort may have been a leading cause of Plato's antagonism to the Sophists.

But the more or less casual observations we have tallied so far, while doubtless important as a cultural phenomenon, do not by themselves constitute a philosophical theory of relativism. The philosophical interest of this topic begins when the observer of differing customs or contradictory opinions asks whether there is, so to speak, a fact of the matter. Is one person right and another wrong? Who is to decide, and how? In the history of philosophy, the term "relativism" has been defined in countless ways; it will be used here to mean the view that things may only be said truly to be some way or another in relation to someone or something else. This kind of relativism thus allows apparently conflicting perceptions and judgments to be equally true; that is, each of them is true for the person whose perception or judgment it is. There is no independent fact of the matter and no court of appeal. We can say of only one Sophist that he may have held such a view, and that is Protagoras.[28]

Discussion begins with DK 80 B 1: "Of all things the measure is a human being, both of the things that are that they are, and of the things that are not that they are not." Intense scrutiny has been applied to every word of this sentence, which is quoted in essentially the same form by Plato and Sextus. Both authors attest that this was the first sentence of one of Protagoras' books, which Plato calls *Aletheia* (*Truth*) and Sextus *Kataballontes* (sc. *Logoi*, a title which, borrowing a metaphor from wrestling, means *Overthrowing Arguments*). Accepting what is nowadays accepted by nearly everyone will allow us to focus on a few of the most interesting points.[29] It is generally accepted that *anthrōpos*, "a human being," means an individual human being, not "humankind." It is possible to ask interesting questions about how Protagoras believed human communities ought to arrive at value judgments, but these should enter the picture only at a later stage. Second, the measurement of things that Protagoras has at least initially in view concerns not their existence or nonexistence, but their possession of certain properties, the perception or judgment that they are (or are not) such and such. Whether or not this is conditioned by the usage of the verb "to be" in Protagoras' day, it is a fair inference from the examples used to illustrate the thesis in all the earliest discussions. Third, what it means for a person to be a measure of a thing is that, according to Protagoras, that thing truly *is* as it *seems* to the person in question. This is Plato's gloss at *Theaetetus* 152a, and he immediately illustrates it with the example of a wind that seems cold to one person but not to another. If we follow Protagoras, he says, we will not say that the wind is cold or not cold in itself, but that it actually is cold for the one person and not cold for the other.

This illustration comes from the realm of perception, and it is here that important divergences in the interpretation of Protagoras begin to occur. It must be emphasized that everything from at least this point forward is more or less educated guesswork, either as to how Protagoras might have illustrated, expanded, and defended his thesis, or how others did so for him. Those others, of course, may have misunderstood or distorted him in the course of their own philosophizing. As we shall see, not the least interesting question to ask when interpreting Protagoras is when to stop.

To take up the matter of perception, while the formulation "to be is to be perceived" (Latin *esse est percipi*) was destined to exercise philosophers in later ages, Protagoras' earliest interpreters, whether fairly or not, clearly extended the range of "seeming" to include judgments about anything at all. That is, they began by at least sometimes treating "the wind seems cold to me" as equivalent to "I judge that the wind is cold," and then, aided perhaps by this formulation (if not by examples actually used by Protagoras), they took Protagoras to be willing to apply his doctrine to any proposition introduced by "I judge that . . ." There are two kinds of evidence that Protagoras was understood to have committed to this formulation of his doctrine. The first is linguistic. The Greek verb that properly means "to perceive" is *aisthanesthai*. If a person *aisthanetai* something, one may equally properly say that the thing *phainetai*, "seems or appears," to the person. But the semantic range of *phainesthai* stretches beyond perception to include judgmental seeming. Another Greek verb often translatable as "to seem," *dokein*, properly refers only to judgmental seeming. Now Plato, after beginning with an example confined to perception (*aisthēsis*), gradually moves by way of the middle term *phainesthai* to formulations in terms of *dokein*. Aristotle and Sextus also use *dokein* some of the time in their discussions of Protagoras.[30]

The second piece of evidence is Sextus' remark that both Democritus and Plato used the argument known as the *peritropē* ("turn-about" or "self-refutation") against Protagoras (*Math.* 7.389 = DK 80 A 15). The measure doctrine must either fall within its own scope or not. If not, Protagoras is claiming that it is true in a nonrelative way, and this means that the doctrine is false, for it began by claiming that a human being is the measure of *all* things. But Democritus and Plato argued that if the doctrine does apply to itself, it commits one to the view that if it seems to anyone that the doctrine is wrong, it is wrong. There are people who think the doctrine is wrong, so if Protagoras is right, he is also wrong. This argumentative strategy requires glossing Protagoras in terms of judgmental seeming.[31]

Aristotle believed that in allowing the same judgment to be true (for one person) and false (for another), Protagoras abandoned the law of noncontradiction (*Metaph.* 11.6, 1062b 13–20 = DK 80 A 19). Most scholars agree that Protagoras would have insisted on maintaining the relativizing expressions "for A" and "for B" throughout the argument. This would appear to provide him at least some initial immunity from the complaint that he tolerates contradiction, and Aristotle is thus taken to task for the inadequacy of his conclusion about Protagoras. Now it has been shown fairly recently that this defense of Protagoras is not ultimately good enough. If he does in fact apply his doctrine to judgmental seeming, then he must at some point commit himself to an absolute truth claim concerning his own doctrine, and this exposes him to the *peritropē*.[32] At the same time, it is probably a fair conclusion that Protagoras did not either deliberately or casually deny the law of noncontradiction as Aristotle understands it. On the contrary, he is said to have held that "it is not possible to contradict" (Pl. *Euthyd.* 286b–c = DK 80 A 19). He would probably have explained this by saying not "because contradictory statements about the same thing are always both true," but rather "because apparently contradictory statements are never truly contradictory." And he would have backed this up by repeating that all statements, whatever their surface form, logically require relativizing expressions such as "for me" or "for you."[33]

Accepting that Protagoras would have responded to Aristotle in this way, modern scholars have described various philosophical positions to which he might have been willing to subscribe. The challenge is to determine exactly what "true for A" means. One position is sometimes called "objectivist," and it explains that according to Protagoras there is after all a single reality that somehow embraces the contrary properties individuals perceive in it. Of course, if there is a single reality, then although Protagoras chooses to highlight situations in which perceptions differ, he is not a relativist in the sense defined earlier. Nor does he abandon the principle of noncontradiction, for what makes opposing *logoi* appear contradictory is merely the fact that each refers to only a part of the underlying reality. Although we do not have him on record to this effect, Protagoras, on this interpretation, would presumably concede that the underlying reality is in some sense truer than individual perceptions of it.[34] In favor of the objectivist view, it is easy to find elements of continuity between it and earlier Greek philosophy. Heraclitus, for example, had insisted on the copresence of opposites, while several thinkers had said that the true nature of things is other than it appears. On the other hand, only one ancient source that discusses Protagoras can be taken as supporting this view of his doctrine. That source is Sextus (*Pyr.* 1.218, part of DK 80 A 14), from whom indeed as many as three interpretations of Protagoras can be wrung. But Sextus seems generally to be so indebted to Plato's *Theaetetus* on this issue that it is hard to believe he is doing anything here other than attributing to Protagoras a view he has mistakenly derived from Plato. Nonetheless, many scholars believe that this view is the one Protagoras is most likely to have held.[35]

A second view holds that Protagoras was indeed a relativist as we have defined the term.[36] That is, every judgment is true just in the sense that it is true for the person whose judgment it is. Ancient support for this view comes from Plato and Sextus whenever they scrupulously include relativizing phrases ("for me," "for you," and so on) in their formulations of Protagoras. Some philosophers see here a challenging doctrine that remains difficult to refute. In most elaborations, it leads to notions of private truth, private worlds, or idealism. The principle that "it is not possible to contradict" is quite easily explained on this view. At the same time, apparent contradiction remains an important part of our experience, and it therefore causes no trouble for this interpretation that we also find Protagoras observing that it is possible to discourse on both sides of every subject (DK 80 A 20). Nor, against the background of his claim that all statements are true for those who make them, need he worry too much about the possibility of making a weaker argument stronger (as, according to DK 80 A 21, he professed to be able to do). He will simply argue that the strength of a *logos* is measured by its ability to persuade those who hear it. He will stake out a similar position for value judgments, his professional concern for which is well attested.[37]

According to a third view, Protagoras is best described as an infallibilist, where this means that every perception is in fact true.[38] Each perception, of course, is a perception by someone at a particular moment. Further, on this view, Protagoras holds that each act of perception changes its object. The qualifications binding each perception to a single observer and moment and asserting that perception changes its object all derive from Plato's *Theaetetus*, where Socrates maintains that Protagoras' thesis is best understood in a Heraclitean context, that is, on the assumption of a world in which observable reality is in constant flux. The main reason for interpreting Protagoras in this light is that, to the extent that any view of him which philosophers still find interesting has textual support, that support comes from Plato. Plato's Socrates says Protagoreanism best supports and is supported by Heracliteanism, and a view that vindicates this judgment has a certain advantage over one which abandons Plato and reconstructs Protagoras unaided by ancient texts (as the objectivist view does) or one which arbitrarily accepts certain Platonic elaborations but not others. The second view just sketched, for which we have retained the label relativist, takes the latter course when it accepts that Protagoras insisted on relativizing expressions but rejects Plato's admixture of Heracliteanism. There is perhaps another reason to take the infallibilist view seriously. It has puzzled commentators that when Plato subjects Protagoras' view to the *peritropē* (*Tht.* 170e–171c), he neglects to use relativizing expressions, although he seems elsewhere to acknowledge that they were important to Protagoras. Likewise, as we have seen, Aristotle simply drops the relativizers when he complains that Protagoras abandons the law of noncontradiction. Now, on Plato's Heraclitean understanding of Protagoras, relativizers begin to appear unnecessary once they are subsumed, in effect, under the assumption of constant flux. If Protagoras made such an assumption, he might have been willing to formulate his doctrine in various ways, including on occasion without relativizing expressions. Plato, then, was on the right track when he examined Protagoras and Heraclitus together, and Aristotle had a better excuse for brusquely dismissing Protagoreanism as tolerant of contradiction.

Plato's Socrates says that his Heraclitean elaboration of Protagoras' view may be what the latter told his pupils in secret (*Tht.* 152c; cf. 155e). This is usually taken as a signal that Plato himself takes responsibility for combining the views as he does. The question relevant to reconstructing Protagoras, however, is whether he thereby admits to distorting the latter's view. He may have found no interesting elaboration at all in Protagoras' book. Each of the views sketched here, then, can claim a different advantage. The objectivist view claims the plausibility of a resort by Protagoras, were he elaborating and defending his view, to ideas we know were in the air. In so doing, it denies him a thesis philosophers still find interesting, but it is easy enough to see how a clever speaker would have used this pronouncement to impress an audience of his contemporaries and advertise his own skill. The view we have called relativist quickly leads down paths most scholars believe were untrodden by ancient Greek philosophy. It honors Protagoras, however, with what some judge the most profound view he might have developed from his preserved point of departure, and also by refusing to let Plato set the agenda. The infallibilist view is best grounded in a text nearly contemporary with Protagoras. This strength is also its weakness, since the text in question is Plato's, and it clearly betrays his own philosophical preoccupations. Whether the infallibilist view has greater philosophical staying power than Aristotle saw in it requires subjecting it to analysis that begins with Plato and goes on far beyond him. No one believes Protagoras had such conversations, but is that a decisive reason for denying him the view? The questions that arise here, which may be answered in more than one way, concerning the purpose of philosophical reconstruction and the appropriate test(s) of its adequacy, are intriguing ones.

Acknowledgments

I would like to offer warm thanks to Chris Shields and Mitzi Lee for careful reading and expert advice; also to Jerry Pendrick for sharing his translation of Antiphon with me in advance of publication, and the Cambridge University Press for permission to quote from it.

Notes

1 Mourelatos 1987, 151. On eristic ("competitive refutation"), see "Language and Rhetoric" below.
2 If Plato was grossly unfair to the Sophists, he did not thereby provoke a reexamination of them by his pupil Aristotle, who defines sophistic simply as "apparent, not real wisdom" and the sophist as "one who makes money from apparent, not real wisdom" (*Soph. el.* 165a 21–3 = DK 79, 3). For more on Aristotle and the Sophists, see Guthrie 1969, 53–4; Classen 1981.

3 On Aristophanes' *Clouds*, the first version of which was produced in 423 BCE and offers a hostile portrait of Socrates as a composite natural philosopher and sophist, see chapter 3. For sketches of modern reception of the Sophists, see Guthrie 1969, 10–13; Kerferd 1981, 4–14; and Hoffmann 1997, 4–10.

4 For fuller narrative and on all matters of detail, the books of Guthrie 1969 and Kerferd 1981 are indispensable; see also de Romilly 1992. On most topics and for most individual Sophists, Kerferd makes the case for maximum philosophical interest and coherence, and his approach has found many followers. Striker 1996 wonders whether the trend towards charitable interpretation has gone too far (cf. n. 17 below). For information about editions, translations, and aids for the student, see the Bibliography.

5 This is only the general picture. Just a few years after Plato's death, the orator Aeschines (*in Tim.* 173) speaks of "Socrates the sophist" (yes, Socrates!), and much later *sophistēs* again comes into general use, more or less as the equivalent of "professor."

6 3.38.4. That Cleon has sophistic *epideixeis* in mind is shown by 3.38.7. The dramatic date of Cleon's speech is 427 BCE.

7 See e.g. Xen. *Mem.* 1.6.13, and Aristophanes' picture of a starving, stealing Socrates who takes money for teaching. On the Sophists' professionalism, Guthrie 1969, 35–40.

8 DK 80–8. For English translations and handbooks based on DK, see the Bibliography.

9 DK 88 B 25. For a recent text, English translation, commentary, and discussion of authorship and genre, see Davies 1989. Those with German should consult Pechstein 1998.

10 See Guthrie 1969, 261–94. For all of these except Antiphon, Plato is the most important source. We are also fortunate to have a few extended texts by Gorgias (see below).

11 W. C. Greene, as quoted by Guthrie 1969, 73.

12 Thomas 2000, a book which demonstrates that the historian Herodotus, too, must be seen against this background, is full of useful insights about the Sophists. See also Wallace 1998, 208–14.

13 Kennedy 1963. For discussion of the Sophists' role in the development of rhetoric as a specialized discipline, which lies beyond the scope of this chapter, see e.g. Cole 1991 and Schiappa 1999.

14 Classen 1976 (1959).

15 Kerferd 1981, 59–67, to whom the discussion in the text is indebted. Nehamas 1990, however, would modify the picture in significant ways.

16 McCabe 1998, however, is a spirited attempt to find in *Euthydemus* a philosophical topic worthy of being treated by Plato at such length. The exemplification in Aristotle's *Sophistic Refutations* of the eristic art he professes to despise raises similar problems; see above, n. 2, and Guthrie 1981, 150–5.

17 According to Striker's re-examination of this terminology, Greek authors not inclined to link dialectic with the theory of Forms or to reserve it piously for Socrates and Plato would have had no reason not to use it to describe the Sophists' characteristic method (Striker 1996). Striker agrees with Plato and Aristotle that the Sophists typically propounded only arguments, not doctrines. Plato therefore denies them the title dialecticians, while Aristotle allows them to be dialecticians but not philosophers.

18 See, besides the annotated editions of MacDowell 1982 and Buchheim 1989, e.g. Mourelatos 1987; Schiappa 1999, 114–32. A recent discussion that concentrates on Gorgias' appropriation of myth is Morgan 2000, 122–8.

19 §8. Here and elsewhere the translation is by G. Kennedy in Sprague 1972.

20 One of the paraphrases, by Sextus (*Math.* 7.65–87), is printed as DK 82 B 3 and accordingly translated by Kennedy in Sprague 1972. Many scholars prefer the other, by the anonymous author of the treatise *On Melissus, Xenophanes, and Gorgias* attributed to Aristotle; a translation appears in Gagarin and Woodruff 1995. Opinions differ as to whether Gorgias should be seen as seriously committed to a philosophy of language which is hard (if not impossible) to reconcile with his practice of rhetoric. For arguments urging both seriousness and compatibility, see Kerferd 1981, 78–82; Mourelatos 1987. On Gorgias and deception, see Segal 1962; Verdenius 1981.

21 *Helen* 3–5; Plato apparently considers Gorgias' treatise beneath notice. To say that it is amusing is not to deny that philosophers, with effort and good will, can find in it anticipations of arguments that still interest them. The approach to *On Not-Being* in this way by Mourelatos 1987 yields impressive results. Striker (1996, 14) judges Gorgias' arguments on the whole no worse than Parmenides'.

22 Readers of German may consult the recent study of sophistic views on justice by Hoffmann 1997. Relevant discussions are scattered throughout the books of Guthrie, Kerferd, de Romilly, and Cassin. On Protagoras' "Great Speech," see e.g. Farrar 1988, 77–98; Morgan 2000, 132–54.

23 Guthrie surveys the *nomos-physis* antithesis in his long fourth chapter (Guthrie 1969, 55–134).

24 For more on these issues, see Guthrie 1969, 107–13; Kerferd 1981, 115–17; Furley 1981; and Caizzi 1999, 323–8.

25 DK 87 B 44 Fr. A = fr. 44(a) Pendrick, col. 2.23–4.22. The translation here and elsewhere is by Pendrick 2002.

26 See recently Hobbs 2000, 137–74; Everson 1998 (on Thrasymachus only); and Beversluis 2000, 221–44 and 339–76 (on Socrates' allegedly weak arguments and Plato's systematic unfairness to Thrasymachus and Callicles).

27 On this topic, see Guthrie 1969, 164–75; Dihle 1981.

28 Bett 1989.

29 For summaries of earlier debates, see Guthrie 1969, 188–92; and the exhaustive survey in Huss 1996.

30 Like the Greek *phainesthai*, many English verbs can express both perceptions and judgments. Thus "seem" itself: "the water seems cold to me" alongside "killing people seems wrong to me."

31 On the *peritrope*, see Burnyeat 1976a and 1976b.

32 Burnyeat 1976b.

33 So Barnes 1982, 547–53.

34 Such a concession might easily lead to a Lockean distinction between primary and secondary qualities, and it is worth noting that the examples most often used by other ancient philosophers to elucidate Protagoras' position are in fact confined to secondary and moral qualities. Protagoras' fellow Abderite Democritus seems to move in the direction of the same distinction when he writes, for example, "by convention sweet, by convention bitter, by convention warm, by convention cold, by convention color, but in reality atoms and void" (68 B 9 DK, cf. B 125). See McKirahan in this volume (chapter 1); and Guthrie 1965, 440.

35 E.g. Kerferd 1981, 87; cf. Woodruff 1999, 302–4. Guthrie 1969, 184–6, argues against Cornford's earlier defense of this view.

36 Guthrie 1969, 186–7; Burnyeat 1976a, 45–6.
37 For various suggestions as to how Protagoras retained a role for wise teachers and orators while holding that all judgments, including value judgments, are true for those whose judgments they are, see Guthrie 1969, 170–5; Cole 1972; Farrar 1988, 66–77; Caizzi 1999, 320–2.
38 Fine 1994.

References and Recommended Reading

Primary Sources

DK. Diels, Hermann 1952. *Die Fragmente der Vorsokratiker.* 6th ed. revised by Walter Kranz. Berlin: Weidmann. The standard collection of testimonia (A fragments) and direct quotations (B fragments) for nine named Sophists (chapters 80–8), the Anonymous Iamblichi (89), and *Dissoi Logoi* (90). Citation takes the form, e.g., DK 80 B 1 for the first-numbered direct quotation of Protagoras. Chapters 80–90 largely abandon the practice followed elsewhere in DK of translating B fragments into German.

The following three works follow the arrangement of DK and provide different kinds of help for the student of the Sophists:

Freeman, Kathleen 1959. *The Pre-Socratic Philosophers: A Companion to Diels, Fragmente der Vorsokratiker.* 2nd ed. Cambridge, Mass.: Harvard University Press. Summarizes what is known about the life and thought of each philosopher included in DK.

Sprague, Rosamond Kent, ed. 1972. *The Older Sophists: A Complete Translation by Several Hands of the Fragments in Die Fragmente der Vorsokratiker, edited by Diels–Kranz. With a new edition of Antiphon and of Euthydemus.* Columbia: University of South Carolina Press. English translation of both A and B fragments, with brief introductions and some additional material (especially for Antiphon), including extracts from Plato's *Euthydemus* presented as "fragments" of Euthydemus of Chios.

Untersteiner, Mario 1967 (1949–62). *Sofisti: Testimonianze e Frammenti.* 4 vols. Florence: La Nuova Italia. Translation of both A and B fragments, with some additional material and fairly full commentary, in Italian. The section on Critias in vol. 4 is by Antonio Battegazzore.

In a few cases, those working closely with the Greek texts should consult more recent or annotated editions.

For Antiphon:
Pendrick, Gerard J. 2002. *Antiphon the Sophist: The Fragments.* Cambridge: Cambridge University Press.

For *Dissoi Logoi*:
Robinson, T. M. 1979. *Contrasting Arguments: An Edition of the Dissoi Logoi.* New York: Arno Press.

For Gorgias:
Buchheim, Thomas 1989. *Gorgias von Leontinoi: Reden, Fragmente und Testimonien*. Hamburg: Meiner. With German translation and commentary.
MacDowell, D. M. 1982. *Gorgias: Encomium of Helen*. Edited, with introduction, notes, and translation. Bristol: Bristol Classical Press.

Secondary Sources

The main secondary works on the Sophists in English are:
Guthrie, W. K. C. 1969. *A History of Greek Philosophy*, vol. 3: *The Fifth-Century Enlightenment*. Cambridge: Cambridge University Press.
Kerferd, G. B. 1981. *The Sophistic Movement*. Cambridge: Cambridge University Press.

The following does a good job of setting the Sophists in their social and historical context but engages rather less with philosophical interpretation:
Romilly, Jacqueline de 1992 (French original 1988). *The Great Sophists in Periclean Athens*. Translated by Janet Lloyd. Oxford: Oxford University Press.

Recent treatments on a large scale, with full bibliography, include:
Cassin, Barbara 1995. *L'effet sophistique*. Paris: Gallimard.
Kerferd, G. B., and Hellmut Flashar 1998. "Die Sophistik," in *Die Philosophie der Antike*, vol. 2/1, ed. Hellmut Flashar. Basel: Schwabe, 1–137. This chapter was completed by Hellmut Flashar and others from a draft written originally in English by G. B. Kerferd and including his revisions up to the year 1992.

Useful collections of articles include:
Cassin, Barbara, ed. 1986. *Positions de la sophistique*. Paris: J. Vrin.
Classen, Carl Joachim 1976. *Sophistik*. Darmstadt: Wissenschaftliche Buchgesellschaft (*Wege der Forschung* 187). (Reprinted essays in German and English and a lengthy bibliography.)
Kerferd, G. B., ed. 1981. *The Sophists and Their Legacy*. Wiesbaden: Steiner (*Hermes Einzelschriften* 44).

Other Works

Barnes, Jonathan 1982. *The Presocratic Philosophers*. London: Routledge & Kegan Paul.
Bett, Richard, 1989. "The Sophists and Relativism," *Phronesis* 34, 139–69.
Beversluis, John 2000. *Cross-Examining Socrates: A Defense of the Interlocutors in Plato's Early Dialogues*. Cambridge: Cambridge University Press.
Burnyeat, M. F. 1976a. "Protagoras and Self-Refutation in Later Greek Philosophy," *Philosophical Review* 85, 44–69.
—— 1976b. "Protagoras and Self-Refutation in Plato's *Theaetetus*," *Philosophical Review* 85, 172–95. (Reprinted in Stephen Everson, ed., *Epistemology* [*Companions to Ancient Thought: 1*]. Cambridge: Cambridge University Press, 1990, 39–59.)

Caizzi, F. D. 1999. "Protagoras and Antiphon: Sophistic Debates on Justice," in A. A. Long, ed., *The Cambridge Companion to Early Greek Philosophy*. Cambridge: Cambridge University Press, 311–31.

Classen, Carl Joachim 1976 (1959). "The Study of Language amongst Socrates' Contemporaries," in Classen, ed., *Sophistik*, 215–47. (First published in *Proceedings of the African Classical Associations* 2, 33–49.)

—— 1981. "Aristotle's Picture of the Sophists," in Kerferd, ed., 7–24.

Cole, A. Thomas 1972. "The Relativism of Protagoras," *Yale Classical Studies* 22, 19–45.

—— 1991. *The Origins of Rhetoric in Ancient Greece*. Baltimore: The Johns Hopkins University Press.

Davies, Malcolm 1989. "Sisyphus and the Invention of Religion ('Critias' *TrGF* 1 (43) F 19 = B 25 DK)," *Bulletin of the Institute of Classical Studies* 36, 16–32.

Dihle, A. 1981. "Die Verschiedenheit der Sitten als Argument ethischer Theorie," in Kerferd, ed., 54–63.

Everson, Stephen 1998. "The Incoherence of Thrasymachus," *Oxford Studies in Ancient Philosophy* 16, 99–131.

Farrar, Cynthia 1988. *The Origins of Democratic Thinking: The Invention of Politics in Classical Athens*. Cambridge: Cambridge University Press.

Fine, Gail 1994. "Protagorean Relativisms," *Proceedings of the Boston Area Colloquium in Ancient Philosophy* 10, 211–55. Much of the same material is in Gail Fine, "Conflicting Appearances: *Theaetetus* 153d–154b," in Christopher Gill and Mary Margaret McCabe, eds., *Form and Argument in Late Plato*. Oxford: Oxford University Press, 1996, 105–33.

Furley, David J. 1981. "Antiphon's Case Against Justice," in Kerferd, ed., 81–91. (Reprinted in D. J. Furley, *Cosmic Problems: Essays on Greek and Roman Philosophy of Nature*. Cambridge: Cambridge University Press, 1989.)

Gagarin, Michael, and Paul Woodruff 1995. *Early Greek Political Thought from Homer to the Sophists*. Cambridge: Cambridge University Press.

Guthrie, W. K. C. 1965. *A History of Greek Philosophy*. Vol. 2: *The Presocratic Tradition from Parmenides to Democritus*. Cambridge: Cambridge University Press.

—— 1981. *A History of Greek Philosophy*. Vol. 6: *Aristotle, an Encounter*. Cambridge: Cambridge University Press.

Hobbs, Angela 2000. *Plato and the Hero: Courage, Manliness and the Impersonal Good*. Cambridge: Cambridge University Press.

Hoffmann, Klaus Friedrich 1997. *Das Recht im Denken der Sophistik*. Stuttgart: Teubner (*Beiträge zur Altertumskunde* 104).

Huss, Bernhard 1996. "Der Homo-Mensura-Satz des Protagoras: Ein Forschungsbericht," *Gymnasium* 103, 229–57.

Kennedy, George 1963. *The Art of Persuasion in Greece*. Princeton: Princeton University Press.

McCabe, Mary Margaret 1998. "Silencing the Sophists: The Drama of the *Euthydemus*," *Proceedings of the Boston Area Colloquium in Ancient Philosophy* 14, 139–76.

Morgan, Kathryn A. 2000. *Myth and Philosophy from the Presocratics to Plato*. Cambridge: Cambridge University Press.

Mourelatos, Alexander P. D. 1987. "Gorgias on the Function of Language," *Philosophical Topics* 15.2, 135–70.

Nehamas, Alexander 1990. "Eristic, Antilogic, Sophistic, Dialectic: Plato's Demarcation of Philosophy from Sophistry," *History of Philosophy Quarterly* 7, 3–16.

Pechstein, Nikolaus 1998. *Euripides Satyrographos.* Stuttgart: Teubner.

Schiappa, Edward 1999. *The Beginnings of Rhetorical Theory in Classical Greece.* New Haven: Yale University Press.

Segal, C. P. 1962. "Gorgias and the Psychology of the Logos," *Harvard Studies in Classical Philology* 66, 99–155.

Striker, Gisela 1996. "Methods of Sophistry," in *Essays on Hellenistic Epistemology and Ethics.* Cambridge: Cambridge University Press, 3–21.

Thomas, Rosalind 2000. *Herodotus in Context: Ethnography, Science and the Art of Persuasion.* Cambridge: Cambridge University Press.

Verdenius, W. J. 1981. "Gorgias' Doctrine of Deception," in Kerferd, ed., 116–28.

Wallace, Robert W. 1998. "The Sophists in Athens," in Deborah Boedeker and Kurt A. Raaflaub, eds., *Democracy, Empire, and the Arts in Fifth-Century Athens* (Cambridge, Mass.: Harvard University Press), 203–22.

Woodruff, Paul 1999. "Rhetoric and Relativism: Protagoras and Gorgias," in A. A. Long, ed., *The Cambridge Companion to Early Greek Philosophy.* Cambridge: Cambridge University Press, 290–310.

Part II

Socrates: Introduction

Socrates is a pivotal but enigmatic figure in the history of Greek Philosophy. His centrality to the history of its development is most readily appreciated by comparing the philosophical climate in Greece before his life with the completely dissimilar situation which followed it. It is, indeed, a testament to his significance that scholars first came to call those before him who philosophized the "Presocratics." The term itself marks something momentous, as do parallel terms such as "pre-industrial" in "preindustrial society" or "post-war" in "postwar economy." Presocratic philosophy is philosophy as it was before it was touched by Socrates; after Socrates, philosophy was not the same. This is why writing some four centuries after the death of Socrates, Cicero could contend without fear of contradiction that Socrates "first called philosophy down from heaven, set her into the cities, introduced her into men's homes, and compelled her to investigate life and customs, good and evil."[1] Cicero means that Socrates first turned philosophy towards matters of morality and ethical conduct, that he personalized it by enjoining each of us to see through the self-constructed psychological barriers which keep us from knowing ourselves and our true motives, that he directed each of us to examine our own lives lest we lead lives not worthy of human beings.

Cicero signifies something more as well: Socrates left a lasting impression on those who knew him, and through them, those who followed him. Indeed, his very name rapidly became the basis of an adjective, "Socratic," and even, in the hands of a comic poet, a verb, "to socratize," that is, to ape Socrates in manner, dress, and demeanor. In its adjectival form, "Socratic" came to be applied to an entire genre of writing, the so-called *Sokratikoi logoi*, the "Socratic writings" or "Socratic compositions," inspired by Socrates' way of conducting himself in life as in philosophical inquiry. Later, in the Hellenistic Period, it became commonplace for schools of philosophy – even those with diametrically opposed points of view – to claim Socrates as their progenitor. Evidently, only those who could claim to be following in the footsteps of Socrates could claim to be engaging in *bona fide* philosophy.

So, who was this man whose very name became an adjective and a verb practically in his own lifetime, whose imprimatur became the stamp of philosophical legitimacy? Only bare essentials are well established. He was born in Athens in

469 BC, lived virtually his whole life without leaving the city, and died in 399 BC, by order of an Athenian court which had tried and sentenced him to death on charges of irreligiosity and immorality. The actual motives of those who brought the charges against Socrates are disputed, though they probably derive at least in part from the company he kept: Socrates consorted with rich young men of oligarchic and antidemocratic tendencies. These men included some who were active, directly and indirectly, in a coup which overthrew the democratic government of Athens and established the rule of the Thirty Tyrants, a group of oligarchs with connections to Sparta who took power in 404 BC, only to be removed and to see democracy restored in 403 BC. Fairly clearly, Socrates' associations with some of the movers behind this coup left him in bad odor with Athenians of democratic leaning. Although a general amnesty had been proclaimed upon the restoration of democracy, and despite the fact that Socrates had not himself supported the Thirty and even opposed them in some particulars, those who disliked Socrates may nonetheless have found a vehicle for retribution and punishment in the form of his eventual trial and execution.

Socrates maintains his own innocence in a dialogue by Plato, the *Apology* (*apologia* = "defense" in Greek), as he does in a different *Apology*, written by another contemporary of his, Xenophon. The samenesses and differences in these accounts of Socrates' trial already introduce the central "Socratic Problem," as it is called, the problem of trying to determine the views held by the actual Socrates. Central to this problem is that Socrates himself wrote next to nothing, and nothing philosophical at all. To make matters worse, when we piece together his views from those who wrote about him, or who presented him as a character in Socratic compositions, we find Socrates presenting himself as modest to the point of knowing little or nothing of lasting value, as a man who has few positive views, who merely helps others through his pointed questioning of them. Thus, in Plato's *Theaetetus*, he compares himself to his mother, who had been a midwife, intimating that though he is himself intellectually barren, he has a knack for helping those with fertile minds give birth to their own ideas.[2] So, we are left wondering whether the philosopher held to be the founder of a number of distinct philosophical schools held positive views of his own, and whether, to the extent that he did, he was ever prepared to develop and defend them in dogmatic detail.

Smith and Brickhouse survey the surviving evidence for Socrates and identify some key theses he was willing to promulgate.[3] They present these theses, several of which are engagingly paradoxical, together with Socrates' famous method, the *elenchtic method*, now often imitated in universities and law schools in many parts of the world, if somewhat loosely, under the name of the "the Socratic method." They also show clearly why Socrates insisted, with his characteristic directness, that "the unexamined life is not worth living."[4]

Notes

1 *Tusculan Disputations* 5.10–11.
2 *Theaetetus* 149a–b. For this sort of citation to a Platonic text, see Part 3, "Plato: Introduction," n. 2.
3 See also Part 3, "Plato: Introduction," for a brief characterization of the chronology of Plato's dialogues, including those which are "Socratic."
4 Plato, *Apology* 38a.

Chapter 3

Socrates

Thomas C. Brickhouse and Nicholas D. Smith

"Socratic Problem" and Sources on Socrates

Nothing written by Socrates has come down to us. Some testimonia claim that he wrote poetry; others claim he wrote nothing. Even if Socrates did occasionally write, whatever he wrote was insignificant. Instead, his influence derived wholly from conversations in which he asked deeply probing questions which left his interlocutors and spectators puzzled, stimulated, disturbed, sometimes amused, and often infuriated. But much was written about Socrates by his contemporaries and members of later generations. So controversial a figure was he that the early part of the fourth century BC saw a vast literary genre of "Socratic" writings come into existence after his death. These "Socratic writings," as they were called, expounded allegedly Socratic doctrines, depicted conversations in which a character named Socrates was the principal speaker, attacked Socrates' character in polemical "accusations," or defended him in various "apologies of Socrates," which purported to be versions of the defense speech Socrates gave at his trial.

Many puzzles surround what has become known as "the Socratic Problem," that is, to decipher who the real Socrates was and what his views are. Much of the evidence has been lost to time and much of what has survived is either fragmentary or plainly partisan. Perhaps the most puzzling thing of all is what we can be confident actually happened to Socrates. In 399 BC, when Socrates was seventy years old, three Athenians (the nominal prosecutor, Meletus, and his two *synēgoroi* [supporting prosecutors] – the powerful politician, Anytus, and Lycon, about whom we know next to nothing) – brought Socrates to trial for impiety. The charge had three specifications: not recognizing the gods of the state; introducing new divine things; and corrupting the youth. The charge of impiety itself was not entirely uncommon, but these specifications of it are quite unusual. At the end of the trial a majority of the jury of 500 members found the old man guilty and sentenced him to death by drinking the poison derived from hemlock (*conium maculatum*). The great puzzle is this: What had this man done to convince the Athenians that he deserved execution?

It is fortunate that a number of complete works by different authors have come down to us in which a figure named "Socrates" figures prominently. Each of the authors – Aristophanes, Xenophon, and Plato – seems to have known Socrates personally and, thus, what they say about the man and his philosophy deserve special attention. Also important is Aristotle's testimony about Socrates, for even though Socrates died before Aristotle was born, and much of what Aristotle tells us may simply have been taken from his teacher, Plato, Aristotle was in a position to tell which of the many stories that continued to circulate about Socrates were true and which were imaginary. Still later reports, such as the one we find in the life of Socrates provided (probably in the third century AD) by Diogenes Laertius (2.18–47), are suspect, and in any case rely heavily on the earlier testimony.

Aristophanes

The earliest of the surviving works in which we find Socrates portrayed is Aristophanes' comedy the *Clouds*. The play was first produced in 423 BC and revised five years or so later by Aristophanes himself; it is the revised version that has come down to us. The *Clouds* burlesques the so-called new education that became popular during the Peloponnesian War, in which natural science and rhetorical skill were more heavily emphasized than the military skills, traditional religion, and social mores featured more prominently in the past. Scholars continue to dispute Aristophanes' motivation in electing to portray Socrates as the exemplar of the "new" educator, a quack who runs the "Think-shop" to which students come to learn absurd and worthless scientific theories as well as the more practical but morally questionable skill to "make the weaker argument appear the stronger."

Most scholars believe that Aristophanes' depiction of Socrates at least to some degree merely assimilates him to a stereotype of the fifth century sophistical intellectual. Moreover, it is likely that Socrates had already developed a considerable reputation in Athens as a thinker who challenged conventional educational practices. Otherwise, Aristophanes would not have been able to achieve the desired comic effect with a character by the name of "Socrates." Recently, a number of scholars have noted distinct dissimilarities between Aristophanes' Socrates and the deeply pious and sincere philosopher of that name we find in Plato and Xenophon. The differences in these authors' portraits, such scholars argue, is most likely the result of the different authors' motives in writing about Socrates. Aristophanes, writing satirical comedy, needed only enough of the real Socrates to appear in his comical character to make his portrayal recognizable, for his real purpose was to lampoon the sophists and nature-philosophers, whose teachings constituted the "new education." And naturally, even this much accuracy would be put in the worst possible light. Many of the particular ways in which Socrates is portrayed by Aristophanes seem to be recognizable caricatures of traits or methods Socrates' apologists themselves assign to him. Where the pictures diverge it is not improbable that the comic poet was stereotyping the philosopher – no one expected accuracy from comedy. But Aristophanes' decision to use Socrates betrayed at least some prejudice – by Aristophanes' audience at least, if not by the comic poet himself – that Socrates was indeed a danger to traditional values and the society such values help to maintain.

One advantage to seeing such a commonality among the sources is obvious: It helps to explain how Socrates could at least to many appear to be enough of a threat to warrant prosecution.

Xenophon

Of the two apologists (Plato and Xenophon), Xenophon's account is the one usually given less weight by scholars, though some reputable scholars have given great credibility to Xenophon as a source for genuine Socratic teaching. The problem with Xenophon's portrait may not be so much its lack of value as history, but rather in the dull and lifeless philosophy Socrates articulates in it. The most detailed portrayals of Socrates in Xenophon occur in four of the latter's works: the *Apology of Socrates*, the *Memorabilia*, the *Symposium*, and the *Oeconomicus*. The latter two are by most scholars agreed to be nearly worthless as history; in the *Symposium* we find Socrates at a light-hearted banquet and drinking party, and in the *Oeconomicus*, we find him giving folksy advice on how best to manage one's property and home.

In none of Xenophon's works do we find Socrates to be especially keen or penetrating in his arguments or professed beliefs; certainly we find little that would have drawn the ire of his countrymen. Reading Xenophon leaves one completely puzzled as to why Socrates would ever have been tried and condemned. Xenophon's Socrates is traditionally pious almost to a fault; he is a philosopher of homilies and platitudes, whose most dangerous views consisted in certain relatively bland criticisms of Athenian democracy, the likes of which were common in the latter part of the fifth century. Xenophon's Socrates always encourages what appears to be a fairly conservative morality, and his arguments appear to most readers to be lacking in subtlety. The one exception to this rule is what appears to be a quite sophisticated argument for the existence of the gods in the *Memorabilia* (1.4.4–18), but we have no independent evidence for attributing this sort of argument to the historical Socrates. Perhaps Xenophon had heard such an argument elsewhere and put it into Socrates' mouth; perhaps Xenophon had a creative moment himself. In any case, as Xenophon himself points out at its conclusion (*Memorabilia* 1.4.19), such an argument would hardly have been the sort of thing to earn its author an accusation of impiety.

Probably the earliest Xenophontic depiction of Socrates is the *Apology*, which explicitly states that it was inspired by other "Apologies" (possibly including Plato's) with which Xenophon found fault (*Apology* 1). Xenophon's *Apology* stresses Socrates' *megalēgoria* (boastful talk) at his trial (*Apology* 2). In Xenophon's account, Socrates had decided that it was better to die rather than face the infirmities of old age (*Apology* 6–9); so at his trial he acted in such a way as to invite condemnation.

In what is in all likelihood a later work, the *Memorabilia*, much the same account is given of Socrates' behavior at his trial. In the *Memorabilia*, however, Xenophon's explanation is explicitly a rebuttal to the charge that Socrates' *daimonion* (deity – elsewhere called a "voice" or a "divine sign") was a sham (*Memorabilia* 4.8.1). In both Plato's and Xenophon's works Socrates claims to have a personal *daimonion* which forewarned him when he was about to do something wrong (Xenophon, *Memorabilia* 1.12–14; *Apology* 4–5, 8, 12–13; *Symposium* 8.5, Plato, *Apology* 31c–d, 40a, c, 41d; *Euthyphro* 3b; *Euthydemus* 272e; *Republic* 6.496c; *Phaedrus* 242b; see also Pseudo-Plato, *Theages* 128d–131a). In Plato the *daimonion's* alarms came merely as warning against some impending error he might otherwise have committed; in Xenophon and Pseudo-Plato, it also guides him to do what is right. In the *Memorabilia* Xenophon denies that Socrates' condemnation showed that the *daimonion* was a delusion – if he had such a prophetic sign, the objection goes, how was he unable to avoid being put to death? Xenophon's answer: He chose to be put to death, rather than face old age, "the most burdensome part of life" (4.8.1).

Other parts of the *Memorabilia* defend Socrates against further charges that Xenophon seems either to have heard or that he anticipated from those bent on attacking Socrates after his death. Perhaps the most notorious example of such an attack was a pamphlet of the sophist Polycrates, which caused a sensation – especially among Socrates' apologists. Indeed, much of the first book of Xenophon's *Memorabilia* is devoted to defending Socrates against charges that had been launched by someone Xenophon simply refers to as "the accuser" (first mentioned at *Memorabilia* 1.2.9) but who scholars now generally believe was Polycrates. Because we cannot be sure of what Polycrates' accusations were or what motivated him to make them, little or nothing can be inferred from Xenophon's responses to them about what led the Athenians to put Socrates on trial in 399.

The rest of the *Memorabilia* is a potpourri of anecdotes Xenophon offers to underscore the piety and plain morality of the philosopher the Athenians put to death. Xenophon's defense of Socrates' virtue is so ordinary that it leaves the Athenians' motives for convicting him mysterious. This, indeed, appears to be part of the design of the *Memorabilia*: Xenophon begins that work with the protest that the trial and condemnation of Socrates were a matter for "wonder" (*Memorabilia* 1.1.1).

Plato

Plato's Socrates is also a man morally superior to others. But his methods and the responses to them Plato portrays help more to explain Socrates' demise than anything we find in Xenophon. In Plato's dialogues Socrates is a man of extreme intellectual agility, capable of reducing even the most resolutely proud and learned men to confusion and self-contradiction. All the while professing his own ignorance, Plato's Socrates is consistently able to reveal the ignorance of others. In Plato's account Socrates spends each day of his life publicly exposing the ignorance of those who claim in some way to be wise (*Apology* 23b). It takes little imagination to see how such a daily ritual would earn Socrates the enmity of many of his victims and their supporters. One can also easily imagine the dismay of parents who hear of young men "examining" their elders Socratically. If there is a puzzle about the trial of Socrates (as he is portrayed in Plato), it is not so much why he is prosecuted, as why it took the Athenians so long to bring charges against him.

Plato wrote numerous dialogues throughout his life. With predictable disagreements about the details, scholars have attempted to arrange these dialogues in chronological groupings, using several approaches, including especially computer-assisted stylometric analysis – by which Plato's diction in each dialogue is carefully scrutinized and compared to what appears in each other dialogue – as well as careful scrutiny of significant commonalities and differences in the philosophical style and content of the various dialogues. Although controversies abound for all such schemes, most of the recent scholarship on Socrates at any rate has focused on the depiction of Socrates in the group of dialogues counted by chronological orderings as the earliest in Plato's writings. This group includes (in alphabetical order): *Apology, Charmides, Crito, Euthydemus, Euthyphro, Gorgias, Hippias major, Hippias minor, Ion, Laches, Lysis, Menexenus, Protagoras, Republic* Book 1. Most also suppose that the *Meno*, too, contains many of the elements common to the early period.

These works allow us, at least to some degree, to understand why a number of bright young minds were attracted to Socrates, on the one hand, and why many other Athenians, on the other, would have regarded him as having a dangerous and corrosive effect on some of the Athenian youth. But most of all, Plato's works pose philosophical problems and questions whose intricacy and difficulty continue to challenge us; and ultimately this is why scholars tend to focus on Plato's works – whether or not they are taken to depict the historical Socrates accurately. From the point of view of the history of philosophy, at any rate, it is Plato's Socrates who asks and explores many of what have become the quintessential questions of philosophy. He asks them in ways that are readily understood; and in Plato's version he asks them in dramatic settings that make such questions even more compelling. Thus, when Plato asks us, in the *Crito*, to consider the duty of each of us has to obey the laws of the state, he does not merely raise the question in an abstract way – he has Socrates discuss it as he awaits execution in jail, condemned to die by what both he and his interlocutor (Crito) agree was a miscarriage of justice and a misapplication of the very laws obedience to which is in question. So too, we learn what the Platonic Socrates thinks about piety, and how much he thinks we do not know about it, in the *Euthyphro*, a dialogue set on the steps of the king-archon's office, where his interlocutor (Euthyphro) had come to press charges against his own father – something Athenians of that time would view as impious in the extreme. So it is that Plato's early portrayals of Socrates continue not only to raise the most serious philosophical questions, but also to stimulate and arouse the reader with their drama. For these reasons, then, though scholars may debate endlessly and never conclusively about their relative value as history, Plato's dialogues deservedly continue to be the most widely read and studied sources on Socrates.

Socrates' "Method" and Moral Viewpoints

Taking Plato as our principal authority, we discover that Socrates was a man with a moral mission, which had its origin in an oracle given by the god Apollo at Delphi.

According to Plato's *Apology*, once Socrates' friend, a man named Chaerophon, asked the oracle whether any man is wiser than Socrates (*Apology* 20e–21a). Socrates was astonished at the news that the god had answered "no," for Socrates thought he had no wisdom at all (*Apology* 21b). Investigating the meaning of the oracle by questioning those he thought were wise, Socrates discovered they were in fact ignorant – and worse, ignorant even of their own ignorance (*Apology* 21b–22e). All but Socrates supposed they had wisdom of the most important things – how to live well, be virtuous, and be happy – yet all were ignorant. Worse, because they supposed they were wise, they did not examine their lives as they should, smugly supposing that their way of living was best. By leading him to this realization, Socrates believed, the god was giving him a mission: He must examine people relentlessly, demonstrating their ignorance to them and encouraging them to care more for virtue than for the reputation and wealth they so prized (*Apology* 29d–e), and above all exhorting them always to open their lives to examination – for "the unexamined life is not worth living for a human being" (*Apology* 38a).

Socrates performed his examinations and his exhortations through what has come to be known as the method of *elenchos*, or "elenctic method," by which Socrates would one way or another reveal inherent absurdities or incoherence in his interlocutors' thoughts on ethical subjects. Typically, these demonstrations would begin when the interlocutor explicitly expressed, or in some other way betrayed, a belief Socrates would target as suspect. By patiently eliciting premises from among what he insisted must be his interlocutor's other sincerely held views, Socrates would show how the targeted view did not cohere with the interlocutor's other views. At least in Plato's dialogues, these "examinations," as he called them, unfortunately only rarely produced the kind of moral chastening that Socrates seemed to seek in his interlocutors: We occasionally find Socrates' interlocutors giving up their incoherent positions; but more often they end up unrepentant and annoyed, thinking that some sort of trick had been played on them. Depending upon their degree of receptivity, though, Socrates might have hoped that at least a seed of self-doubt had been planted, whose germination would vitiate to some degree his interlocutor's ignorant self-confidence. We might guess from his eventual trial and execution, however, that much of what Socrates attempted to plant in his interlocutors never bore worthy fruit.

Although the Socrates found in the pages of Plato makes it his mission to question others and professed no special moral expertise of his own, it is nonetheless possible to isolate a number of moral positions in which he appears to have great confidence. How he arrives at some of his views is not entirely clear. However, he suggests that the repeated and consistent failures in arguments with him, of those who accept views opposed to his own, is informative (*Gorgias* 508e–509b). For example, he finds that anyone who urges that injustice with impunity is really a good thing can never successfully defend his view in elenctic discussion (see, e.g., *Gorgias* 472e ff.; *Republic* 1.336b ff.). Thus, Socrates concludes that injustice with impunity cannot be a good thing. That he believes that justice and virtue invariably brought the greatest rewards are things we are lucky enough to find Socrates saying explicitly in a number of passages (e.g., *Apology* 30b; *Crito* 48b; *Gorgias* 507b–c;

Republic 1.353d–354a). Similarly, he tells us that he believes one ought never to harm another or do evil, and hence, one ought never to return harm for harm or evil for evil (see, e.g., *Apology* 25c–26a, 29b, 37a–b; *Crito* 49a–c; *Gorgias* 469b ff. [esp. 479c–e], 527a–b; *Republic* 1.335b–e); accordingly, it is always better to suffer than to do evil or harm (see, e.g., *Gorgias* 469b–c, 474b ff., 508c).

Some of these principles would have struck many of Socrates' contemporaries as incredible. His theory of motivation, however, rests on less controversial convictions: first, the greatest good for human beings is *eudaimonia* (happiness or well-being, see, e.g., *Crito* 48b) and, second, the agent's belief that a certain action will best promote his or her conception of happiness is sufficient to produce that action (see, e.g., *Protagoras* 358d; *Euthydemus* 278e). Socrates believes, in other words, that every action people ever undertake aims at what they believe to be in their best interest in their pursuit of happiness. Scholars differ about whether Socrates recognizes any desires that aim at anything (e.g., pleasure) other than the agent's good or benefit. But even if he does allow for such "good-independent" desires, it is clear that he thinks that we nonetheless always act out of our desire for what is good for us (that is, what is conducive to our happiness) – if there are other desires, these can work only by somehow influencing us to believe, at the time we act, that pursuing their objects will bring us some advantage in our pursuit of happiness.

What Socrates takes happiness to consist in is the subject of intense and ongoing scholarly debate. Based on an extended *elenchos* developed in the *Protagoras* (351b ff.), a crucial premise of which is the claim that happiness is pleasure, some scholars take Socrates to be a hedonist. But Socrates in the *Gorgias* launches a withering attack on hedonism. Some scholars have taken this to express *Plato's* rejection of the Socratic view of happiness expressed in the *Protagoras*, or have argued that the form of hedonism Socrates attacks in the *Gorgias* is different from the form he seems to endorse in the *Protagoras*. But other scholars deny that Socrates ever actually endorses hedonism in the *Protagoras*. Instead, they take him to be merely showing what most people, and perhaps his interlocutor Protagoras, are committed to by *their* acceptance of hedonism.

Whatever the truth of the matter, there is little doubt that Socrates believes the best way to pursue happiness is through the cultivation of the virtue of one's soul and by acting virtuously in one's daily affairs (see, e.g., *Apology* 28b, 30a–b; *Crito* 48b–d). If we think of a real good as that which is always conducive to happiness and never productive of wretchedness, the only real good is the virtue of one's soul, which Socrates identifies with the traditionally recognized moral virtues of piety, justice, wisdom, self-control, and courage. Other things that people often regard as far more precious – health, honor, wealth, good looks, and the like – are, for Socrates, mere instruments, in themselves neither good nor bad. If they are put in the service of virtuous ends, they become good. If they are put in the service of evil ends, they become evil (see, e.g., *Euthydemus* 281a–e; *Meno* 78c–d).

Some commentators have taken Socrates to believe that not only is moral virtue the only thing that it is always good; it is actually sufficient for happiness – in other words, that the possession of moral virtue is all by itself a complete guarantee that one will be happy. Such a position is certainly suggested by some texts (e.g., *Republic*

1.353d–354a and *Gorgias* 507b–c). But there is also reason to doubt that this is what Socrates believes, for he sometimes suggests that life would not be worth living if one contracted a chronic and painful disease (*Crito* 47e and *Gorgias* 512a–b). It seems obvious that such a condition could befall even the most virtuous of people and if it did, even if moral virtue could protect one against ever harming one's own soul through the commission of injustice and so could shield one from wretchedness, moral virtue could not guarantee happiness. If so, it seems preferable to think that when Socrates seems to be suggesting that virtue is sufficient for happiness he be taken to mean that *under normal conditions, when there are not great evils sufficient to make one's life not worth living,* moral virtue will guarantee one's happiness. The pursuit of moral virtue, then, is always rational, for it is the best protection against preventable evils. But it can never make one invulnerable to various evils that would, if suffered, have a catastrophic effect on one's well-being.

Many scholars argue that, for Socrates, virtue is at least necessary for happiness, and indeed, they have strong textual support for their claim. At *Gorgias* 507c–e Socrates states unequivocally that no one can be happy who lacks moral virtue. It is worth noting that if this is indeed Socrates' considered view, he must also think that no one, at least no one he has ever known, including himself, is happy – for no one, including himself possesses the knowledge that constitutes moral virtue. But Socrates' position on this issue is not as plain as many have taken it to be, for in at least one passage, *Apology* 41b–c, Socrates states equally plainly that engaging in uninterrupted philosophical discussion in the afterlife (if there is an afterlife) would bring one enormous happiness. Since Socrates is suggesting that such activity would be available to him in the afterlife, and because he lacks the knowledge that constitutes moral virtue, he seems to think that virtue is not necessary for happiness.

Two of the views for which Socrates is best known are especially counterintuitive. The first of these "paradoxes," that weakness of will, or *akrasia*, is an illusion follows directly from Socrates' view, referred to above, that all action is motivated by a desire for one's own happiness. If one always acts from a desire for one's own good, then it cannot be the case that one ever acts contrary to one's knowledge (or even one's belief) about what would be the better course of action. It is impossible, as Socrates argues in the *Protagoras* (351c), that one's knowledge of what is best "could be dragged around like a slave." Socrates' denial of the possibility of weakness of will has an important corollary. Since Socrates believes that virtuous action is always in one's interest and viciousness is never in one's interest, then anyone who understands this fact and who recognizes an opportunity to engage in virtuous action, will necessarily pursue it. It follows, of course, that all failures to promote one's own good generally, and all failures to do what is morally correct, are directly attributable and only attributable to wrongdoers' ignorance of what is in their interest. If so, all wrongdoing is involuntary. (See also, *Apology* 25c–e; *Gorgias* 460b–d, 468c; *Meno* 77b–78b; *Protagoras* 345c, 358c, 360c.) It is worth pointing out that however counterintuitive Socrates' denial of *akrasia* may appear, it follows from premises each of which seems, taken by itself, not at all implausible.

The second "paradox" is that all of the virtues (courage, piety, justice, temperance, and wisdom) form a unity. In the *Protagoras* Socrates argues that it is not possible for a person to possess one of the virtues without possessing each of the others. Although the precise sense in which the virtues form a unity has been vigorously contested over the years, there is widespread though not universal agreement today that throughout the early dialogues Socrates holds that all of the virtues are in some sense one and the same thing. "Moral virtue" is another name for moral knowledge and each of the "parts" of moral virtue as a whole is constituted by the same knowledge.

That Socrates thinks that moral virtue is constituted by moral wisdom would seem to derive some support from the many comparisons he makes between moral virtue and craft, or *technē* (e.g., *Laches* 198d–199a; *Charmides* 174b–175a; *Euthydemus* 291d–e). Socrates' use of the "craft analogy," as it is frequently called, suggests that he thinks that moral virtue has a "product," or *ergon*. The possessor of moral virtue is able invariably to pick out and create examples of virtue's *ergon* in just the same way that a skilled artisan can pick out and create examples of what his or her particular craft serves to produce. Moreover, just as the craftsperson can give an account of how the product is brought about and can teach that knowledge to others, so would anyone who possesses moral virtue be able to explain how the product of the craft of virtue is rendered and would be able to provide that knowledge to others.

Plato's early works reveal a Socrates who is himself willing to raise vexing questions about the craft analogy. What exactly does he think the *ergon* of virtue is (e.g., *Euthyphro* 13e–14c)? Does he think that the various individual virtues can have different products and yet still be essentially the same moral knowledge? Can the craft of virtue be used expertly for an evil purpose in the way that other crafts can be used expertly to bring about the contrary of their proper products (*Hippias minor* 366b–376b; *Republic* 1.333e–334b). Whether the fact that Plato puts questions such as these before the reader indicates that Socrates never really accepted the craft analogy or whether Plato presents them as puzzles for his audience to figure out for themselves is a matter of continuing debate among scholars.

Socrates' exploration of these issues might not in themselves have attracted the ire of his fellow Athenians, though in them may be found a number of subversions of contemporary common morality. But the aggressiveness with which he attacked opposing views and exposed the ignorance of those who held them would certainly have made such views seem greatly more innovative and dangerous than they actually were. In any case, it is not at all clear that Socrates' moral views were on trial in 399; it is more likely that something else about the man who held those views, or the way in which he presented them, led to his trial and condemnation.

Socrates' Religious Views

Given that Socrates was formally charged with the religious crime of impiety, it is worth asking to what extent or in what ways his religious beliefs and practices were substantially unorthodox. As noted above, Socrates claimed to have a personal divine "voice" or "sign," and there is at least some reason to believe that the charge of introducing new divine things reflected Socrates' belief in his private oracle (see Plato, *Apology* 31c–d; *Euthyphro* 3b; Xenophon, *Apology* 12, *Memorabilia* 1.1.2). But even if his belief in his "sign" would have qualified as unusual, it is not at all clear that all by itself it would have prompted Socrates' prosecutors to bring legal charges against him (see Plato, *Apology* 27b ff.; Xenophon, *Apology* 12–13; *Memorabilia* 1.1.2–9).

As for his other religious beliefs, it appears clear that like most of his contemporaries, Socrates put faith in the oracle of Apollo at Delphi (see Plato, *Apology* 20e ff.; Xenophon, *Apology* 14), as well as in a number of other modes of divination (see Plato, *Apology* 33c; Xenophon, *Apology* 12; *Memorabilia* 1.1.9). He is also portrayed as somewhat passively accepting the mythical accounts of nature and natural phenomena. In Plato's *Apology*, for example, he dismisses Anaxagoras's view that the sun and moon are not gods as "absurd" (26d–e). Even when such accounts struck his intellectual contemporaries as unlikely, Socrates is shown to regard as vain and pointless the attempt to provide naturalistic explanations of the traditional myths – he says that those who do this reveal a "bumpkinish kind of wisdom" (*Phaedrus* 229e). He did have his doubts about myths portraying the gods as immoral, but even these he could not bring himself to deny outright (*Euthyphro* 6a–b). His religious views, in short, appear to be well enough within the norm as not to be likely sources of the charges against him. At any rate, in the defense he gives in Plato's *Apology* he does not bother to address such a concern in the part of this speech explicitly given to considering what issues had led to his being prosecuted.

But we would do well to recall that corruption of youth was considered an apt specification of the charge of impiety, and that this corruption is supposed to have derived from Socrates' philosophical examinations of others in the public places of Athens. Aristophanes, too, appears to have made Socrates' argumentative style the principal source of his corruption of others. If this is seen as the essence of the widespread prejudice against Socrates, we need not look for an additional *religious* rationale to the charge – corruption of youth was, for the Athenians, a religious crime. The prosecution's attempt to tie this accusation to ones involving additional religious crimes need only be seen as specifying accusations contained within the stereotype of the fifth century sophist – a stereotype our sources agree was applied by the prosecution to Socrates himself. That Socrates did not regard himself as in any way guilty of this sort of irreligion is made amply clear in his defense speech in Plato's *Apology* (see esp. 26a–27e).

Socratic Irony and Rhetoric

One feature of Plato's Socrates has received a great deal of attention from modern readers – so much so that it has come to be taken by some as virtually definitive of the man. Socrates' interlocutors often accuse him of being ironical (see, e.g., *Gorgias* 489e; *Republic* 1.337a; *Symposium* 216e; see also *Apology* 38a), and Aristotle later confirms their accusations (*Nicomachean Ethics* 1127b22–6). It is extremely difficult to know, however, just when an attribution of irony to Socrates is justified, for as noted above, some of his more deeply held convictions would strike many as quite implausible on first hearing. In saying that Socrates is being ironic, accordingly, one risks dismissing as insincere something that Socrates truly believes. One guideline in particular for attributing irony to Socrates should be followed. Socrates clearly says (in Plato's *Apology*) that he construes his philosophizing as a religious mission given him by Apollo, the god of the Delphic oracle. Whatever Socrates' rhetorical strategies may be, then, they must cohere with his mission – that is, they must not interfere unnecessarily with his and his interlocutor's pursuit of truth and virtue. If Socrates pointlessly annoys or provokes his interlocutor to the point of unreason, or simply spends his time toying with others, he has violated his own mission. Similarly, though he may not merely flatter his interlocutors, or employ other rhetorical strategies that seduce them into believing what is false, Socrates' mission would appear to require that he attempt to make them as receptive as he can to his "examinations." Thus it is that he maintains an amiable attitude even when his interlocutors become hostile (e.g., at *Gorgias* 486e ff.; *Republic* 1.336e ff.), insisting, despite their current anger, that each is his "friend" (*philos*) and "comrade" (*hetairos*).

But irony may often be compatible with the serious pursuit of truth, especially if and when its use encourages this pursuit. Socrates thus regularly praises his interlocutors for their wisdom, no doubt to encourage them not to be reticent about engaging in conversation with him. Having done so, they soon discover just how little wisdom they have. Socrates' initial praise, however, was not gratuitous. Those praised are rather more likely than not to speak freely and unguardedly with the one praising them. This consequence is vital if Socrates is to examine *them*, as opposed merely to wrangling about words – so it is that he insists that his interlocutors only argue from premises they themselves sincerely believe (see, e.g., *Crito* 49c–d; *Euthyphro* 9d; *Gorgias* 458a–b, 495a; 499b–c, 500b–c; *Protagoras* 331c–d; *Republic* 1.349a.). Whether or not we assume that the same restriction applies to Socrates, it is clear that his "irony" must never interfere with his philosophical mission.

Socratic Ignorance and Socratic Knowledge

Socrates frequently confesses his ignorance (see, e.g., *Apology* 20c, 21d, 23b; *Charmides* 165b–c, 166c–d; *Euthyphro* 5a–c, 15c, 15e–16a; *Laches* 186b–e, 200e; *Lysis* 212a, 223b; *Hippias major* 286c–e, 304d–e; *Gorgias* 509a; *Meno* 71a, 80d; *Republic* 1.337e); yet he seems invariably able to reduce his proudest interlocutors to confusion and self-contradiction. The apparent disparity of his abilities in argument with his assessment of his own cognitive capacities is what leads his interlocutors (and many scholars) to accuse him of irony. Socrates, moreover, is frequently quite willing confidently to affirm any number of principles and maxims, even to the point of claiming them as knowledge (e.g., at *Apology* 29a–b; see also 37b).

What Socrates confesses, however, need not and should not be construed as a general cognitive uncertainly about all propositions. Some things, as we can readily see, he is willing to affirm with the utmost confidence. And Socrates admits that many people do have a form of wisdom. The craftsmen, he says, "know many fine things" (*Apology* 22d). But their wisdom, he finds, is only in knowing how to practice their crafts well; they also suppose that they are wise in what Socrates calls "the most important things" (such as virtue), as well, and this false supposition renders them more ignorant than if they had no wisdom at all. But in granting some wisdom to the craftsmen, Socrates shows that he regards wisdom as the kind of knowledge that enables its possessor to act flawlessly in a certain area, or to produce certain goods capably. Given this "craft analogy" (discussed above), we can understand that what Socrates repeats again and again in his confession of ignorance is that he is lacking in the kind of knowledge or wisdom that would constitute a moral craft – the ability to render infallible judgments about what Socrates calls "the most important things", and thus flawlessly to practice morality.

Many of Plato's dialogues sooner or later involve attempts to provide adequate definitions for moral terms: "What is piety?" they ask, or "What is courage?" or "What is friendship?" Fully successful answers to such questions are never given in the early dialogues. Complete answers would provide definitions according to which the essence of the moral item in question would be exposed and articulated. An understanding of such a definition would enable one to identify its instances with expertise. Socrates is also an intellectualist – that is, he believes that human action always follows human cognition: we always do what we *think* is best for us. Accordingly, he supposes that what one needs to be virtuous is the knowledge of virtue. Given the ability invariably to identify the instances of morality, one would never fail to be moral. But Socrates does not have this ability, for he lacks the relevant wisdom/craft. Socratic ignorance, then, is neither feigned, nor does it consist in general philosophical skepticism; it is the view that whatever else one knows, one does not know the essential nature of virtue or how to put such knowledge to work so as to perfect one's life.

Socrates' Influence on Later Philosophers

The circumstances of Socrates' life and trial were themselves sources of a vast literature in the ancient world, whose influences on later writers may never be fully known to us. But various aspects of Socratic thought and method were explicitly adopted by, or adapted to, later philosophies. Socrates' best-known admirer, Plato, was most patently originally influenced by his mentor's relentless elenctic method and the ceaseless quest for moral understanding. As we said earlier, Plato's earliest dialogues are often thus understood as his attempts to capture the essential method and message of Socrates. But other philosophies came to influence Plato's philosophy, among which were those of the Eleatics, who argued for a suprasensible reality, and the Pythagoreans, whose mathematical studies he came to admire for their methodological clarity and confidence.

The Socratic search for definitions included a variety of conditions according to which answers would be tested for adequacy: A proper definition must cover all and only cases of what it defines, and must identify the essence of the item to which the word it defines refers. In coming to know the definition, moreover, one must be enabled thereby to pick out all of the instances of things having the quality being defined. Plato never forgot either the search for definitions or the conditions according to which such a search might be counted as successfully concluded; but both the methods and the products of such searches undertaken in Plato's later works are very different from what we find in the early dialogues. In these dialogues, Socrates does not just refute his interlocutors' expressed views – he generally enlists their help in arguing *for* various positions. The product of this revised Socratic search for definitions was Plato's renowned Theory of Forms (or Ideas), according to which there exist supranatural realities that are the purest instantiations of each general quality. Thus, in Plato's view, the term "beauty" refers directly to the Form of Beauty – the Beautiful Itself. In virtue of a metaphysical relation (called "participation") to each Form, each participant came to resemble the Forms to some degree, and accordingly can be compared to the Form and determined to be more or less an instantiation of the relevant quality. Thus equal things are more or less equal, according to the degree to which they resemble the Equal Itself, through participation in it; just things are more or less just, according to the degree to which they resemble the Form of Justice, through participation in it. To Socrates' question, then, "what is piety (or justice, or the good)," Plato gave the answer "the Form of Piety (or Justice, or Goodness)," and supposed that such an answer could satisfy the Socratic conditions of adequacy for such an answer.

Plato's Theory of Forms remains one of the most significant theories ever offered in the philosophical literature of the West. Criticisms and defenses of it or some variety of it soon became preoccupations of philosophy. Even now it remains the subject of intense scholarly debate. But other philosophical tenets have been traced to Socrates, as well, often by philosophers with a dubious understanding of the man they took themselves to be following. The Cynics found in Socrates a model of their disdain for material things, though it is not clear that Socrates himself absolutely disdained material goods. Similarly, the Skeptics saw the Socratic *elenchos* as a method for purging its victim of all convictions – whereas Socrates himself had been a man of many, quite firmly held convictions, and who was not at all shy about exhorting others to hold the same convictions.

Throughout the centuries, Socrates has been held by admirers as an exemplar of nearly every philosophical and moral trait taken by such admirers to be admirable ones. He has been seen both as deeply pious and religiously conventional, and as a man of extreme religious skepticism; he has been accounted a martyr for truth and a model of righteous teaching, yet each generation has offered a noticeably different account of precisely what the truths were for which he died, and what it was exactly that he taught. No doubt his style of asking, but only rarely answering questions, has helped to make his philosophy more amenable to conflicting interpretations and "sympathetic" amendments. Certainly his unflappable dignity is beyond question, whatever its substantive sources may have been. This, and his unwavering confidence in the value of philosophy, even as he went to his death for having practiced it, will continue to fire our imagination and provoke the kind of admiration that will lead great and disparate varieties of thinkers to claim him as a spiritual and intellectual ancestor.

References and Recommended Reading

Primary Sources

Aristophanes, *Clouds*, tr. with notes by Alan H. Sommerstein (Chicago: Bolchazy-Carducci; Warminster, UK: Aris & Phillips, 1982).

Plato: Complete Works, ed. John M. Cooper (Indianapolis: Hackett, 1997).

Xenophon, *Xenophon IV: Memorabilia, Oeconomicus, Symposium, Apology*, tr. E. C. Marchant and O. J. Todd, Loeb Classical Library (Cambridge, Mass.: Harvard University Press; London: William Heinemann, 1923).

Secondary Sources

Commentaries in English: general

Hugh H. Benson (ed.), *Essays on the Philosophy of Socrates* (New York: Oxford University Press, 1992).

Thomas C. Brickhouse and Nicholas D. Smith, *Plato's Socrates* (New York: Oxford University Press, 1994).

——, *The Philosophy of Socrates* (Boulder, Colo.: Westview, 1999).

W. K. C. Guthrie, *Socrates* (Cambridge: Cambridge University Press, 1971).

Terence Irwin, *Plato's Ethics* (Oxford: Oxford University Press, 1995), chs. 1–9.

Mark L. McPherran (ed.), *Wisdom, Ignorance, and Virtue: New Essays in Socratic Studies* (Edmonton: Academic Printing and Publishing [Supplement, *Apeiron* 30], 1997).

William Prior (ed.), *Socrates: Critical Examinations*, 4 vols. (London: Routledge, 1996).

Gerasimos Xenophon Santas, *Socrates: Philosophy in Plato's Early Dialogues* (London: Routledge & Kegan Paul, 1979).

Gregory Vlastos, *The Philosophy of Socrates* (Notre Dame, Ind.: University of Notre Dame Press, 1980, repr. of first edition by Anchor Books: Garden City, N.Y., 1971).

——, *Socrates: Ironist and Moral Philosopher* (Ithaca, N.Y.: Cornell University Press; Cambridge: Cambridge University Press, 1991).

——, *Socratic Studies* (Cambridge: Cambridge University Press, 1994).

Eduard Zeller, *Socrates and the Socratic Schools*, tr. O. J. Reichel (New York: Russell & Russell, 1962).

Commentaries in English: special topics

R. E. Allen, *Socrates and Legal Obligation* (Minneapolis: University of Minnesota Press, 1980).

Hugh H. Benson, *Socratic Wisdom* (New York: Oxford University Press, 2000).

Thomas C. Brickhouse and Nicholas D. Smith (eds.), *The Trial and Execution of Socrates: Sources and Controversies* (New York: Oxford University Press, 2001).

Anton-Hermann Chroust, *Socrates, Man and Myth* (Notre Dame, Ind.: University of Notre Dame Press, 1957).

Alfonso Gomez-Lobo, *The Foundations of Socratic Ethics* (Indianapolis: Hackett, 1994).

Mark L. McPherran, *The Religion of Socrates* (University Park: Pennsylvania State University Press, 1996).

M. J. O'Brien, *The Socratic Paradoxes and the Greek Mind* (Chapel Hill: University of North Carolina Press, 1967).

Coleman Phillipson, *The Trial of Socrates* (London: Stevens & Sons, 1928).

Arthur Kenyon Rogers, *The Socratic Problem* (New York: Russell & Russell, 1971).

George Rudebusch, *Socrates, Pleasure, and Value* (New York: Oxford University Press, 1999).

Nicholas D. Smith and Paul Woodruff (eds.), *Reason and Religion in Socratic Philosophy* (New York: Oxford University Press, 2000).

Commentaries and discussions in English: individual dialogues

David Bolotin, *Plato's Dialogue on Friendship* (Ithaca, N.Y.: Cornell University Press, 1979) [*Lysis*].

Thomas C. Brickhouse and Nicholas D. Smith, *Socrates on Trial* (Oxford: Oxford University Press; Princeton: Princeton University Press, 1989). [*Apology*]

John Burnet, *Plato's Euthyphro, Apology of Socrates, and Crito* (Oxford: Oxford University Press, 1924).

Thomas Chance, *Plato's Euthydemus: Analysis of What Is and What Is Not Philosophy* (Berkeley: University of California Press, 1992).

E. R. Dodds, *Plato: Gorgias* (Oxford: Clarendon, 1959).

Terence H. Irwin, *Plato: Gorgias* (Oxford: Clarendon, 1976).

Jacob Klein, *A Commentary on Plato's Meno* (Chapel Hill: University of North Carolina Press, 1965).

Richard Kraut, *Socrates and the State* (Princeton: Princeton University Press, 1984). [*Crito*]

C. D. C. Reeve, *Socrates in the Apology* (Indianapolis: Hackett, 1989).

Alexander Sesonske and Noel Fleming, *Plato's Meno: Text and Criticism* (Belmont, Calif.: Wadsworth, 1965).

C. C. W. Taylor, *Plato: Protagoras* (Oxford: Clarendon, 1976).

T. G. Tuckey, *Plato's Charmides* (Cambridge: Cambridge University Press, 1951).

Lazlo Versenyi, *Holiness and Justice: An Interpretation of Plato's Euthyphro* (Lanham, N.Y.: University Press of America, 1982).

Paul Woodruff, *Plato: The Hippias Major* (Indianapolis: Hackett, 1982).

Part III

Plato: Introduction

As pursued in many universities throughout the world today, Philosophy is recognizably the discipline of study inaugurated by Plato. He was the first to write and think systematically and comprehensively about issues now investigated under the distinct headings of metaphysics, epistemology, ethical theory, political theory, aesthetics, philosophy of language, and philosophy of mind. Perhaps this is what induced the distinguished British philosopher Alfred North Whitehead to assert Plato's preeminence in this way: "The safest general characterization of the European philosophical tradition is that it consists of a series of footnotes to Plato."[1] To be sure, like Socrates, Plato has had a profound influence on those who followed him; but unlike Socrates, his fame derives from his own writings. Whereas Socrates wrote nothing philosophical, Plato wrote a great many works, all of which, uncharacteristically for an ancient author, have evidently come down to us in their entirety. It is principally through his own writings, then, that we know Plato's views.

We also know some things about the man from his own writings, though he refers to himself explicitly only twice in his entire corpus,[2] and then only in passing.[3] We have, unfortunately, only scanty ancient evidence regarding Plato's life, much of it clearly composed with the dubious intention of providing a sort of biographical backdrop to the views found expounded by the various characters in his dialogues, and some of it plainly scurrilous. Still, the rudiments of Plato's life are clear enough. He was born of aristocratic parentage in approximately 429 BC, lived most of his life in Athens, with a few trips abroad, to Sicily and perhaps to as far away as Egypt, though sources for this latter visit are rather late and unreliable. However that may be, after returning from some travels, Plato founded a school in Athens, probably in the 380s BC. This institution was less a school or university in our sense of the term than an association of fellow searchers under the general guidance of Plato as leader, established near a shrine, an olive grove dedicated to the legendary Greek hero Academos, whence our word "Academy." Plato's Academy, remarkably, operated continuously until 529 AD, though it underwent changes which Plato could hardly have envisaged.[4] During his own time there, Plato associated with many of the leading intellectuals of his age, including, most notably, Aristotle, who came to Athens to study when Plato was in the later stages of his life. Plato, unlike Socrates, died peacefully in old age, in 347 BC.

What we know about Plato from his own writings is primarily intellectual rather than biographical. This is in part because Plato rarely refers to himself expressly, but mainly because his writings are composed almost exclusively in dialogue form, with all but one of them featuring Socrates as a character. Still, it is possible, relying principally on stylistic considerations and ancient testimony, especially that of Aristotle, to divide Plato's writings first into those that are "Socratic," that is, into those whose primary intent is to recapitulate the views of the historical Socrates, and then among those which are genuinely Platonic, to establish a rough order of those which are earlier and those which come later. Although sometimes disputed, the following rough division of Plato's main writings provides a reliable overview of the relative dates of those of his compositions usually encountered by beginning students:

1. Socratic Dialogues: *Euthyphro, Apology, Crito, Alcibiades, Charmides, Laches, Lysis, Euthydemus, Hippias major* and *Hippias minor, *Protagoras, and *Gorgias* (* = probably transitional, in the sense that they incorporate some features of early Platonic dialogues)
2. Platonic:
    a. Earlier Dialogues: *Meno, Phaedo, Cratylus, Symposium, Republic, Phaedrus,* and *Parmenides*
    b. Later Dialogues: *Theaetetus, Timaeus, Philebus, Critias, Sophist, Statesman, Laws*

Although the novice is better advised to immerse herself in Plato's works than to join scholarly questions regarding their relative dating, it is nonetheless worth bearing in mind that Plato, like almost all other philosophers, revised, refined, and replaced his views as he moved through his long life. It is also especially important to bear in mind that the Socratic dialogues have as their principal aim the characterization of Socrates – his method, manner, and general intellectual demeanor – rather than the promulgation of positive Platonic theses. In particular, it is noteworthy, as Aristotle points out, that the Socratic dialogues limit themselves almost exclusively to questions in ethics and the conduct of life, whereas the Platonic dialogues range widely into all areas of metaphysics and epistemology. The chapters which follow only sometimes engage questions regarding the relative dating of Plato's dialogues; mainly, they rely on the general framework presented here.

In any case, as Devereux and White make clear in their chapters on Plato's metaphysics and epistemology, throughout his Platonic dialogues, Plato makes central use in his positive philosophizing of his Theory of Forms, a theory concerning the proper objects of human knowledge, evidently conceived as mind- and language-independent entities which exist of necessity as immutable essences known only after deliberate and extended philosophical study. Plato argues for the existence of Forms in various dialogues; he also subjects them to searing criticisms in another. They seem never far from the center of his philosophy, though he does not dwell on them at all times, as Silverman and Santas reveal when investigating Plato's views on the soul and on justice. When read together, the authors of all four chapters on Plato help illustrate the deep interconnections among the various strands of Plato's thought. He was, par excellence, a constructive philosopher whose towering genius has rarely been equaled in philosophy's long subsequent history.

Notes

1   Whitehead (1929: 39).

2   *Apology* 38b and *Phaedo* 59b. These citations employ the so-called Stephanus numbers, named for the canonical Greek edition of Plato by Henri Estienne (Latinized as "Stephanus") published in Paris in 1578; the numbers correspond to the pages and sections of Estienne's text. For practical purposes, a student need only know that every good modern edition of Plato's writings employs Stephanus pagination, usually in the margins, to facilitate reference. So, for instance, to find the passages cited here in their appropriate contexts, a student has only to open a translation of the *Apology* or *Phaedo* and skim the margins until the relevant Stephanus number is found.

3   This discounts as spurious the Seventh Letter, ostensibly by Plato and addressed to one Dion, a contender for political ascendancy in Syracuse in the mid-350s BC. This letter purports to provide a first-person account of Plato's own early political ambition, as well as his subsequent disillusionment and turn towards philosophy as the only true source of justice and understanding.

4   On the fate of Plato's Academy, see Part 5, "Hellenistic Philosophy: Introduction," as well as chapter 14 below.

Chapter 4

Plato: Metaphysics

Daniel Devereux

Introduction

The heart of Plato's metaphysics is his famous "Theory of Forms." This theory holds that there is a higher reality beyond the world of change which we come to know through sense experience. This "transcendent" reality consists of *Forms*: that is, eternal, unchanging entities which are grasped by the intellect, not by the senses. Whatever reality our world of experience has it gets from these Forms. What is "real" for Plato is not just what is permanent and unchanging, but, more importantly, what is intelligible or knowable. It is chiefly because of the Forms' perfect intelligibility that they are more real than the things we grasp through sense experience. This fusion of the real with the knowable is distinctive of Plato's metaphysics: as we shall see, his metaphysics is inseparable from his epistemology, that is, from his views concerning knowledge and what is knowable.[1] Plato is interested in other metaphysical topics, such as the nature and existence of the divine, and the nature of the soul or mind and its relationship to the body; but his Theory of Forms dominates his metaphysical speculation, and it must therefore be the central focus of our discussion. Plato arrived at his Theory of Forms by coming to grips with problems he perceived in the views of his predecessors, especially the views of his mentor, Socrates. Thus it will be appropriate to begin our discussion with a brief look at some of the distinctive views of Socrates.

Socrates' Search for Definitions

Aristotle reports that Socrates focused his inquiries on the ethical virtues and sought to define them "universally"; but he did not "separate" the universals he was seeking to define. He says that Plato, on the other hand, *did* separate the universals, calling them Forms, and that his investigations, in contrast with Socrates', ranged over a wide variety of philosophical questions and topics.[2] It is interesting to note that these differences between Socrates and Plato are reflected in differences among

Plato's dialogues. In his shorter dialogues, such as the *Protagoras, Laches, Charmides*, and *Euthyphro*, Plato portrays Socrates as an inquirer into the nature of the virtues and their interrelations. The Socrates of these dialogues shows no interest in the "metaphysical" questions discussed by some of his predecessors: for example, Whether what exists is one thing or many (Parmenides); Whether change and motion are possible (Parmenides, Zeno); Whether anything remains self-identical over time (Heracleitus). Even in the case of the objects he seeks to define, Socrates shows no interest in exploring questions of a metaphysical nature; he does not, for instance, ask what it means to say that justice is a single *thing* (*Prot.* 330c), or how this thing might be related to the many things that are called just. However, in a number of his longer dialogues, Plato examines the key doctrines of the earlier metaphysicians, especially Parmenides and Heracleitus, and opens up many new areas of philosophical inquiry. In four of these longer dialogues, the *Republic, Phaedo, Symposium*, and *Phaedrus*, he portrays Socrates as a philosopher who not only seeks definitions of the virtues, but wants to know whether these things exist in the same way as the things encountered in our everyday sense experience, how they are related to the things that possess them, and what it is to have knowledge of them. The Socrates of these dialogues is metaphysician and epistemologist as well as moral philosopher. His answers to the questions about the nature and existence of the objects of definition comprise Plato's celebrated Theory of Forms: the Forms are stable, unchanging objects of knowledge that are somehow separate from things in the sensible world – things that we grasp through sense experience. The Socrates of these dialogues seems to fit Aristotle's description of Plato, whereas the Socrates of the *Protagoras* and the other shorter dialogues fits his description of Socrates. In view of these correspondences between the two groups of dialogues and Aristotle's report, many scholars have suggested that Plato's own views and interests are reflected in the longer dialogues, while the views and interests of the historical Socrates are reflected in the shorter dialogues (for this reason these dialogues are often called "Socratic"). This suggestion seems plausible, and it may serve as a basis for understanding how Plato arrived at his metaphysical views, especially his Theory of Forms.

Let us begin by considering some aspects of Socrates' search for definitions which may be relevant to Plato's metaphysical speculations. Although Socrates (in the shorter "Socratic" dialogues) does not take up any metaphysical questions in his investigations of such things as justice, piety, and courage, his searches do reveal some interesting assumptions about what these things are like. For instance, in searching for an account of the nature of courage, he assumes that there is one thing named by "courage," and therefore the definition he is searching for will be an account of one thing. By making this assumption, he implicitly rejects some other possible views about the nature of courage. We might suppose, for instance, that there are several different sorts of courage manifested in different situations, and though these different sorts resemble each other there is no single notion that unifies them. According to this view, the best account of courage would be one which specifies the different sorts and perhaps also points out their resemblances. Socrates, however, assumes that there is a single notion or "essence" running through all the different sorts of courage, and he therefore expects a unified definition

(*Lach.* 191c–192b). We might express this assumption by saying that all instances of courage, however different they may be in other respects, are exactly alike insofar as they are correctly described as "courageous" (*Meno* 72b–d). But Socrates' assumption is stronger than this. For one might hold that instances of courage resemble each other insofar as they are courageous, but deny that there is some single thing that they share in virtue of which they are called "courageous." Socrates, however, believes that "courage" refers to a single thing which is shared by all things that are courageous; it is through their possession of this thing that courageous things are courageous (*Prot.* 330d; *Euthyphr.* 5c–d, 6d–e; *Hipp. maj.* 287c–d).

For the sake of convenience, let us express Socrates' assumption in more general terms. In the case of the things for which he seeks definitions, there are on the one hand the many things that are F (e.g., pious, just), and on the other hand there is one thing, Fness (piety, justice), which all the F things have in common. Socrates' assumption, then, is that *There is, in addition to the many F things, a single thing, Fness, which all of the many F things have in common.* Let us call this the Unity Assumption.[3] We noted a moment ago that, in the Socratic dialogues, Socrates does not say what sort of view one would be committed to if one denied this assumption. In the *Republic*, however, he distinguishes between philosophers and those he calls "sight-lovers," and one of the differences he mentions is that the latter "believe in" many beautiful things but not in beauty itself, whereas the philosophers believe in beauty itself and are able to distinguish it as one thing apart from the many beautiful things (476a–c, 479a; cf. *Hipp. maj.* 300e–301a). Socrates also says that the "sight-lovers" mistake resemblance for identity: they believe that beauty is identical with the many beautiful things, whereas in fact the many beautiful things *resemble* beauty. The "sight-lovers" thus deny the Unity Assumption by holding that Fness is nothing but the many things that are F. Although this argument in the *Republic* reflects Plato's views rather than Socrates', the sight-lovers' denial that Fness is one thing might be the sort of view that Socrates means to deny when he affirms that Fness is one thing, distinct from the many Fs. In the light of this passage in the *Republic*, we might formulate the Unity Assumption as the claim that *Fness is one thing, not many.*

Another interesting aspect of Socrates' search for definitions of the virtues is a pattern of moving from types of actions to the internal source of such actions. For example, in his inquiry into the nature of courage in the *Laches*, the first definition offered by Socrates' interlocutor, Laches, is a type of action – "standing firm in battle" (190e). Socrates first points out that there are many other ways of displaying courage, and that not every instance of standing firm in battle counts as courageous. He then suggests that, rather than searching for an action-type that is common to all the different ways of displaying courage, they look for a certain capacity or *power* which is the inner source of courageous actions (192a–b). There is some one thing that is the same in all courageous actions (191e), but it is not something that could be captured in a general description of a type of action ("doing such and such"); rather what unites courageous actions is their common source – a certain capacity or power within the soul.

This pattern of beginning with action-types and moving to an inner source of action is repeated in a number of Socrates' searches for definitions of the virtues.

The pattern indicates Socrates' belief that it is a mistake to try to define the virtues in terms of action-types; but it also indicates that his contemporaries were strongly inclined to think of the virtues in just this way. Socrates' opposition to this way of characterizing the virtues is understandable if we bear in mind that he took quite seriously the view of Protagoras and other Sophists that the virtues should be understood as skills or crafts. It would plainly be a mistake to define a craft like carpentry simply in terms of certain actions – to say, for instance, that carpentry is choosing appropriate woods, and putting them together to make tables, chairs, and so on. Carpentry is the *skill* or *capacity* that enables one to do these things. If the virtues are skills, or closely analogous to skills, then we would reasonably expect them to be capacities that enable one to perform certain types of actions.

But the "craft analogy" is not the only reason for Socrates' opposition to definitions of the virtues in terms of action-types. His arguments against definitions of this sort strongly suggest that he believed that any action-type proposed as a definition of a virtue will have both that property and its opposite: Fness, if defined as an action-type, will be both F and not-F. For example, consider the definition of justice as "paying back what one owes" (*Rep.* 331c–d). While it is true that paying back what one owes would normally be a just action, there are some instances, as Socrates points out, in which it would not be right to do this – for example, if one had borrowed a weapon, and its owner wanted it back, indicating that he was going to kill himself. If paying back what one owes is sometimes unjust, this action-type could not be identical with justice: it could not tell us what it is to be just. If we could point to some action that was always just and never unjust, then this type of action might be a viable candidate for a definition of justice.[4] But Socrates consistently argues in the case of the virtues that no action-types satisfy this requirement. If we are seeking an answer to the question What is justice? we must look for an inner source of just action.

It is worth noting that, according to Socrates' argument, it is actions of a certain *type* that may be either just or unjust, depending on the circumstances: the action-type, "paying back what one owes," may be just in one set of circumstances but unjust in a different set. He does not suggest that the same individual act might be both just and unjust; for instance, my paying off a loan in a timely fashion would be a just action, and would not be in any way unjust. In fact, in the *Euthyphro*, he regards it as an unacceptable consequence of a definition of piety that the same act would be both pious and impious (7a–8b). And he never suggests that a *person* might be both just and unjust, pious and impious. These points will be relevant later on in our discussion of the Theory of Forms.[5]

For an action-type to serve as a definition of Fness (where Fness is some virtue), it would have to be always F and never not-F; it could not be both F and not-F. We might wonder whether Socrates would insist on this requirement even if the proposed definition specified a capacity or state which was the source of virtuous actions. It seems that he would. He claims, for instance, that if temperance, understood as an inner state or capacity, is such as to make its possessor good, then it must be good itself (*Charm.* 160d–e; cf. *Gorg.* 497e). He also says that it is *through* temperance that temperate people are temperate and act temperately (*Prot.* 332a–b;

cf. *Hipp. maj.* 287c). Thus if temperance is an inner state or capacity which makes its possessor temperate, it must itself be temperate; that is, temperance must have the property which it causes other things to have. We might generalize Socrates' requirement as follows: Fness is that which makes F things F, and because of this it must itself be F and can never be the opposite of F. In view of these considerations, it is not surprising to find Socrates making statements like the following: "Justice is such as to be just and not unjust," and "Piety by its nature cannot be impious but must be pious." To support the claim that piety must be pious, he says that "If piety itself is not pious, it is hard to see how anything else could be pious" (*Prot.* 330c–d; cf. *Hipp. maj.* 288c); in other words, it is necessary for piety to be pious (and not impious) if it is to *make* other things pious (cf. *Phaed.* 100c).

Socrates' view that justice is just, piety is pious, and so on, is often referred to as the "Self-Predication Assumption." But as we have seen, Socrates seems to regard the claim that Fness is F as a consequence of a couple of other views: first, that Fness is something that makes other things F, and second, that something that causes other things to have a property must itself have that property. If Fness is an "F maker," and an F maker must itself be F, it follows that Fness must be F. It would therefore be more helpful to formulate Socrates' Self-Predication Assumption, not simply as *Fness is F*, but rather as: *Fness is an F maker, and because of this it must itself be F and cannot be the opposite of F.*

We noticed earlier that Socrates holds that temperance makes its possessor temperate; that is, people who are temperate are so through the possession of temperance.[6] Here again, we might generalize the point in the following way: It is through the possession of Fness that F things are F. But we need to be careful here. Socrates does not make this point in regard to temperate actions: he does not say that it is through the possession of temperance that temperate actions are temperate. If we recall that Socrates regards temperance as a capacity or power to perform certain actions, then it will be obvious why he would not want to say that temperate actions possess temperance; if temperate *actions* possessed temperance, they would have the power to perform temperate actions, and these would have the power to perform other temperate actions, and so on *ad infinitum*. Temperate actions are temperate not because they possess temperance but because they have a certain character through being the expression or exercise of temperance. Temperance is *manifested* in temperate actions in the way that a cause is manifested in its effects. Socrates typically speaks of Fness as something that is *in* the many F things, but at least in the case of the virtues he does not mean that Fness is in all F things in the same way. Fness is in a person in the sense that it is possessed by that person, but Fness is in actions in the sense that it is manifested in those actions (and perhaps it is in other things in yet other ways). Given the way Socrates speaks about the various things he seeks to define, it seems reasonable to say that he regards Fness as *immanent in* F things. We might label this the Immanence Assumption: *Fness is a one in many.* But we should keep in mind that he does not hold that Fness is in F things in the same way in all cases.

These assumptions that Socrates makes about the objects of his philosophical investigations raise interesting questions of a metaphysical nature: How can Fness be one thing and yet be *in* the many F things? Does Fness depend for its existence on the things it is in, or does it somehow exist independently of them? More generally, What sort of relationship does Fness have to the many F things? In modern philosophy, these questions are grouped together under what is called "the problem of universals." Plato's Theory of Forms is the first attempt to provide a solution to this problem. But Socrates deserves credit for at least raising the problem through his searches for definitions.

Before we turn to the Theory of Forms, let us list the assumptions we have uncovered in our brief examination of Socrates' search for definitions:

S_1 (the Unity Assumption): *In addition to the many F things, there is a single thing, Fness, which all of the many F things have in common ("Fness is one thing, not many").*

S_2 (the Self-Predication Assumption): *Fness is an F maker, and because of this it must itself be F and cannot be the opposite of F.*

S_3 (the Immanence Assumption): *Fness is in the many F things (Fness is a "one in many").*

Plato's Theory of Forms: Epistemological Separation

Aristotle reports that Plato separated Socrates' "universals" from the particulars of which they are predicated, and that he called these things *Forms*. Aristotle also has a story about what led Plato to make this separation:

> Those who put forward the theory of Forms were led to it because they were persuaded of the truth of the Heracleitean doctrine that all sensible things are in constant flux, so that if there is to be knowledge or understanding of anything, there must be some other stable entities apart from sensible things – for there is no knowledge of things in flux. (*Metaph.* 1078b12–17)

The theory that Aristotle refers to is the theory that figures so prominently in the *Republic, Phaedo, Symposium,* and *Phaedrus* – the so-called middle dialogues. In these dialogues Plato sketches a dramatic picture of reality divided into two realms: the realm of Being, consisting of eternal, unchanging Forms – perfect objects of knowledge – and the realm of Becoming, consisting of the ever-changing objects of our everyday sense experience. When we compare Aristotle's story with the theory that Plato presents in these dialogues, we find substantial agreement. As Aristotle reports, Plato makes a sharp distinction between sensible and nonsensible objects, the latter being the proper objects of knowledge. This distinction between the two kinds of entities is found in virtually all of the passages in which Forms are discussed. There is also clear evidence in these dialogues for the claim that Plato's view of the sensible world was influenced by Heracleitus. In a number of passages he characterizes the objects of the sensible world as constantly changing, and contrasts them with nonsensible Forms, which are eternal and unchanging (*Phaed.* 78c; *Rep.* 585c). And in at least one passage, he indicates that if everything is constantly changing, then there would be no possibility of knowledge (*Crat.* 439d–440c).

The implication of these contentions is that if knowledge is possible, there must exist some other objects besides those in the sensible world, objects which are stable and unchanging. And, in particular, if the objects which Socrates sought to define are to be knowable, they must be separate and different from the objects of the sensible world. It is thus surprising that we do not find any direct arguments for the existence of Forms in the middle dialogues along the lines suggested by Aristotle. What we find instead is a development of a line of reasoning we have already noticed in the Socratic dialogues. The first step is to distinguish the Form Fness from the many F things. Any one of the many F things may be both F and not-F and therefore cannot be identical with Fness, for Fness is always F and never not-F. In the Socratic dialogues, the things that are both F and not-F are restricted to action-types (e.g., returning what one owes may be both just and unjust, depending on the circumstances).[7] In the middle dialogues, the range of things that are considered to be both F and not-F is broadened to include all sensible objects.[8] Any sensible object which is thought to be beautiful will appear not-beautiful or ugly when compared with something else, or when looked at from a different perspective; therefore no sensible object could be identical with beauty or the essence of the beautiful (cf. *Phaed.* 74b–c; *Symp.* 211a–b). In the *Republic* Socrates introduces an intriguing new claim: no sensible object can be said to *be* F because it is no more F than not-F (479b–c); only Fness itself can be said to *be* F since it is always F and never not-F. He infers that the many sensible Fs are "between being and not-being," partaking of both, whereas the Form Fness has pure, unadulterated being. Not only are the many sensible Fs not identical with Fness itself, they are also inferior to Fness with respect to their being.[9] Because of their ambivalence and lack of pure being, Socrates concludes that the many sensible Fs should be assigned to opinion rather than knowledge; the only true objects of knowledge are the Forms, because only Forms have the kind of being appropriate for an object of knowledge (476e–477b).

In the middle dialogues Socrates does not claim in so many words that we must posit the existence of separate Forms in order to preserve the possibility of knowledge.[10] He does claim that sensible objects lack the kind of being required of objects of knowledge, but he does not use this as a basis for saying (what we might expect from Aristotle's report) that there must be other objects that have the required kind of being.[11] He argues in effect that since the sight-lovers do not acknowledge the existence of Forms, the best they can hope for is *opinion*. So Socrates implies that there can be no knowledge without Forms: if knowledge is possible, Forms must exist. Although Plato does not argue for the existence of Forms in the way suggested by Aristotle's report, his arguments nevertheless indicate that Aristotle was basically right: Plato thought that we must posit Forms "if there is to be knowledge of anything."

But there is another respect in which Aristotle's report might be questioned. The reason Socrates gives for claiming that sensible objects are not fit to be objects of knowledge is their *ambivalence* – the fact that they are both F and not-F, which means that they have an inferior kind of being. Although he claims that sensible objects are constantly changing, he does not give this (as we might expect him to from Aristotle's report) as the basis for disqualifying them as objects of knowledge. And it seems that ambivalence and being subject to change are distinct and separate characteristics: the fact that the same object may be F in one context and not-F in another is no indication that it has undergone change. Thus there seems to be the following discrepancy between Aristotle's report and the arguments concerning Forms in the middle dialogues: the reason Plato gives for denying that sensible objects can be known is that they are both F and not-F, not that they are constantly changing.

Perhaps Aristotle's report is simply inaccurate. However, I believe there are some telling indications in the dialogues that provide support for his claim that it was the changeability of sensible objects that led Plato to posit separate Forms. For in the argument against the sight-lovers in the *Republic*, Socrates, immediately after pointing out the ambivalence of sensible objects, describes these things as "tumbling about" and "wandering" between being and not being, and contrasts them with the things that are "always the same and unchanging" (479d–e; cf. *Parm.* 135d–e). And a couple of pages further on, he characterizes things of the sensible world as "wandering about" insofar as they are always in the course of coming-to-be and passing away (485b). He seems to see a connection between the ambivalence of sensible things and their "wandering" and "becoming."[12] And even if it is unclear what the connection might be, the fact that Plato saw such a connection means that Aristotle was not off the mark in saying that it was the changeability of sensible objects that led Plato to posit separate Forms. Perhaps the connection is related to the fact that Socrates first says that sensible Fs *appear* both F and not-F (while Fness itself does not appear both F and not-F), and then infers that they no more *are* F than not-F (479a–b). Something might appear beautiful in one context or from one perspective, and appear not to be beautiful in another context or from another perspective: now it appears beautiful, but change the lighting and it no longer appears beautiful. The appearances of sensible objects can in this way shift from one moment to the next. But why should change of appearance lead us to suppose that there is change in the object (that the object is "wandering")? Perhaps Plato believes that the way things appear to us is a part of their "being" – just as it is part of the being of beauty itself that it always appears beautiful, never ugly (*Phaed.* 74c; *Hipp. maj.* 291d; 292e), it is part of the being of a thing that appears beautiful to the senses that it will also appear ugly.[13] So if a thing appears F at one moment and not-F at the next, this will mean that the thing has undergone a change. *If* we suppose that Plato thought along these lines, we would be able to understand why he would think that a thing's appearing F and not-F means that it is "wandering" and changing (cf. *Tht.* 154b). But whether or not we suppose something like this, it seems that Plato sees a connection between the changeability of sensible objects and their appearing both F and not-F. Aristotle was right after all: Plato held that sensible objects cannot be objects of knowledge because of their changeability.

Since Plato's separation of Socrates' objects of definition from the sensible world is based on epistemological considerations – what objects must be like if they are to be knowable – we might call this the "epistemological separation" of Forms. In the Socratic dialogues we find a rudimentary distinction between knowledge and opinion (Gorg. 454d); but there is no hint that the objects of knowledge must be different from those of opinion. On the contrary, in the Meno Socrates suggests that true opinions can be transformed into knowledge by the addition of supporting reasons (97c–98a), which seems to imply that we could first have true opinion and then later acquire knowledge of the same objects. Nowhere in these dialogues do we find indications of a distinction between things which we grasp through the senses and other things which we apprehend by some other means.[14] The thought behind the epistemological separation of Forms seems to be independent of the concerns and assumptions of the Socratic dialogues, which fits with Aristotle's suggestion of a "Heracleitean" influence.

In the Phaedo the distinction between sensible and nonsensible objects is closely related to a distinction between the senses, which pertain to the body, and the faculty of thought, which pertains to the soul (65a–c; 79c–d). Socrates contends that justice, beauty, and the other objects of his searches can only be apprehended by the soul's faculty of thought when it operates independently of the bodily senses (65d–66a). According to the arguments in the Phaedo, the soul continues to exist after the death of the body, and it is only in its disembodied state that the soul is able to attain an apprehension of the objects it seeks to know (66d–67a). Thus the separation of nonsensible from sensible objects is correlated to a separation of the soul's faculty of thought from the bodily senses; the soul must not make use of the senses in its search for knowledge – to achieve its goal it must separate itself as much as possible from the body and the senses, and conduct its investigation using pure thought by itself. As we shall see in a moment, Plato's conception of the nature of the soul and its relationship to the body is closely correlated to another separation: the "ontological separation" of Forms from their participants.

Plato's Theory of Forms: Ontological Separation

Aristotle's statement that Plato "separated" the Forms involves more than the claim that he distinguished Forms as intelligible, nonsensible objects from the objects accessible to us through the senses; it involves the further claim that Plato treated the Forms as *existing separately* from sensible objects. In other words, Forms do not depend for their existence on objects in the sensible world. This is clear from the way in which Aristotle uses the term "separate." For instance, he says in a number of places that the properties of objects (e.g., justice, beauty) are not "separate," but depend on the things they are predicated of for their existence.[15] If justice were "separate," it would not depend on the many just things for its existence. In claiming that Plato regarded the Forms as separate, Aristotle is therefore implying that he regarded the Forms as existing independently of the things that partake of them (the many Fs).

The claim that Forms have separate existence – that they are "ontologically" separate from their participants – is different from, and is not implied by, the claim that they are epistemologically separate. One could deny that Forms exist independently of their participants, while still holding that they are inaccessible to the senses. Aristotle, for instance, holds that the proper objects of knowledge are inaccessible to the senses, but are not ontologically separate from sensible things (cf. *Posterior Analytics* I 31). And in the *Republic* Socrates maintains that powers of the soul such as knowledge or opinion cannot be grasped by the senses, but he does not hold that these powers can exist independently of the things that possess them (477c–d).

Although Aristotle claims that Plato regarded Forms as ontologically separate, scholars have disagreed over whether there is clear evidence in the dialogues to support this claim.[16] But the *Phaedo*, at least, seems to contain indirect evidence that Aristotle's report is trustworthy. As we have already noted, Socrates argues in this dialogue for the immortality of the soul, that is, he argues that the soul does not depend for its existence on the body. The final argument of the dialogue, which is apparently regarded by Socrates as the most convincing, relies on a principle which is similar to one of the assumptions we discovered in the Socratic dialogues (S₂): *Fness is an F maker, and because of this it must itself be F and cannot be the opposite of* F (the "Self-Predication" Assumption). In the argument in the *Phaedo* Socrates sets out the following causal principle: if something is an "F maker," that is, the cause of another thing's being F, then the F maker must itself be F and exclude the opposite of F (105b–c). He then applies this principle to the soul, arguing that since the soul is the cause of the body's being alive, it must itself be alive and exclude the opposite of life: death. The soul is therefore "deathless" or immortal (105c–e).

According to the *Phaedo*, the soul has two modes of existence. During certain periods it has "embodied" existence: that is, it exists within a body and is the animating principle of that body. At other times, the soul has disembodied existence: it exists on its own, separated from any corporeal object. When the soul is disembodied and has separate existence, Socrates describes it as being "itself by itself" (64c, 66e–67a). In the final argument of the dialogue, Socrates makes a distinction between Forms and "immanent characters," between Fness itself and the Fness *in* a particular F thing (102d–e, 103b).[17] In the case of the Form itself, Socrates describes it as being "itself by itself": that is, he applies to the Form the same description which he applies to the soul when it has separate existence. The implication seems to be that insofar as Forms exist "themselves by themselves," they exist separately from the things that participate in them. And since Forms have separate existence, they are like souls in that they do not depend for their existence on the things that participate in them. However, in contrast with souls, Forms do not have two modes of existence: they do not sometimes exist *in* things and sometimes exist separately, on their own; they always exist on their own, separately from the things that partake of them. Immanent characters (the "Fness in us"), on the other hand, always exist *in* things, never on their own.

Socrates seems to treat existing "itself by itself" and existing *in* something as mutually exclusive modes of existence. It is only when a soul is not *in* a body that it exists "itself by itself." So if the Form, Fness itself, exists "itself by itself," it cannot be *in* its participants.[18] What is *in* the Form's participants is the immanent character corresponding to the Form (the "Fness in us"). The ontological separation of Forms entails that they are no longer a "one *in* many." The Immanence Assumption of the Socratic dialogues (S_3 above) no longer applies to Forms, for they are now regarded as a "one *over* many."[19]

We have seen that Plato's separation of Forms involves two claims: first, that Forms are nonsensible objects of knowledge, distinct from sensible things which are objects of opinion; and second, that Forms have separate existence and do not depend on their participants for their existence. Although it is controversial whether the second claim should be attributed to Plato, there is evidence in at least some of the middle dialogues for the separate existence of Forms.[20] According to Aristotle, Plato separated Forms from sensible objects because of his belief that things in the sensible world are in constant flux, and that if there is to be knowledge there must be stable, nonsensible objects. It is clear how these considerations lead to the epistemological separation of Forms. But one might wonder whether Aristotle has given us Plato's reason for the *ontological* separation of Forms from their participants. As we saw before, the separate existence of Forms does not follow from their epistemological separateness; the objects of Socrates' search for definitions might be nonsensible properties of sensible things – properties which do not have separate existence but do have enough fixity to qualify as objects of knowledge. So the failure of sensible objects to meet the strict conditions for being objects of knowledge does not explain why Forms must *exist* separately from their participants. It therefore seems that Aristotle's report does not give us a full explanation of Plato's reasons for separating Forms from their participants.

We noticed that the ontological separation of Forms from their participants involves abandoning the Immanence Assumption of the Socratic dialogues: if Forms exist separately from their participants, then they cannot be *in* those participants. But what considerations led Plato to the view that a Form cannot be *in* its participants? If we can answer this question, we should be able to see why he thought that Forms must exist "themselves by themselves," that is, separately from their participants. Let us begin with the supposition that the many F things participate in Fness by having Fness *in* them. According to the Unity Assumption of the Socratic dialogues (S_1 above), "Fness is one thing, not many"; that is, Fness is a single thing which the many F things have in common. Beauty, for instance, is a single thing, and it is found in both the Parthenon and the paintings of the Sistine Chapel. But does this single thing, beauty, *exist as a whole* in the Parthenon and the Sistine Chapel? It does not seem possible that a single thing could exist as a whole in two separate places at the same time.[21] Perhaps, then, there is a part of beauty in the Parthenon and a part in the Sistine Chapel (cf. *Euthyd.* 301a). But would beauty be one thing if it consists of parts that are scattered in this way? Plato apparently does not think so, as the following passage from the *Parmenides* indicates:

"Then," said he, "the Forms themselves, Socrates, are divisible into parts, and their participants partake of a part, and in each of them there would not be the whole, but only a part of each Form."

"So it appears."

"Are you then willing to say, Socrates, that a single Form is actually divided and will still be one?"

"By no means," he replied. (131c)

When we reflect on the Unity Assumption of the Socratic dialogues (the assumption that Fness is a "one *in* many), we are confronted with difficulties which are not considered in those dialogues: can we consistently hold that Fness is one thing and that it exists as a whole in distinct and separate places at the same time? Or is it consistent with the unity of Fness to suppose that it is divisible into parts and that these parts are scattered among things in different places? It is clear that in the *Phaedo* Plato is concerned with questions of this sort. One of the arguments for immortality rests on an analogy between Forms and the soul. Socrates argues that souls are like Forms in that they are not divisible into parts in the way that material things are, and there is therefore no danger that they will be "scattered" to the four winds at death (78b–c). Socrates conceives of the Form as a unity, not only in the sense that there is only one Fness corresponding to the many F things, but also in the sense that it cannot be "scattered" – it cannot exist, either as a whole or as divided into parts, in distinct and separate spatial locations at the same time. And since it is true of the many Fs that they exist in different places at the same time, it follows that Fness cannot be *in* the many Fs. If Fness is to have the sort of unity that a Form must have, then it must exist separately from its participants.[22]

Aristotle tells us that Plato held that Forms are "numerically" one. He also says that if something is one in this way it cannot exist in many places at the same time.[23] His notion of numerical unity thus seems to capture the sort of unity that Plato has in mind when he claims that a Form's being one is incompatible with its being "scattered" among its participants. If something is numerically one, it must exist either in one place only at a time, or in no place at all. A Form, since it does not exist *in* anything, presumably does not have any spatial location. We may recall, however, that Plato distinguishes between "Fness itself" and the "Fness *in* us" (*Phaed.* 102d–e, 103b; cf. *Symp.* 210b with 211a–b). The Fness in something, for example, the Largeness in Socrates, obviously does have a particular spatial location; but since it does not exist in distinct, separate places at the same time, it satisfies the condition for being numerically one. So both Fness itself and the Fness *in* us are numerically one: Fness itself is a "*one over* many" while Fness in us is a "*one* in one." In order to preserve the strict, numerical, unity of a Form, Plato no longer conceives of the Form as a "one *in* many"; the Form becomes a "one *over* many," and thus exists separately from its many participants.

Aristotle reports that Socrates did not separate the objects he was seeking to define, but that Plato did separate them, and called these objects Forms. As we have seen, Aristotle means by this that Plato held that Forms are not *immanent* in their participants – they exist separately, "themselves by themselves." However, the reasons

Aristotle gives for Plato's separation of Forms apply only to the epistemological side of the separation: they explain why Forms must be nonsensible, but not why they must be ontologically separate from their participants.[24] To fill in this gap, we suggested that it was Plato's reflections on the Socratic Unity Assumption and its relationship to the Immanence Assumption that led him to make the ontological separation. In order to preserve the strict unity of Forms, Plato decides that he must reject Socrates' assumption that Fness is *in* the many F things; his Forms must exist "themselves by themselves," apart from their participants.

The *Parmenides*: Plato's Second Thoughts about the Theory of Forms

The *Parmenides*, which is generally considered to have been written after the "middle" dialogues, contains a series of intriguing and powerful attacks on the Theory of Forms. Most scholars believe that these arguments indicate a crisis of confidence in the Theory on Plato's part. Some scholars believe that these arguments mark a turning point in his conception of Forms: that after the *Parmenides* Plato jettisoned the ontological separateness of Forms. Before considering these arguments and their possible ramifications, let us summarize some of the main theses of the Theory of Forms.

Plato holds that Forms are objects of knowledge, and since knowledge requires stable, unchanging objects, Forms must have these attributes. Forms must also be nonsensible (they must be grasped through reasoning and intellect rather than through sense experience) since it is characteristic of sensible objects to "wander" and undergo change. If Forms are unchanging they cannot undergo generation and destruction: they must be eternal as well as unchanging.

Since Plato views Forms as causes of their participants having certain properties (Fness is the cause of its participants being F), he holds that the Self-Predication Assumption of the Socratic dialogues (S_2) must apply to Forms: since the Form, Fness, is an "F maker," it must itself be F and exclude the opposite of F. Plato also continues to maintain the Unity Assumption of the Socratic dialogues (S_1): there is one and only one Form, Fness, for each group of "the many Fs." But we have seen that there is another kind of unity that must be possessed by Forms: Forms must be *numerically one*, that is, they cannot be "scattered" among their participants since they cannot exist in spatially discontinuous locations. This means that Forms cannot be *in* their participants. Thus Plato rejects the Immanence Assumption of the Socratic dialogues (S_3) and adopts the view that Forms are ontologically separate from their participants and do not depend on them for their existence. While a Socratic object of definition is a "one *in* many," a Platonic Form is a "one *over* many." The thesis that each Form is a "one *over* many" combines three claims about the unity and existence of Forms: (1) each Form is "unique" in the sense that there is just one Form for each group of F things; (2) each Form is "numerically one" in the sense that it does not have scattered existence; (3) since a Form does not have scattered existence, it must exist separately from its participants, and hence it does not depend on its participants for its existence.

One advantage of the Socratic view that Forms are immanent in their participants is that there are familiar analogues for understanding the relationship of participation. Just as we can explain the paint's being white by its having white pigment in it, so (it seems) we can explain something's being F by its having the Form of Fness in it. Once Forms are separated from their participants, the relation of participation becomes more of a puzzle. Plato acknowledges the problematic nature of participation in the *Phaedo* and does not offer any suggestions as to how it might be understood (100d). In other dialogues like the *Republic*, however, he suggests that we might understand the relationship between F things and the Form of Fness by analogy with the relationship between images or copies and their original: F things are F by resembling the Form of Fness in the way that images resemble their original. In line with this suggestion, he sometimes speaks of Forms as "paradigms," that is, as models or patterns to be copied (*Rep.* 500d–e, 540a). In general, the middle dialogues represent participation in terms of resemblance between image and original, but the admission of unclarity in the *Phaedo* is probably an indication of a nagging worry about this aspect of the Theory of Forms. Not surprisingly, several of the arguments in the *Parmenides* focus on participation.

The most famous of the attacks on the Theory of Forms in the *Parmenides* is the so-called Third Man Argument (TMA).[25] Though the argument is very brief and elliptical (only thirteen lines in the standard Greek text), its importance for understanding Plato's attitude towards the Theory of Forms is indicated by the fact that the many interpretations of the argument which have appeared since the 1950s would fill several thick volumes. The following interpretation of the argument should therefore be regarded as a "one *among* many."

There is general agreement that the aim of the TMA is to show that certain elements in the Theory of Forms are inconsistent with the thesis that there is a unique Form for each group of F things.[26] Exactly which elements of the Theory are involved in the argument is a matter of scholarly debate, as is the question whether the argument is a serious threat to the Theory. Let us begin with an outline of the argument:

1. The venerable philosopher, Parmenides, enunciates Socrates' thesis that there is a single Form, say "Largeness itself," over the many large things that we see.
2. Parmenides then suggests that if we consider Largeness itself together with the other large things, there will appear another Largeness by which all of these are large.
3. Thus there will be another Form of Largeness over the [first] Largeness itself and its participants, and then another over all of these by which they are large.
4. The result, according to Parmenides, is that there will not be just one Form of Largeness, but an unlimited number of them. (132a–b).

The crucial move in the argument is step 2. Step 1 is simply a particular instance of the claim that there is just one Form, Fness, for each group of the many Fs. In step 2, Parmenides groups the Form of Largeness together with the many large things, and then infers that there must be another Form of Largeness "over" the group consisting of the original Form of Largeness and its participants. But is it fair to the Theory of Forms to lump together the Form of Largeness and the many large things, and to consider this an expanded class of large things? After all, the Form seems to belong to a different order of reality. And even if we agree to this, why is it necessary to posit a second Form of Largeness?

In connection with the first question, we should note that step 2 of the argument implicitly relies on the Self-Predication Assumption (SP): If the Form of Largeness can be considered a member of the class of large things, then it must itself be large. At least this much of step 2 seems fair to the theory. What seems problematic is the treatment of the Form as a large thing *on a par with* other large things. As we have noted, Forms are nonsensible, unchanging, eternal entities; in these respects, the otherworldly Forms are strikingly different from their worldly participants. On the other hand, the Form of Largeness is like its participants in being a *large thing*: it is a separate entity in its own right, and, given SP, it has the same property of largeness that its participants have.[27] So, even though it is true that Forms and their participants belong to different orders of reality, it is a consequence of SP and the "one *over* many" thesis that Forms are like their participants in the respects relevant to the argument: these elements of the Theory of Forms apparently justify treating the Form of Largeness as a member of the class of large things.

Once the Form of Largeness is placed within the class of large things, Parmenides claims that there must be "another" Form of Largeness in virtue of which all of these are large. What is the basis for positing a second Form of Largeness? It may be helpful to consider a brief passage in the *Republic* in which Socrates considers whether there could be more than one Form corresponding to a set of F things, for example, more than one Form corresponding to the set of all beds. He claims that this is impossible. For suppose, he says, that there are two Forms of "Bedness," Bedness$_1$ and Bedness$_2$; necessarily, another Form would appear over these, and this would be *the* Form of Bedness, and not Bedness$_1$ and Bedness$_2$ (597c–d).[28] (We might call this the "Third Bed Argument.") Although this argument is designed to show that there can be no more than one Form for a given set of F things, it paradoxically leaves an opening for a counterargument along the lines of the Third Man Argument. It seems that the only reason for positing another Form of Bedness in addition to Bedness$_1$ and Bedness$_2$ is that these two constitute a plurality. According to Socrates' reasoning, if there is a plurality of things which share the property of being F, then we must posit a Form of Fness over these things – even if these things are not sensible particulars. Thus the principle which drives the Third Bed Argument is that whenever there is a plurality of things that are F, whether these things are sensible particulars or nonsensible Forms – or a combination of the two – there must be a single Form over them. This principle apparently justifies Parmenides' claim that there must be a second Form of Largeness, over the set consisting of the first Form and its participants. The same steps can be reiterated, yielding as many Forms of Largeness as one likes – an *infinite regress* of Forms. The argument thus shows that SP and the "one *over* many" thesis generate a multiplicity of Forms for each set of things that are F, and this is of course inconsistent with the thesis that there is only one Form for each set of F things.

What does the Third Man Argument show about Plato's attitude towards the Theory of Forms? The argument seems to reveal an important inconsistency in the theory, and it is worth noting that Plato does not offer a reply to the argument in the *Parmenides* or in any other dialogue. Aristotle cites the argument as an effective critique of the Theory of Forms, and makes no mention of any response by Plato to the argument. In view of these facts, it seems likely that the TMA caused Plato to have second thoughts about the theory. In the 1950s the British scholar G. E. L. Owen argued that Plato abandoned the Theory of Forms as a result of the arguments in the *Parmenides*.[29] Owen tried to show that in dialogues written after the *Parmenides* (e.g., *the Theaetetus, Sophist, Statesman, Philebus,* and *Laws*) we do not find evidence of a commitment to the Theory of Forms which is so prominent in the middle dialogues; in particular, we do not find evidence of a commitment to what Owen called the "paradeigmatic" conception of Forms – the conception of Forms as separately existing paradigms or models, and the associated view that sensible particulars participate in Forms by resembling them. Owen concluded (on the basis of this and other considerations) that Plato was persuaded by the arguments in the *Parmenides* to give up his earlier conception of Forms as separately existing paradigms. The reason that Owen's view did not strike earlier scholars as a viable option is that the *Timaeus,* traditionally considered among the latest of Plato's dialogues, contains a clear affirmation of the separate existence of Forms. Owen took the bull by the horns, and argued that, for a variety of reasons, the *Timaeus* should be considered a middle dialogue. If the *Timaeus* is grouped with the middle dialogues, then we have a sharp contrast between the dialogues written before and after the *Parmenides*: in the dialogues that come before the *Parmenides* (the *Phaedo, Republic, Symposium, Phaedrus,* and *Timaeus*) Plato is a firm and forceful advocate of separately existing Forms, while in the dialogues that come after the *Parmenides* (the *Theaetetus, Sophist, Statesman, Philebus,* and *Laws*) there are discussions of Forms but there is no mention of their separate existence or of the idea that Forms are paradigms.

Owen's view that the *Timaeus* was written before the *Parmenides* has not found favor among current scholars. Those who have addressed the question have tended to accept the traditional late dating of the *Timaeus,* and therefore believe that Plato never gave up the conception of Forms as separately existing paradigms. Tending to support this traditional view is the fact that Aristotle, who discusses the Theory of Forms extensively, does not give any indication that Plato had a change of heart in later years.[30] Some would point to the fact that the separate existence of Forms is not mentioned in other late dialogues as evidence that Plato's confidence was somewhat shaken by the arguments of the *Parmenides*, even though, as the *Timaeus* shows, he continued to maintain the theory to the end. Other scholars believe that Plato had answers to the arguments of the *Parmenides* (even though they went unrecorded by Aristotle), and never saw those arguments as serious threats to his theory.

Before concluding our discussion of the Theory of Forms, it may be of interest to take a closer look at the idea that Forms are *paradigms*. In recent discussions of Plato's theory, scholars often describe Forms as paradigms, and they take the paradigm–copy relation to be a standard feature of the theory. However, Plato actually refers to Forms as paradigms in only two dialogues, the *Republic* and the *Timaeus*;[31] further, there is an interesting difference between these two dialogues in regard to the way in which Forms are viewed as paradigms. In the *Republic* Plato speaks of the philosopher-rulers of the ideal state *using* Forms, especially the Form of the Good, as paradigms in producing justice and the other virtues in the souls of their fellow citizens (500d–e, 540a–b). If the rulers are successful in making their fellow citizens just and good, then these instances of justice and goodness will be related to the corresponding Forms as copies are to paradigms. In the *Republic* it is only when Forms are *used* as paradigms that the paradigm–copy relation will obtain; in cases where things come to be F in some other way (e.g., a tree comes to be large), the relation between participant and Form will be different.[32] In the *Timaeus*, on the other hand, we find the view that Forms are by their very nature paradigms. In specifying the most basic kinds of entities, Timaeus mentions three types: (1) the Forms which are paradigms; (2) the copies or likenesses of these paradigms; and (3) the place or "receptacle" in which these likenesses come to be and pass out of existence (48e–49a). Participation in general is here understood in terms of the paradigm–copy relation. Thus it is only in the *Timaeus* that we find the notion that a Form is *essentially* related to its instances as a paradigm is to its copies.

One of the arguments against the Theory of Forms in the *Parmenides* takes as its target a certain view of participation based on the idea that Forms are paradigms. The argument is a response to the following proposal put forward by Socrates:

> But Parmenides, it seems to me that the most likely view is that these Forms are established in nature as paradigms, and that the other things resemble these and are likenesses of them; and the participation of these things in Forms is nothing other than their being modeled after them. (132c–d)

This proposal is clearly a formulation of the view that to participate in a Form is to be related to it as a copy is to its paradigm. Parmenides' regress argument against this proposal is different from the TMA in that it attacks a particular conception of participation whereas the TMA leaves participation unspecified and focuses on problems arising from the combination of the "one *over* many" thesis and SP.[33] It seems that Parmenides' second regress argument is aimed specifically at the *Timaeus* for it is only in the *Timaeus* that we find the view that participation as such is to be understood in terms of the paradigm–copy relation.

If it is true that Parmenides' second regress argument alludes to a view which is found only in the *Timaeus*, this would seem to support Owen's view that the *Timaeus* was written before the *Parmenides*. For the second regress argument, like the TMA, seems to be a damaging critique of the theory, and there are no hints in the *Timaeus*, or in other late dialogues, as to how the argument might be countered. Furthermore, as Owen notes, the view that Forms are paradigms does not appear in any of the dialogues that are considered to be late (leaving aside the *Timaeus*, of course). The traditional view that the *Timaeus* was written after the *Parmenides* involves a couple of awkward consequences: first, it would mean that the second regress argument of the *Parmenides* attacks a conception of participation (that Forms are *essentially* related to their participants as paradigms to copies) which does not appear in any of the discussions of Forms in the middle dialogues; second, it would mean that this conception of participation is built into the metaphysics of the *Timaeus* without any indication of how it might be defended against Parmenides' apparently damaging attack. Owen's view seems more plausible: Parmenides' second regress argument attacks a conception of Forms which has already been articulated by Plato; and since Plato does not see how to answer the argument, he abandons the idea that Forms are related to their instances as paradigms to copies in the dialogues written after the *Parmenides*.

If at the time of writing the *Parmenides* Plato abandoned the view that Forms are paradigms, does this mean that he also rejected the Theory of Forms of the middle dialogues (as Owen apparently thought)? There are good reasons for skepticism about the proposal that Plato, in his latest works, abandoned the Theory of Forms of the middle dialogues. For instance, there is evidence in such late dialogues as the *Sophist* and *Philebus* that Plato still regards Forms as eternal, unchanging, nonsensible entities. And, as the following passage from the *Philebus* indicates, he still takes seriously the idea that Forms are numerically one and therefore exist separately from their participants:

> SOCRATES: The first question (1) is whether we should believe that such unities [= Forms] really exist; and then (2), how these things, each being one, always the same [= unchanging], and admitting neither generation nor destruction [= eternal], can nevertheless most assuredly be declared a unity; and again (3), [how] being in things that come to be and are unlimited (whether it should be considered broken up into many parts and scattered, or as a whole separate from itself – which would seem most impossible), each being one and the same will simultaneously be in one and in many. It is these puzzles about the one and many, and not those others, Protarchus, which cause the greatest perplexity if they are not well resolved, but lead to progress if they are well resolved. (15b–c)

Socrates' third question harks back to our discussion of the Socratic Immanence Assumption. If a Form is immanent in its participants, then either the whole Form is in each participant or the Form must be divided into parts and the parts dispersed among the participants; neither of these possibilities seems compatible with the principle that each Form is a unity (*Parm.* 131a–c). If these are the only possible ways for Forms to be immanent in their participants (131a), then we must conclude that if Forms are unities they cannot be immanent in their participants. The passage quoted from the *Philebus*, in which Socrates wonders how a Form can be one thing and at the same time "in many," indicates that Plato still has grave doubts about the notion that Forms are immanent in their participants. Neither in the *Philebus* nor in any of the other late dialogues does he attempt to solve this "puzzle about the one and many." In his latest works, Plato seems to be caught in a dilemma:

Forms must either have separate existence or be immanent in their participants; but separate existence leads to the Third Man Argument, while immanence is incompatible with the strict, numerical unity of Forms. It seems that he is not ready to abandon the separate existence of Forms, but neither is he ready to commit himself to it.

If it is true that Plato did abandon the *Timaeus'* conception of Forms as paradigms in his latest dialogues, this does not mean that he rejected the Theory of Forms of the middle dialogues. Since he was unable to solve the "puzzle about the one and many," his attitude towards the separate existence of the Forms remained ambivalent to the end. Plato's brilliant young student Aristotle came up with his own solution to the puzzle. He opted for immanence, and gave up the strict, numerical unity of Forms (or Universals). But his immanent, "scattered," universals would not have appealed to Plato.

Late Developments in Plato's Metaphysics

In his latest dialogues, Plato's metaphysical interests branch out to include, for example, (1) a critical examination of the metaphysical views of his predecessors, Heracleitus and Parmenides; (2) inquiry into the basic constitution of material objects; and (3) consideration of whether generality is a hallmark of substance – whether the most general kinds such as *being, sameness,* and *unity* are more of the nature of substance than specific types of entities, for example, *human being,* or *horse.* I can give only a brief sketch of each of these topics, along with some indications of where the reader can look for more detailed discussion:

1. One of the views examined in the *Theaetetus* is Heracleitus' Doctrine of Flux, that is, the view that everything is constantly changing (179c–183b). We noticed earlier that Plato agrees with the Heracleitean doctrine as applied to things in the sensible world, but he holds that there are nonsensible Forms that are free of change. In the *Theaetetus* he looks more carefully at the Heracleitean doctrine, and distinguishes different ways in which it can be understood. An extreme version of the doctrine holds that things are constantly changing in all respects: there is no stability whatsoever in things. A more moderate version holds that things are constantly changing, but not necessarily in all respects: someone lying in the sun is not changing with respect to location, but is gradually getting darker. Plato argues that the extreme version of the doctrine is incoherent and self-defeating, for if it were true, it would be impossible even to say "this thing is changing" since "this thing" implies that there is something that *remains the same* through the change (183b; cf. *Soph.* 249b–d). We may infer that if Plato continued to hold that things in the sensible world are constantly changing,[34] it is the more moderate view that he accepted.

In another late dialogue, the *Sophist*, Plato comes to grips with Parmenides' famous dictum that nonbeing cannot be thought of or conceived. By giving a careful analysis of negation, Plato shows that we can coherently speak and think about "what is not"; for instance, we can ascribe nonbeing to X by saying that it *is not* F, and what is meant by this may be expressed as "there is something, X, which is different from the things that are F" (254b–259a).

There is evidence in Aristotle that Plato tackled another puzzle posed by one of Parmenides' claims. In Book I of his *Physics* Aristotle criticizes a Platonic account of change which was designed to answer Parmenides' arguments against the possibility of change. Plato's account, like Aristotle's, involved the notion of "matter" as an underlying continuent through change.[35] Although there are passages in the *Timaeus* and *Philebus* which indicate that Plato had a concept of matter which was a precursor of Aristotle's, there do not seem to be any passages that give the account of change which is criticized in the *Physics*.[36]

2. In his discussion of substance in Book VII of the *Metaphysics*, Aristotle mentions certain unnamed thinkers who hold that the "limits" or dimensions of bodies are substances, and indeed are more of the nature of substance than the bodies themselves.[37] It is generally believed that he is referring to Plato and his followers, but, as in the case of his report of Plato's account of change, it is not clear whether Aristotle is reporting a doctrine contained in Plato's writings, or rather a view defended by Plato in discussion but not explicitly set forth in any of the dialogues. In the *Philebus* we find an analysis of various sorts of things into two factors: a "material-like" factor which in its nature is without definite limits or dimensions, and a "formal" factor which consists of "limits" imposed on the unlimited; the things that come about as a result of the combination of these factors are either products of art or things that are naturally generated (23c–27c). This passage in the *Philebus* undoubtedly contains part of the doctrine that Aristotle attributes to Plato in the *Metaphysics*. In the *Philebus*, as also in the *Timaeus*, we see indications of a change of attitude towards the sensible world: in his later years, Plato apparently became more open to the possibilities of understanding and explaining the world of change and coming-to-be.

3. Aristotle, again, is our primary source for another of Plato's later views in metaphysics. In his *Metaphysics* he criticizes the view of certain thinkers who hold that to be a substance is to be a universal or *genus*. He says that the universal or genus is closely connected to the Forms or Ideas since they are thought to be substances for similar reasons (VIII 1, 1042a13–16). It seems that the view he is referring to is Plato's (cf. XII 1, 1069a26–30). According to this view, both a universal genus like "animal" and a species like "horse" are substantial entities, but the genus is more of a substance than the species.[38] Aristotle's criticism of this view is separate from his criticism of the Theory of (separate) Forms (cf. VIII 1, 1042a21–4). In his critique of the view that universals are substances, he does not treat them as necessarily having separate existence; but when he attacks the Theory of Forms he says that it is their separate existence that is the cause of all the difficulties (XIII 9, 1086b2–7). Thus, for Aristotle at least, the view that the genus or universal is substance is distinct from the Theory of Forms.

We find some traces of the view that the genus or universal is substance in several of Plato's late dialogues. In the light of Aristotle's attribution of this view to Plato, it is significant that in these dialogues the term "genus" (*genos*) is used interchangeably with "Form," and seems to be used in preference to the latter term. In the *Sophist*, for example, the Eleatic Stranger (who is described as a philosopher: 216a–c) focuses his main investigation on the "greatest *genera*" (or "kinds"), for example, "being," "motion," "rest," "sameness," and "difference" (254c–260a). The Stranger holds that Dialectic is the science which enables one to "divide things according to their genera or kinds," and this ability is a defining condition of the philosopher (253b–e). If these genera are to qualify as proper objects of knowledge, they must have fixed essences (249b–c). But the Stranger does not say that these genera, which are the objects of the science of Dialectic, exist apart from the sensible things that partake of them – nor does he say that they do *not* exist apart; he adopts a neutral stance vis-à-vis the contentious issue of the separate existence of the objects of Dialectic. According to the Stranger's conception of Dialectic, both those who believe in separately existing genera or Forms and those who reject them may qualify as dialecticians and philosophers; what is required is acceptance of the view that the genera or Forms investigated by Dialectic have fixed, permanent essences. The *Sophist* thus provides some evidence that Plato, in his later works, regarded universals or "genera" as substances, and that this doctrine is independent of the Theory of (separate) Forms.

Plato continued to grapple with metaphysical problems to the end of his long life. As he became older, he seems to have mellowed in certain respects. In his conception of philosophy, for example, he put aside partisanship and became more accepting of diverse points of view. Recall that in the *Republic*, philosophy is identified with the highest form of knowledge – the science of Dialectic – and the objects of this science are Forms, that is, entities which exist in a separate realm distinct from the sensible world. In his later dialogues, like the *Sophist* and *Statesman*, Plato still regards Dialectic as the highest form of knowledge, the special possession of the philosopher. But he now characterizes the objects of Dialectic as "genera" or "kinds," and sees Dialectic as especially concerned with the most universal genera.[39] To be a dialectician, one does not need to accept the doctrine of the separate existence of these genera; one only needs to hold that these entities have fixed, stable essences. Plato may have continued to believe that Forms must have separate existence, but he refuses to treat this belief as a dogma. The ranks of philosophers include not only the "Friends of the Forms" (*Soph.* 248a), but also those who (like Aristotle) might be opposed to the separate existence of Forms. By avoiding dogmatism and welcoming debate and disagreement, Plato set a fine example for future philosophers.

Acknowledgments

I would like to thank Tom Brickhouse, Jim Cargile, and especially Christopher Shields for helpful comments on an earlier version of this chapter.

Notes

1 See White 1992.

2 See Aristotle's *Metaphysics* XIII 4, 1078b17–36. Cf. *Apology* 38a, where Socrates describes his daily conversations as "about virtue."

3 This is at the same time an assumption of the *existence* of a single entity, Fness, over and above the many F things.

4 Cf. *Euthyphro* 8a–b.

5 Only in the *Hippias maj.* among the Socratic dialogues, does Socrates claim that the same individual may be both F and the opposite of F (288e–289c).

6 Socrates does not hold that in all cases Fness makes its possessor F; see *Lysis* 217c–e; cf. *Euthydemus* 300e–301b.

7 For a possible exception, see *Hippias maj.* 288e–289c.

8 The *Phaedo* recognizes a few exceptions, fires are always hot, never cold, snow is always cold, never hot (103c–e).

9 For another way of understanding the argument, see Fine 1990, 85–115.

10 This claim *is* made in the *Timaeus* (at 51b–52a), but the *Timaeus* is usually considered to be a late rather than a middle dialogue. We will discuss the relationship between the *Timaeus* and the middle dialogues in "Plato's Theory of Forms: Ontological Separation," below.

11 Note that in the passages in the *Republic* and *Phaedo* in which Socrates introduces and discusses Forms, his interlocutors at that point already accept the existence of Forms. In the *Republic* the "sight-lovers" (of 476a–480a) reject the existence of separate Forms, and many interpreters believe that Socrates' argument is aimed at winning them over to his and Glaucon's view. But it seems unlikely that Socrates is trying to persuade the sight-lovers that there must be separate Forms, for he says that these people "cannot be led by another" to grasp that there are such things (479e; cf. 476c). He says that he will try to persuade them that their state of mind is opinion rather than knowledge, and he does this by showing that the objects which they believe in can only be objects of opinion (476d–e; 479d–480a); he does not get them to acknowledge the existence of separate Forms.

12 My view is similar to the view of Terence Irwin ("The Theory of Forms" in Fine 1999, 168–70) and Fine 1993, 54–7. They argue that Plato regards the "compresence of opposites" is part of what is meant by the claim that things are in flux: things can be in flux either by changing over time or by partaking of opposites at the same time ("compresence" of opposites). My view differs in that I (will) suggest that, for Plato, the fact that sensible objects are both F and not-F is an indication that they undergo a kind of change.

13 Beauty itself "appears" beautiful to the mind or intellect: since it is a nonsensible object, we have no access to it through the senses.

14 Reflection on Socrates' belief that the virtues are *powers* of the soul might lead to the idea that the virtues are not things that can be grasped through the senses. While we may perceive the external manifestations of these powers, i.e., virtuous actions, the powers themselves do not seem to be accessible to the senses; as Socrates points out in the *Republic*, psychic powers do not have sensible properties (477c–d). However, there are no signs in the Socratic dialogues that Socrates gave any thought to the question whether the things he sought to define were accessible to the senses.

15 See, e.g., *Physics* I 2, 185a31–2; *Metaphysics* VII 1, 1028a33–4; XII 1, 1069a21–4.

16 For the claim that there is not clear evidence in the middle dialogues for Forms as ontologically separate, see Fine 1986, 71–97; for arguments on the other side, see Devereux 1994, 63–90.

17 See Devereux 1994, 70–7, for support for this claim.

18 See *Parmenides* 133c: "Socrates, I believe that you or anyone else who posits an essence of each thing, itself by itself, would agree in the first place that none of them exist in us." "Yes, for how could it still be itself by itself," said Socrates. (Cf. 159c.) Confirmation of this view is found in Aristotle: "For the Form is separate and itself by itself, whereas the common character inheres *in* all; the latter cannot be the same as the separate [Form], for that which is separate and by its nature itself by itself could not be *in* all" (*Mag. mor.* 1182b12–16).

19 Aristotle frequently mentions that Forms are not regarded by the "Platonists" as *in* their participants: see, e.g., *Metaphysics* I 9, 991a12–14; XIII 5, 1079b15–18, 1079b35–1080a2; he also indicates that the Platonists regard Forms as a "one over many": see *Metaphysics* VII 16, 1040b27–30; I 9, 990b13.

20 In addition to the evidence already cited from the *Phaedo*, see *Symposium* 211ab, *Timaeus* 51e–52a.

21 Cf. *Philebus* 15b: "are we to suppose that a unity [a Form] remains one and the same even though it is afterwards found again among the things that come to be and are unlimited, so that it finds itself as one and the same in one and many things at the same time? And must it be treated as scattered and multiplied, or *as a whole separated from itself*, which would seem most impossible of all?" See also Armstrong 1989, 98.

22 See *Parmenides* 131a–c, and Devereux 1994, 83–8.

23 See *Metaphysics* VII 16, 1040b25; for the claim that Forms are numerically one, see *Topics* VI 6, 143b29–31; *On Ideas* 98.4 (Barnes 1984, p. 2440).

24 Aristotle may have thought that if Forms must be free of change to be proper objects of knowledge, then they must also exist separately from their participants; for he notes that if Forms are "in us" they must be subject to change, i.e., change of place (*Topics* 113a25–30).

25 The name of the argument derives from Aristotle: in a number of places he refers to an argument exactly like the one at *Parmenides* 132ab as the "Third Man Argument" (cf. *Sophistical Refutations* 22, 178b36–179a10).

26 For a different view of the aim of the argument, see Rickless 1998, 501–54.

27 Cf. Aristotle, *Nicomachean Ethics* I 6, 1096a34–b5: "One might wonder what in the world they mean by *a thing itself*, if in man himself and in a particular man the account of man is one and the same. For as men, they will not differ; and if this is so, neither will they differ in so far as they are good. But again it will not be good to a greater extent for being eternal, since the white which is longlasting is no whiter than that which perishes in a day."

28 Although Plato uses the Form Bed (or "Bedness") as an illustration in this passage, many scholars would claim that he does not actually believe that there are Forms of artifacts. It seems likely that Plato did not have a fixed view about the range of things for which there are Forms when he wrote the middle dialogues; cf. *Parmenides* 130b–e; also Nehamas 1973, 461–91.

29 See Owen 1953, 79–95.

30 See Fine 1993, 37–8.

31 Cf. Fine 1993, 63, n. 83.

32 One might object that, while the use of the term "paradigm" is infrequent, the paradigm–copy relation is implied whenever Plato speaks of participants as *images* of Forms, or as *resembling* Forms, and these terms are used in virtually all contexts in which Forms are discussed. However, Plato speaks of Forms as paradigms only in cases in which instances come about in a certain way: viz., through the productive activity of an intelligent agent who uses a Form as a pattern or guide. (Aristotle also understands Forms as paradigms in this way; cf. *Metaph.* A 9, 991a20–3.) This is obviously not a necessary feature of the relation between an image and that of which it is an image – consider, e.g., reflections in water (*Rep.* 509e–510a). To say that a Form is a paradigm is not simply to say that a Form is that of which other things are images; it is to ascribe to the Form a certain role in the coming-into-being of its instances – the Form as paradigm is not directly responsible for its participants being F; something else is directly responsible, and it "looks to" the Form in bringing about its effect.

33 The second regress argument may also be different in generating multiple Forms of Likeness rather than multiple Forms of the original Fness; see Schofield 1996, 49–77.

34 Aristotle mentions that Plato continued to hold the Heracleitean doctrine as applied to sensible things "even in later years" (*Metaph.* I 6, 987a32–b1).

35 See *Physics* I 9, 191b35–192a16.

36 See *Timaeus* 49a–51b; cf. *Philebus* 25d–27b; 54bc.

37 See VII 2, 1028b16–18; cf. V 8, 1017b17–21; III 5, 1002a4–13.

38 See *Metaphysics* VIII 1, 1042a13–15; cf. III 3, 998b14–21; XI 1, 1059b24–31. In the *Categories*, Aristotle argues for the antithesis of this view, i.e., that the species is more of a substance than the genus; cf. 2b7–22.

39 Cf. Aristotle, *Metaphysics* III 1, 995b18–25.

References and Recommended Reading

Allen, R. E. 1965. *Studies in Plato's Metaphysics*. London: Routledge and Kegan Paul.

Armstrong, D. M. 1989. *Universals: An Opinionated Introduction*. Boulder: Westview Press.

Bambrough, R. 1965 (ed.). *New Essays on Plato and Aristotle*. London: Humanities Press.

Barnes, J. 1984. *The Complete Works of Aristotle: The Revised Oxford Translation*, 2 vols. Princeton: Princeton University Press.

Cherniss, H. F. 1957. "The Relation of the *Timaeus* to Plato's Later Dialogues." *American Journal of Philology* 78 225–66 (reprinted in Allen 1965, 339–78).

Cohen, S. M. 1971. "The Logic of the Third Man." *Philosophical Review* 80 448–75 (reprinted in Fine 1999, 275–97).

Devereux, D. T. 1994. "Separation and Immanence in Plato's Theory of Forms." *Oxford Studies in Ancient Philosophy* 12 (reprinted in Fine 1999, 192–214).

Everson, S. 1990 (ed.). *Epistemology*. Cambridge: Cambridge University Press.

Fine, G., 1984. "Separation." *Oxford Studies in Ancient Philosophy* 2 31–87.

—— 1986. "Immanence." *Oxford Studies in Ancient Philosophy* 4 71–97.

—— 1990 (ed.). "Knowledge and Belief in *Republic V–VII*" in Everson 1990, 85–115 (reprinted in Fine 1999, 215–45).

—— 1993. *On Ideas*. Oxford: Clarendon Press.

—— 1999 (ed.). *Oxford Readings in Philosophy: Plato 1*. Oxford: Oxford University Press.

Gallop, D. 1975. *Plato's Phaedo*. Oxford: Clarendon Press.

Gill, C., and McCabe, M. M. (eds.) 1996. *Form and Argument in Late Plato*. Oxford: Clarendon Press.

Irwin, T. 1999. "The Theory of Forms" in Fine 1999, 143–70.

Kraut, R. 1992. *The Cambridge Companion to Plato*. Cambridge: Cambridge University Press.

Meinwald, C. 1992. "Good-bye to the Third Man" in Kraut 1992, 365–96.

Nehamas, A. 1973. "Predication and Forms of Opposites in the *Phaedo*." *Review of Metaphysics* **26** 461–91.

—— 1975. "Plato on the Imperfection of the Sensible World." *American Philosophical Quarterly* **12** 105–17 (reprinted in Fine 1999, 171–99).

Owen, G. E. L. 1953. "The Place of the Timaeus in Plato's Dialogues." *Classical Quarterly* NS **3** 79–95 (reprinted in Owen 1986, 65–84).

—— 1986. *Logic, Science and Dialectic*. ed. M. Nussbaum. Ithaca: Cornell University Press.

Rickless, S. 1998. "How Parmenides Saved the Theory of Forms." *Philosophical Review* **107** 501–54.

Scholfield, M. "Likeness and Likenesses in the *Parmenides*" in Gill and McCabe 1996, 49–77.

Strange, S. K. 1985. "The Double Explanation in the Timaeus." *Ancient Philosophy* **5** 25–39 (reprinted in Fine 199, 397–415).

Vlastos, G. 1954. "The Third Man Argument in the Parmenides." *Philosophical Review* **63** 319–49 (reprinted in Allen 1965, 231–63).

—— 1965. "Degrees of Reality in Plato" in Bambrough 1965 1–18 (reprinted in Vlastos 1981, 43–57).

—— 1969. "Plato's 'Third Man' Argument (Parm. 132a1–b2): Text and Logic." *Philosophical Quarterly* **19** 289–301 (reprinted in Vlastos 1981, 342–65).

—— 1981. *Platonic Studies*, 2nd ed. Princeton: Princeton University Press.

White, N. 1992. "Plato's Metaphysical Epistemology" in Kraut 1992, 277–310.

Chapter 5

Plato: Epistemology

Nicholas White

Introduction

Plato's epistemology is the direct ancestor of virtually all contemporary philosophical reflections on knowledge. Most current accounts of knowledge owe something substantial to his views. At the same time, however, his approach is not the same as most recent ones. For one thing, his thinking about knowledge is far more closely linked with metaphysics than present-day epistemology is. For another thing, he is less intensely concerned than recent epistemology has been with whether knowledge is correctly defined as justified true belief. In addition, he tends to take it for granted that we do have knowledge, and accordingly is less concerned than epistemologists nowadays to refute skepticism. Nevertheless his views about knowledge, even when they have a different focus from recent epistemological theories, bear importantly on these modern issues.

To most philosophers, such phrases as "Plato's theory of knowledge," "Plato's epistemology," and "epistemological Platonism" bring to mind two main theses about knowledge – "knowledge" being the standard translation of the Greek noun *epistēmē*. One of these theses says that human beings do indeed have knowledge, and that it concerns something "real" or "objective." The other says that knowledge concerns, mainly or exclusively, nonsensible, nonphysical objects. The former thesis is the more fundamental. The latter has seemed to many philosophers, including Plato, to follow from the former together with certain other claims.

The former thesis obviously combines two subtheses. One is that we do have knowledge, that is, that some people sometimes know this or that. The other subthesis is that our knowledge is about "reality" or "what (really) is, *to (ontos) ón*, or – in another possible formulation, which incorporates a bit of interpretation of what the subthesis amounts to – what is 'objective' or 'objectively so.'"

In addition to the two main theses about knowledge, it is necessary to include in any discussion of Plato's epistemology a further set of issues. These concern, not knowledge in the sense of that term that is now usual, but rather what we call "understanding." This is not to say that the Greek words usually translated by the English word "know" (esp. *epistasthai*, *gignōskein*, *eidenai*) should be translated instead by the word "understand" (though in some contexts that is advisable and is indeed sometimes done). Rather it is to say that Plato's views about what we call knowledge are inextricably bound up with his thoughts about understanding.

The understanding in question is of two types. One is the understanding of things and facts and the like – the kind of understanding that is provided by what we now think of as scientific "explanation." For example we might speak of someone as understanding superconductors or their structure, or the movements of the planets, or bacteria, or how some bacteria survive high temperatures. Here we see a link between Plato's epistemology and what would nowadays be called his "philosophy of science" – "science" being another common translation, suited to some contexts, of *epistēmē*. Plato himself drew no distinction between the philosophy of science and epistemology. Equally, while considerations concerning mathematics play a major role in his thinking about these issues, and mathematical knowledge as a premier case of knowledge, he marked no separation between epistemology and the philosophy of mathematics.

A different-seeming type of understanding that is relevant here has to do with the understanding of propositions, with the contents or meanings of statements, or with sentences, or other such linguistic and conceptual understanding. Here a connection with the notion of knowledge is not hard to see. In order to know a certain proposition, it seems to be necessary to understand that proposition, or in some sense to know what it is or means.

Plato plainly believed that these two general types of understanding are closely connected, and indeed scarcely distinguished them at all. Accordingly one cannot separate his theory of knowledge from what one might call his theory of understanding or his – as it is sometimes called – philosophy of thought. Indeed, the best way to investigate this whole area of Plato's philosophy – and in fact almost all of it – is to regard it as a philosophical explanation of thinking, especially of reasonable and successful thinking broadly construed.

A further departmental boundary that Plato did not draw and would not have wished to draw is the boundary between epistemology and what is often called "metaphysics." There are two reasons for this that are worth mentioning here. One is this: Plato maintained, as noted, that knowledge concerns what is "real" or objective; but the notion of reality, *to ón*, has been assigned by Aristotelian usage to "metaphysics," or the science of "the real *qua* real" (*to ón hei ón*), or, as we might say, the investigation of "what it is (for something) to be objective."

The second reason is this. Plato believed, and indeed took it as virtually axiomatic, that humans do sometimes have knowledge. He also believed that in order for humans to have knowledge, certain broad states of affairs must necessarily obtain, concerning the human mind or soul and also other things that exist. The investigation of such states of affairs is normally assigned to metaphysics. There is accordingly no distinction for Plato to draw between metaphysics, so construed, and the investigation of the conditions necessary for human beings to have knowledge.

(Accordingly it is rather misleading to claim, as is sometimes done, that Plato accepted something much like the twentieth-century tripartite account of conditions necessary and sufficient for knowledge, as found, for example, in G. E. Moore, namely, that if *S* knows that *P*, then it must be the case that (1) *P* is true, (2) *S* believes that *P*, and (3) *S* has good grounds for his belief that *P*. Even if we should agree to this claim, which is dubious, we must note that Plato's conception of what is involved in these conditions involves far more metaphysics than is normally taken, in recent times, to be attached to these conditions.)

The rest of this article will sketch some of the philosophically important features of this area of Plato's philosophy, the main questions with which he deals, and the relationships between them. Such a specification is necessary. It is not possible to comprehend his thinking through an account that relies on the unexplicated use of standard translations of his terminology. Rather one must focus largely on the problems that he was trying to address.

Some Differences Between Plato and Descartes

Many of Plato's reflections, as Aristotle tells us in Book I of his *Metaphysics*, take their start from a Socratic project of trying to reach definitions of various terms, especially terms that figure in ethical discourse. These unsuccessful efforts are recorded both in works that most scholars regard as having been written relatively early in Plato's career, such as the *Laches*, the *Charmides*, the *Lysis*, and the *Euthyphro*, and in some other Platonic works which, though perhaps written somewhat later, record thoughts that were evidently stimulated by Socrates' efforts, such as the *Protagoras* and the *Meno*.

One of the ideas that are brought to mind by these works is the following: that when people disagree about whether something (a person, an action, or whatever) possesses a certain feature *F* (being just, being courageous, being a shape) and when, as indicated by this disagreement, people do not seem to *know* whether the thing in fact possesses that feature or not, the first line of investigation to follow is to pose the question "What is *F*? so as to elicit a definition of *F* or an account of "what *F* is."

Contrast this reaction to disagreement and lack of knowledge with the reaction that we observe in Descartes's *Meditations*. Several points of difference suggest themselves. First, Descartes wonders in a solitary way whether he is correct in believing that he is sitting by a fire. He is not involved in a disagreement with someone else, who maintains that he, Descartes, is not sitting by a fire. Second, when Descartes wonders whether he is in fact sitting before a fire, he does not ask such a question as what a fire is, or what sitting is. Third, the issue upon which Descartes focuses from the very start, whether he is sitting by a fire, is an issue about which it would for various reasons seem odd to raise such questions of definition. Rather Descartes's issues involve words or concepts which, it seems plausible to assume, we all understand unproblematically and without disagreeing about them.

Socrates and Plato, by contrast, focus on issues where the difficulty of knowing may plausibly be taken to arise from a failure to understand what is meant, in some sense, by some general term or terms. This is indicated by the fact that not only do the interlocutors in these Platonic dialogues disagree about whether the thing in question is *F*, but they also begin with little or no general agreement about what to say *F* is, or how the term *F* is to be defined. Such terms include "courage" (the *Laches*), "temperance" (the *Charmides*), "friendship" or "attachment" (the *Lysis*), and "piety" (the *Euthyphro*).

Next and perhaps most important, the failure of the interlocutors in a Platonic–Socratic dialogue to have knowledge is indicated by *disagreement*. In the Cartesian situation, in contrast, we have to do with a single investigator who is made to entertain *doubts* about what he is initially inclined to believe. In a Platonic work disagreement sometimes does, to be sure, lead one or both of the parties to a disagreement to have doubts about their initial beliefs (though the notion of "doubt" plays no significant role in Plato and indeed scarcely appears). But this is not always so; often the parties seem to hold onto their beliefs, and the fact of disagreement itself, not the occurrence of doubt on anyone's part, is what generates the subsequent discussion. This fact is closely connected with Plato's emphasis, to be explained below, on the notion of *perspective*.

Plato's focus on the phenomenon of disagreement is to be connected with three important characteristics of his epistemology. First, discovering what *F* is, or arriving at a "definition" of *F*, is treated as an essential preliminary to determining whether or not a particular thing has the characteristic of being *F*. This fact highlights one reason why, as remarked above, Plato does not make a sharp break between discussions of knowledge and of understanding. (Indeed he goes so far as sometimes, it appears, to assimilate the conditions of the understandability of a statement and the conditions of its knowability, and thus also of its truth.) For Plato, the chief obstacle to our knowing whether or not something is *F* usually seems to be our failure to understand the term *F*. However, for reasons that will emerge, he does not believe that this obstacle can be removed by consulting a dictionary.

Furthermore Plato often takes for granted that in the case of such a disagreement there must be some single correct answer to questions like "What is *F*?" and "What does the term *F* mean?" He never responds to such disagreements about whether a thing is *F* by saying simply, "Well, one of us means one thing by *F* and the other means something else, and that is all there is to it." This is a striking fact, especially in the context of present-day discussions, in which philosophers often raise questions about whether people who disagree do understand their terms in the same way, and about whether there is any right answer, even within the context of a single conversation, to the question what the *real* or *correct* meaning of a term is.

Plato's main way of attacking this matter is to develop a theory of reality – his so-called theory of "Forms" (*eidē*; sing. *eidos*), which includes his theory of the workings of the "soul" (*psychē*). (Beside the word "Form" the word "Idea" is also sometimes used here, as a translation of the Greek term *idea*, which is nearly equivalent to *eidos*; but that translation is misleading, because it makes one think that Forms are subjective entities in the mind, which is certainly not Plato's view.) This theory aims to state both necessary and sufficient conditions for our having knowledge and understanding.

Plato's Opposition to Perspectivism

Does Plato assume that we sometimes do possess knowledge and understanding, and infer on that basis that his theory about the conditions for our doing that is correct? Or does he think that he can first establish the correctness of his theory, and then infer on that basis that we possess knowledge and understanding?

In favor of the idea that Plato simply presupposes that we have knowledge and understanding, rather than arguing for this claim, one may cite *Parmenides* 135b–c and *Timaeus* 51d. In the former passage, Plato seems to say that if Forms did not exist (as his theory maintains they do), then we would not be able to think or engage in the kind of discourse that we do. In the latter, he argues for the existence of Forms on the basis of the claim that there is an obvious difference, which we all grasp, between knowledge (here *nous*) and true belief (*alethes doxa*), making the tacit presupposition that we do sometimes have each.

Moreover, although Plato plainly regards the conditions laid down in his theory as sufficient for the possibility of our possessing knowledge and understanding, there is no reason to suppose that he thinks he can use his theory as a basis for *inferring* that we do possess knowledge and understanding. Rather, as noted, our possession of knowledge (as contrasted with belief) and of understanding (so that we may think and engage in discourse) is, in the aforementioned passages (and also, it seems clear, in such passages as *Republic* 476–80), explicitly taken as a given, or perhaps simply as obvious.

Here we see another contrast with what appears to be going on in Descartes's thinking. Descartes seems intent on combating skepticism, at least concerning certain matters. Plato, on the other hand, evidently has little or no interest in combating skeptical hypotheses. Rather, he takes it to be obvious that we know and understand certain things, and then he proceeds, through his theory, to try to describe what things in general must be like if that is to be so. We must once again conclude that Plato regards the philosophical tasks of epistemology otherwise than Descartes did.

Nevertheless in a way we can regard Plato as combating, not skepticism of the sort that preoccupied Descartes, but instead a different sort of opposition, namely, the perspectivist or relativist thinking of Protagoras and others. This kind of thinking is one of Plato's main targets in his most concentrated attack on problems concerning knowledge, his *Theaetetus*, and perhaps also (though this is controversial) in his *Protagoras*. Relativist thinking is also on his mind in many other places, including *Republic* V–VII, especially in 479–80 and 505–6. Here and elsewhere he wishes to attack the view that a person's understanding of the term *F* is exhausted by what is contained in his own experience. This view would say, for instance, that a person's understanding of the term "equal" consists exclusively in the experiences that he or she in some way associates with that word. But each person surely has had different experiences associated with such a word, since each of us sees perceptible things under different conditions and from different vantage points. This view therefore implies that each of us must have his or her own understanding of each such term.

To that extent the view is clearly relativist in a sense. Moreover the view seems to imply that one cannot know just what meaning another person attaches to a term.

Plato's theory of Forms is in part an effort to show how, to the contrary, it can be the case that we all can attach the same concept to a given term, or, in other words, that we all mean the same thing by the term F. (It thus bears an important resemblance to certain elements of Frege's theory of "thoughts," namely, Frege's insistence that for "science" it is necessary that investigator A be able to assert or deny precisely what investigator B asserts or denies.) Especially in the *Theaetetus*, Plato is concerned to make much the same point. Plato, however, is particularly concerned with the case in which A and B are the same person at different times – that is, with the possibility of one and the same person's grasping the same concept, or having the same thought, at different times (cf. *Symposium* 211a–b, 207d–208a).

Notice that a certain obvious-seeming kind of response to this problem which is widespread in present-day discussions would seem to Plato to be plainly unsatisfactory in principle. This response says, roughly, that our concept of F ("yellow," for instance) is the concept of what would appear F to a normal observer in normal circumstances, and that that is what we express when we say that something is F. One of Plato's objections would be that there is no adequate way of determining the relevant sort of "normality."

This objection is not presented by Plato as a response to precisely this proposal, since he does not formulate the proposal in this way. Nevertheless the substance of the objection follows immediately from objections that he frequently makes, and that Socrates had made before him (and that are registered in works as early as the *Apology* and the *Crito*), to the view that the truth about things could be determined by the fact of consensus (a view that is implied by the "Great Speech" of Protagoras at *Protagoras* 320–8). Plato tirelessly stresses the claim that we should not trust what most people say (e.g., *Theaetetus* 172–7). What counts as the "normal" view, and also (as we shall see) what counts as the "normal" perspective, is in Plato's view always hostage to arbitrary contingency, especially the contingency of the perspectives from which most people's experiences happen to have arisen, and also to the presumed incapacity of most people to deploy their perceptual and cognitive faculties with due care and competence. (Cf. the idea enunciated and illustrated at *Cratylus*, 436–40, that internal consistency is not truth; and also the seeming basis of Plato's dissatisfaction with the "Great Speech" in the *Protagoras*.)

In this connection it should also be remarked that Plato exhibits no interest in or sympathy for the idea, also common in recent times, that whereas we may not be able to obtain "objectivity" in our knowledge or understanding of our concepts, we may reasonably settle for "intersubjectivity" – for example, for a kind of "agreement" in practice. Once again, Plato does not directly attack this proposal, but it is clear enough wherein his opposition to it would consist. Just as he rejects the view that the internal consistency of an individual's beliefs is not tantamount to truth, he would deny likewise that truth is exhausted by the mutual consistency of different people's beliefs. Otherwise the fact of general agreement among people would, after all, weigh at least somewhat in favor of accepting what they say – which, as noted, he repeatedly insists it does not.

Surprisingly enough, Plato is prepared to maintain that his position on this topic is not merely obvious but even uncontroversial, in spite of the fact that it is seemingly opposed by what appears to be the sincerely held perspectivist views of Protagoras. This is shown by *Republic* 505–6. Here Plato notes that according to the "majority," pleasure is the good, and that many people are satisfied with what merely appears beautiful or just. But, he says, *no one*, not even such a person, is content to acquire what is merely believed to be good, "but everyone wants to have what really *is* good, and despises mere belief in this case." One implication of this passage is worth stressing. It is that in the view of *everyone*, there *is* a distinction to be drawn between what really is good and what merely seems so. But this is an extraordinary statement. One would have thought that this simply could not be true, on the ground that at least Protagoras had maintained, as Plato well knew, that for a thing to be good can amount to nothing more than its appearing good to someone, and thus being, at best, good "for" that person (*Theaetetus* 151–2, 169–71). And this would seem tantamount to a denial that there really is, in Plato's sense, any such thing as a thing's really *being* good as opposed to merely seeming good.

However, just as *Republic* 505–6 declares, Plato believed that even Protagoras and his ilk, in spite of what they professed, actually did accept the notion of what is good rather than merely appearing so. This fact emerges also from *Theaetetus* 178–9. Here Plato argues that Protagoras himself maintains that his advice will *in fact* seem good to those who follow it. This, Plato claims, must be construed as an attempt to advance a true claim about a future that is objectively a certain way. One of the conclusions that Plato seems prepared to draw from this is that Protagoras himself *has the concept* of a thing's being thus-and-so in a way that goes beyond its merely appearing thus-and-so. That is to say, *Theaetetus* 178–9 appears to give part of Plato's reason for taking it, in *Republic* 505–6, that everyone has that concept.

Plato's willingness to follow this line of thought is no doubt linked in some way to his view, prominent in the *Republic*, that the concept of goodness possesses preeminent philosophical importance. He expresses this preeminence in mainly metaphorical terms (507b–517e), by comparing the Good to the sun, or to something that is brighter in a way even more impressive than the sun is, and by saying that the good is "beyond Being" (*epekeina tēs ousias*). It seems plausible to conjecture that one of the thoughts intended by Plato to emerge from these pregnant sayings is that the concept of the good is, in Plato's view, the concept in which the distinction between reality and mere appearance shows itself to our minds most clearly and universally.

The argument against Protagoras' relativism in *Theaetetus* 169–71 also seems to present a further reason for saying that even according to Plato, the notion of reality, as opposed to appearance, is a concept that we all understand. For that argument accepts the idea that according to Protagoras, his own position *disagrees* with the position of his opponents. Plato takes that admission to imply, in turn, that even according to Protagoras himself there is such a thing as a relation of disagreement and therefore contradiction between one belief and another (170a–b). It seems that in Plato's view someone who has the concept of such a contradiction must have the concept of things really being so or not so, or in other words, of reality. For Plato assumes that the relation of disagreement implicates the notion of holding, so to speak, opposing judgments about how things are. And Plato seems also to conclude that Protagoras himself has that concept, in spite of his attempt to avoid it, and also actually applies it to particular cases. Not all philosophers would accept Plato's arguments here, or concede that someone like Protagoras must own up to using such concepts. Nevertheless it is plain that Plato focuses on precisely these issues.

At this level, then, Plato does confront the challenge of trying to show that we do possess certain particular concepts. He does this inasmuch as he tries to show that even someone who denies that we possess the concept of a thing's being a certain way, as opposed to merely appearing a certain way, must turn out himself actually to possess that concept and to attempt to apply it.

Conditions on Knowledge and Understanding

Now let us turn to Plato's account of the conditions for possessing knowledge and understanding. It must be borne in mind that Plato's theory was not a static thing. Rather it seems in certain respects to have been developed and altered over the course of his lifetime. At the same time, however, it does not seem to me likely that, as some have maintained, he first fully developed a theory and then, in the middle of his career, abandoned or very radically revised it. The similarities between the thinking presented in the *Phaedo* and what is said in such later works as the *Philebus* and also, most likely, the *Timaeus*, seem too strong for that to be probable. Without going into details on this vexed issue, I shall presuppose a moderate developmentalist interpretation, according to which the main goals and outlines of Plato's theory were pretty clearly marked out by the time of his so-called middle dialogues, notably the *Phaedo*, the *Symposium*, and the *Republic*, and after that remained in place, even while various features of it, including some important ones, were more fully articulated or even altered in order to meet difficulties that arose as he pursued his philosophical thinking.

In order to present a philosophically somewhat unified picture of Plato's thinking, I shall concentrate on what I take to be its leading ideas, which concern the relation between sense perception and intellectual cognition. To organize the exposition I shall present his position as consisting of three main theses:

1. Our understanding of our terms and concepts cannot be explained as the result merely of our sensory apprehension of the sensible things that fall under them. That is, one's possession of the notion of F-ness, construed as the notion of something's *being F*, cannot be the result *merely* of one's having observed sensible things that are F. The reason is that any sensible thing that presents itself to sense as appearing F also presents itself as appearing non-F.
2. Rather, our understanding of terms and concepts are to be explained by a kind of cognition of nonsensible things, namely "Forms." According to Plato's middle works,

Forms do not present contrary appearances when we think about them, and it is for this reason that cognition of them enables us to gain understanding and knowledge. (Because Plato later held that Forms can indeed present contrary appearances to thought, he seemingly was obliged to revise his thinking on this point.)

3. A common misapprehension to the contrary notwithstanding, Plato never held that all there is to a sensible object is the appearances that it presents, and thus he never held that all that we can judge about physical objects concerns merely the appearances that they present to us. (That is a position espoused by his main opponents, "relativists," which he wished to attack.) Rather he believed that our grasp of forms enables us to understand the difference between a sensible thing's being F, at least to a degree, and its merely appearing F. Thus we can understand the notion that a sensible object may be F, at least to a degree, in a way that does not consist simply in the fact that it presents certain appearances. (Plato continued to develop views on this matter, especially in his account in the *Philebus* of the way in which both sensible and intelligible objects can be understood as a combination of "limit" and "the unlimited.")

In addition to 2, there are some further points that need to be made about Forms. Plato's thesis that we understand our general terms through cognition of forms involves some complex ontological subtheses. One of them says that forms are nonsensible entities. Another says that the entity that enables one's understanding of the term F is in some sense or other an idealization of what it is to be F. Further parts of Plato's theory – his treatment of the "method of hypothesis" and the "method of collection and division" – discuss the relations between the cognitions of different forms.

The Understanding of Terms

First let us consider 1. As already noted, Socrates traced disagreements and failures of knowledge primarily to people's failure to understand fully the terms that figure in their judgments. This failure is manifested, he thought, in people's inability to discover adequate definitions of those terms. However, as also noted, he also believed that there is such a thing as arriving at a correct definition of a term, and thus as gaining the understanding requisite for reaching well-based judgments in which those terms figure.

For purposes of comprehending what Plato thinks are the conditions for knowledge and understanding, the most important aspect of his theory concerns his diagnosis of why people disagree in their judgments, and are at a loss to articulate general definitions for the concepts that figure in those judgments. Part of his theory of Forms explains what causes those deficiencies.

The main weight here falls, as Plato's frequent emphasis on definitions indicates, on issues concerning the understanding of terms. Though Plato's theory of Forms is also a theory of knowledge, it is broached first as a theory of the understanding of concepts.

What, according to Plato, makes for the understanding of a term or a concept (we may for the most part use these expressions indifferently here)? His answer is, in brief, a particular kind of cognition of a Form, which corresponds in a certain way to that term or concept. This answer, however, is uninformative as it stands. It gains its main significance from the contrast between it and the view which Plato regards as his main opposition, namely, the thesis that our apprehension of physical objects (especially through perception or sensation), or the way in which sensible or perceptible things appear to us, is by itself enough to provide such understanding. (Note that Plato's word *aisthēsis* means both "sensation" and "perception," in spite of the different connotations of these English words.)

Plato's thinking about this matter consists of two main steps. The first is to argue (1) that sensory apprehension of physical objects is by itself insufficient to give us understanding of our concepts. (To reiterate, he takes it to be obvious, and supported by his argument against Protagorean relativism, that we do possess such understanding.) The second step is to show that (2) our understanding of concepts can arise only from the cognition of Forms. This idea involves what is traditionally thought of as ontological Platonism, according to which there exist not merely physical objects but also Forms.

Perception and Perspective

Prominent in Plato's mind here are thoughts about how sensory perception takes place. These have to do with perspectives or points of view from which human beings experience or perceive things, form judgments, and arrive at concepts. Both perceivers and perceived things are embedded within space and time, and also within more complex networks of relationships that arise from the experiences and thoughts that perceivers have. Because this is so, perceptions take place in a way that allows a perceptible thing to present different aspects to different viewpoints, which affect how it appears. As a result, the notion or thought that is brought to mind by a perception of a given thing, as apprehended from one perspective, will often be different from the notion or thought that is brought to mind by the perception of that thing from a different perspective. Moreover, a thing apprehended from one perspective may bring to mind precisely the contrary notion to the one that it brings to mind when it is apprehended from a different perspective. This is because one and the same thing may appear F from one viewpoint and non-F from another.

It is because of this phenomenon, according to Plato, that sensory apprehension cannot by itself constitute or generate our understanding of concepts. Loosely expressed, Plato's first point is this: precisely because any putative sensible sample of what it is to be F presents to sense not only the property of being F but also the property of being non-F, therefore we cannot come by a grasp of what it is to be F from merely such presentations to sense. Thus something further must be involved beyond merely the presentation of appearances. Plato's second point is that this something is a certain kind of cognition of the nonsensible entities which he calls

Forms. These do not, according to the works of his middle period (see *Phaedo* 74; *Republic* 476–80; and *Symposium* 211–12), present these sorts of contrary appearances.

The point may be elucidated by means of an example used by Bertrand Russell. If you always looked at round pennies from oblique angles and never straight on, they would not bring the notion of roundness to mind but rather the notion of ellipticality. And if you looked at elliptical wafers from particular angles they would bring roundness to mind. But the notions of roundness and ellipticality that we have, Plato insists, are the notions of a thing's *being* round and *being* elliptical. But to bring these notions to mind in the right way, we must recognize, when we look at a round coin, for example, that we *are* looking at it from straight on, in such a way that it looks to be shaped as it really is shaped. (To be sure, the notion of a thing's "looking the way it is" is problematic, as is shown by Wittgenstein's scornful question, "How large does the sun look when it looks as large as it is?")

Plato wishes to make a point that is broader than Russell's and so he uses a broader range of types of examples. All of them are vulnerable to philosophical objections, but let us begin by simply laying out three of the types.

Spatial — One relatively simple sort of case involves differences in spatial perspective. Plato's example involves the notion of equality. Even if we suppose that two sticks or other such perceptible things are equal, Plato says (*Phaedo* 74b–c), they nevertheless will appear equal to one person and unequal to another. The reason is the familiar one that the angle from which one looks at two such things can make them look either equal or unequal. (The interpretation of this passage is controversial, but the cases that Plato adduces in various passages seem to me to show with reasonable certainty that he has this sort of issue about perspective in mind here.) Plato also says that the sticks *are* both equal and not equal, and therefore constitute a deficient case of equality. Note also that at *Republic* 476–80 Plato gives the impression of passing nonchalantly from saying that a thing "appears both *F* and non-*F*" to supposing that it is both *F* and non-*F* (see 479a–b, "each of them always participates in both contraries").

time — Another kind of case can be thought of in terms of what we might call "temporal perspective." This is a matter of the time at which an object is perceived and judgments are formed about it. This is a bit like thinking of one's experience of an object as taking place "from the point of view of" two different times rather than two different spatial positions. Something that you consider at one time, for example some water, may appear hot to you, whereas when you consider it at another time it may appear cold (e.g., *Timaeus* 49c–e; *Symposium* 211a–b). Here again we can thereby come to the judgment that the thing both is hot at one time and is not hot at the other time.

Judgment — A third very general sort of case has to do, not with spatial or temporal perspective, but rather with the way in which a judgment that a person makes can be affected or conditioned by the experiences that he has had, and by the thoughts and concepts that he brings to bear in making that judgment. For instance Plato (somewhat like Berkeley much later) is struck by the fact that a thing can appear in one way as compared to one thing but in a seemingly opposed way as compared to some other thing. For instance in the *Hippias major* (289a–c) Plato says that a girl can be beautiful as compared with a pot but not beautiful as compared to a goddess. And at *Parmenides* 129c–d he states that Socrates is one man, of the seven men gathered for the conversation, whereas he is also many in view of the fact that the parts of him on his right or in front, or his upper parts, are different respectively from the parts of him on his left or behind or below.

All of the foregoing cases involve particular sensible objects which present contrary appearances from different perspectives. In other passages, however, Plato perhaps has in mind a different sort of case, in which a concept or general feature possesses another sort of general feature only under certain circumstances and not others. For instance at *Republic* 331 it is stated that repaying what one owes is sometimes just and sometimes unjust, depending on the circumstances. This is not plausibly interpreted as a case in which one and the same particular action is both just and unjust. It is not evident how Plato sees the relationship between this sort of case and the three types of cases described above. It seems safe to say, however, that those three cases constitute the core of Plato's thinking about this contrast between Forms and sensibles.

From consideration of cases of this kind Plato draws two main conclusions. The first conclusion is (1) that the sensory apprehension of sensible things cannot by itself provide us with our understanding of the general terms that we use and the concepts that we understand. The second conclusion is (2) that what does provide this understanding, and indeed all of the knowledge that we have, is a particular kind of cognition of nonsensible objects, which Plato calls "Forms" (*eidē*).

Thesis 3: the Contrast Between Being and Appearing

Let us consider the first conclusion by linking it to some more recent philosophical debates. Here we are approaching thesis 3 of Plato's position.

To the modern empiricist knowledge of the physical world can be thought of as maintaining that if statements or beliefs about it can be known at all, they can be known only by inferring them from statements or beliefs about sensory appearances. This is the empiricism of Locke, for instance. This is the normal way of thinking of our knowledge of the world as "based in experience." Plato certainly does not accept this view, but it is not the main target of his criticism.

A related but distinct view is the doctrine that the concepts that we apply to things in the physical world can be defined in terms of the concepts that we apply to sensory appearances. This is, pretty nearly, the view that Plato wishes to attack. One version of this view says, for example, that what it is for a thing to be blue can be defined in terms of "looks blue." I have already mentioned that Plato would reject one version of this view, namely, the version that says that "is blue" amounts to "would look blue to a normal observer under normal conditions." But Plato would reject *any* version of this view. He seems to offer two lines of argument.

First, he argues (as has also been done in recent times) that the notion of a thing's appearing F implicitly makes use of the notion of a thing's being F. For a thing's appearing *F* is tantamount to its appearing as a thing appears if it *is F*. So if you are to understand the *notion* of a thing's appearing *F*, you must already understand the notion of a thing's (not necessarily, *that* thing's) *being F*. This seems to be a part of the point of the claim at *Phaedo* 74–5 that sensible equals are equal only deficiently, because they can appear both equal and unequal, but "strive to be" nondeficiently equal. (As noted, the interpretation of this passage is controversial, but it seems to me to have to mean something like this if it is to make good sense at all.) But if this is so, then we cannot suppose that we begin with the mere notion of a thing's appearing thus-and-so and then subsequently arrive, on the basis of sensory appearances alone, at the notion of a thing's being thus-and-so. (This is one of the reasons why, in the *Meno* and *Phaedo*, Plato advances his notorious theory of "recollection," which says in part that we "recollect" our concepts from a time before we were born.)

A second line of argument for the same conclusion runs as follows. Suppose that we try to explain informatively the conditions under which an *F*-appearing thing *is F*, so that we can say when a person – beginning with mere sensory presentations of things' appearing *F* and without, as yet, any notion of a thing's being *F* – can arrive at that notion. If we try to do this we shall find that within the explanation itself we must already use, overtly or covertly, the notion of something's being thus-and-so (as opposed to appearing thus-and-so). It seems that some such line of thought is present in the *Theaetetus*, at 184–6. At any rate that passage maintains that when we know or understand anything, we make use of concepts, notably the concept of *being*, which are not available to sensory experience alone. (In this regard Plato's argument is somewhat like modern arguments against phenomenalism, the doctrine that descriptions of how the physical world is can be translated into, and thus shown to amount merely to, discourse that describes only experiences; for these arguments hold that the ostensibly phenomenalist translations actually require concepts – counterfactuals, for example, or in the construction in Carnap's *Der logischer Aufbau der Welt* a primitive relation "is at" – which goes beyond what a phenomenalist language may be thought to include.)

Notice that we are already implicitly ascribing statement 3 to Plato. For we are implicitly supposing that in his view, we can make sense of the notion of a sensible object's *being*, rather than merely appearing, thus-and-so. And that notion is, by 1, not merely a matter of apprehending appearances.

We can best approach what Plato is doing in this argument by considering some objections to what he says. The most significant objections turn on the idea that he here neglects his very own distinction between how sensible things appear and how they are, and that he mistakenly infers that because sensibles appear in contrary ways, they must therefore *be* contrary ways or actually have contrary features.

In the example in the *Phaedo*, as noted, he implies that the two sticks *are* equal (it is hypothesized that they are "equal sticks"), though they merely look unequal from some angles. In the cases involving temporal perspectives, on the other hand, one might well protest that the water *is* hot at one time and *is* cold later. And similar qualms may arise concerning the third kind of case. Here we may say that what is in question is not a property, *being beautiful*, but rather two relations, *being more* and *less beautiful than* something-or-other.[1] In all of these cases Plato seems to have ignored or fudged the distinction between a thing's appearing *F* and its being *F*. But it seems wholly implausible that of all people Plato, who worked so hard to uphold this distinction, should have fumbled it so badly. Better to interpret him in some other way.

The natural alternative is to suppose that the distinction is fudged not by Plato but by his opponents. After all, he frequently criticizes others for confusing how things appear with how they are. Let us suppose, then, that he interpreted his opponents as treating a thing's appearing *F* and its being *F* as equivalent. This interpretation turns out to make good sense of what he argues in various passages.

For suppose he took his opponents to maintain that (as *Theaetetus* 151 puts it) "knowing amounts to nothing more than perceiving." Now if what is known is taken to be what is so, as Plato usually supposes, then for a thing to be *F* amounts to nothing other than its appearing *F*. In that case, any relevant case of appearing *F* would be a case of being *F*. It would result from the proposed assumption that sensibles, if we go merely by the appearances that they present, would "be" however they appear. But that leads to the conclusion that sensibles, taken in this way merely as sensibles, are both *F* and non-*F*, because they appear in both those ways.

Now although the interpretation of Plato's thinking on this point is intensely problematic and certainty about it is beyond reach, there is substantial reason to accept this interpretation of Plato's opponents. Plato's position on this matter, by contrast, is twofold. First, he maintains that (1) if *that* is *all* there is to say about sensibles, that is, if all there is to them is their appearances, then we cannot gain our understanding of concepts merely from our sensory experiences of them. Second, he holds that (3) there must be and indeed is another way to think about sensibles, and in particular about what a sensible thing's being a certain way amounts to.

This way of reading Plato seems to be supported by an argument that he gives at *Theaetetus* 181–3. That argument seems to maintain that if we think about sensibles in this way, then nothing can be intelligibly said or thought about anything. To be sure, according to one traditional interpretation of his doctrine, it says that we can have no knowledge or understanding of, or even intelligible judgments about, facts concerning the physical world at all. But it seems highly unlikely that he should have wished to uphold such a view. For one thing, he recommends his scheme of education in the *Republic* partly on the ground that it enables the rulers of his ideal city-state to govern the city better (Book VII, *passim*). This would make little sense if all judgments about the physical world were thoroughly misguided.

Rather it seems that, according to Plato, such a view would make nonsense of all claims about the sensible world, including the minds that are in it and that try to think about it. This, at any rate, is the upshot of a plausible interpretation of the passage of the *Theaetetus* just cited.[2] Rather than being an argument that the sensible world is wholly unknowable and unintelligible, as some interpreters maintain, *Theaetetus* 181–3 appears to argue that if all there is to say about objects in the sensible world (including the people or minds that try to apprehend them) is that they are both *F* and non-*F*, for any term *F*, then no intelligible statement can be made about anything, not even the statement that this is how the sensible world is.

This seems a reasonable enough conclusion. For what do we learn, after all, from the thesis that everything about the sensible world is both thus-and-so and not thus-and-so, besides that there is nothing to say about how it is?

The conclusion to be drawn, then, is (3) that this is the wrong way to think about the sensible world. There must be something more to be said about sensibles than merely that because they appear both *F* and non-*F*, all there is to say about them is that they are so too. Thus we must refrain from saying that for a sensible object to be a certain way is simply for it to appear that way. Not only in the *Theaetetus* but also in the *Phaedo* and the *Republic*, Plato maintains that there is a way in which a sensible thing can be said to be thus-and-so, which does not amount simply to its appearing thus-and-so. On the contrary, when we claim in this mode that a sensible thing is *F*, we (*a*) presuppose a distinction between its being *F* and its merely appearing *F*, and we (*b*) take account of the fact that it will present certain appearances when it, and the person considering it, *are in fact* situated vis-à-vis each other in particular ways and not when they are situated in other ways. This way of making judgments about sensibles incorporates awareness of the *structure* of the sensible world that leads to various appearances. This is just the sort of matter that the latter part of the *Timaeus* investigates. And it is also analogous to the scientific rhetoric that *Phaedrus* 277–9 recommends and that the *Republic* also suggests, namely, a general accounting of the conditions under which particular kinds of music, rhetoric, and so on, will have particular psychological effects.

Thesis 2 and Plato's Ontology

Let us now return to thesis 2 of Plato's position, and to its more specifically ontological aspects. Here Plato's reasoning becomes more difficult to accept, and takes us into metaphysical questions that modern epistemologists tend to skirt.

Even if Plato is right that (1) grasping our concepts and understanding our terms involves more than sensory apprehension of sensible things strictly construed, it is a large and dubious additional step to maintain the ontological thesis that (2) such understanding involves cognition of some other *entities*, namely, the special non-sensible entities that Plato calls "Forms," which do not present contrary appearances in the way in which sensibles do. What could justify this further step into a fully "Platonic" ontology? Interpreters differ about what his response was, and philosophers differ about whether any response could be satisfactory.

One response that might be attributed to him brings notorious problems. Does Plato perhaps suppose that if a person is to understand what it is for a thing to be *F* without being non-*F*, he must as a general matter do so by having apprehended an object that fits precisely that description?[3] That supposition would raise several problems, including one that is often labeled "self-predication" – the idea that what enables us to understand the notion of being *F* must be the cognition of an object that is, so to speak, entirely or ideally *F*. Suppose it is admitted that we cannot gain the notion of what it is to be a horse *merely* from observing things that sometimes appear like horses and sometimes do not, and that we need to take some additional conceptual step beyond those sensory apprehensions. But that step need not require that we apprehend an actual thing that always appears like a horse and never any other way – a horse that is ideal, so to speak, in that it appears horselike from every angle and under all circumstances. Plato does, however, seem to write as if he thought this, and much criticism has been directed at him for doing so from Aristotle onward.

But regardless of how Plato might have hoped to respond to the difficulty created by this way of writing (also a controversial matter), he seems to have clung, even late in his career (in the *Timaeus* and also, e.g., at *Philebus* 58–60), to two tenets that have ever since often been associated with the term "Platonism" in epistemology. One is that we understand terms by somehow cognizing nonsensible Forms. Another is that the Form of *F* is in some sense, however attenuated, an *idealization* of a thing that is *F* – at least in the sense that it does not have the misleading character that makes a sensible *F* thing insufficient support for the understanding of the term *F*.

Plato's account of Forms raises several other topics that must be briefly touched on. One is a second point on which he faced difficulty. As already noted, he concedes in works like the *Sophist* that – in spite of his earlier suggestion (*Phaedo* 74) that Forms do not present contrary appearances in the way that sensible things do – Forms in fact *do* in an important way possess or seem to possess contrary features. Just like sensible things, Forms can be thought about, in various contexts and in reference to various things, in such a way that they present contrary aspects – or at least they do so no less than sensible things can. But if this fact seems to mean that errors about Forms can arise from their presenting contrary appearances, then we should wonder why cognition of Forms can provide us with understanding of our terms any better than sensible objects can.

Insofar as Plato has a response to this question, it lies in such works as the *Theaetetus* and the *Sophist*. There he deals with the possibility of error (though much of the *Sophist* discusses false statement and false belief, its official topic is deception and error), including the possibility of error about Forms (see esp. *Theaetetus* 195–200). It is usually thought that he is there trying to vindicate the possibility of error across the board. Perhaps, however, he wishes still to exclude the possibility of at least certain kinds of error about Forms, that is, error concerning their essential natures, or whatever allows cognition of them to yield our understanding of terms. It seems likely that the distinction drawn in the *Sophist* between what a thing is "by itself" and what it is "in relation to something else" (*Sophist* 255c–d) is meant to play a role here. Perhaps Plato wishes to say that a Form can be considered "by itself" whereas a sensible thing cannot (or anyhow not in the same way), and that that is why the Form of *F* can be used to understand a general term *F* whereas a sensible thing that is *F* cannot. But uncertainty and controversy surrounds passages in these works.

Plato's account of Forms does not suppose that Forms are cognized one by one. He generally, in fact, thinks that they are to be investigated in groups or even all together. Throughout his works he is concerned with what might be called the structure of knowledge or science, and of particular branches thereof. This concern manifests itself primarily in his talk of "dialectic" and "hypothesis," especially in the *Meno*, the *Phaedo*, and the *Republic*, and in his discussion of "collection" and "division" in the *Phaedrus* and the *Philebus*. Here there is space for only a brief mention of some pertinent issues.

One of the most important issues has to do with the question to what extent he thought of knowledge and understanding as manifested in propositions or statements, and to what extent he took knowledge to involve a kind of nonpropositional "grasp" of certain entities. On the whole there is little sign that he drew a very sharp distinction between the two, and he often writes in both ways without marking a contrast between them. Mathematics in Plato's time had made some progress toward showing how some propositions could be *demonstrated* from others, and how a body of mathematical propositions could be organized into assumptions or axioms and derived propositions or theorems. At the same time, however, mathematicians also thought in terms of the *construction* of one mathematical entity out of others. Here too there is a mixture of propositional and nonpropositional formulations.

Plato certainly attached importance to being able to say that a certain proposition is *true*, rather than merely that it is true *given* some assumption or on a hypothesis (see esp. *Republic* 505–41, *passim*). Plato seems to maintain that whereas special sciences can properly assert their theorems hypothetically or conditionally, philosophy or "dialectic" can do better, and can bring us to discover that certain things are flatly true. Plato connects this capacity of dialectic with its capacity to deal explicitly with things other than sensibles, that is, with Forms (*Republic* 510, 527). However, it is unclear and controversial exactly what Plato takes this connection to be. Evidently Plato thinks of the proper knowledge of mathematics (as of knowledge in general) as having to do with some kinds of idealizations of the sensible figures that geometers draw in the sand, and the kind of idealization that is involved here is plainly close to the kind already mentioned above. The exact nature of the connection, however, is difficult to pinpoint on the basis of Plato's texts.

The procedures of collection and division plainly have to do with relationships among Forms – in particular, the structure or structures in which Forms figure. Plato investigates this matter in part to determine which Forms are the same as and different from which (see esp. the *Sophist*). As noted, we here have cases of Forms' presenting contrary aspects, as when a Form is "the same" when considered in relation to one Form, itself, and different when considered in relation to others. Plato seems to have held, or at least to have taken seriously the view that, such relationships can and should be expressed in mathematical terms. If Aristotle's indications in *Metaphysics* XIII–XIV and elsewhere are accurate, Plato's epistemological thinking here merges once again with his philosophy of mathematics.

In addition, Plato brings quasi-mathematical considerations to bear in the *Philebus* when he invokes notions of "limit" (*peras*) and "unlimited" or "indefiniteness" (*apeiron*), the "mixture" of the two, and the cause of the mixture. What he says is obscure, but it evidently has to do with the realization of structure in, or the imposition of structure on, something unstructured, and also with the distinction between vague concepts and making them precise. It is to be observed in this connection that the concepts that figure in most middle dialogues are vague concepts, like large and good and the like. In both the *Philebus* and the *Timaeus* Plato seems to recommend an explication of vague concepts (both quantitative and otherwise) by more precise, mathematical concepts, or at least the investigation of how the two are related. Moreover he seems to be investigating how the instantiation of a precise concept in a particular sensible thing can lead to cases of vagueness or indefiniteness. He plainly regards all of these issues as open to discussion only by virtue of our recognition of features that go beyond what is presented to sense alone.

Notes

1   It is not plausible, however, to say that these features simply are relations; see references in White 1992.
2   The interpretation is due to G. E. L. Owen, in his "The Place of the *Timaeus* in Plato's Dialogues," *Classical Quarterly* NS 3 (1953) 79–95.
3   This seems a far more plausible explanation of Plato's self-predicative locutions than the account which says that it arose from a confusion of adjectives and their corresponding abstract nouns.

References and Recommended Reading

Primary Sources

The best collection of Platonic dialogues:
Cooper, J., ed., *Plato: Complete Works* (Indianapolis: 1997).

Secondary Sources

Carnap, Rudolph, *Der logischer Aufbau der Welt* (Berlin-Schlachtensee: 1928).
Fine, Gail, ed., *Plato 1: Metaphysics and Epistemology* (Oxford: 1999).
Kraut, Richard, ed., *The Cambridge Companion to Plato* (Cambridge: 1992).
White, Nicholas P. (1992), "Plato's Metaphysical Epistemology" in Kraut 1992, 277–310.

Chapter 6

Plato: Ethics

Gerasimos Santas

Introduction

Plato began the discipline of ethics, the study of the good and the right, and developed it to a surprisingly sophisticated level. How did he accomplish this pioneering feat?

In his stimulating early dialogues he has Socrates sharply and persistently question his contemporaries' beliefs about the virtues, wisdom and happiness. In these dialogues, Socrates uses sophisticated arguments intended to refute popular and conventional Greek conceptions of courage (*Laches, Protagoras*), temperance (*Charmides*), piety (*Euthyphro*), and justice (*Republic* I); and to throw serious doubts on popular conceptions of the good as identical with pleasure and on happiness as the satisfaction of the usual human desires for wealth, power, and honors (*Gorgias*). The effects of these Socratic endeavors on the "experts" he questioned were perplexity and a realization that they had opinions but no *knowledge* of virtue and happiness, contrary to what they first thought.

In addition to these critical arguments, Plato also has Socrates pursue a new kind of question, a request for "real" definitions (not stipulations or lexical definitions) of the virtues. Socrates had to instruct his interlocutors about what kind of question this was and insisted that their answers conform to it: that they not merely give examples of each virtue, but discover from the examples what is common to them that make them instances of courage, or temperance, or piety, or virtue itself (*Meno*). The interlocutors catch on, but they are not able to defend successfully the *truth* of the formally correct answers they give, because Socrates regularly reveals to them inconsistencies between their answers and other firm beliefs they have, which they are reluctant to give up.

Now this Socratic Method, raising the so-called "What is X?" question, and testing answers by consistency of beliefs, the so-called Socratic Elenchus, suggests that if we were able to discover and successfully defend such answers about virtue and happiness, our ethical beliefs about how to live and how to act would be on a firmer foundation.

This suggestion is confirmed by Aristotle (*Met.* 1078b) who attributes to Socrates the first pursuit of universal definitions of the virtues, and approves of the effort because definitions, he says, are the beginning of knowledge. So, if we wish to have an art or science of ethics, knowledge, or defensible beliefs about how we should live, then we need at the very least to be able to discover and defend definitions or analyses of the main choice guiding concepts, virtue and happiness, or more abstractly the good and the right.

This suggestion is also confirmed by Plato himself in the comprehensive philosophical masterpiece of his middle period, the *Republic*. This work contains crucial questions and pioneering theories in ethics, political philosophy, epistemology, metaphysics, psychology, education, and aesthetics. As in earlier works, in the *Republic* Plato criticizes his contemporaries' beliefs and theories about the virtues and about happiness; but he also produces constructive analyses of the cardinal virtues, and accounts of the good used to construct and defend *these* Platonic virtues.

In all these works we can see how Plato began and developed the art or science of ethics, by introducing and using *methods* for critically examining our existing beliefs about virtue and happiness, and for discovering and defending analyses of the crucial choice guiding concepts of ethics, the good and the right. Plato invented or borrowed other constructive methods in ethics, such as the methods of hypothesis (from mathematics, *Meno*), and thought experiments (*Meno, Republic, Philebus*). A measure of the breadth and influence of Plato's methods might be the relative difficulty of finding methods he did not use in the ethical writings of, say, Henry Sidgwick or G. E. Moore, some twenty-four centuries later; though the same might not be true of John Rawls, a measure of *his* originality.

Plato developed the study of ethics also by locating and focusing on the central *subject matter* of ethics: virtue, happiness, and the good. He takes it for granted that the first question of ethics is How *should* we live? That is, assuming we have options among different kinds of lives, which of these lives should we choose? – a question no human being capable of reflection can forever leave unexamined. The *general* answers he found agreement on were the *best* of these lives; or, the life in accordance with *virtue*; or, the life which most promotes *happiness*; or some combination thereof. And if this is so, then the good, virtue, and happiness are the central choice guiding concepts of ethics.

But these general answers left plenty of room for disagreements about these main concepts – what they are and how they are related – which Plato portrayed in his dialogues and tried to resolve by his methods. The *Gorgias,* for example, portrays, dramatizes and tries to resolve disputes whether justice brings us happiness and whether the good is the same as pleasure. Thus Plato staked out the main questions of *normative* ethics.

But he even raised questions now thought to belong to *metaethics,* the study of the meaning and justification of ethical concepts. Thus in the *Euthyphro* he has Socrates question Euthyphro's second definition of piety, as what all the gods love, by asking whether something is pious because the gods love it *or* something is loved by the gods because it is pious. This is an issue about the objectivity of that virtue, as well as about the gods as sources of value. Socrates' question has been influential, because it can be generalized to all value concepts and to several authorities other than gods: is something good because human beings desire it or do they desire it because [they think?] it is good? Plato can be usefully compared here with the twentieth-century Nobel prizewinning economist and philosopher, Amartya Sen, who discussed this very question in his Dewey lectures and tried to find room for both answers (see Sen 1985). A similar question can be raised about justice: is a law or constitution just because society approves of it, or does society approve of it because it is just?

Also belonging to metaethics is the question Socrates raises and answers in the *Crito*, how he is to decide whether he should escape from prison and the sentence of death: not by considering what most people would say about it, but by "following the argument that seems best to me" (46); and he proceeds to make his decision by arguments which apply general principles and the facts of his case. Since arguments are the instruments of reason, this passage has rightly been taken to mean that Plato thinks that ethics is amenable to reason, and ethical issues can and should be resolved by reason, not by appeal to common opinions or sentiment. The critical and constructive methods sketched above are the works of reason.

In the rest of this article I shall briefly sketch, by way of example, Plato's discussion of justice, happiness, and the good in the *Republic*, because it is by far the central and most comprehensive text for Plato's critical and constructive ethics. Plato's ethics is above all the ethics of the *Republic*. But the reader must keep in mind that Plato developed some new ideas about the good life in some later dialogues, such as the *Philebus* and the *Laws*.

The Great Questions of Ethics in the *Republic*

At the end of the first book of the *Republic*, Socrates says that they have been debating unsuccessfully answers to three questions: what is justice, whether it is a virtue, and whether justice is good for or brings happiness to the just person. The first and last of these questions are pursued in the rest of the work, so we know they are central questions of Plato's ethics.

Socrates also says that their discussion so far was unsatisfactory because unless they know what justice is they can hardly know whether it is a virtue, or good for us or brings us happiness. For example, earlier Socrates had refuted Thrasymachus' analysis of justice as what is to the interest of the stronger, ruling, party in each society; and yet he went on to "defend" justice by also refuting Thrasymachus' view that we are better off or happier being unjust provided we can get away with it. But since Socrates did not agree with Thrasymachus' analysis of justice, what account of justice was Socrates defending? Socrates sounded a similar theme in the beginning of the *Meno*: we can hardly know whether virtue is teachable before we know what virtue is.

Thus Plato has some priorities for the order of investigation: we must first settle disputes about and learn what the virtues are, before we can settle whether the virtues are good for us or make us happy. The Socratic dialogues acknowledged this rule but failed to produce a satisfactory answer to the first question – they merely refuted unsatisfactory answers. The *Republic* also undertakes positive analyses of the virtues, and only after that does it try to defend justice by showing how it is good for us or makes us happy.

Now this priority rule seems equally applicable to happiness and the good. Unless we know not only what justice is but also what is good for us and what happiness is, we can hardly know whether justice is good for us or makes us happy. This extension seems reasonable because there were and even today there remain disputes about what is good for us and what happiness is, as there were and are disputes about what justice is. Plato himself confirms this priority when he tells us, later in Republic VI, that unless we know the good, the analyses and defense of the virtues Socrates gave earlier would not be secure. There is also evidence that Plato thinks good is prior to happiness; what happiness is depends on what things are good, their uses, and their rankings (*Symposium, Euthydemus, Gorgias*).

Thus, the *Republic* puts the central questions of ethics in the following order:

[What is good?], What is the good?
[What is happiness?]
What is justice? Later, What is Wisdom, Courage, temperance?
Is Justice good, or at least better, for the just person?
Does justice bring happiness to the just?

The questions in brackets are not raised explicitly in our texts, but since there are answers to them in the texts, we can say the questions are implicit.

Theories of Justice and Happiness Plato Opposes and their Methods

When Socrates first broaches the issue of justice, the wealthy old man Cephalus cites two rules of honesty in word and deed: telling the truth and keeping one's promises. And tells us that a main use of wealth is to make reparations if one has broken these rules. Cephalus speaks on the basis of his experience and in view of his advanced age.

Faced with counterexamples to the universality of these rules, Cephalus leaves the discussion to his son Polemarchus, who appeals to a poet's wisdom, that justice is rendering to each man what is due or appropriate to him. Pressed for clarification, he says that what is due or appropriate to friends is benefit, to enemies harm: thus justice is benefiting friends and harming enemies. Socrates responds with a famous argument, that it cannot be the function of a just person, or a function of a person's justice, to harm another human being, enemy or not.

When Thrasymachus is asked what justice is, he does not appeal to his own experience or to the poets, but proceeds as an empirical political scientist studying comparative government. If we want to find out what justice is, we should study various societies, find out what justice each one of them has, and generalize accordingly. When we do so, he claims, what we discover is that in each society, whether democratic, tyrannical, or oligarchic, the stronger or ruling party makes laws to its own interest, and lays it down that justice is conduct in accordance with these laws. Therefore, in all societies, justice is what is in the interest of the stronger, ruling party. (In *Politics* III 6, Aristotle, who conducted an extensive empirical study of ancient constitutions, confirms that some, but *not all* consititutions – he calls them deviant – display the justice of Thrasymachus). Socrates produces many interesting arguments against this definition; and against its implication that justice is not good for the weaker or nonruling parties or citizens. But since they don't agree on what justice is, it is not clear what justice Socrates is defending, and thus his complaint at the end of *this* discussion is very understandable.

Plato's brothers, Glaucon and Adeimantus, are not satisfied with Socrates' defense of justice against Thrasymachus. Glaucon proceeds to give a new account of justice and a new defense of injustice within that account. But he does so, not on the basis of his own experience, nor by appeal to the poets, nor yet by Thrasymachus' empirical method. He uses a *contractarian* method, to construct a theory of justice, and defends its implications by a *thought experiment*.

He claims that we can find out what justice is by discovering the origin of justice; and this origin is found in a contract men who seek to promote their own interests made in a certain circumstance. The circumstance, which the moderns call a "state of nature," is a state of moderate scarcity and without governments and laws. In such a state men come into conflict with each other. Usually unable to take the possessions of others or injure them and avoid even greater retaliation, they see that they would be better off giving up the freedom to take the possessions of or injure others in exchange for the security of not having done that to them. Accordingly they make a compact with each other not to injure others in return for others similarly agreeing not to injure them. Justice is then defined by the laws which are in agreement with this fundamental compact.

In such a system of justice men are usually better off than they were in a state of nature, since they have security from being robbed or injured by others. In that sense justice is good for them. But they are not best off, since they have given up the freedom to do and take whatever they want, including robbing and injuring others and the chance of getting away with it. This theory seems to assume that the freedom to do whatever one pleases without retaliation or the fear thereof is the best and happiest condition for an individual.

That justice is such a compromise, good for us but not best for us, and that men practice it due to lack of power and with reluctance, is shown by a thought experiment: if we imagined two men, one just up to now and the other unjust, and gave them each a magic ring, the ring of Gyges, which made them invisible and thus able to avoid retaliation, we would find them both acting unjustly, taking whatever they wanted even if it belonged to others and was contrary to laws. Socrates and Thrasymachus would use their rings to engage in the same unjust conduct and in the pursuit of the same goods of wealth, power, pleasure, and honors.

Of course there are no such magic rings in nature or society. But there is a social equivalent to them, secrecy of unjust conduct and the deception of a just reputation. When successful with such devices, one can avoid the social equivalent of natural retaliation, just punishment. Then one can do and have everything one wants and be happy.

The theory of justice introduced by Glaucon differs significantly from that of Thrasymachus. It differs not only in its methods (the use of thought experiments and the contractarian model), but also more importantly in its content. Glaucon's justice limits the freedom of all equally in exchange for equal security, whereas Thrasymachus' justice systematically favors the stronger or ruling party. But they do have in common a certain defense of injustice: in Thrasymachus' justice, the weaker or nonruling parties or citizens would be better off being unjust, breaking the laws of the rulers, provided they can get away with deception or violence. And in Glaucon's justice, anyone would be better off breaking the laws he agreed to, provided he could get away with it by secrecy and deception. Bright young men raised in such societies understand this, and might reasonably think that it is not justice that is praised, when their elders praise justice, but the reputation of justice. And they might act accordingly, if they can. This, Plato might be ironically suggesting, is the Achilles heel of such theories. But can we do better?

Plato's own Theory of Justice and Happiness and his own Methods

In his criticisms Plato rejected the views of justice and happiness of his contemporaries. Less evident but equally true, he also rejected or at least abandoned their methods. In his first argument against Trasymachus, Socrates rejects the identification of justice with legality, an identification which makes Thrasymachus' empirical study of justice possible: it may be true that we can find out what justice a society believes and practices by looking at its laws; but its laws might be mistaken and unjust even by its own lights, since legislators can make mistakes no matter what end they have in view. It is also clear enough that in his own constructive analysis of justice and the other virtues Plato does not use the contractarian method. Even more striking, he does not even use the method Socrates was suggesting in the earlier dialogues: applied to justice, this method would direct us to gather several examples of things, whether persons, their actions, laws or institutions, which we are confident are just, and then try to discover what is common to all of them that makes them just. This method is simply not present in the *Republic*, at least not for justice.

How then does Plato build up his own theory of justice? The informal dialogue style which Plato so masterfully used makes for wide accessibility, readability, and even the intellectual excitement that belongs to great ideas. These are virtues of the first order in any book, and the *Republic* has proved to be one of the most popular books of all time. But Plato's style does not favor evident answers to this fundamental question. And yet unless we find some answer to it, do we understand what Plato is doing? Or do we read on excited, beguiled, and even charmed, but really wandering in a cave with a flickering light and a lot of dancing shadows? The late Gregory Vlastos may not have been far off the mark when he called Plato's style an "artful chiaroscuro."

But Plato does leave some clues. The most obvious is his telling us, though only long after he has constructed his theory of social and individual justice, that unless we understand the good we will not understand the virtues or their benefit (505AB). A second clue is that the theories of justice he rejects assume some account of what things are good for us and what happiness is: Thrasymachus and Glaucon take it for granted that the things men usually desire and pursue are the good things of life and the things whose possession makes us happy: wealth, power, pleasure, and honors (as well as the things some men are born into – prominent family, good looks, health and strength). A third clue is a little sketch of what makes things good that Socrates gives and uses as a premise in his last defense of justice against Thrasymachus – what we shall call his functional account of the good (352E–354).

Finally, we know from later important books on justice, from Aristotle's *Politics* (VII 1) to Rawls's *A Theory of Justice* (ch. 3), that no theory of justice, teleological or not, can be built or defended without some account of the good. In teleological ethical theories this is evident, since they hold that the right, including justice of course, is what maximizes the good; so they must have some account of the good, whether it is pleasure, desire satisfaction, perfectionist good, a set of "ideal goods," or a set of major instrumental goods. But even in nonteleological theories, which deny this maximizing principle, some account of good is required, since it is the role of social justice to regulate the distribution of social advantages (and burdens); as in the theory of John Rawls justice regulates the distribution of the "primary goods" of liberties and rights, income and wealth, social powers and opportunities.

What theory of good then does Plato have, which he uses to build up and defend his theory of justice? Well, he propounds a metaphysical account of *the form of the good* in *Republic* VI, and he tells us that unless we understand *that* good, we shall not be secure in our understanding of justice and its benefits. However, it is equally plain that he in fact does *not* use this account of the good in building up his theory of justice, from *Republic* II to the middle of book V; nor yet in his defense of this justice in books VIII and IX. When we look at how in practice he builds up his theory of justice (*Rep.* II, III, IV, V) we find that he uses the functional account of the good, and this provides him with a procedure or method for discovering justice in cities and individuals.

Some things have functions, Socrates says (352E), and he gives examples of animals (horses), organs (eyes and ears), and artifacts (pruning knife). The functions of some of them, organs for example, are the work only they can do: we see only with the eyes, hear only with the ears; let us call these exclusive functions. The functions of artifacts, on the other hand, are the work they can do better than other things can do or the work they can do better than other work they can do: one can prune with a pruning knife better than one can prune with a saw; and a pruning knife prunes better than it can saw; let us call these optimal functions. A thing with functions is good of its kind if it performs well the function(s) of things of that kind. And a thing with functions has the virtue(s) of its kind if it has the "qualities" (properties, structure, composition) which enable it to perform its function(s) well. Thus the presence of the virtues appropriate to a thing of a given kind makes it good of its kind and enables it to perform its functions well. The logical home of this theory was (and is) the productive arts and the art of medicine, in all of which artifacts and organs are evaluated by how well they perform their functions.

This theory of goodness of kind and of virtue clearly suggests a three-step procedure for discovering the virtue(s) of things with functions. First, discover the function(s) of a thing of a given kind; second, discover (or imagine) things of that kind that function well (and others that perform poorly); and finally, discover the qualities of the thing which enables it to perform its function(s) well (and in the absence of which it performs poorly), and these will be the virtues of the thing.

And indeed this is the procedure Plato actually follows in constructing his own theory of social justice (from 369A to 434). Before he does that, he assumes that justice is a virtue, and points out that it is a virtue of both city-states and of individuals. He also makes the unusual claim that the justice of cities and the justice of individuals are isomorphic, mirror images of each other; and since, he says, city-states are larger and more public it would be easier to discover justice in a city first (368–9). To do so, he then applies the three-step procedure to the city. First, he determines the functions of cities: one basic function is to provide themselves with the economic needs for food, shelter, and clothing; a second to defend themselves; and a third to govern themselves. Socrates and Glaucon then imagine and describe a city that performs these functions as well as possible (given certain assumptions about human circumstances and human nature), which (by the theory) would then be as good a city as possible – "a completely good city" Socrates calls it (427E).

The construction of this completely good city proceeds by putting together the abstract and formal theory of function and virtue and empirical assumptions about the human situation and human nature; for example, the empirical propositions that human beings have to labor to satisfy their basic needs; that no individual is self-sufficient with regard to such needs; that human beings come together and cooperate to better satisfy their needs; that human beings are born with different abilities and talents for the various functions required for satisfying human needs; and that in view of all this, division of social labor by inborn abilities and talents and subsequent appropriate educations is the best way to achieve the well functioning of city-states. Given the threefold general division of the city's functions, Plato divides the population into three classes, on the basis of assumptions about what kind of inborn (natural) ability and education would serve each function best; and then matches by optimal function classes of citizens and social functions: the optimal function of citizens of high intelligence is ruling the city, those of high spirit defending the city, those with knacks for producing and trading provisioning the city (*Rep.* II–IV).

Finally, in *Republic* IV Socrates and Glaucon search for the qualities of this city which enable it to perform its functions as well as possible, and these qualities will be the virtues of the city. They easily agree that wisdom is knowledge of what is good for the city as a whole, and it is this that enables the rulers to govern best. Courage is the ability of the soldiers, due to their high spirit and training, to defend the city best by acting according to the counsel of the rulers about what the city should fear and dare. Temperance exists when the three classes agree on who is to rule and who to be ruled. And finally, justice is the very principle of organization which makes possible all these functioning well, that citizens are assigned that social function for which they are best suited by nature and subsequent appropriate education (433).

Plato then exploits his unusual assumption that the justice of a city and of an individual human are mirror images of each other (isomorphic) to transfer his account of justice in the state to justice in the individual. He sees that this assumption requires that a human psyche (soul) has a complexity similar to the complexity of the city his social justice requires. Reasonably enough, he assumes that the individual also has bodily needs, needs to defend herself and needs to rule herself, and corresponding tasks or functions to satisfy these needs. He then argues, independently of his theory of social justice, for his pioneering analysis of the human psyche into three parts: the faculty of *appetite*, for such things as food, drink, and sex; the faculty of *reason*, which, for example, reasons, calculates, constructs and tests hypotheses; and the faculty of *spirit* by which we feel anger and indignation. Arguably, this division uses the concept of exclusive functions, applied now to the psyche: only reason can reason and calculate, so these are the functions of reason, just as seeing is the function of the eyes because only with the eyes can we see; and so with the other psychic parts and functions.

Now the functional theory, the isomorphism, and the theory of justice of cities at hand, together entitle Plato to assign the psychic functions of providing for one's bodily needs, defending oneself and ruling oneself, to parts of the psyche on the basis of inborn (natural) ability and appropriate education of each part. But which of these psychic functions is the optimal function of which psychic part? In actual procedure, Plato assumes that reason corresponds to the class of the *rulers* (perhaps because high intelligence is what picks out this class), spirit to the class of *defenders* (perhaps because high spirit is what picks out this class), and appetite to *artisans*. And from these premises, he validly concludes that a person is just when her personality (psyche) is so organized or structured (by inborn ability and appropriate habituation and education) that her reason rules (e.g., makes choices), her spirit helps her defend herself according to the counsel of reason, and appetite is obedient to reason on when, how, and by how much to satisfy her bodily needs. Similarly, she is temperate when there is agreement and harmony in her about the rule of reason and the obedience of appetite, brave when her spirit is so habituated as to help her defend herself effectively, and wise when her reason knows or at least truly believes what is good for her as a whole individual.

But the functional theory of good can also provide a justification of the Platonically just matching of psychic parts to psychic functions, independently of the isomorphism which is a very disputed and unusual assumption. If reasoning, discovering truths, constructing and testing hypotheses, are exclusive functions of reason, then ruling oneself, that is, making choices, are things that reason can do better than spirit or appetite can do; at least if the best choices are selections of what is best for us as means and ends. The appetites for food, drink, or sex, for example, may give us signals of bodily needs and motivations for their satisfaction, but without reason they are blind on what, how much, and how often it is beneficial to eat, drink, and make love; and significantly Plato often appeals to the physicians of the day to so testify. Similarly, spirit can produce anger, which may or may not be justified, or which can be bad for us to express or act upon.

In addition to these fairly plausible propositions, it should be noted that both the functional theory of good and the metaphysical theory of the form of the good which Plato puts forward in the *Republic* favor reason as the ruler of our lives. For clearly only reason can discover a thing's functions, whether it performs such functions well; or what form or structure a thing has and how far such a form or structure resembles a geometrical ideal; for example, the structure of a wheel and how far it resembles the geometrical ideal of a circle. It might be noted that Hume, who disputes Plato's rule of reason, might argue that these judgments of reason do not go beyond what is instrumentally good, to what is good as ultimate end.

In his first defense of his analysis of justice in individuals, at the end of *Republic* IV, Plato appeals to an analogy between his justice and health in the body: since it is universally granted that bodily health is good for us, and certainly better than disease, Platonic justice is good for us and better than injustice, *if* Platonic justice is to the soul what health is to the body. But Plato does not explain the analogy sufficiently to convince us that this last proposition is true. We can strengthen it if we bring in his functional theory of good and his analysis of bodily organs in the *Timaeus* (69–92), so that we can at least see why he thinks it is true. The physicians of Plato's day, as can be seen in the Hippocratic writings, had already discovered that the human body is naturally divided into parts, such as organs and substances (humors and elements), which have specific functions; and they thought that health obtains when these organs and elements perform their functions well; while disease occurs when they are prevented from performing their functions by, for example, violence; or performing their functions well by, for example, excessive food intake. The analogy between health and justice is based on the supposition that the human soul also is naturally divided into parts with functions, and that a just soul is one in which the parts are allowed to perform their functions and perform them well. One might dispute the isomorphism and the account of psychic justice that goes with it. But in this argument Plato takes these as established. And if the human soul is naturally divided into parts with natural functions, as the human body is, it can be hardly disputed that Platonic psychic justice is good for us, and injustice bad.

After this first defense of justice, Plato proposes several revolutionary institutions, such as the equality of women, common property, and extended family (for the upper classes), on the basis of his theory of justice and certain empirical assumptions. He also puts forward his "metaphysical epistemology" and the metaphysical theory of the form of the good, to answer questions about the possibility of his just city and the possibility of knowledge of the good, propounding his famous paradox of the philosopher-king: that the key to approximating the completely good city is a union of political power and knowledge. He also proposes a very demanding higher education, portrayed in his Allegory of the Cave as a difficult journey from the darkness of a cave to the light of the Sun, for the rulers of his completely good city. After all this, Plato undertakes a second defense of justice, both in his criticism of several forms of injustice in *Republic* VIII, and his positive account of the happiness and even the pure and genuine pleasures of the just person (*Rep.* IX).

Conclusion

The reader should be aware that this very short sketch leaves out much of importance in our texts, and much of significant scholarly controversy. (See the References and Recommended Reading at the end of the chapter.) For example, the isomorphism or analogy between just city and just soul has been attacked and defended in many able essays. Plato's defense of justice against Glaucon has been criticized and defended in fine books and famous articles. The relation between justice and happiness in the Socratic dialogues and the *Republic* has been extensively discussed: is justice (and all of virtue) necessary or sufficient for, means or "dominant" part of, happiness? The "eudaimonism" allegedly universal in Greek ethics has been questioned in the case of "the rulers' choice." The very structure of Plato's ethical theory has been much in dispute: is it teleological or a virtue ethics? Plato's theory of social justice has been attacked as antidemocratic and has been downplayed by many scholars. The metaphysical theory of the form of the good has been under attack since Aristotle and also downplayed recently by scholars. It is understandable that some scholars downplay the more disputed and unpopular parts of the *Republic*, and try to show that Plato still has valuable things to teach us, in his questions, his moral psychology, his theory of individual virtue, his methods of argument, and in his exciting dialogue style. But, arguably, this downplaying of some parts of his views makes it more difficult to understand and defend him, since in effect it takes away some of his resources and weapons.

Whatever the truth of this matter, Plato's major works in ethics, especially the Socratic dialogues and the *Republic*, remain a fruitful source of ideas and arresting comparisons in the history of ethics and contemporary ethical theory, and an exciting and effective way to introduce and even advance the study of ethics in our classrooms, in our seminars, and in conferences around the world.

References and Recommended Reading

Primary Sources

The best collection of Platonic dialogues:
Cooper, J., ed., *Plato: Complete Works*, Indianapolis, 1997

Secondary Sources

Annas, Julia, *An Introduction to Plato's Republic*, Oxford, 1981

——, *Plato's Ethics, Old and New*, Ithaca, N.Y., 1999

Benson, H., ed., *Essays in the Philosophy of Socrates*, Oxford, 1992

Brickhouse, T. C., and Smith, N. D., *Socrates on Trial*, Princeton, 1989

——, *Plato's Socrates*, Oxford, 1994

Cooper, J. M., *Reason and Emotion*, Princeton, 1999

Ferejohn, M., "Socratic Thought Experiments and the Unity of Virtue Paradox," *Phronesis*, 29, 1984

Gosling, J. C. B., and Taylor, C. C. W., *The Greeks on Pleasure*, Oxford, 1982

Irwin, T. H., *Plato's Gorgias*, Oxford, 1979

——, *Plato's Ethics*, Oxford, 1995

Kahn, C. H., *Plato and the Socratic Dialogue*, Cambridge, 1996

Kraut, R., *Socrates and the State*, Princeton, 1984

——, ed., *Cambridge Companion to Plato*, Cambridge, 1992

——, *Plato's Republic: Critical Essays*, Lanham, Md., 1999

Penner, T., "Desire and Thought in Plato," in Vlastos, *Plato II*

——, "Desire and Power in Socrates," *Apeiron*, 1991

Rawls, John, *A Theory of Justice*, Cambridge, Mass., 1971

Reeve, C. D. C., *Philosopher-Kings*, Princeton, 1988

Rudebusch, G., *Socrates, Pleasure, and Value*, Oxford, 1999

Santas, G., *Socrates*, London, 1979

——, *Goodness and Justice*, Oxford, 2001

Sen, Amartya, "Well-Being, Agency, and Freedom," *Journal of Philosophy*, 82, 1985

Vlastos, G., *Platonic Studies*, 2d ed., Princeton, 1981

——, *Socrates*, Ithaca, N.Y., 1991

Vlastos, G., ed., *Plato II*, Garden City, N.Y., 1971

——, *The Philosophy of Socrates*, Garden City, N.Y., 1971

White, N. P., *A Companion to Plato's Republic*, Indianapolis, 1979

——, "The Rulers' Choice," *Archiv fur Geschichte der Philosophy*, 86, 1986

Young, C., "Polemarchus and Thrasymachus' Definition of Justice," *Philosophical Inquiry*, 2, 1980

Chapter 7

Plato: Psychology

Allan Silverman

Introduction

A psychology is an account of the soul. A Platonic psychology would then be Plato's account of the soul. Ideally, perhaps, we could turn to some dialogue to discover what Plato thinks is the essence of soul, and then the other properties soul has in virtue of its essence, and lastly, perhaps, all the properties it has in virtue of its relations to other things. As it turns out, there is no such dialogue. Indeed, there is not even the prospect of looking to a handful of dialogues for such an account. Plato's conception of soul is so rich and varied, and its role is so central to all of his thought, that an account of his psychology would be nothing less than an account of his entire philosophy.

Plato's reflections about the soul pervade almost every aspect of his thought. Consider the ancient tripartition of Philosophy into Ethics, Logic – understood as the way knowledge is (and is not) acquired – and Physics. Plato's ethics has as its focus virtue and happiness, both of which are simply and exclusively a state or condition of soul, or involve the relation of soul to body. Knowledge, belief, and recollection, the fundamental elements of Plato's epistemology, are also transparently capacities of the soul. And insofar as physics concerns the nature of change and motion in general, Plato's physics also has soul as its first principle, since soul, as self-mover, is the source of all motion. If one's concern is persuasion, madness, love, desire, language, thought, immortality, transmigration, likeness to God, or Plato's use of myth, we again find ourselves confronting capacities of soul. Because one cannot neatly compartmentalize Plato's writings about soul, one needs a selective focus in order to isolate his distinctive theses about this multifaceted entity.

Despite, or rather because of, the range of topics and dialogues involving the soul, let us begin from a Socratic question: What, for Plato, is soul? This is a question about the metaphysical essence, the *ousia* of soul. Its ultimate answer is that a soul is a self-mover. In attempting to answer this question, I will, perforce, leave much out (see the essays on Socrates and the other parts of Plato's Philosophy), in order to consider whether the soul is simple or complex, that is, in what sense the soul has parts, especially rational and "arational" (*alogon*) parts, and whether Plato's account of the soul changes. Limitations of space dictate that I concentrate on only a few dialogues and passages which discuss the essence of soul, especially those discussions which pertain to soul's immortality. The *Phaedo* is the best introduction to the metaphysics of soul and the core text on immortality, that aspect of Plato's psychology which strikes many a modern reader as most fantastic. The *Sophist* will serve as the vehicle to study the nature of soul as self-mover.

Phaedo

Plato's Psychology begins with Socrates. In the *Apology* Socrates is made to declare that his sole interest in practicing philosophy in the manner he does is care of the soul (*Apology* 29d–30b, 31b, 32d, 36c, 39d; *Laws* 186a). Proper care of the soul will lead to happiness (*eudaimonia*), the aim of each of us. We will be happy if and only if we are virtuous. Virtue, in turn, is a state of one's soul, namely knowledge of goods and evils. Variation in the way one lives is, then, according to Socrates, a function of the location of one's soul in the continuum of ignorance to knowledge. By engaging in critical discussion with one another about key ethical notions and through rigorous self-reflection, one can come to be virtuous and to act accordingly. It thus appears that, according to Socrates, each of us has a soul that is without parts: soul is the rational capacity (*nous*) of a human being. Each of us is responsible for the care of his soul in this life. Although there is reason to believe that the soul is something divine, Socrates is famously noncommittal as to whether the soul survives the death of the person. (*Apology* 40c ff.)

The *Phaedo* is Plato's eulogy to Socrates. Socrates claims that in doing philosophy, he has not only been properly caring for his soul in this lifetime, but has been "practicing death," which is simply the separation of the soul from the body (*Phaedo* 63e–64c). Socrates is his soul and one's soul is immortal. Thus Socrates is not dead; he has merely departed this earthly existence. Like all eulogies, the *Phaedo* is meant to console, both the close associates of Socrates and the rest of us. In order to console us and, in accordance with Socrates' injunctions, to move us to care for our souls in this life, it is simply *assumed* that each of us has a *distinct, individual soul*. Plato aims to "prove" that every soul is immortal. For the Greeks the immortality of the soul is certainly controversial – witness Socrates' aforementioned reticence to assert immortality at his trial. To be sure, the focus of all the arguments in the dialogue is the issue of (personal) immortality. However, some of the arguments of the *Phaedo*, as well as remarks of other Greek thinkers, seem to suggest that a person's soul is really just a "part" of a larger world-soul and upon the death of a body this part is reabsorbed back into the larger whole. (Consider the meaning of the term "pan-psychism," a doctrine some would date back to Thales, if not earlier.)

Socrates opens his defense (63e–69e) with the claim that the (philosophical) soul seeking truth wishes to be separate from the body. The human body, and everything material, is condemned as the source of confusion and falsehood. The soul achieves its desire when, disdaining the physical/sensible world, it regains knowledge of the Forms, the ultimate truth-bearers or truth-makers.

When he focuses on the soul in its own right, Plato describes it as something "itself by itself" – *aut kathê autê*, using for the first time in the dialogues the special locution (*auto kath auto*) that will become one of his most distinctive formulations for speaking of Forms. The *auto kath auto* epithet applies initially to a soul when it is *separated* from a body and implies that the soul can be what it is when it is by itself, that is, apart from the body. It is then assigned to a function of the soul, *logismos* or reasoning, and finally to the objects of the soul's reasoning, the Forms. Plato then expands the import of the notion: the soul is an *auto kath auto* entity even when it is incarcerated in a body. The expanded sense of the epithet is that the soul, and a Form, *is whatever it is in its own right or in virtue of itself.* Thus by the end of the opening argument we find that being *auto kath auto* implies that a soul, and a Form, is what it is in virtue of itself, regardless of whether it is or is not separated from material particulars.

These opening remarks also intimate that for something to be *auto kath auto* need not entail that it has or is exactly one property. When separated from the body and most truly what it is, a soul is endowed with a special power, namely reasoning or intelligence (70ab). The soul, prior to its initial incarceration, in and of itself studies the Forms. Thus each soul in this situation knows exactly the same things. When incarcerated, on the other hand, the soul acquires and gains properties. For instance, souls can be just or unjust, fearful or not, and desirous of different things. Here one soul will differ from another. (Because souls differ when incarcerated, Plato and Socrates must adopt different strategies to persuade members of the audience to eschew the bodily and pursue philosophy, or, failing that, use different approaches to encourage them to believe in the soul's immortality, for example, Pythagorean or Orphic myths.) Thus a soul, in that it has the capacity to conjoin with a body, has the capacity to change. All souls are victimized by their imprisonment in the "tomb" that is the body. If a soul can eschew the desires of the body and reject the temptations of the sensible world, it can be purified and reclaim its prior condition.

The *Phaedo*, then, introduces the soul in the company of Forms, marking both as *auto kath auto* entities and implying that on its own and in its own right a soul is simply something that reasons and reasons about Forms. From this basic tenet Plato never deviates. The soul is fundamentally the home of reason and, insofar as reason is directed at the Forms, the nature of the soul imbricates with the nature of Forms. A second feature of soul highlighted in this passage is not so secure. Initially, the soul seems not to be responsible for the desires and perceptions of the person; rather, it is the body with which it cohabits that is the source of these malign influences on the soul. Perhaps this tenet is a reflection of Socrates' own beliefs, or perhaps it is a consequence of Plato's eulogistic endeavor. As we shall see, it is unclear how long Plato adheres to this tenet.

Plato next tries to prove that such a soul both predates and postdates its incarceration in a body. The Argument from Recollection (72e3–77a5) is designed to prove that the soul *preexists* its incarceration. The argument here fleshes out how it is that the soul, in the guise of reason, allows an individual eventually to learn, that is, to recollect, the Forms. In a disembodied state, every (human) soul, it seems, once saw the Forms. Once incarcerated, a soul can regain a clear knowledge of the Forms by reflecting on the perceptions, beliefs and language it uses in its dealings with the material or sensible world. Its original vision of the Forms thus seems to furnish the human soul with an "innate grammar" with which to learn language and a "conceptual filter" that causes it to react in predetermined ways to the perceptions of the world furnished by its body. Initially unaware of these features of its own design, through philosophical reflection an incarcerated soul can regain explicit knowledge of the Forms.

Having proved that the soul predates its incarceration, Plato turns next to show that the soul exists after separation from the body. In the so-called Affinity Argument (78b4–84b8), Plato begins from the proposition that what is divisible is complex. He then suggests that what is simple, that is, not complex, is, therefore, not fit to be divided or to "scatter." The material and visible, for example, the body, is then declared to be complex and divisible, whereas the invisible, immaterial Forms are asserted to be indivisible and simple (*monoeidēs*). Then Socrates claims that since the soul, also being invisible, is like these simple Forms (recall that the soul and the Forms were introduced in tandem), that it too "is most like the divine, deathless, intelligible, uniform, indissoluble, always the same as itself" (80ab).

The Affinity Argument reinforces the kindred relationship between Forms and the soul and emphasizes that the soul is simple (The Greek *monoeidēs* can also be translated "of one [*mono*] kind [*eidēs*]." The fact that *eidos* is one of the Greek expressions Plato uses to denominate his Forms reinforces the affinity between the Forms and the soul.) Plato's point seems to be that soul suffers change only when joined with the body; in its own right the soul is something simple and pure, that is, a pure reasoner. Our earthly task is to *purify* the soul by distancing ourselves from everyday desires and commerce with the physical so that we, that is, our souls, may regain the company of the divine. The theme of becoming like the divine through purification suggests that Orphic and Pythagorean doctrines are clearly part of the backdrop to Plato's psychology.

At the conclusion of the Affinity Argument (78b4–84b8), Simmias and Cebes author objections to Socrates' defense of immortal souls. Cebes contends that a given soul may eventually wear out, like a cloak that, while it may have many owners, and thus predate and postdate any one, eventually unravels. An adequate response, Socrates declares, requires "a thorough inquiry into the whole question of the reason for coming-to-be and passing away" (95e–96a). The so-called Final Argument and its preliminaries (95a4–107b1) is the culmination of the *Phaedo*'s effort to prove the immortality of the soul. But Socrates embarks on this course of argumentation only after he explains why he came to despair of the efforts of the natural philosophers to explain generation and destruction. Even Anaxagoras, who declared that "Mind directs and is the cause of everything," had relied on physical causes. What is needed is a teleological account, requiring appeal to the Mind and what is for the Best. Plato thus drops a broad hint that soul, Mind, and The Good are somehow responsible for all generation and destruction. Since Socrates cannot (here) provide that proof, what follows is a second-best sailing on the subject (97b–100b).

The actual argument for the soul's immortality comes at the conclusion of a series of complicated and controversial arguments that introduce the "Theory" of Forms, the distinction between Being and Participating, the notions of simple and clever causes (*aitia*) and the Method of Hypothesis. Little is clear in the Final Argument (including in what fashion this second sailing is connected to the desired teleological account). Of particular concern is the relation between the status of the soul and the status of the items that figure in participation. In the participation relation there appear to be a Form, which *is* what it is in a special way that marks a Form's relation to its essence (*ousia*), and a particular, which participates or partakes of a Form and becomes appropriately characterized: Beauty Itself (just) Is beautiful, whereas Helen has beauty or comes to be beautiful in virtue of partaking of Beauty – because Beauty Is beautiful Helen can come to be beautiful by partaking in it. (The " '[just]' " reflects the possibility that the only thing a given Form is is itself – Justice is just and only just; Beauty only beautiful. Recall from the Affinity Argument that Forms are simple. Call the way of being enjoyed by Forms "Being" – note the capital "B." Forms, then, are Beings. Anything that is a Being is an *auto kath auto* entity, that is, it Is what it is in virtue of itself. Let anything that is a Being be called a "substance.")

However, some passages (102b–103e, 104b–c, 106a–d) suggest that a third kind of item is involved in participation, a form-in-us, for example, the-beautiful-in-Helen. For those who believe in them, the forms-in-us, or form-copies, are the actual (unit-)properties had by particulars: what is *present to* Helen is not Beauty Itself but the beautiful-in-Helen. Since the soul is also present to a particular, in order to determine the nature of the soul we need to know whether it is analogous to a Form, a form-copy, or a particular. One problem is to decide whether Plato thinks that there are form-copies and how they differ from Forms. A second problem is to decide on the range of Forms, that is whether or not there is a Form corresponding to every property mentioned in the argument. While no one contests that there is a Form of Largeness and a Form of Beauty, there is no agreement on whether there are Forms for Snow, Fire, Man, Three, or Soul! (Cf. *Parmenides* 130c.) Accordingly, there is uncertainty over the status of certain particulars. Perhaps some particulars are themselves *auto kath auto* beings; that is, each respectively *is* in the same strong fashion that a Form Is what it is; that is, Socrates, a particular, is essentially or completely a man in his own right, that is, without partaking of the Form of Man, for there is no such Form. Socrates would then be a substance. He partakes only when his possession of properties like Beauty is in question. Perhaps souls, like Socrates, are also substances: souls are essentially what they are without partaking of a Form. On the other hand, there may be Forms for every property. If so, then particulars would acquire all their properties via participation in Forms. On this reading, a particular is nothing but a bundle of Forms or, if there are form-copies, a bundle of form-copies. If souls are like these particulars, then, at a minimum, they must partake of a Form, Soul Itself, in order to be anything at all. Even worse, they may turn out to be complex, thus contradicting the thrust of the Affinity Argument.

In addition to this basic or simple account of property possession, Plato constructs a second, cleverer account. The crucial move in this second account is to introduce the idea that certain properties or Forms occupy something *and* in virtue of what they respectively are "bring with" them other properties and exclude the presence of other properties. For instance, Snow must be Cold and cannot be Hot; Three must be Odd and can't be Even. What Three occupies must be three and odd and cannot be even, so long as it is three.

The last phase of the final argument applies to the soul the distinctions adumbrated in the clever *aitia* analysis. The opposite properties are Life and Death. Plato aims to show that Life excludes death and brings with it Imperishability. Note that the very structure and number of Forms seems different from that found in the clever *aitia*. There we had a Form or occupier, Fire, that brought with it an opposite, Heat, and excluded its opposite, Cold. Here we seem to have soul which brings with it Life and excludes Death, and also brings with it a third property, Imperishability.

Where is soul to be located in analogy with the accounts of the simple and clever *aitia*: is a soul an occupier or what is occupied? Many have thought that in the final argument the soul is a substance. While the *Phaedo* itself offers no detailed account of what a substance is, we can safely claim that a necessary condition for being a substance is possession of an *ousia* or essence. If soul is a substance, then the question is whether it is general in the same fashion as the Forms, which are the only substances universally accepted in the *Phaedo*; or whether it is somehow like the particulars such as Simmias, items which some think also qualify as substances; or whether it is like the form-copies. If soul is a Form, that is, a universal of some kind, then Plato would seem to fail in his aim of proving the immortality of *individual* souls. But the very presence of the Final Argument suggests that soul is not a Form; for given that all Forms are immortal, he would not need the elaborate argument of the last pages to prove its immortality. Since no one thinks that Plato wants to prove that the Form of Soul is immortal, the logic of the dialogue dictates that at the end of the day Plato admits into his ontology an individual substance, that is, an individual endowed with an essence. Because it is an individual, a soul is unlike a Form. What would it be for something to be at once both individual and essentially what it is, an item, moreover, that is capable of withdrawing from what it is present to?

The soul, when present to a body, makes it alive. It makes the body alive because the soul itself is alive in virtue of its relation to the Form of Life. Were the soul a particular like Socrates, then it might be said to *partake* of Life. Given that Death is the opposite of Life, the alive soul excludes Death, just as the cold snow excludes heat. The soul is thus deathless. And if, as is conceded without argument, what is deathless is indestructible, then the soul is immortal and indestructible. The problem, according to the classic objection, is that nothing justifies the move from the claim that what is alive cannot die and still exist to the claim that the soul cannot die. Just as Socrates is a man, and if we like, essentially a man, as long as he exists, so too then a soul might be alive, and essentially alive, as long as it exists. But Socrates can cease to be a man, and a soul, accordingly, can cease to be alive.

Crucial to this objection is the notion that a soul is to be treated as a particular, a contingent entity in the same fashion as Socrates or any particular that acquires its property/properties via partaking or by being occupied in the manner in which Fire occupies a log. It is noteworthy that Plato never says, let alone argues, that Socrates is essentially man; and he never asserts that any particular is what it is essentially or in virtue of itself, that is, he never says that a particular is an *auto kath auto* being. Similarly, he is never explicit about whether snow occupies something or is occupied. Lastly, he never says that soul partakes of the Form of Life. Souls, then, are not like particulars because particulars do not occupy things, because particulars are on any account contingent beings, and because on some accounts particulars are whatever they are in virtue of partaking in the requisite Forms. Since a soul cannot be a Form, what is needed is a kind of entity that, like the particular, is individual, that can nonetheless occupy something, and that, like a Form, is a necessary being, that is, a being which not only is essentially what it is so long as it exists, but also a being that in virtue of its peculiar relation to its essence cannot fail to possess its essence, that is, cannot fail to exist. And there is such an entity in the Final Argument of the *Phaedo*, the forms-in-us. If form-copies are as strongly tied to their essence in the same fashion as Forms, that is, if they Are their respective essences, then they are necessary beings. The beautiful-in-Helen does not partake of Beauty: it is (Is) beauty. So, too, then the individual souls do not partake of Life Itself: they are (Are) alive. In virtue of *being* what they are in the same manner as the Forms and form-copies, individual souls are immortal and indestructible. (It should be said that this altern- ative not only admits form-copies as bona fide members of the ontology, it further contends that form-copies always depart and thus do not perish when an opposite form-copy approaches the particular whose form-copy it is. This is a controversial claim that cannot be defended here.)

From the *Phaedo* we can draw few strong conclusions about the soul. While clearly Plato wants to insist that each person's soul is immortal, its ontological status is uncertain. It appears that it is an incomposite or simple entity, a being that is what it is in its own right (*auto kath auto*). From the initial arguments, it seems that in its own right, especially when it is free from earthly entanglements, the essential and sole property of soul is its power to grasp Forms. When combined with a body, its prior grasp of Forms conditions all experiences. In certain cases, that is, in those who devote themselves to philosophy, knowledge of Forms can be regained through recollection. In the Final Argument, on the other hand, it appears that its essential quality is being alive, not being rational. Each soul is essentially alive, bearing its essence in a special way enjoyed only by Forms and perhaps form-copies. The question is, can the soul as a principle of life be reconciled with the soul as the power of reasoning. Does Plato, implicitly at least, accept a conditional such as Necessarily, if something is capable of reason, then it is alive? Lurking in the back- ground is the "first sailing," the teleological account which shows how mind, or soul, can "direct and be the cause of everything."

Middle Period Dialogues

In the *Republic*, *Phaedrus*, and *Symposium*, the powers of the soul are expanded. The crucial difference in the *Republic* and *Phaedrus* is the apparent division of the soul into three parts. Reason is only one part of soul, accompanied now by appetite and spirit. Though it is traditional to refer to this as a tripartite psychology, there is also reason to think of a tripartition of desire, for each of the parts of the soul seem to have their own desires and thus their own pleasures. This desiderative aspect of soul is also emphasized in the *Symposium* and the myth of the winged soul in the *Phaedrus*, where the soul by nature has an erotic attraction for the Good and the Beautiful. While there can be no question that the soul is assigned powers (*dynameis*) seemingly reserved for the body in the *Phaedo* and perhaps also in the Socratic dialogues, it is less clear that these parts or their desires are independent of one another. (The tripartition of the soul is often aligned with Plato's effort to revise the moral psychology of Socrates, or the Socratic dialogues, in part to explain how, *pace* Socrates, weakness of will is possible.) In particular, two aspects of the *Republic* suggest that reason remains the fundamental power of the soul, or better, perhaps, what soul is in its own right. First, the rational capacity is capable of influencing and redirecting the drives of the other two parts in any individual. In the just and moderate person, reason, by looking out for the "good" of each of the parts, has sovereignty over the other parts with the result that all three parts will want the same things. Thus even if the soul is fractured in ways inconsistent with the *Phaedo*'s depiction of it as simple and uniform, reason is capable of *unifying* the parts into a whole (See *Republic* X, 611b ff.). (The full story behind unification is better told in the entry on Plato's ethics.)

The second, related, facet is Plato's emphasis that a human's goal is to become like God. Throughout these works, and equally in the *Philebus, Timaeus,* and *Laws,* the divine is depicted as purely rational. Thus in achieving our best state, we humans try to become as rational as possible. This cannot be viewed as either the elimination or the complete suppression of emotion, spirit, or desire, for that is to confuse being like God for being a God. Our goal, rather, is to organize our parts in such a fashion that reason is allowed as much unfettered time to pursue knowledge as is humanly possible. In keeping with this program, the various desires of the three parts are ordered such that the desires and pleasures of the rational capacity are deemed most pleasant, and only those properly educated can understand reason's desires and experience the highest pleasures. Nonetheless, each of the parts has their own desires and pleasures. The fact that these parts are independent of reason, though somehow persuadable by it, leaves a rather large problem for the Platonic doctrine of immortality; to wit: is the immortal soul to be identified with all three parts of the soul, or only with the rational part? Insofar as the spiritive and desiderative parts of the soul are inextricably intertwined with the body, it is difficult to picture how they can survive the separation of the soul from the body. It does seem, however, that they do survive, since Plato's eschatological myths (most famously, The Myth of Er, *Republic* X, 614b–621d, and the concluding myth of the *Phaedo* 113d–115a) suggest that the soul separated from a person carries with it the burdens of the life lived by that individual. Hence, one who has lived a less than virtuous life takes a soul filled with the desires and attitudes of his life with him when faced with his choice of next lives.

The doctrine of the tripartite soul also complicates our picture of Plato's epistemology. Broadly speaking, the desiderative and spiritive parts of the soul are irrational.

Reason, or thought in general, is reserved for the rational part. On the other hand, it sometimes seems that each of the *Republic*'s parts has beliefs and issues judgments, just as each of the parts has its own desires. The finger passage (523 ff.), as well as 602c–603a, implies that these judgments are potentially at odds with the judgments of reason. The parts of the soul thus appear to be homunculi, distinguished from one another by the objects about which they judge and the aims towards which their desires are directed.

The tripartite and homuncular character of the *Republic*'s soul seems at odds with the simple or uniform soul of the *Phaedo*. In the view of many scholars, one of Plato's aims in the *Theaetetus* is to repair the *Republic*'s epistemologically fragmented soul. In the concluding argument against Theaetetus' first definition that knowledge is perception (151d–e) (a definition Plato expands by adding to it a Protagorean epistemology and a Heraclitean ontology [152a–183e]), Socrates appears to argue that the senses themselves make no judgments (184b–186e). Rather, the "reports" of the senses are delivered to the same soul that issues judgments about both the (special) objects of the senses, for example, "The cheese is green" (where green, a color, is special to sight), and everything else, for all judgments about anything require "common" notions, for example, being, or same or different, unavailable to the senses. Plato thus anticipates the Kantian "unity of the perceiving consciousness" and relocates all rational, cognitive, and judgmental activities in one (part of the) soul. The appetitive and spiritive aspects remain "irrational."

The "change" recorded in the *Theaetetus* depends on one's reading of the epistemologies of the *Republic* and the argument at 184–6 of the *Theaetetus*. It is not necessary to regard the senses in the *Republic* as capable of issuing judgments, which is to say that the senses are not cognitive agents. Similarly in the *Theaetetus*, it is unclear what powers are assigned to the senses and what to the thinking soul, in no small measure because the crucial claim at 186 concerns what it means to deny to the senses a grasp of *ousia*. If the senses are not cognitive agents, that is if, as in the *Timaeus*, the senses seem to be part of the irrational (*alogon*) soul, then, as in the *Phaedo*, their deliverances will always be material for the rational soul to use in making judgments about perceptual properties. On this reading, there may be no change in the Plato's epistemology from the middle to the late dialogues.

Later Dialogues

Let us return to the metaphysical nature of the soul. Three related questions need to be addressed. The first is what is the nature or essence of soul? The second is whether soul is a primitive in Plato's metaphysics or, rather, whether the soul is a construct of some kind. The third question concerns the relation of individual souls to the universal or collective notion of a world-soul or Demiurge. Throughout the dialogues, Plato never wavers from the notion that fundamental to soul is its power to know the Forms. In this respect, each soul strives to achieve the same state, alternatively describable as knowing (all) the Forms, or being like God, or being (completely) virtuous. Since no soul in such a state will differ from another soul in this state, any qualitative differences between souls will be a function of the different experiences or pleasures or histories that result from its incorporation(s) in a given body, whether an animal or human.

If souls are constructed, then perhaps one could individuate them by appeal to their different components. But this prospect has little going for it. In the *Timaeus* the Demiurge is said to construct the world-soul and derivatively the rational souls (of rational creatures) from a mixture of divisible and indivisible Being, Sameness, and Difference (34c–37c). These ingredients seem designed to enable intelligent activity on the part of all souls and cannot serve to distinguish one soul from the next. If there are rational souls, then their individuality is primitive, that is, unable to be explained by appeal to other factors.

Timaeus' depiction of the construction of soul, like the construction of the cosmos, is subject to dispute. Literalists, that is, those who maintain that Plato believed that the cosmos was created, contend that souls are not primitive items, though they may differ over the elements from which souls are constructed. (Kinds of Being, Sameness, and Difference, different motions, a substrate of some kind which then partakes of a Form, for example, Life Itself or the Soul Itself). Fictionalists, that is, those who believe that the genesis described in the *Timaeus* is a myth created for the sake of instruction, point out that since the construction of the soul is an intelligent action on the part of the Demiurge, and since intelligence lives only in soul, the Demiurge must be a soul that intelligently constructs the world-soul. I prefer the fictionalist account. The World-soul just is the Demiurge. Individual rational souls are primitive elements in Plato's ontology. Indeed, I think that the Demiurge and his intelligent construction of a unified complete Cosmos is a continuation of the themes of the rational human soul attempting to be as like the Divine as possible in its effort to unify its various elements into a virtuous life. The Demiurge is just the idealization of the various rational souls, yours, mine, and everybody else's. But what then is this primitive rational soul?

In the *Timaeus* (41d1–3, 42d5–e4; cf. *Laws* 895b, 897a and Book X, *passim*) the rational and the irrational soul are assigned different "makers" (the Demiurge for the former, the lesser Gods for the latter). How the two souls or the parts of souls can be melded into a unity remains rather opaque in these late dialogues, though the *Philebus'* account of mixtures and the *Timaeus'* depiction of the regulation of the various psychic motions indicates that Plato continues to uphold the *Republic's* doctrine that the complex soul can be unified. Whether the irrational soul departs with its rational brother is not definitively answered.

Apart from the *Phaedo*, the nature of the soul is discussed only in passing. In the *Phaedrus*, however, Plato explicitly assigns to the soul a nature: a soul is a self-mover; and insofar as soul is a self-mover it is responsible for *all* other motions. This account of soul is reiterated in Book X of the *Laws* and in the *Timaeus'* (35–44d) depiction of the movements of the soul, where the circular motions of the rational soul are an attempt to depict how the soul can continuously move. Taken together, the Demiurge and individual rational souls are ultimately responsible for all motion and thus finally give fulfillment to Socrates' wish to discover how mind directs and is the cause of everything.

But passages in the *Statesman, Laws,* and especially the *Timaeus,* suggest that there may be sources of motion other than rational souls. It is arguable that the *Timaeus* (47e–53c, esp. 52d ff.) maintains that there are moving bodies in the precosmic chaos prior to the intervention of rational souls or the Demiurge. These motions are often ascribed to Necessity or the Wandering Cause. Similarly in the *Laws* (896d10–e6) and *Statesman* (272b–274e), an Evil or Irrational counterpart to the Demiurge or World-soul is sometimes thought to be responsible for the chaotic or disorderly motions (of elements) of the universe. Ultimately the interpretation of these passages turns on two issues: What are the sources of evil in Plato; and is the cosmos in fact created from primitive matter and its motions?

The key to understanding at least the late Platonic doctrine of soul is to determine the relation between the rational capacity of soul and soul as the source of motion in the physical cosmos. The idea bridging the two questions is that evil or chaos in the cosmos ultimately results from the activity of self-moving souls who act out of ignorance, that is, souls who have not regained knowledge of the Forms and thus are less than perfectly rational. The soul's self-motion is perfect when the soul is perfectly rational; and a soul is perfectly rational only when it is contemplating Forms. Thus whenever the soul has commerce with the bodily, that is when it is incarcerated and when it is involved in perception of the external world, the potentially perfect motions of the soul are threatened. Nonetheless, the self-motion of the soul never ceases, because the soul's nature, it's unchanging essence, is to move itself. To the extent that a rational (part of a) soul can bring order to, that is, unify, the perturbations caused by its commerce with the bodily, it can engage in contemplation of the Forms and thus liken itself as much, as is humanly possible, to it's divine counterpart.

Throughout the dialogues, then, the activity and nature of soul is imbricated with the Forms in general and with one Form in particular, the Form of Motion Itself. In the *Phaedo* we saw that a soul is a principle of life and stands in some relation to the apparent Form of Life Itself. In the *Phaedrus, Timaeus,* and *Laws* the soul is said to be essentially a self-mover and thus, at bottom, responsible for the motion of everything else. Plato, alas, never offers a precise account of the relation between soul, the Form of Motion itself, and the motions of matter. However, an extended, but intricate discussion of Motion and soul is found in the *Sophist*'s account of the materialists and idealists. The Stranger describes a battle between the Gods and Giants (245e6–249d4), where the Giants are introduced initially as materialists who deny the existence of (immaterial) Forms: what there is, is matter. In a remarkable act of rehabilitation, the Stranger reforms the Giants so that they ultimately accommodate immaterial entities into their ontology, namely particular souls and forms of knowledge (246d4–247d6). In light of this reform the Stranger proposes a new definition of being designed to embrace matter, souls, and knowledge, the power to act or be acted upon (*dynamis*).

With the new mark on the table, the materialists are dismissed in favor of the idealists. The Gods were originally (246b6–7) introduced as maintaining that true being is confined to some intelligible and bodiless kinds, dismissing all the rest, all matter, as mere becoming (*genesis*). The Stranger, just as he had surprised the materialists with his reformation, next complicates the idealists' doctrine by grafting the soul on to it:

> And you claim that by our body through perception we have communion with genesis, and that with our soul through reasoning we have communion with real being, which you say always holds in the same way with respect to the same things, whereas genesis holds differently at different times. (248a10–13)

The Stranger, on behalf of the Gods, points out that they will not accept the new definition of being as *dynamis*, because the idea of communing with anything is appropriate only for what becomes, not for what truly is. Soul, according to the idealists, must then be motionless. The problem, the Stranger goes on to illustrate, is to decide what to say about knowledge and what is known. If what is (*ousia*) is known, and if knowing is an activity, then it seems that *ousia* is acted upon: "and insofar as it is known, to that extent it is moved on account of its being affected which we say could not come to be concerning that which is at rest," that is, concerning what truly is (248e1–4). In the background is the cardinal Platonic thesis that the Forms are what truly is. Thus it seems that the Forms cannot be the objects of knowledge and the soul cannot be what knows.

Both the Gods and the Giants, then, are victimized by the Stranger's insertion of knowledge and soul into the account. Both the Gods and the Giants, that is, both those who are materialists and idealists, cannot accommodate the possibility of knowledge. But, for Plato, it is not an option to deny that there is knowledge. The Stranger and Theaetetus agree that there must be knowledge, life, and soul (all three must belong to what completely is [245d7–249a1], and thus one must agree that motion and what moves are (beings). But equally, the Stranger declares, there must be motionless beings if there is to be knowledge, for its objects must be stable and unchanging. The conclusion is that what is *is both what is at rest and what moves* (249d4).

In light of the arguments in the *Phaedo, Republic, Phaedrus, Timaeus* and the other dialogues, we know what the moral of the Battle is: There must be self-moving souls, that is, souls capable of knowing, and there must be motionless objects of knowledge, that is, Forms. The critical chain of inferences in this passage encapsulates the central elements of Plato's psychology: Nous *implies life, life implies soul, and soul implies motion* (cf. *Phaedrus* 247d, 249c6 and *Laws* 896e–897b). *Nous* is the soul's ability to see the Forms. To account for the nature of the rational soul and its ability to know, Plato thus introduces in the *Sophist* the Forms of Motion and Rest and assigns them to the ranks of the *greatest kinds*. The greatest kinds are those Forms, for example, Being, Sameness, Difference, which every Form, in virtue of being a Form, must partake of. Hence every Form must partake of both Motion and Rest.

In partaking of Rest, Plato does not mean to indicate that a Form is not moving through space or in time, since Forms are not in space and time. Nor does it mean that Forms are free from alteration or generation or destruction in the manner of particulars, though they are free. When introduced in the Battle of Gods and Giants, the Rest at issue is freedom from affect when a Form serves as an object of knowledge (or thought or language). The same line of reasoning compels Plato to postulate a form of Motion. It is much harder to see what it would be for *a Form* to partake of Motion. Certainly a Form is not subject to change of properties, translocation, or generation and destruction. But we need not and should not view it in terms appropriate to describe the motions of particulars. Motion, like Rest, is introduced to "save" psychic (self-)motion, and in particular the form of psychic Motion that is rational activity. The Form of Motion is identical *neither* with soul nor with knowledge. Rather, Motion seems to be responsible for explaining how Forms can be the objects of the rational soul insofar as the self-moving soul communes (*Sophist* 248a11) with Forms in thought and language. Motion allows Forms to serve as the object of knowledge. Since all Forms can be known, including Motion itself, all Forms partake of Motion. Rest, conversely, is responsible for the imperviousness of those same Forms to being altered by this communion.

If the Form of Motion explains how Forms can be known, that is not its only function. Souls are self-movers and self-movement is the primary type of movement in that it is responsible for the subsequent or secondary movements of bodies. Thus soul is an intermediary between the Forms and the motions of physical bodies. A soul is, it seems, a substance that moves itself in virtue of its relation to the Form of Motion. However, just as Plato refrains in the *Phaedo* from claiming that souls partake necessarily in Life, nowhere in the late dialogues does he assert that they partake of Motion itself. The reason, I suspect, is that he wants neither to claim that a soul causes movement in itself nor that it is anything prior to its participation in the Form of Motion. Rather, souls are primitive beings whose self-moving nature draws them towards (knowledge of) Forms. They fashion their activities, that is, their lives, in pursuit of this knowledge and their actions set in motion the bodies with which they consort and the other bodies with which they come into contact. Unlike "freed" souls, or divine souls, they are hindered in their activities by the material world. They set bodies in motion and once set in motion these bodies then interact with each other in ways outside of the control of rational souls. These random, secondary motions of bodies are the Wandering Cause of the *Timaeus*. Inevitably these secondary motions rebound on the souls themselves, marring their attempts to give order to their world and thus inhibiting their efforts to regain knowledge of the Good and the other Forms. Platonic souls then are self-moving rational substances or beings, at once gifted with the power to revisit the Forms and cursed by fate to often commingle with matter that can never ultimately yield to their suasion. Insofar as each soul seeks to separate from this matter, to be a pure thinking thing, to be like the divine, each soul seeks assimilation with the World-soul or Demiurge. Had Plato a concept of the person, his souls might well be Cartesian egos.

References and Recommended Reading

General Reading

All of these suggested readings contain references to other worthwhile readings.

Begin with
Guthrie, W. K. C., "Plato's Views on the Nature of the Soul," in *Plato*, vol. 2, ed. G. Vlastos (New York: 1971), 230–41.

Also basic is the section on psychology in
Shorey, P., *The Unity of Plato's Thought* (Chicago: 1903).

For advanced readers:
Cherniss, H. F., *Aristotle's Criticism of Plato and the Academy* (Baltimore: 1944; reprinted New York: 1962).
McCabe, M. M., *Plato's Individuals* (Princeton: 1994), ch. 9.

A number of excellent articles:
Wagner, E. (ed. with intro.), *Essays on Plato's Psychology* (New York: 2001).

Phaedo

There are many fine translations, commentaries, and editions of the *Phaedo*, such as the following, in which one can find discussions of the various arguments:
Bluck, R., *Phaedo; a Translation with Introductory Notes and Appendices* (London: 1955).
Bostock, D., *Plato's Phaedo* (Oxford: 1982).
Gallap, D., *Plato: Phaedo*, trans. with notes (Oxford: 1975).
Hackforth, R., *Phaedo*, trans. with intro. and commentary (Cambridge: 1955). (This one is not a translation, but rather a commentary on the Greek text.)
Rowe, C. J., ed., Phaedo (Cambridge: 1993).

On the Affinity Argument:
McCabe, M. M., *Plato's Individuals* (Princeton: 1994), ch. 2.

Fine works on the role of Forms in the final argument:
Rowe, C., "Explanation in the *Phaedo* 99c6–102a8," *Oxford Studies in Ancient Philosophy* 11 (1993) 49–69.
Stough, C., "Forms and Explanation in the *Phaedo*," *Phronesis* 21 (1976) 1–30.

On the attempt to prove the immortality of the soul:
Frede, D., "The Final Proof of the Immortality of the Soul," *Phronesis* 23 (1978) 24–41.
O'Brien, D., "The Last Argument of Plato's *Phaedo*," *Classical Quarterly* (1967) 189–213; (1968) 95–106.

Middle Period Dialogues

The literature on Plato's *Republic* is vast. My favorite introduction to the *Republic* is
Annas, J., *An Introduction to Plato's Republic* (Oxford: 1981).

On the evolution of the soul from the Socratic dialogues to the *Republic*, the best place to start is
Irwin, T., *Plato's Moral Theory* (Oxford: 1977).

See also
Irwin, T., *Plato's Ethics* (Oxford: 1995).

For the more advanced reader interested in the change of doctrine evidenced in the epistemology of the *Theaetetus*, the classic account is
Burnyeat, M., "Plato on the Grammar of Perceiving," *Classical Quarterly* (1976) 29–51.

In response, see
Silverman, A., "Plato on Perception and 'Commons'," *Classical Quarterly* (1990) 148–75.

For those interested in the relation between Plato and Freud, see chapter 6 of
Lear, J., *Happiness, Death and the Remainder of Life* (Harvard: 2000).

Late Dialogues

There is, alas, no easily accessible commentary on the *Sophist* or *Timaeus*. Perhaps the best places to start are the Hackett editions of each:
Plato's *Sophist*, ed. by N. White; Plato's *Timaeus*, ed. by D. Zeyl.

For the more advanced reader:
McCabe, M. M., *Plato's Individuals* (Princeton: 1994).
Moravcsik, J., *Plato and Platonism* (Oxford: 1992).

On the Battle of Gods and Giants:
Cherniss, H. F., *Aristotle's Criticism of Plato and the Academy* (Baltimore: 1944; reprinted New York: 1962).
Keyt, D., "Plato's Paradox that the Immutable is Unknowable," *Philosophical Quarterly* 19 (1969) 1–14.

On the sources of evil:
Cherniss, H., "The Sources of Evil According to Plato," in *Plato*, vol. 2, ed. by G. Vlastos (Garden City, N.Y.: 1971), 244–58.

Part IV

Aristotle: Introduction

Although in some rare instances abstruse, Plato's dialogues are consistently fun to read. They have, to be sure, an uncommon philosophical depth and rigor; but they are also polished in their presentation, supple in their prose, and regularly amusing in their repartee. A student who moves from Plato to Aristotle, accustomed to such engaging writing, is bound to be put off: Aristotle's writings are mainly dry, crabbed in style, and often airily magisterial in tone. They are, moreover, in many instances so compact and technical that a novice reader is likely to turn away from them bewildered. Opening Aristotle's collected works at random, one is apt to read, for example, "The universal negative converts universally; each of the affirmatives converts into a particular. If it is necessary that A belongs to no B, it is necessarily also that B belongs to no A."[1] Elsewhere, one encounters the suggestion that "Some things exist only actually, some potentially, some potentially and actually – some as beings, some as quantities, others in the other categories."[2] Still elsewhere, one learns from Aristotle that

> The horse has forty teeth. It sheds its first set of four, two from the upper jaw and two from the lower when two and a half years old. After a year's interval, it sheds another set of four in like manner, two upper and two lower, and another set of four after yet another year's interval; after arriving at the age of four years and six months, it sheds no more.[3]

These samples, it must be said, are representative. It is therefore understandable that beginning students, particularly those coming to Aristotle from their first exposure to Plato, do not immediately find much to inspire their interest.

It is a pity that some students do not persevere with Aristotle. For Aristotle left a legacy to Western civilization that is surely unparalleled. As the quotations presented attest, his works encompass not only logical theory and metaphysics, but areas which are today no part of philosophy, not even natural philosophy or philosophy of science. He wrote a great many works in biology, much of it taxonomical and much of it simply observational. He also wrote works in political theory and the history of politics; in aesthetic theory; in ethical theory; in "physics," where this extended not only to puzzles about change, time, and causation, but to meteorology and astronomy as well; in psychology, both philosophical and empirical; in rhetoric; and, to judge from some ancient catalogues which mention works of Aristotle no longer extant, on such diverse matters as the river Nile and the finer points of drunkenness. He was a tireless researcher and writer in an astonishing array of fields. In some cases, he originated the disciplines in which he investigated; in others, he set the agenda for many hundreds of years after his death. In general, his was a formidable intellect, of a sort rarely equaled and never since surpassed.

Because of their alien character, Aristotle's writings require some brief explanation. In antiquity, Cicero, someone who knew beautiful prose when he saw it, judged Aristotle a superior writer to Plato. It seems plain, then, that Cicero was not reading the works of Aristotle which have come down to us. For although they do contain flashes of stylistic brilliance, the writings we possess are for the most part compressed and ungainly. It is overwhelmingly likely, therefore, that Aristotle's surviving writings are not those which he himself prepared for a public audience, as pieces to be made available to the general reading public. Rather, they seem to be akin to the lecture notes kept and revised by a university professor from year to year: they contain correction, interpolation, expansion, and revision – all without too much care given to matters of presentation or accessibility. Since they were for the most part not intended for public consumption, Aristotle's surviving writings, unlike those read with an appreciative eye by Cicero, require a bit of effort from their readers. The only justification for such expenditure can be their eventual philosophical payoff.

Students can best approach Aristotle for the first time by bearing in mind two features of his writing: (1) his philosophical work regularly takes as its point of departure puzzles and problems bequeathed him by his predecessors, including most notably Plato, with whom he associated for a full two decades; and (2) he makes free use of a technical terminology which he rarely pauses to explicate, especially *the doctrine of the four causes*, an explanatory framework which pervades virtually all of his work, whether philosophical or biological.

His extended association with Plato took place in Athens, in Plato's Academy, where Aristotle came to study as a young man, probably at the age of eighteen. He had been born in Stagira, in what is now northeastern Greece, in 484 BC, some fifteen years after the death of Socrates. He was the son of a doctor and a wealthy mother, though since both his parents died while he was still a young boy, Aristotle was raised by a family friend or relative in accordance with his father's wishes. Although there is no direct evidence to support it, it seems overwhelmingly likely that he came to Athens with the express intention of studying with Plato, who was at that time a famous and controversial figure throughout Greece and beyond.

Aristotle's relationship with Plato has been an irresistible subject for speculation. Some ancient lives, mainly late and mostly untrustworthy, portray Aristotle as a noisy thorn in Plato's side, as a sort of precocious but insufferable genius with an overweening demeanor. Others treat Aristotle as a dutiful student who with time came to establish himself as an independent thinker, often at variance with Plato, sometimes even caustically so, but mainly reverential in his attitudes. Neither of the portraits is likely to be wholly accurate, though we do find shards of evidence for both in Aristotle's surviving works. What matters for our current understanding of Aristotle is this: he plainly takes Plato's philosophy very seriously – so seriously, in fact, that he very often feels the need to address Plato's views when advancing his own philosophical theories. This tendency has two roots, the first of which is perfectly general and the second of which is slightly more personal. In the first instance, Aristotle quite rightly insists that we best begin grappling with a given philosophical problem by determining what our intellectual forebears had to say about it. This is not only because we should wish to avoid reinventing the wheel, but also because the very formulation of a philosophical problem requires reflection and precision, both things afforded by surveying the approaches of other philosophers. When engaging in such activity, Aristotle naturally looks first and foremost to Plato. Plato was not only Aristotle's primary teacher, but a manifest genius whose views carry a special weight with him. When approaching Aristotle's works, therefore, it is often advisable to read them with an eye on Plato. It is often the case that we can understand him better when we appreciate how he is reacting to a Platonic point of view.

One key to understanding his reaction to Plato is Aristotle's contention that Plato erred in a serious way in postulating Forms. His criticisms are myriad. One, a milder one, is especially noteworthy for novices. Aristotle contends that Platonic Forms cannot explain some obvious facts about change and generation. Even if we think, for instance, that a statue is a statue of Hermes and not of Galateia because of its *form*, that by itself will do nothing to explain how the statue came to have the form it has. Platonic Forms do not, and indeed cannot, explain change and generation. In fact, contends Aristotle, in order to mount complete and satisfying explanations, we need to appeal not merely to forms, nor even merely to matter, as the Presocratics had been inclined to do, but rather to *four causes*. The authors of the chapters in this volume make free appeal to this technical apparatus, whose essentials, then, must be fully appreciated.

Aristotle's doctrine is most fruitfully first approached as he himself approached it first, by means of an example. Suppose we come to the university one day and discover a statue erected somewhere in the main quadrangle. To explain completely what it is, we will need to know what it is made of, what sort of a statue it is (a statesman, a horse, a soldier, a shabby professor), how it came to be made, and the purpose for its being erected. These four appeals correspond to Aristotle's four causes:

1. *Material Cause*: the matter of which the statue is made, e.g., bronze.
2. *Formal Cause*: the structure of the statue, taken in one way, its shape, though taken more robustly, its essence or nature, e.g., the attribute of being a statue.
3. *Efficient Cause*: the actual agent which brought it about that the matter, the bronze, came to have the form it has, e.g., the sculptor.
4. *Final Cause*: the function or purpose of the statue, what the statue is for, e.g., to honor a president.

Aristotle makes twin claims about the four causes: (1) explanations are incomplete when they fail to specify one of the causes; and (2) an explanation which cites all four causes at the appropriate level of specificity is both complete and satisfying. When reading Aristotle, or when reading the chapters which follow, it is essential to keep this framework in mind, since it structures a great deal of Aristotle's thinking.

Thus, for example, Bolton makes clear that Aristotelian explanation requires an appreciation of essence, a notion which in Aristotle's mind is closely connected to formal and final causation. Loux too makes free use of this terminology in discussing Aristotle's metaphysics. His doing so is appropriate, even inevitable, since when Aristotle himself talks about substance, the keystone in his metaphysical system, he frames his discussion in terms of form and matter. One immediately connected application of Aristotle's theory of substance provides the subject of Matthews' chapter. Aristotle thinks that just as a statue is a sort of complex of form and matter, so a human being is a complex of a soul and a body, which Aristotle in turn characterizes as related as form to matter. The soul is the form of the body; the body the matter of the soul. Here, as in so many other places, Aristotle deploys his technical framework in an effort to explain a central philosophical problem – the relation of soul and body – in a strikingly anti-Platonic manner. The same sort of appeal to the four-causal framework finds its way even into Aristotle's ethical and political writings. As Miller makes abundantly clear, it is not possible to understand Aristotle's conception of the state without having a prior appreciation of the four-causal schema. Aristotle wants to know what states are *for*, because he wants to know what form the best civic institutions should take. He even conceptualizes a state's constitution as its form and its citizens as its matter. When conducting political theory, Aristotle thinks he can rely on his four causes because he thinks that their explanatory success in other domains is unassailable.

In these ways, then, Aristotle is a highly systematic philosopher, one who draws the framework of much of his thinking from a relatively straightforward explanatory schema. Still, his writings range over topics so disparate that no one today could pursue them at the level of professional engagement exhibited by Aristotle. This is in part, of course, because the arts and sciences have marched on and progressed since Aristotle's day. It is also, though, to some degree simply a testament to Aristotle's restless mind. He claimed, in the beginning of his great *Metaphysics*, that "all humans, by nature, desire to know." Surely what he says of everyone holds true, in an especially vivid way, of Aristotle himself.

Notes

1   *Prior Analytics* I.3, 25a29–32. These page numbers are the so-called Bekker numbers of Aristotle, a pagination which derives from Immanuel Bekker's standard Greek edition of Aristotle, published in 1831. All good subsequent translations cross-reference these pages. The Bekker numbers thus provide a common form of citation used by almost all scholars, including those in this volume. The citation at the beginning of this note means that the quotation from the text is excerpted from Aristotle's work, the *Prior Analytics*, book I,

chapter 3, Bekker page 25, column a, lines 29–32. In practical terms, to read the quotation in its appropriate context, a student need only open any good translation of the *Prior Analytics* and scan along the Bekker pagination, usually given in the margins along the side of the text, until reaching the appropriate passage.

2   *Metaphysics* XI.9, 1065b5–6.
3   *History of Animals* VI.22 576a7–12.

Chapter 8

Aristotle: Epistemology and Methodology

Robert Bolton

Aristotle's approach to epistemology, and to the methodology of inquiry more generally, is very different from the one with which we are now most familiar. In modern and contemporary epistemology the central interest or objective, as a starting point, has typically been to give a *general* account of *knowledge*. For instance, it has been common to take knowledge to be something like *justified true belief* or, more carefully, *warranted true belief*, where *warrant* is whatever needs to be added to true belief to secure knowledge. On this type of account, the debate then mainly focuses, reasonably enough, on what is required for warrant, since the notions of truth and belief seem, by comparison, relatively unproblematic.

One main question, then, about warrant is how it is achieved, and how this may differ in, say, the case of a priori knowledge, where warrant is not directly tied to any appeal to perceptual experience, from the case of a posteriori knowledge where it is. Then one may ask, further, how warrant may differ for different types of a priori and a posteriori knowledge. For instance, is a priori knowledge always knowledge of *analytic* truths, so that a priori warrant is always based on a grasp of semantic or conceptual connections; or are there other types of a priori knowledge and warrant? Equally, we can ask, is all a posteriori knowledge *internally* warranted, on the basis of explicit reasoned justification or proof which the knower can in principle supply on demand? Or is there *externally* warranted a posteriori knowledge which is achieved simply in virtue of the knower's standing in the appropriate relations to the external environment? These are very typical main questions considered by epistemologists in modern and contemporary discussion.

It is most striking that Aristotle shows no explicit interest at all in this type of approach to questions about knowledge. This does not mean as we shall see that one cannot reasonably ask what his views might be on such matters as these and construct some plausible answers. But Aristotle does not himself directly approach things in these terms. How do we explain this, and what are the implications of this for our understanding of Aristotle's own views and their interest for us? Some might try to explain this simply by saying that, after all, Aristotle lived in distant primitive times, philosophically speaking, before the light dawned as to how to properly do epistemology. But we cannot say anything like this because, in fact, Aristotle's teacher Plato is very interested in this type of general approach to epistemology. The *Meno*, a relatively early Platonic dialogue, already offers a general account of knowledge as something like justified or warranted true belief, and the *Theaetetus* arguably explores in detail various aspects of and difficulties for this type of view. In his *Phaedo* and *Republic*, Plato explores the difference between a priori and a posteriori warrant and, on a plausible interpretation, argues that all genuine warrant is a priori internal warrant. (Plato does not of course use the terms a priori and a posteriori, since he did not know any Latin, but he is clearly very interested in these topics.)

So the fact that Aristotle does not take our general approach to epistemology cannot be simply due to the fact that no one had thought of it. Another deeper explanation that many would offer is this. The general approach that we and Plato follow fits very naturally with an interest in skepticism. An account of knowledge that makes *justification* or *warrant* the central topic of interest directly reflects the skeptic's concerns and strategy, since the skeptic's main objective is to lead us to feel that *warrant* is exactly what we lack for all of the types of beliefs where we might initially feel quite certain that we have it. One can see already in his early dialogues, where Socrates strives mightily for totally irrefutable beliefs, that warrant and the certainty that might accompany it is of intense interest to Plato. And Plato knows well the main skeptical strategies, as one can see not only from the modes of refutation used in the Socratic dialogues but also in the *Theaetetus*. There Plato introduces a version of the powerful skeptical challenge to any confidence we might have in any a posteriori warrant, at least, on the ground that for all we know our experiences might always be only dreams (158bff).

Also, some would argue, since modern epistemology gets going, in the seventeenth century, partly in response to a strong revival of interest in skepticism in the sixteenth century, it is natural that it comes to have the focus on justification or warrant that has continued to this day. The revival of skepticism in the sixteenth century was, of course, related to an interest at the time in curbing the power of various social institutions such as the church. One convenient way to try to do that was to undermine the *epistemic* authority which the church claimed, and the standard skeptical strategies were handy for that purpose. Similarly, the very strong interest of both Socrates and Plato in challenging established authority in ancient Athenian society helps to explain their strong interest in this approach; and a continuing interest in challenges to the authority of, for instance, the state or of certain social structures, may help to explain our continuing attachment to the early modern focus in epistemology. If, on the other hand, one does not take skepticism seriously, for whatever reason, as many scholars have claimed Aristotle does not, then one will not so easily be attracted to ways of approaching epistemology in general on which warrant is a main focus.

However, this line does not take us very far either toward understanding Aristotle's own distinctive approach, since certain passages in the *Posterior Analytics* (I.3, II.19) and *Metaphysics* (IV.5–6) make it clear that he does take the skeptical challenge quite seriously. He is not obsessed with this as later Hellenistic philosophy came to be, or as Socrates perhaps was, but he does clearly understand this challenge and he wants to answer it. A more positive explanation is needed, in any case, for Aristotle's own very distinctive approach. This explanation has to do with what we may term Aristotle's *naturalism* in epistemology. This should not be confused with the view sponsored today by some advocates of so-called naturalized epistemology, that epistemology should be taken out of the hands of philosophers and put where it properly belongs, in the hands of those scientists, specifically psychologists, who study human cognition. Though he has interests in the scientific study of our cognitive states and in how this meshes with and supports his epistemological views, Aristotle is not a strong naturalist in this sense. His discussions of knowledge and the methodology of inquiry in the *Posterior Analytics* and *Topics*, for instance, do not proceed from the perspective of a cognitive psychologist. Rather, Aristotle's own starting point in considering knowledge is *human nature* or our distinctive natural capacities as human beings. What he mainly wants to understand is the various *forms of knowledge* that figure in our distinctive activities as possessors of a distinctively human nature. These forms of knowledge that we pursue and achieve are so important, and so importantly different for him, as they are not for Plato, that Aristotle's main focus is on their differences rather than on what they may have in common as forms of knowledge.

This comes out right away when we consider what is in fact Aristotle's most general discussion of knowledge, which comes not in the *Analytics* but rather in the *Nicomachean Ethics*. There, in Book VI, Aristotle's interest in knowledge, at the most general level, is primarily an interest in the *intellectual virtues*. What most strongly attracts Aristotle's attention in the area of epistemology broadly speaking is the various forms of intellectual excellence, the forms of highest achievement, epistemologically speaking, of which we, as human beings, are capable. So, for instance, Aristotle offers us an account of technical knowledge or skill (*technē*), that form of intellectual excellence by virtue of which we are able to *produce* various valuable results – as medicine produces health or architecture produces museums. He also offers us an account, in *Ethics* VI, of the intellectual virtue of scientific knowledge (*epistēmē*), such as we have in mathematics or physics, which is pursued, he argues, for its own sake independent of any practical applications it may have. The *Posterior Analytics* is mainly concerned with this, so we can see from the *Ethics* how Aristotle's interests elsewhere in this intellectual virtue fit into his broader way of thinking about topics in epistemology. Also, Aristotle discusses, in *Ethics* VI, moral wisdom (*phronēsis*) as another very distinct form of human intellectual excellence, and a good portion of the *Ethics* itself is devoted to the study of this.

So Aristotle's interests in epistemology are determined to a significant degree by his primary concern to understand all the specific *forms* of knowledge that we value most, and must value most, given our nature and our capabilities as human beings. He gives no special epistemic priority to any one form over the others, contrary to what some have suggested. It is this that largely explains Aristotle's deviation from the more unified Platonic approach that we have recently been more influenced by.

However, it would be a serious mistake to think that Aristotle's approach, which starts from a certain view of our natural cognitive capacities, dictates that his interests in epistemology are confined to the intellectual virtues. Nor would he himself be sympathetic to a *general* account of knowledge based on the notion of intellectual virtue, as some have recently suggested. Aristotle is fully aware that the knowledge that we enjoy and employ, and must employ most of all, in the major portion of our ordinary day-to-day activities does not fall within the scope of any intellectual virtue or excellence. Aristotle introduces this point most emphatically in the opening lines of his *Rhetoric*:

> Rhetoric is a partner of dialectic. For both of them are concerned with the sorts of things which it is common, in a certain way, to absolutely everyone to know and which require no specialized knowledge. Thus, everyone in a certain way takes part in both dialectic and rhetoric. For everyone on a limited basis engages in examination and in submitting to argument; and also in defending himself and accusing others. Ordinary people do this either in a random way or due to practice and habit. (1351a1–7)

Here Aristotle clearly recognizes that in various standard human activities such as our normal everyday consideration or examination of the claims of others, and our everyday submission to the examination of our own claims by others, we mainly do not employ or rely on knowledge of the sort that we acquire in the attainment of any of the intellectual virtues. Rather than relying on one of these forms of *special* knowledge or expertise, Aristotle says, we rely on what it is *common to everyone* to understand. So in addition to the type of knowledge that constitutes one or another of the intellectual virtues there is also what Aristotle calls common knowledge. This, he says in the passage above, is the knowledge which we exercise paradigmatically in two closely correlated activities or techniques, rhetoric and dialectic. Rhetoric, for him, is what we use for the examination or prosecution of others, and for the advocacy and defense of our own position, in a *public* forum such as the courts or the media. Dialectic is what is used for the consideration and examination of claims in more *private* one-on-one situations – which include instances of self-examination. These two types of activities are, Aristotle says, both based on common knowledge as opposed to some form of expertise or intellectual virtue. They are sufficiently important to him, in view again of their natural place in human life, that he devotes two of his longest books – his *Rhetoric* and his *Topics* – to the study of them and of how to master them.

In modern and contemporary epistemology also the main examples of knowledge considered that usually guide the discussion have not been examples of special expertise but rather examples of what Aristotle would call common knowledge. As one might expect from this, in his consideration of common knowledge Aristotle comes closest to some of our own recent epistemological interests, so his views in this area are particularly worth our attention. Aristotle identifies common knowledge, as we have seen, with the basis for the most common forms of dialectical reasoning. So to explore his views we may ask the question: What *is* dialectic as Aristotle understands it? One might think that this should be a rather easy question to answer, since, as we have noted, Aristotle wrote a whole book on dialectic and dialectical reasoning, namely the *Topics* (which includes the so-called *Sophistical*

Refutations). But this turns out to be not at all an easy question to answer and the chief reason for this does not have to do with problems that we encounter in the interpretation of the *Topics* itself, though many of these problems are real enough. The main difficulty comes when we try to fit together what we find in the *Topics* with things that Aristotle says or implies about dialectic in other works. To grasp the main features of this problem we may begin by returning to the opening lines of the *Rhetoric*.

There as we have seen Aristotle tells us that the most widespread uses of dialectic are not based on the possession of any expert knowledge but rather on "things which it is common (*koina*), in a certain way, to absolutely everyone to know (*gnōrizein*)." This explains, he then goes on to say, why dialectic is in fact used with some success by everyone – either on an occasional random basis or in a regular way, due to practice and habit (*dia synētheian*). The first question to ask about this sort of characterization of dialectic, however, is whether Aristotle does indeed mean to describe the standard basis for dialectical argument of the most common sort as a type of knowledge. The verb that he uses here is *gnōrizein*, and this could mean, some might argue, not *to know* but only *to be familiar with*. In this case dialectic *need* not be based in its most common uses on what is genuinely *known*. To decide this matter we need to turn first to a passage in Aristotle's *Physics* I.2. There Aristotle is discussing and trying to refute the view of Parmenides that "*what exists* is one and unchanging." But, he says:

> To inquire whether *what exists* is one and unchanging is not an inquiry for physics. For just as there is no further proof for the geometer to give to someone who has rejected his principles, but this proof will proceed from some different type of knowledge, or from knowledge which is common in relation to all disciplines, so neither is there [a proof to use against one who denies principles] for anyone [whose subject is] governed by principles. (184b25ff)

Here, just as in the *Rhetoric*, Aristotle contrasts discussion and argument based on *expert* knowledge, and in particular on the known scientific principles of physics or geometry, with discussion and argument based on common (*koinē*) information (185a3). It is the latter, he says, that must be used to refute those who deny the *principles* of a given science, at least when this science is not subordinate to some higher science whose principles are not in dispute. And here the word that Aristotle uses to describe this common information is *epistēmē*, a word that he would not use for just any information that is commonly *familiar* but only for what is genuinely *known*.[1]

Still, some would argue that despite the similarity of the distinction here in *Physics* I.2 to Aristotle's distinction at the beginning of the *Rhetoric* they are not the same distinction, since the common *epistēmē* that Aristotle has in view in *Physics* I.2 is actually the science of metaphysics, not the common basis for dialectic that he has in view in the *Rhetoric*.[2] However, two later remarks in the *Physics* passage rule this interpretation out. First, Aristotle says that the procedure based on common *epistēmē* is just like the one to use, quite generally, in discussion with those who are maintaining any position for the sake of argument (*logou heneka*), and also in exposing any eristic arguments (185a5–8). This can hardly be the science of metaphysics. Eristic arguments, for instance, include fallacious arguments that beg the question or commit the fallacy of equivocation. It does not require mastery of the science of metaphysics to show that someone begs the question or is guilty of an equivocation. Aristotle also further suggests that this procedure, based on common *epistēmē*, is the one to use to refute Antiphon's attempt to square the circle but not the attempt that uses lunes or segments (185a14–17).

If we look now at a closely related passage in the *Sophistical Refutations* we can see clearly that the procedure that Aristotle has in view, the one that is to be used for exposing eristic arguments, and to refute Antiphon, is in fact dialectic. There Aristotle indicates that Antiphon's proof, like Bryson's, *is* an eristic argument, unlike the attempt to square the circle which uses lunes (11 172a2ff). The difference between the two, he says, is that the latter draws on the special principles of geometry while the procedure of Antiphon is based simply on what is common (*koinos*, 172a9). If we look further we can see that in Aristotle's view the procedure to use to expose a false argument based on what is common (*koina*) is simply dialectic (9 170a35–b5). So when Aristotle says in *Physics* I.2 that the procedure of arguing from common knowledge (*koinē epistēmē*) that is to be used to refute Parmenides is just like the procedure to be used in exposing any eristic argument, or Antiphon's argument, he must mean not that this always requires the use of the scientific principles or results of metaphysics but rather that this is the business of dialectic. This confirms, then, that Aristotle does genuinely mean in the *Rhetoric* to characterize the basis for dialectic, at least in the most widespread ordinary uses he mentions there, as common knowledge. He makes this claim again in *Sophistical Refutations* 11 where he says of the common things on which the most common uses of dialectic are based that ordinary people "know these things themselves no less than" the experts (172a22ff at a33).

The opening lines of the *Rhetoric* also give us some indication of how, according to Aristotle, we come to have this common knowledge so that we are able to use it in standard ordinary situations. In some cases, he says, this happens in a random or haphazard way, but ordinary people also acquire the settled ability (*hexis*) to operate from this common knowledge by habituation and practice (*dia synētheian*, 1354a6–11). As he goes on to indicate, the ability that Aristotle chiefly has in mind here in the *Rhetoric* is the ability to produce what he calls *pisteis*, or compelling rhetorical arguments (1354a11ff; cf. 1355a3ff). So, Aristotle is supposing, we have the capacity to build up simply by a process of habituation (*synētheia*) the settled ability to regularly produce credible arguments (*pisteis*) that typically convince people about various ordinary matters about which we wish to persuade them. The basis for this procedure is what Aristotle refers to as common knowledge.

Now, it seems reasonable enough for Aristotle to claim that people in general, to a significant degree, have the capacity to pick up by habituation an ability to produce compelling arguments on various ordinary matters of common concern. Without this, normal socialization would be impossible. What is less clear is how it is that Aristotle can claim that the standard basis for this is appropriately called common *knowledge*. The main problem here, of course, is that what counts as knowledge must be *true*. How can Aristotle claim that what people standardly find rhetorically most compelling in the most ordinary everyday situations is likely to be true? He directly addresses this question in a quite remarkable passage in *Rhetoric* I.1, where he says:

> To discern what is true and what is like to it is the function of the same capacity. At the same time, people are, sufficiently, naturally inclined toward the truth, and mainly reach the truth. Therefore, anyone who can proceed effectively on the basis of what is generally accredited (*ta endoxa*) does so equally on the basis of the truth. (1355a14–18)

Aristotle has it in mind here that rhetorically convincing arguments (*pisteis*) are based on what is *generally accredited* (*ta endoxa*) and thus are persuasive. So how do people acquire by habit the settled ability to hit on the *endoxa* or what is generally accredited? The remarkable answer that Aristotle gives is that people in general have a *natural* tendency to acquire *true* beliefs which is *sufficient* to guarantee that they mainly *do* acquire true beliefs. He must mean also, for his argument to work, that this natural tendency leads people in general to mainly acquire the *same* true beliefs, at least on the matters with which, as he has indicated, rhetoric and dialectic most commonly deal. (See 1155a24–9 with *Topics* I.2 101a31ff.) Due to this *natural* tendency and process the beliefs that are most *accredited* (most *endoxa*) and thus most *like to* the truth, that is, the beliefs to which people in general are in fact most attracted *as being true*, will largely *be true*.

So if we simply come to rely by habit on the beliefs that we most of all as a group *naturally* acquire and use, in trying to convince and persuade people in ordinary rhetorical or dialectical situations, as we can hardly avoid doing, then we will be rhetorically and dialectically quite successful, so Aristotle argues, and in addition we will normally be arguing from what is true. Given this, there is no major difficulty posed by Aristotle's assumption that the common information that people in general standardly find most compelling in the kinds of situations in which rhetoric and dialectic are most commonly used counts as knowledge, based on concerns about its truth. It seems clear, in addition, that what Aristotle is prepared to call knowledge, in these cases, is just *true* belief generated by a certain *natural* process that reliably leads to true belief. This knowledge, for Aristotle, is not tied to any intellectual virtue. On this point, moreover, his views clearly anticipate one main strand in contemporary epistemology according to which knowledge should be understood in just this way.

The main problem to further explore here is raised by a comparison between what Aristotle says about dialectic in the *Rhetoric* and also in the *Physics*, and what we find in the more official account of dialectical reasoning presented in the *Topics*. As we have already seen, in the *Rhetoric* Aristotle equates reasoning from *common knowledge*, in rhetoric or dialectic, with reasoning from certain *generally accredited beliefs* or *endoxa* (*Rhetoric* I.1 1355a18; cf. *Sophistical Refutations* 9 170a40). Aristotle explains in some detail what he means by the *endoxa* in *Topics* I.1 (100a30ff). According to his description, there are just five types of *endoxa*: the views of everyone, or of the preponderant majority, or of the recognized experts – either all the experts, or most, or the most famous.

But given this explicit account of the five types of beliefs that count as *endoxa* it is *very* difficult to see how dialectic, as reasoning from *endoxa*, can be identified with reasoning from common *knowledge*. To begin with, the *endoxa* as described in *Topics* I.1 obviously can conflict. The views of the many are often inconsistent with the views of the experts, and any views of the experts, especially those who are most famous, are almost always inconsistent with the views of other experts (see I.11). So the *endoxa*, as described here in *Topics* I.1, simply cannot be identified with the naturally generated *reliably true* information that Aristotle calls common knowledge and describes as the standard basis for the most ordinary uses of dialectic and rhetoric in the *Rhetoric*. In the *Rhetoric* itself, if we look closely, we find much the same difficulty. There Aristotle says, "None of the other arts deduces opposites, only rhetoric and dialectic do this" (I.1 1355a33–5). If one is normally able however, by dialectical argument, to deduce opposite conclusions, and thus inconsistent conclusions on a wide variety of matters, then the premises for dialectical argument, namely the *endoxa* – the generally accredited opinions – must themselves be massively inconsistent. But then they cannot all or mainly be true and they cannot then, as a body, count as common knowledge. Aristotle does say that it is naturally *easier* to deduce what is true by rhetorical argument than what is false (1355a21ff). But it is hard to see how this can be right in view of what he says in the *Topics*.

To try to deal with this problem it is useful to begin with some further reflections on the first chapter of the *Topics*, where Aristotle both characterizes dialectic as reasoning from *endoxa* and details for us which propositions or beliefs count as *endoxa*. Given the familiarity of this description of dialectic to us now it is easy for us to fail to realize how very unusual it is. The description of dialectic in *Topics* I.1 is *not* a standard traditional description of dialectic. Plato, for instance, talks a great deal about dialectic, in many of his dialogues, but he never describes it in this way, as reasoning from *endoxa*. He only even uses the word *endoxos* once, at *Sophist* 223b5, not in describing dialectic but in the standard sense of *esteemed* or *honored*. Plato himself describes dialectic simply as "the ability to ask and answer questions" – successfully, he must mean (*Cratylus* 390c). That is, on Plato's description dialectic is just skill in locating things that others will agree to on the basis of which you can refute or persuade them and on the basis of which you can yourself avoid refutation or persuasion by them. This, if anything, is the traditional description of dialectic. So Aristotle is introducing in the *Topics* a completely new way of describing a traditional practice and he is adopting for this purpose an ordinary term, *endoxos*, rarely used at all in previous philosophical writings, and giving it a rather precise characterization in his account in *Topics* I.1.

What then is it that leads him to do this? Our best clue here comes from the very last chapter of the *Topics* where Aristotle recalls the beginning of the opening chapter and the statement of his general purpose in the *Topics* which he had offered there (see 183a37–b1; cf. I.1 100a18ff). This passage confirms to us, first, that the codified account which Aristotle offers us in the *Topics* overall of the materials on which dialectic is properly based, and of how to properly use these materials, is, in all its details, his own discovery which, he says, it took a great deal of time for him to reach, by trial and error (183b34ff). He also indicates in this final chapter what criterion he was employing in judging the adequacy of his efforts along the way. Aristotle says that his general purpose was to describe that skill (*dynamis*) on the basis of which one can examine others and defend oneself in argument on any topic at all, on the basis of *endoxotata*, on the basis of the most widely accredited things that there are (183a37ff).

So this, it would seem, was in effect Aristotle's first thought in attempting to fill out Plato's formulaic description of dialectic as the ability to successfully ask and answer questions. Aristotle understands this ability, in the first instance, as the skill that enables one to find, as premises for argument, things that would be most of all generally regarded as worthy of credit or note (*endoxotata*). If one had such a skill then one could, as much as possible, successfully ask and answer questions on all subjects with all comers. This is how the term *endoxa* comes to be used in Aristotle's account.

The next question to ask would naturally be this: How can one *systematically* describe the materials available to anyone who has this skill so that one could learn this skill as an *art*, and not simply rely on accumulated habit for success? Our best indication of Aristotle's general approach here comes again from the opening chapter of the *Rhetoric* where he indicates his interest in providing an art, or a *systematic* account of how it is that people in fact come to be successful – by habit for instance without art – in the practice of both dialectic and rhetoric (1354a7ff). The *Rhetoric* provides us with Aristotle's results on this score in rhetoric, and the *Topics*, it seems clear, gives us Aristotle's results for dialectic. In view of this, then, what Aristotle is in effect saying in the opening chapter of the *Topics* is this: The way people are able to ask and answer questions successfully on all matters with all comers or, in other words, the way that they are able to reason in all situations from what is as accredited as possible (from *endoxotata*) is by possessing the ability to reason from the specific types of beliefs that he calls *endoxa* – that is, either the views of everyone, or of most people, or of the experts. Successful dialecticians, from habit for instance, need not introduce the premises of their arguments *as* the views of the many or the experts. They may not even be aware that their premises have this standing. But the reason that their habitual practice is successful, Aristotle is claiming, is that their premises are views of these types. So Aristotle's account of dialectic in *Topics* I.1 is his first attempt at describing not how people intentionally have proceeded in successful dialectical practice but how they in fact have proceeded when they were successful, whether they were aware of it or not.

If this is Aristotle's approach, however, then it is right away subject to question. The *endoxa* include the views of famous sages. The views of famous sages, or reputedly wise men, include the view of Zeno that motion is impossible. But, to take an example from *Sophistical Refutations* 11, if one attempted to dialectically refute someone's claim that taking walks after dinner is good for one's health, by trying to get that person to concede as a premise Zeno's view that motion is impossible, one would not be likely to achieve much success. That is, it is not at all plausible that just any view that Aristotle would list among the *endoxa*, as described in *Topics* I.1, will regularly serve as the basis for successful ordinary dialectical argument or refutation.

But, it is also not clear that Aristotle means to suggest even in *Topics* I.1 that it will. At the end of that chapter he clearly warns us that he has only offered there a rough sketch (*hos typo*) of dialectical reasoning, not an exact account (101a18ff). In fact, moreover, we find a much more precise account later, starting in I.10, where Aristotle tells us more specifically what counts as a proper dialectical premise (*protasis*).

We can see from this later discussion that not just any *endoxon*, as specified in *Topics* I.1, counts as a proper dialectical premise. The beliefs of the experts that are *paradoxical*, for instance, do not count as dialectical premises, Aristotle says. The reason for this, he indicates, is just that they would not be readily granted in discussion in the way the nonparadoxical beliefs of the experts would be (104a8–12). This shows us one way in which the specification of the proper basis for dialectical argument in *Topics* I.1, simply as the *endoxa* as listed there, was indeed only rough and sketchy. Aristotle does not say precisely what he means by a para-doxical belief. One example, clearly, is a view of the wise that is opposed to the views of the many (104a12). This would, of course, rule out Zeno's doctrine as a proper dialectical premise. But it is evident from a later passage in I.11, where he discusses what he calls a *thesis*, that the class of excluded paradoxical *endoxa* is wider than this (104b29–35). It is clear from this passage that anything that Aristotle calls a *thesis* is for him a paradoxical belief. And this includes not only the beliefs of the wise that conflict with common opinion but also any view of the wise that conflicts with other views of the wise.

Here, then, Aristotle seems to be wanting to collect together, as proper dialectical premises, a *consistent subset of* the *endoxa*, as described in *Topics* I.1, with preference given in case of conflict to the most widely accredited.[3] His thought then is, quite reasonably, that this consistent subset will constitute the set of premises that are most likely to be effective in dialectic since these things are either generally accepted, or they are recommended without significant dissent by those who have the stand-ing of sages or experts and, as Aristotle says at 104a11: "one would accept the view of the wise if it is not opposed to the view of the many."

It seems, further, from the *Rhetoric* again, that Aristotle regards material of this type as very likely indeed to be true. There Aristotle says that the reason why rhetoric is valuable is *because* what is true is naturally stronger – in its persuasive force he means – than what is false (I.1 1355a21ff). That is, when we locate the "common things" that do have the most common credit or persuasive appeal, in rhetoric or dialectic, they are very likely indeed to be true.[4] It is also important to notice that we can see, further, from the more precise discussion in *Topics* I.10 that anything else that has a *similar* common appeal to the actual *endoxa* will be treated by Aristotle in the same way (104a12ff). This passage is of special importance because it shows us that there are proper dialectical premises for Aristotle which do not belong to *any* of the original classes of *endoxa* listed in *Topics* I.1. What is important for such a dialectical premise, Aristotle says, is that it be appropriately "similar to" those *endoxa* or at least, we should no doubt say, to the nonparadoxical ones. If it is it will have the same common appeal and we can locate such items by seeing what is "similar to" the nonparadoxical *endoxa* in ways that Aristotle lists (*Topics* I.10 104a5ff).

What is most important in Aristotle's account in the *Rhetoric*, however, is that for the items that have this common appeal there is a *natural* guarantee of truth. That is, Aristotle is not taking what some would now call an *internal realist* position. He is not supposing that the fact that some belief comes to be a part of our collective understanding *makes it true* or is constitutive of its truth. Rather he believes that we are *naturally set up* so that it comes about that our items of most common agreement on ordinary matters are true, or sufficiently so. We have, as it were, a *gene* for truth on the matters which are most effective for us in our most ordinary uses of dialectic and rhetoric. Given this, it is not at all unintelligible, or indefensible, that Aristotle should think of these items as matters of common *knowledge*. So what distinguishes skill in dialectic from the intellectual virtues is that dialectic is standardly based in its most common successful uses on this common knowledge. Aristotle's discovery of this does not diminish his interest in the intellectual virtues. Our development of these for him is still the realization of our highest natural capacities. But though our capacities for these virtues are natural, their realization, Aristotle tells us in the *Ethics*, does not come to us by nature (II.1 1103a 14ff). This sharply differentiates them from our common knowledge which does so accrue. This crucial but often ignored divide is central to Aristotle's epistemology.

Notes

1. At 185a3 the understood noun with *common – koinē*, in the feminine – clearly must be *epistēmē*.
2. The subsequent discussion in *Physics* I.2 might be held to support this since Aristotle seems to go on there, at 185b20ff, to make use of aspects of his metaphysical doctrine of categories in refuting Parmenides.
3. Notice also that he substitutes here in characterizing a dialectical premise, no doubt in the interest of greater precision, the weaker term *endoxos* – accredited, for *dokounta* – accepted, which he used for this purpose in *Topics* I.1. Cf. 104a8–11 with 100b21–3. To say, for instance, that some view is *endoxos* for all of the wise is to say in effect that it is taken very seriously by all the wise, but not that it is necessarily accepted by all of them.
4. We can see from a comparison with the passage in *Topics* I.2 to which Aristotle refers here that by "common things" he means "the opinions of the many" (101a30–4). These things are the basis for the most common uses of dialectic, which we have been considering here. In the other uses of dialectic discussed in I.2, the basis can be different.

References and Recommended Reading

Barnes, J., "An Aristotelian Way with Skepticism," in *Aristotle Today*, ed. M. Matthen (Edmonton, 1987).

Bolton, R., "Scepticism et véracité de la perception dans le *De Anima* et la *Métaphysique* d'Aristote," in *Corps et Ame: Sur le De Anima d'Aristote*, ed. G. Romeyer-Dherbey (Paris, 1996).

——, "The Epistemological Basis of Aristotelian Dialectic," rev. ed., in *From Puzzles to Principles: Essays on Aristotle's Dialectic*, ed. M. Sim (Lanham, Md., 1999).

Irwin, T., Aristotle's Discovery of Metaphysics," *Review of Metaphysics*, 1977–8.

Smith, R., "Aristotle on the Uses of Dialectic," *Synthese* 1993.

Taylor, C., "Aristotle's Epistemology," in *Companions to Ancient Thought*. Vol. 1: *Epistemology*, ed. S. Everson (Cambridge, 1990).

Chapter 9

Aristotle: Metaphysics

Michael Loux

Introduction

The treatise known as the *Metaphysics* provides the focus for any attempt to characterize Aristotle's views on what we call metaphysical issues; but it is not the only text where Aristotle deals with such issues. Two other treatises stand out here – the *Categories* and *Physics* I. Both are presumably earlier than the *Metaphysics*, and both provide background requisite for understanding the later treatise. In the *Categories*, Aristotle is concerned to identify the primary substances. These are the ontologically basic items, the things such that they do not depend on anything else for their existence, but everything else depends on one or more of them for its existence. What Aristotle tells us is that the primary substances are the ultimate subjects of predication; that is, the things that are subjects of predication, but not themselves predicated of anything else; and he identifies these ultimate subjects with familiar concrete particulars like "a certain man" and "a certain horse" (2ᵃ11–13).

Now, Aristotle's primary substances are things that come to be; and in the philosophical context in which Aristotle operated, the claim that anything could come to be was suspect. It was thought that coming to be would constitute a radical and mysterious form of emergence unrooted in anything that precedes. The idea is that if something were to come to be, there would be some completely novel entity just "popping" into existence *ex nihilo*. Since this was thought to be impossible, coming to be along with the things that come to be was consigned to the realm of mere appearance. Primary substances, by contrast, are the full-blooded realities. Accordingly, if Aristotle is to vindicate the *Categories* account of substance, he must take the mystery out of coming to be. It is in *Physics* I where he attempts to do this.

Aristotle begins by examining a sample case of coming to be, the case where the product of the change is a musical man. He denies that this case involves any kind of radical emergence *ex nihilo*. Instead, he tells us, for the musical man to come to be is for some antecedently existing thing – the man – to come to be musical. So the apparently problematic

(1)   The musical man comes to be

is to be analyzed by way of the benign

(2)   The man comes to be musical.

The suggestion, then, is that the coming to be of the musical man is to be under-stood as the coming to obtain of a predication whose subject is some antecedently existing thing (190^{b}20–3), and what Aristotle wants to claim is that an analogous account is possible for the case where what comes to be is one of Aristotle's primary substances – a thing like "a certain man" or "a certain horse" (190^{b}1–2).

The paradigm of an Aristotelian substance is a living being. Accordingly, Aristotle looks to the case where we have the generation of an individual plant or animal; and he tells us that such generation always originates in a seed and that there is a mater-ial continuity between the seed and the organism that develops out of it (190^{b}3–4). But, then, what happens in the case where a living being comes to be is that some antecedently existing stuff comes to exhibit a new structure and functional organ-ization, so that the coming to be of a primary substance is a perfectly intelligible form of transformation rather than a radical emergence *ex nihilo*. What happens is simply that some antecedently existing stuff has some new feature or attribute predicated of it; and Aristotle pins labels on the antecedently existing stuff and what gets predicated of it as a result of the change, calling the former *matter* and the latter *form*.

So matter and form are the principles of the coming to be of a primary substance; but Aristotle insists that they are as well the principles of the being of a primary substance once it has come to be (190^{b}17–18). The idea here is straightforward. If what is involved in the coming to be of a primary substance is the coming to obtain of a certain predication, then it is perfectly natural to suppose that what is involved in the continued existence of that substance once it has come to be is simply the continued obtaining of that same predication. The upshot is that the familiar par-ticulars the *Categories* takes to be the primary substances are things with an internal predicative structure. They are matter–form composites. The existence of a primary substance of this or that kind is grounded in a predication, a predication whose subject is the matter constitutive of the substance and whose predicated entity is the structure and functional organization characteristic of substances of that kind. And this picture provides the backdrop for what occurs in the *Metaphysics*.

Aristotle's Treatise the *Metaphysics*

What is supposed to tie the fourteen books of the *Metaphysics* together is the conception of a single discipline. We use the title of the text as the label for the discipline. That term, however, is not Aristotle's, but the creation of later thinkers. He used a variety of labels to pick out the discipline: "wisdom," "theology," "the

science of truth," "first philosophy," and just "philosophy." This discipline is supposed to be the most honorable or noble of disciplines, and the fourteen books
are all supposed to be exercises in the discipline. Nonetheless, they appear to be
something of a hotchpotch. The first six books have an introductory cast: they seek
to identify the subject matter for the discipline, to characterize its methodology, to
identify the problems it must resolve, and to provide us with a vocabulary for
research in the discipline; but these books do not proceed consecutively. They
appear to have been composed independently; they make little reference to each
other; and their positive contributions can seem flatly inconsistent. The remaining
eight books are more substantive, but arguably even less unified than the first six.
Books VII and VIII provide an account of the ontological structure of material
substances; Book IX focuses on the notions of potentiality and actuality; Book X
turns to the notion of unity; and Book XI is itself just a compilation and abbreviation of other texts from the *Metaphysics* and the *Physics*. Book XII takes the Prime
Mover or God as its target; and the last two books deal with topics in the philosophy of mathematics.

Now, it may turn out that there is more unity to the *Metaphysics* than initial
appearances suggest, but not even the most enthusiastic defenders of a unitarian
approach to the text would want to claim that the *Metaphysics* presents us with a
single line of argument with a clearly identifiable beginning, middle, and end. In
discussing the overall shape of the text, we have little option but to approach the
Metaphysics topically; and that is how I will proceed. I will deal with three sets of
issues. In this section, I will address topics from the first six books focusing on the
subject matter and methodology of what Aristotle calls first philosophy. In the
following three sections, I will discuss the theory of material substance developed in
what are often called the middle books, Books VII and VIII. Finally, in the last
three sections, I will examine Aristotle's views on immaterial or separated substance.
Here, I will make a few comments on Aristotle's views about the subject matter of
mathematics, but the focus will be Book XII's theology.

One aim of the first six books of the *Metaphysics* is the identification of the subject
matter for the discipline the treatise is supposed to instantiate. Unfortunately, the
books provide what look like two incompatible accounts of that subject matter. If
we take "first philosophy" to be a neutral label for the discipline, then we can say
that in Book I Aristotle introduces us to first philosophy under the title "wisdom."
We are told that whereas the familiar sciences all seek to identify causes and principles, wisdom is the knowledge of first causes and first principles ($981^{b}29$); and
Aristotle goes on to tell us that wisdom is a "divine knowledge" since, first, God will
most of all have it and, second, "God is thought to be among the causes of all things
and to be a first principle" ($983^{a}8$–10). In Book VI, the idea that first philosophy is
a "divine knowledge" gets reaffirmed. There, Aristotle calls first philosophy "theology"; and after telling us that the proper object for theological investigation is what
exists separately and is unchangeable, he remarks that "if the divine is present
anywhere, it is present in things of this sort" ($1026^{a}19$–20).

Aristotle's wisdom or theology, then, seems to be what is called a special or departmental discipline. It seems to mark off a particular genus or kind – unchangeable

substance – and to investigate that. The difficulty is that in other places Aristotle describes first philosophy in what appear to be quite different terms. Thus, at the beginning of *Metaphysics* IV, Aristotle tells us that first philosophy "investigates being qua being and the attributes which belong to it in virtue of its own nature" (1003^{a}21), and he goes on to deny that it is any of the departmental disciplines (1003^{a}23–5). On the contrary, it has universal scope; its subject matter spans the subjects of the various special sciences. It investigates everything that there is, and it does so from the most general perspective: it investigates the things that are precisely insofar as they are things that are. Now the concept of being can seem to be a rather thin notion; and that might suggest that there's not much for a discipline investigating being as being to tell us. Towards countering this suggestion, Aristotle reminds us of the distinctions marked by the categories (substance, quantity, quality, relation, etc.). Those distinctions, he tells us, represent a division of being itself. Accordingly, the categorial distinctions will fall under the purview of this universal discipline (1003^{b}20–2 and 1026^{a}35–6). The same is true of the contrast between actuality and potentiality (1026^{b}1–2). But the focus on being does not exhaust the discipline. As Aristotle sees it, a discipline that seeks to understand being will deal as well with any concept necessarily coextensive with being. Unity is such a concept, so it too provides material for this discipline; and like being, it takes different categorial forms – unity in substance or sameness, unity in quality or similarity, unity in quantity or equality – so these notions too will fall under the science that studies being (1003^{b}33–5). And since one and the same science studies opposites, this science will deal with notions like nonbeing, plurality, difference, dissimilarity, and inequality (1004^{a}9 ff.). Finally, it will deal with any principles that hold true of things just in virtue of their being beings (1005^{a}20–4). Since the most general principles underlying all demonstration (for example, the principle of noncontradiction – the principle that "the same attribute cannot at the same time belong and not belong to the same subject in the same respect" (1005^{b}18–20)) are such principles; it is the role of this discipline to inquire into them.

So we have two different characterizations of first philosophy. Aristotle seems to be saying that it is both a departmental discipline concerned with first causes or unchangeable substance and a universal discipline concerned with everything that there is. It is difficult to see how the two characterizations can be anything but flatly incompatible. One and the same discipline cannot be both a departmental/special discipline and an inquiry into everything. A departmental discipline considers only a proper subset of the things that are, so it cannot be identified with a discipline that inquires into the nature of all the things there are. The apparent inconsistency demands explanation. Providing that explanation is one of the most ancient problems in the interpretation of Aristotle. A popular strategy here is to explain the incompatibility in developmental terms: the two characterizations are supposed to represent two different stages in Aristotle's philosophical career. This strategy has been especially popular in the twentieth century. Often, the proposed stages get characterized in terms of what are alleged to be Aristotle's changing reactions to Plato. The details here vary, but we are typically told that the conception of first philosophy as wisdom or theology represents an earlier conception of the most honorable discipline, a conception that ultimately gets displaced by the more mature idea of a universal discipline. Frequently, this story gets extended beyond the first six books to the rest of the *Metaphysics* in the form of a "patchwork" theory. The claim is that so far from being a unified treatise, the *Metaphysics* is a collection of independently composed and doctrinally inconsistent texts from different periods in Aristotle's career. Corresponding to the idea of wisdom or theology is Book XII's picture of a transcendent God in the person of the Prime Mover; whereas, corresponding to the idea of a universal science is the text encompassing Books VII and VIII, where we meet a straightforwardly naturalistic ontology including only material substances.[1]

As I have said, virtually no one would want to claim that the *Metaphysics* is a text that runs smoothly and without interruption from Book I to Book XIV pursuing along the way a single train of argument. But conceding that the composition of the *Metaphysics* involved compilation hardly commits one to the view that the core texts making up the "book" embody flatly inconsistent metaphysical doctrines. Indeed, even a quick reading of the middle books and Book XII suggests a picture quite different from that developed by "patchwork" theorists. In Books VII and VIII, we find Aristotle repeatedly telling us that our discussion of sensible, material substance is meant to prepare us for the investigation of nonsensible, immaterial substance (see 1029^{a}34–1029^{b}13 and 1041^{a}6–9), and the Aristotle of Book XII develops his account of the Prime Mover only after spending five chapters reviewing the main themes of Books VII and VIII, the implication being that the doctrine of the Prime Mover is intelligible only against the background of the theory of material substance developed in Books VII and VIII.

The fact that Aristotle himself seems to think that the metaphysical pictures expressed in the two contexts constitute a consistent whole suggests that we should look more closely at his accounts of the nature of first philosophy. When we do, we find that the apparent tension between the idea of a science of first causes and the idea of a science which investigates being as being disappears. When Aristotle first presents us with the idea of a body of knowledge that focuses on first causes and first principles, he tells us that the body of knowledge will have a universal dimension (982^{a}21–3). In grasping what is primary, he suggests, we will have an implicit handle on all the items to which it is prior. Furthermore, it becomes clear as we move beyond Book I that the science that investigates the divine also deals with the propositions that constitute the first principles of the sciences (996^{b}26–997^{a}14); but these just are the propositions that hold true of beings insofar as they are beings. Hence, they fall under the purview of a universal discipline. And when Aristotle tells us that there is a science that "investigates being as being," he tells us that this discipline is the target of anyone concerned to identify first causes and first principles (1003^{a}26–32). The idea is that our interest in first causes/principles is an interest in the causes/principles in virtue of which things are beings. What makes a cause primary, presumably, is that it is a cause responsible for that feature of things that is prior to every other feature they exhibit – their being or their existing. This idea gets repeated at the beginning of Book VI (1025^{b}1 ff.); and, then, Aristotle concludes his discussion of the subject matter of first philosophy by telling us that theology, the science concerned with unchangeable, separable substance, is universal precisely because it is primary (1026ª23–32). So the two characterizations look like characterizations of a single discipline. The universal science will study everything – God included; and the discipline that identifies and characterizes the Prime Mover cannot be a merely departmental discipline. It has to be a discipline that is concerned with being qua being; for what it does is identify the cause or principle on which the being of everything else depends.

Substance and the Science of Being

When Aristotle introduces us to the science that studies being as being, he implicitly concedes that the idea of a universal discipline of this sort can appear problematic. The difficulty is that being is not a genus. There is no single kind encompassing all the things there are. The highest kinds are the categories, and the term "being" is equivocal over the categories. Substances, qualities, quantities, and so on are, in turn, each said to be in a unique and distinct sense of the term. But, then, the suggestion that all the things that are said to be beings constitute the subject matter for a single science seems bizarre. It is as though one were to insist that there is a single science whose subject matter is whatever is picked out by the word "bank" – a science whose inquiry spans the geology of river edges and the economics of financial institutions concerned with borrowing and lending money.

Aristotle's reaction to this problem is to argue that while "being" is not univocal, it has a special kind of equivocity, one that is compatible with there being a single science of being (1003ª32–1003ᵇ18).[2] Although "being" is equivocal, its different senses are not like those of the word "bank" – totally unrelated to each other. "Being" exhibits what Aristotle calls *pros hen* equivocity or focal meaning. One of its senses is primary and its other senses get explained by reference to that primary sense. Aristotle's stock example of a *pros hen* term is "healthy." While "healthy" has a variety of different meanings, the sense of "healthy" in which it picks out the metabolically sound organism is the core or primary meaning of the term. It provides the focus for the other, secondary meanings. Thus, some things (e.g., a certain complexion or a certain red blood count) are said to be healthy because they are signs or symptoms of what is healthy in the core sense; other things (a certain diet or a certain kind of vitamin) are said to be healthy because they are productive of what is healthy in the core sense. In the same way, the term "being" has a primary sense – that in which it picks out substances. Everything else is called a being by reference to the being of substance. Thus, some things are said to be beings because they qualify what is a being in the primary sense; other things, because they are quantitative determinations of what is a being in the core sense; still others, because they are actions of what is a being in the focal sense.

So "being" like "healthy" has *pros hen* equivocity; but, Aristotle tells us, the case of "healthy" shows that there can be a single discipline concerned with all the things picked out by a *pros hen* term (1003ᵇ11–13). There is, after all, a single science dealing with all the things that are said to be healthy – the science of medicine or, perhaps, physiotherapy; and Aristotle thinks that what the example of that discipline shows us is that where a single discipline takes everything in the extension of a *pros hen* term as its subject, it makes the items picked out by the term in its primary use the focus of its investigation. Thus, while physiotherapy deals in complexions, diets, vitamins and the like, the primary concern of the discipline is the metabolically sound organism. It deals with the other things called healthy only insofar as they are related to the focus of the discipline. But, then, there can be a single discipline concerned to investigate all the things that are; and while the discipline will deal with everything, it will have a focus-substance; and it will consider other things only insofar as they stand in some ontological relation to substance.

So we get the result that the science that investigates being is the science of substance; and Aristotle tells us that what follows is that the perennial metaphysical question "What is being?" turns out to be the question "What is substance?" (1028^{b}2–4). Substances, we have seen, are the ontologically basic things. To attempt to answer the question "What is substance?" we have said, is to attempt to identify the things that do not depend on other things for their existence, but are such that everything else depends on one or more of them for its existence; and as we have seen, that project is one that occupied the Aristotle of the early treatise, the *Categories*. When, in Book VII, he turns to the question "What is substance?" Aristotle begins by examining the answer he gave to that question in the early treatise. The *Categories*, recall, tells us that the primary substances are those things that, while not predicated of anything else, are the subjects of which everything else is predicated. *Physics* I, however, tells us that since they are things that come to be, the familiar particulars of the *Categories* have an internal structure: they are matter–form composites, where the relationship between matter and form is that of subject and what gets predicated of it.

The Aristotle of *Metaphysics* VII.3 argues that in light of these facts, the *Categories* criterion for substantiality fails to do what it was intended to do: to identify familiar particulars like "a certain man" as the primary substances. Given that those particulars are matter–form composites, what turns out to be the ultimate subject of predication is a matter that "in itself is neither a particular thing nor of a certain quantity nor assigned to any other of the categories by which being is determined" (1029^{a}20–1). Aristotle thinks that we will agree that anything meeting that austere characterization is a woefully inadequate candidate for status as substance; and, consequently, he believes we will join him in rejecting the *Categories* account of substance.

If we endorse the picture underlying the subject criterion of substantiality, we will think that what gets presented to us in experience is a kind of complex that includes a whole host of predicated features. On this view, the strategy for isolating substance is to engage in an abstraction in which we "strip away" (1029^{a}11) from the complex anything that can be construed as something predicated of something else. What survives the abstraction, presumably, will be the "something else" of which all the features are predicated and, hence, by the early theory, an instance of primary substance. So we take the sort of thing we meet in our everyday encounters with the world – something like that pale, 6 foot, 200 pound offspring of Diares; and we "think away" the qualitative features, the quantitative determinations, the relational properties, and so on. According to the author of the *Categories*, what remains is "a certain man"; a thing like that, he wants to say, is ontologically basic.

But is that right? It is true that the man provides a subject for the predication of all the accidents associated with him; but the man himself has a structure involving an ontologically more basic subject of predication. He is a thing that comes to be, so he is a matter–form composite; and his matter provides a subject for the predicated form. By the subject criterion, then, the matter constitutive of the man has a better claim than the man to status as substance. But, by that same criterion, there is something with a still better claim to that status. The matter constitutive of our man is, let us suppose, something like flesh and bones; but flesh and bones are themselves things that come to be, so they too must have a matter–form structure. Accordingly, we have some still more fundamental subjects of predication; and assuming the generability of those subjects, we are led on to even more basic subjects of predication. According to the chemical theory Aristotle borrows from Empedocles, this process of analysis continues until we reach the four elements (fire, earth, air, water). They are supposed to be the qualitatively most fundamental stuffs; but Aristotle takes it to be an empirical fact that they can be transformed into each other (see *De Generatione et Corruptione* II.1, 329^{a}24–329^{b}3). So they too have a matter (it is called "prime matter"); but it appears at a level below that at which even the most primitive qualitative characterizations apply, so it is the sort of thing that conforms to Aristotle's austere characterization of the ultimate or final subject of predication;[3] and what the Aristotle of VII.3 is telling us is that anyone who endorses the *Categories* criterion for substantiality is committed to making this matter substance.

But Aristotle takes this result to constitute a reductio of the subject criterion. He tells us that a constraint on our notion of substance is that what is ontologically primary must be a "this something" and separable (1029^{a}27–8). These are not easy notions, but we can understand Aristotle's appeal to them as a gesture towards the notion of essence. The claim is that a substance is something with an essence. To say that a thing is a "this something" is to say that *what* it is is something like "this man" or "this horse" – something involving a determinate conceptual content that can be isolated and articulated ("separated") in a definition. And obviously a matter that falls under no category lacks that kind of conceptual content.

There is, then, a conflict between the subject criterion for substantiality and an essentialist interpretation of substance. Accordingly, if the critique of the early theory of substance is to be decisive, we need a clearcut formulation and defense of substance essentialism. We get these things in VII.6, where Aristotle argues for a very strong thesis about the connection between substance and essence (1032^{a}5–6). What he tells us is that each primary substance is necessarily identical with its essence. So the primary substances do not have essences; they *are* essences – their own essences; and Aristotle defends this thesis (we can call it the VII.6 Identity Thesis) not by reference to premises idiosyncratic to his own metaphysical theory. He argues that it is a constraint on any metaphysical theory – any attempt to identify the primary substances. To identify the primary substances, we have said, is to identify the ontologically basic things – those things that are prior to everything else. However, were it to be the case that a thing and its essence are always distinct and separate, then the attempt to identify the primary substances would be doomed from the start. Any entity one might want to select as ontologically primary would fail to have that status. Something else – its essence – would have a better claim to the status. After all, the essence of a thing is prior to that thing: it makes the thing be what it is. But given the separation of thing and essence, our new candidate for status as primary substance would likewise fail to be ontologically basic; for its essence would be prior to it. If thing and essence are always distinct, the primary substances would be forever elusive, and the central project of metaphysics – that of identifying primary substance – would be impossible. That project requires that there be things – the ontologically basic things – that just are their own essences. It requires that the VII.6 Identity Thesis be true.[4]

Substance as Form

We have seen that one implication of VII.3's critique of the subject criterion is that the search after substance cannot terminate in matter. A consequence of the VII.6 Identity Thesis is that no concrete particular like the man or the horse of the *Categories* can be a primary substance. The Identity Thesis tells us that each primary substance is identical with its essence; but all the familiar particulars of a single kind or species exhibit the same essence. Accordingly, the claim that things like Plato and Socrates are ontologically basic commits us to holding that they are numerically identical with each other. More generally, the supposition that familiar particulars are primary substances yields the result that there is just one member of each species – a clearly unsatisfactory consequence. But if VII.3 excludes matter from the inventory of primary substances and VII.6 entails that no composite particulars are primary substances, the only things remaining as possible candidates for status as primary substances are the substantial forms of concrete particulars. And the fact is that from the early chapters of VII, Aristotle makes little secret of the privileged role that form will play in the theory of the middle books. It is not, however, until very late in VII and in VIII that we find Aristotle providing a formal statement and defense of the thesis that form is primary substance.

As he formulates the thesis, Aristotle uses the term "substance" in a special sense. In this sense, it functions as an abstract singular term, and its characteristic use is in the context "the substance of x." So the idea is that certain things have something else as their substance. Which things? In the middle books, Aristotle is interested in identifying the substance of the familiar particulars of the *Categories* – things, again, like "a certain man" and "a certain horse"; and the attempt to identify their substance is part of an explanatory project. As Aristotle tells us, the substance of a familiar particular is that constituent of the particular that is "the cause of its being" (1017^b14–15); and in attempting to clarify what the search for such a thing consists in, Aristotle explicitly denies that the attempt to identity the substance of a thing, x, is the attempt to explain the truth of the bald existential claim "x exists" or the trivial identity claim "x is identical with x." It is rather the attempt to explain why some predication obtains (1041^a11-17). Which predication? The predication that marks out x as *what* it is or as the kind of thing it is (1041^b5-6). So what we seek to explain when we try to identify the substance of a familiar particular is a kind-predication like

Socrates is a human being

or

Secretariat is a horse;

and our explanation is to take a special form; we are to explain the kind-predication by reference to constituents of our chosen familiar particular. In our discussion of VII.3, however, we have seen that what grounds the fact that an ordinary particular belongs to the kind it does is the fact that the substantial form associated with the kind is predicated of the matter constitutive of our chosen particular. So it is because the appropriate form-predication obtains that the relevant kind-predication obtains. And Aristotle tells us just that in VIII.2:

> For example, if it is a threshold that is to be defined, then we should say, "Wood and stones lying in this way"; and if it is a house, we should say "Bricks and boards lying in this way"; and if it is ice, "Water frozen or solidified in this way . . ." (1043^a7-11)

The predication that does the explaining in each of these cases involves both matter and form; and both can be construed as constituents of the thing whose "being" we seek to explain. Accordingly, both its matter and its form should count as the substance of a familiar particular. And Aristotle concedes as much (1042^a26-8). Nonetheless, it is the thesis that substantial form is the substance of a thing that is the centerpiece of VII and VIII. It is not difficult to see why Aristotle construes form as preeminent here. What leads us on the search after the substance of a familiar particular is the fact that it fails to be what Aristotle calls a *kath hauto legomenon* – something "said to be what it is in its own right." Its being what it is depends on something ontologically more fundamental than it – the form-predication in question. But the matter constitutive of a familiar particular is no more a *kath hauto legomenon* than the particular itself. As we saw in our discussion of VII.3, the matter making up an ordinary individual has an internal structure of its own; and its being what it is gets explained by reference to that structure. It is, recall, because some lower level stuff has a form predicated of it that the matter constitutive of a human being is what it is – flesh or bones, say; and the analysis continues until we reach the matter for the four elements, what we called prime matter. That matter has no constituents on which it depends; but it has no *what* or essence either. There is no saying what it is; it is no *legomenon* at all, so it too fails to be a *kath hauto legomenon*.

But being a *kath hauto legomenon* is a requirement on anything that is to play the role of primary substance. Nothing can be a primary substance if it depends on something else for its "being," that is, for its being what it is or for its having the essence it does. But while he denies that anything that plays the role of matter satisfies this condition, Aristotle thinks that all substantial forms satisfy it. As he sees it, there is nothing external to a form that serves to explain why it is what it is; and he denies that substantial forms have any internal structure involving distinct entities standing in any kind of ontological relation. He has nothing like transcendental arguments for these claims; but he thinks that the central reason for attributing an internal structure to particulars and their matter does not apply here. It is because a thing can come to be and pass away that we take it to have a matter–form structure; but Aristotle insists on the ingenerability and incorruptibility of substantial form (1033^b5–9); and he thinks that an examination of the procedures for defining forms confirms the absence of internal structure here (see *Metaphysics* VII.10). Substantial forms are unanalyzable simples.

So substantial forms are *kath hauta legomena* – things whose "being" depends on nothing else; but the "being" of everything else depends on the predication of substantial form. Accordingly, substantial forms are the primary substances; and no sooner has Aristotle issued the formal statement of this thesis than he points out that the VII.6 Identity Thesis holds for substantial form (1043^b1). Each form just is its essence: the form is identical with what the form is.[5]

Substantial Unity: Matter and Form

Although the claim that form is primary substance may be the pivotal thesis of the middle books, its statement does not provide us with the culmination of Books VII and VIII. Indeed, its formulation only serves to give rise to what is the central problem occupying Aristotle in the middle books. What concerns Aristotle is the fact that in attributing this privileged status to substantial form, we seem to be undermining the core intuitions motivating the metaphysical theory of the *Categories*. There is a good bit of technical machinery at work in the early treatise, but that machinery is presented in the service of an intuition that is anything but technical; for what motivates Aristotle in the *Categories* is simply the belief that, despite the claims of his predecessors to the contrary, the familiar individuals of commonsense (in particular, individual living beings) are fully real; and that belief gets expressed in the thesis that things like "a certain man" and "a certain horse" are the primary substances, the paradigmatic instances of things that are. In arguing that the matter and form constitutive of familiar particulars are prior to those particulars and in claiming that forms are the primary substances, however, the Aristotle of VII and VIII seems to be rejecting the core intuition at work in the *Categories*. He seems to be saying that the familiar particulars of commonsense are just assemblages or heaps of ontologically more basic entities; and he appears to be telling us that, in the final analysis, the only thing that is genuinely real is substantial form. We have, then, what looks like a conflict between the ontological theory of the middle books and the commonsense conception of the world defended in the *Categories*. Books VII and VIII appear to be defending a reductionism about familiar particulars of precisely the sort that the Aristotle of the *Categories* sought to combat.

Now, some philosophers would not be concerned by the kind of conflict we appear to have here. They would not find a conflict between our metaphysical theory and our commonsense conception of the world problematic. But Aristotle is not one of these philosophers. He believes that there must be harmony between our philosophical theories and those prephilosophical beliefs we find irresistible (see 211^a6-11 and 1145^b1-7). And, surely, the belief that things like cats, dogs, and human beings are fully real is irresistible. Indeed, *we* can make no sense of *our* denying the claim that *we* are real.

So for Aristotle at least, the possibility of a tension here is a serious problem; and a central aim of the middle books is to show that the tension is not real. Throughout VII and VIII, Aristotle is at pains to show that we can endorse the claim that form is primary substance while continuing to hold on to the beliefs motivating the *Categories*. Thus, he assures us that despite the privileged status of substantial form, ordinary objects continue to be substances – real things; and he denies that this is a matter of mere stipulation (1042^a24-32). Familiar particulars are, after all, things that are paradigmatically instances of the "this something" formula: each is a particular human being, a particular horse, or a particular oak tree. Furthermore, concrete particulars satisfy the other condition VII.3 associated with substance: they are separable. Here, Aristotle insists on two different notions of separability. There is what he calls separability in formula and unqualified separability. To have the former is to have an essence that can be defined independently of a reference to anything else; whereas the latter is separability in existence or existential autonomy. And while only substantial forms have separability in formula, only familiar particulars have unqualified separability. They are things that come into existence at a time; they pass out of existence at a later time; and they enjoy a career in between, a career that makes up a chapter of the history of the natural world.

Forms, by contrast, do not enjoy this kind of existential autonomy. They do not come into existence or pass out of existence; and they do not undergo other kinds of change either. Accordingly, they do not have what we can think of as a career. They are essentially predicable entities. They do not exist independently; they exist merely as items predicated of something else. As Aristotle puts it, they are "suches" and not "thises." They are not things that can be picked out and pointed to; they aren't objects of ostension in the way even their matter is. They are, on the contrary, *how* some parcel of matter is, the way that matter is; and they can exist only if there is some matter that is that way. So while substantial forms have one kind of separability, there is another kind of separability that only the composite particular has; and that, Aristotle wants to say, warrants the claim that familiar particulars are full-blooded realities.

And they are genuine unities as well. On Aristotle's analysis, the matter and form constitutive of a familiar particular turn out to be categorically different kinds of things. The one is something suited to play the role of subject and the other, the role of predicated item. And Aristotle wants to insist that because they have these categorically different structures, they can constitute what is a unified subject of predication. Familiar particulars are not just piles or heaps of things that are connected by a merely additive process. They are rather predicative structures; and, for Aristotle, a predicative structure is more than a mere assemblage of nameable ingredients or what Aristotle calls elements ($1041^{b}12$–13). To get a familiar particular, we need the appropriate material ingredients or elements, but we need more. Those material ingredients need to be put together in the right way; and their being so put together is not a matter of an additional ingredient. It is something categorically different from those nameable ingredients or "thises"; it is what Aristotle calls a principle ($1041^{b}30$). It is the way those ingredients are structured or organized; and the relevant principle is form

So matter and form are, so to speak, made for each other. They fit together in such a way that what they constitute is a substantial unity. Indeed, at the end of Book VIII, Aristotle tells us that what is unique about his hylomorphic analysis of the structure of familiar particulars is just that it leaves us with no problem about the reality and unity of those particulars ($1045^{a}23$–5). By their very nature, matter and form are things such that the latter's predication of the former results in what is a genuine unity and a genuine reality. And if one has doubts about this, Aristotle implies, it is only because one supposes that being and unity are genera, that there is some one thing that is just plain being and some one thing that is just plain unity ($1045^{b}6$–9). But there are no such properties. The only notions of being and unity that we have are those associated with kinds; and the pivotal kinds here are the kinds of substances, kinds like *human being, horse,* and *oak tree.* But where the appropriate form is predicated of the appropriate matter, that fact alone results in what is *one human being* and *a real human being; one horse* and *a real horse;* or *one oak tree* and *a real oak.* These sorts of things constitute the paradigmatic kinds of unity and reality; and matter and form are sufficient to deliver them.[6]

Science and Separation

In Book VI of the *Metaphysics,* Aristotle tells us that the science that studies being as being is distinct from physics only if there is what he calls separated substance, substance that exists apart from the material and sensible world of change. Aristotle, of course, thinks that there is such a separated substance – the Unmoved Mover he calls God. But the Prime Mover represents just one candidate for status as separated substance. The Platonist adds both forms and mathematical objects to the list. From the perspective of the middle books, the Platonic separation of form rests on a mistake, the mistake of construing a "such" as a "this" ($1033^{b}19$–30). Although substantial form is separable in formula, no form is separable in existence. Forms are always predicable entities. For a form to exist is for it to be predicated of something else. As we put it, a form is *how* some matter is. It is a way matter is and exists only if there is some matter that is that way.

The case against the Platonic separation of mathematical objects is developed in *Metaphysics* XIII and XIV. There, we find that an important source of the view that mathematical objects are immaterial substances is the idea that no object in the material world matches the mathematician's characterization of the subject matter of geometry and arithmetic. As the mathematician describes them, geometrical objects and numbers are things whose only properties are those fixed by the axioms and theorems of geometry and arithmetic. Nothing in the sensible world, however, has geometrical or arithmetical properties and no others. Ordinary material objects have a host of properties over and above their specifically mathematical properties. They have colors, give off odors, undergo changes, and so on. Accordingly, the Platonist concludes that no ordinary objects can be the things arithmetic and geometry are about and posits immaterial substances with purely mathematical natures as the truthmakers for mathematical claims.

Aristotle thinks that this line of reasoning embodies a deep misunderstanding of the nature of science. The view is that for the propositions of a science to be true, there must be objects that have the properties specified in the axioms and theorems of the science and no other properties; and that view conflicts with what we know about the sciences ($1077^{b}17$–31). What the Platonic view overlooks is the obvious fact that every science has a particular focus ($1077^{b}33$–$1078^{a}2$). A science selects certain features of objects for its investigation while prescinding from others. Accordingly, no object has only the properties constituting the focus of the science. The objects that have those properties have other properties that are not considered by the science; but despite that fact, those objects constitute the truthmakers for the science – the things the science is about. And that is how it is with both geometry and arithmetic. Neither science characterizes items separate from the sensible physical world. Both characterize ordinary physical objects, but they do so by focusing on selected features of those objects. As Aristotle puts it, both geometry and arithmetic deal exclusively with sensible objects, but neither science deals with them insofar as they are sensible. The two sciences examine sensible objects insofar as they exhibit, respectively, geometrical and arithmetical properties ($1078^{a}2$–13). The geometrician deals with physical objects insofar as they have extension and are things like pyramids, cubes, and spheres. Arithmetic, by contrast, examines groups of physical objects from the perspective of their ennumerability or countability.

Geometry, then, is the science of continuous quantities; and it is ordinary objects that are continuous quantities. Arithmetic is the science of numbers; and for Aristotle numbers are just countable pluralities or groups:

> "number" means a measured plurality and a plurality of measures . . . The measure must always be some identical thing predicated of all the things it measures, e.g. if the things are horses, the measure is *horse*, and if they are men, *man*. If they are a man, a horse, and a god, the measure is perhaps *living thing* and the number of them will be a number of living beings. ($1088^{a}4$–11)

So just as physical objects are continuous quantities, groups of physical objects constitute discrete quantities. The relevant quantitative features of those objects and groups of objects will, of course, be coinstantiated with all sorts of other properties; and the way the mathematician will proceed in characterizing the relevant objects and groups of objects is

> by setting up by an act of separation what is not separate . . . For a man qua man is one indivisible thing; and the arithmetician supposed one indivisible thing, and then considered whether any attribute belongs to a man qua indivisible. But the geometer treats him neither qua man nor qua indivisible, but as a solid. (1078^a21-6)[7]

Towards the Prime Mover

So neither forms nor mathematical objects provide us with examples of separated substances. But the Prime Mover does. In Book XII, Aristotle arrives at this conclusion by reflecting on the nature of time. There is, he assumes, a single all-embracing time, a time of which all other times are proper parts. That single temporal framework cannot, however, begin to apply or cease to apply (1071^b6-8); for if time in general were to come into being, then it would be true that *before* it *came* into being there *was* no time. But that is incoherent. Accordingly, if we take time to have a beginning, then what we construed as time was not time, but rather a part of some longer time; and, of course, precisely the same argument applies in the case of that longer time. Similarly, if time were to cease to exist, then it would be true that *after* its corruption time *will* no longer exist. Again, we have incoherence, so that the period of time we took to be time was not time, but just a part of some longer time. Temporal facts cannot fail to obtain, and the times those facts import are necessarily parts of a single, all-embracing time. So we have to concede both that there is a single time with neither beginning nor end of which all times are interrelated parts and that this is necessarily the case.

Now, Aristotle thinks that what a time is is just the number of some change; it is what we count or measure in the change when we say how long the change takes. A time, then, is the duration of a change (219^a3-8). Accordingly, for each stretch of time, there is some change whose duration that time is; and what holds the time together, what makes it one time is just that it is the duration of some one change. So if there is to be a single all-inclusive time, there must be a single change whose duration it is; and if the single all-inclusive time is necessarily without beginning or end, then the one change whose duration it is must likewise be necessarily without beginning or end. Now, Aristotle holds that only one kind of change can, in the required way, be eternal – change in place of a circular sort (1071^b10-11). All other kinds of change involve movement between contraries and so must come to an end; but in the case of circular motion, there are no states which, in a nonarbitrary way, can be said to initiate or terminate the motion. A body undergoing uniform circular motion is such that at any point in its motion what counts as completing the motion is always different; and if the change is eternally occurring, there is nothing that counts as its starting point.

We can conclude, then, that necessarily there is at least one case of eternal circular motion; and since numerically one change is possible only if there is numerically one substance undergoing the change, we can conclude that there is at least one necessarily existent substance – the substance undergoing the eternally occurring change. All of this follows on strictly philosophical grounds, but Aristotle believes that the philosophical arguments have empirical confirmation in the never failing regularity of the movement of the heavenly bodies (1072ª22).

Now, Aristotle tells the story of the Prime Mover in terms of the model provided by Eudoxian astronomy. On this model, the heavenly bodies are attached to a series of concentric crystaline spheres with motion conveyed inwards from the outermost sphere. There are all kinds of complications involved in setting out the details of the model. We can, however, ignore these and focus merely on the motion of the outermost sphere – the "first heaven." That sphere moves the spheres within it, but it too undergoes a kind of change – the necessarily eternal circular motion of the outermost heavenly bodies, the fixed stars. So the first heaven is a mover that is itself in motion; and for Aristotle that entails that it is a moved mover; and although Aristotle would concede that, theoretically at least, it is possible that what moves the first heaven is itself another moved mover, he wants to deny the possibility of an infinite series of moved movers. He thinks that if each mover in the series were moved by a moved mover, there would be no First Mover and, hence, no motion at all (994ª1–18). So there is an Unmoved Mover, something that "moves without being moved, being eternal, substance and actuality" (1072ª24–6), and Aristotle, for his part, is satisfied that this Prime or First Mover just is the being that directly causes the first heaven to move.

There is, however, a problem here. The Prime Mover causes the locomotion of the outermost celestial sphere, but it is difficult to understand how anything could cause something else to move in place without being in some sort of physical contact with what it moves and, hence, without being itself affected or moved by the causal interaction. But if this is how it produces motion, then what was supposed to be the Prime or First Mover is not that at all. It is just another moved mover; and if there is no other way of producing motion, then the very idea of a First Mover seems to be threatened with incoherence. Towards showing that there can be something that causes change in place without being in contact with anything, Aristotle reminds us that "the object of desire and the object of thought move in this way": they move without being moved (1072ª26–7). So there is a familiar way things can cause motion without being moved or affected themselves. They can motivate by being objects of thought and desire; and Aristotle wants to claim that the causation of the First Mover is an instance of this form of causation. The First Mover "produces motion by being loved" (1072ᵇ3). None of the details of all this get spelled out precisely; but it seems, first, that Aristotle took the first heaven to be endowed with intelligence, to have some sort of cognitive access to the Prime Mover, and to find the Prime Mover a good worthy of emulation in the form of eternal rotatory motion, and, second, that since Aristotle took these facts to underlie the necessary motion of the celestial bodies, he construed them as holding of necessity.

The Nature of the Prime Mover

As we have already indicated, Aristotle characterizes the Prime Mover as "actuality." He denies that the Unmoved Mover has any unactualized potentialities: it actually is everything it can be. Given the connection between the concepts of matter and potentiality, it follows that the Prime Mover is entirely lacking in matter (1074^a36); and Aristotle infers a number of claims from the immateriality of the Prime Mover. Since it is by way of matter that things with a single essence are diversified (1034^b5–7), Aristotle concludes that there can be just one substance with the essence of the Unmoved Mover (1074^a36–8). Furthermore, he invokes the immateriality of the Prime Mover to conclude that it is a being without parts, that it is through and through simple (1073^a5–6). He does not, however, say that the Prime Mover is form; and it is no accident that he fails to invoke the familiar connection between actuality and form in his characterization of the Prime Mover. The Prime Mover agrees with substantial forms in being one with its essence; like those forms, it is separate in definition or essence. But unlike the forms of familiar objects, the Prime Mover is also separate in existence. It has the existential autonomy that forms lack: it is a "this" and not a "such." Accordingly, the Prime Mover is categorically a different kind of entity from any form.

So the Prime Mover enjoys both kinds of separability or independence; and this fact suggests that the ontological theory of Book XII enables us to resolve a nagging difficulty associated with the metaphysics of the middle books. In Books VII and VIII, we meet a gap between the things (substantial forms) that are independent or separate in essence and those (familiar particulars) that are existentially independent or separate in an unqualified way; and that gap can appear disconcerting. How can it be that the beings that are supposed to be the primary substances are not themselves things capable of standing alone, of existing in their own right? Book XII tells us that, in the final analysis, this cannot happen. It closes the gap between things that are separable in formula and separable in existence; for it tells us that when we look beyond the material world that provides the context for the middle books, we find a being that is at once independent in essence and independent in existence; and that being is the substance that is prior to everything else: it is the primary substance par excellence.

But what is this being? What kind of essence does the First Mover have? Aristotle's answer is that it is a being engaged in intellectual activity. It is a being that thinks. Indeed, he tells us that the Prime Mover just is its acts of thinking; and he argues that since thinking is a form of living, the Prime Mover is a living being, a being whose essence is to think and, therefore, to live. The Prime Mover, then, is alive; and since its life is the best life, the Prime Mover deserves the title "God."

So the Prime Mover is a living being whose life is the best any substance can aspire to; its life is a life of unchanging intellectual activity. What it thinks of is just itself. Accordingly, Aristotle claims, the Prime Mover or God is thinking that is thinking of thinking (1074^b34). This characterization of the Prime Mover has been roundly criticized.[8] Thus, we are told that Aristotle's God is narcissistic or that since it focuses merely on itself, the Unmoved Mover's intellectual life is severely impoverished; and we meet with the more radical claim that Aristotle's description of God incorporates an incoherent conception of thinking. Thinking is essentially object-directed: for any act of thinking, there is some object that the thinking is about; and that object gives the act its character and identity. It is, however, unclear whether Aristotle's formula gives us any object for the Divine thinking. He claims that God is the act of thinking; but what is the thinking a thinking of? Aristotle's answer: the thinking that it is. But if the first use of "thinking" was problematic on the grounds that it failed to identify the object of the act we were attempting to pick out, Aristotle hardly helps things by identifying that object as what we initially picked out by the term "thinking."

These criticisms would be just were the claim that God is a thinking that thinks of thinking Aristotle's last word on God; but it is not. It is rather a template for an account of God's essence, a template offered as a solution to a problem about God's thought. If God's life is in the best kind of life and consists in intellectual activity, that activity must take the best thing as its object; but, then, it looks as though there is something more perfect than God – the object of God's thinking. We can avoid this conclusion, however, if we say that God is the object of God's thinking; and that is what Aristotle's formula tells us. But the formula needs an interpretation; and we meet with the required interpretation in a doctrine from the *De Anima*, the idea that the act of thinking and its object are one and the same (430^{a}3–5). The claim is that the intelligible in actuality just is the intellect in actuality. What the doctrine implies is that, in a way, every act of thinking is self-directed. The intellect becomes its objects when it thinks, so every act of thinking is a case where the intellect in act is its own object (1075^{a}1–4). But, then, the thinking that is God can grasp all the intelligibles there are and still be thinking of itself. We have, then, the interpretation of the formula and an answer to Aristotle's critics as well. God's thought encompasses all the essences or universals there are and is, nonetheless, a thinking of what is best.

But if we can make sense of Aristotle's characterization of the Divine thought, we need to realize that his conception of the Prime Mover is very different from the Judeo-Christian conception of God. It is, for example, doubtful whether the Prime Mover has cognitive access to the contingent particulars making up the material world; and it is fairly clear that Aristotle's Unmoved Mover is not a creator. The material world is eternal and uncreated. It can seem, then, that the dependence of the world on God is indirect and remote. It can seem that the physical universe is an independently existing, self-sufficient whole that merely needs to be kept moving. Some comments, however, at the end of Book XII suggest a deeper form of dependence:

> We must consider also in which of two ways the nature of the universe contains the good and the highest good, whether as something separate and by itself, or as the order of the parts. Probably in both ways, as an army does; for its good is found both in its order and in its leader, and more in the latter; for he does not depend on the order, but it depends on him. And all things are ordered together somehow, but not all alike

– both fishes and fowls and plants; and the world is not such that one thing has nothing to do with another, but they are connected. For all are ordered together to one end . . . (1075ᵃ11–19)

Here, Aristotle is saying that there is a universal order that ties the workings of the various natures together, and he is telling us that this universal order is like the order in an army. The order found in an army derives from the thought of its general; it is simply an expression of the overall strategic plan the general has formulated. The upshot of Aristotle's analogy, then, seems to be that the order or harmony he wants to impute to the natural world is an expression of the intelligible order and structure of the Divine Thought. He does not tell us just how the dependence of the natural harmony on God's thought works itself out. But if we pursue the analogy Aristotle offers, we will find it plausible to suggest that it is the movement of the first heaven that provides the causal mechanism for the expression of the natural order and harmony that originates in the Divine Thought. It is, after all, by the efforts of his subordinates that a general's strategic plan gets implemented.

It is tempting, then, to suppose that the first heaven grasps the intelligible order at work in the Divine Thought and moves as it does so as to realize that order in the natural world. But if something like this is what Aristotle means to be telling us, then even though his Prime Mover is not the creating God of the Judeo-Christian tradition, the dependence of the world on Aristotle's God is not the very remote sort of dependence it can seem to be. Aristotle does not see the world as an independently existing, self-sufficient whole that merely needs a "jump start" from an otherwise unrelated substance. The very order of the world – its general nature and structure – derives from God. That order is just a reflection or expression of the Divine Thought. It is because that order constitutes the intelligible content of God's thinking that it constitutes the intelligible structure of the world. So it is in a strong sense that the Prime Mover is "the first cause and first principle" of all things (981ᵇ29).

Acknowledgments

Parts of this chapter are taken from my "Aristotle's *Metaphysics*," previously published in *The Classics of Western Philosophy*, edited by J. Gracia, G. Reichberg, and B. Schumacher (Oxford: Blackwell), 2002.

Notes

1   The most detailed and most influential statement of the sort of view I outline here is found in Jaeger 1923. A very different developmental picture is presented in Owen 1960. For criticisms of both views, see Code 1996.

2   See Owen 1960 for an important discussion of the doctrine of focal meaning and its role in the *Metaphysics*.

3   Some scholars, however, question the attribution of a doctrine of prime matter to Aristotle. See, e.g., King 1956, Charlton 1970, and Gill 1989. For a more detailed discussion of the issues surrounding the topic of prime matter, see chapter 7 of Loux 1991. For a more detailed discussion of the argument of VII.3, see chapter 2 of the same work.

4   The account outlined here is developed in chapter 3 of Loux 1991. Other approaches to VII.6 are discussed in Bostock 1994. One especially influential account is presented in Owen 1966.

5   In the interests of avoiding complications, I do not discuss one of the central debates about the theory of the middle books. In my presentation I assume that substantial forms are universals. Not all commentators, however, would concede that assumption. Many scholars have taken VII.13 and the chapters following it to entail that there is a numerically distinct form for each member of a given species. For a detailed defense of my reading of the text, see chapter 6 of Loux 1991. For the opposing view, see Lesher 1971, Frede 1983, 1985, and chapter 12 of Irwin 1988. For readings that agree with mine, see Woods 1967, Code 1978, Furth 1988, and Lewis 1991.

6   For a more detailed discussion of these themes, see Loux 1995.

7   My brief discussion here barely scratches the surface of XIII and XIV. Much of those books is devoted to detailed criticisms of highly technical material in Plato's philosophy of mathematics. Good introductions to these issues are found in Annas 1976 and chapter 6 of Lear 1988.

8   See chapter 29 of Copleston 1946, where one meets the sorts of criticism I mention here.

References and Recommended Reading

Annas, J. 1976. *Aristotle's Metaphysics M and N* (Oxford: Oxford University Press).

Aubenque, P., ed. 1979. *Etudes sur la Metaphysique d'Aristote* (Paris: J. Vrin).

Barnes, J. 1984. *The Complete Works of Aristotle: The Revised Oxford Translation*, 2 vols. (Princeton: Princeton University Press).

Bostock, D. 1994. *Aristotle's Metaphysics Z and H* (Oxford: Oxford University Press).

Charlton, O. W. 1970. *Aristotle's Physics Books I and II* (Oxford: Oxford University Press).

Code, A. 1978. "No Universal is a Substance: An Interpretation of *Metaphysics* Z.13," *Paideia* 7.

—— 1996. "Owen on the Development of Aristotle's Metaphysics" in Wians 1996.

Copleston, F. 1946. *A History of Western Philosophy*, vol. 1 (Westminster, Md.: Newman Press).

Frede, M. 1983. "Individuals in Aristotle" in Frede 1987. First published in German in 1983.

—— 1985. "Substance in Aristotle's Metaphysics" in Gotthelf 1985. Reprinted in Frede 1987.

—— 1987. *Essays in Ancient Philosophy* (Minneapolis: University of Minnesota Press).

Furth, M. 1988. *Substance, Form, and Psyche* (Cambridge: Cambridge University Press).

Gill, M. 1989. *Aristotle on Substance* (Princeton: Princeton University Press).

Gotthelf, A. 1985. *Aristotle on Nature and Living Things* (Bristol: Mathesis).

Irwin, T. 1988. *Aristotle's First Principles* (Oxford: Oxford University Press).

Jaeger, W. 1923. *Aristotle: Fundamentals of the History of His Development* (Oxford: Oxford University Press), trans. by R. Robinson, 2nd ed., 1948. First published in German, 1923.

King, H. 1956. "Aristotle without *Prima Materia*," *Journal of the History of Ideas* 17.

Lear, J. 1988. *Aristotle: The Desire to Understand* (Cambridge: Cambridge University Press).

Lesher, J. 1971. "Aristotle on Form, Substance, and Universal: A Dilemma," *Phronesis* 16.

Lewis, F. 1991. *Substance and Predication in Aristotle* (Cambridge: Cambridge University Press).

Loux, M. 1979. "Form, Species, and Predication in *Metaphysics* Z, H, and ϑ," *Mind* Ser. 2 vol. 88.

—— 1991. *Primary Ousia* (Ithaca: Cornell University Press).

—— 1995. "Composition and Unity: An Examination of *Metaphysics* H.6" in Sim 1995.

Moravscik, J. 1967. *Aristotle: A Collection of Critical Essays* (Garden City, N.Y.: Doubleday).

Norman, R. 1969. "Aristotle's Philosopher-God," *Phronesis* 14.

Owen, G. 1960. "Logic and Metaphysics in Some Earlier Works of Aristotle" in Owen 1986. First published in Owen and During 1960.

—— 1966. "The Platonism of Aristotle" in Owen 1986. First published in *Proceedings of the British Academy*.

—— 1986. *Logic, Science, and Dialectic* (Ithaca: Cornell University Press).

Owen, G., and I. Düring 1960. *Aristotle and Plato in the Mid-Fourth Century* (Göteborg: Studia Graeca et Latina Gothaburgensia), 11.

Owens, J. 1963. *The Doctrine of Being in the Aristotelian Metaphysics*, 2nd ed. (Toronto: Pontifical Institute of Mediaeval Studies).

—— 1979. "The Relation of God to the World in the *Metaphysics*" in Aubenque 1979.

Ross, W. 1924. *Aristotle's Metaphysics*, 2 vols. (Oxford: Oxford University Press).

Scaltsas, T. 1994. *Substances and Universals in Aristotle's Metaphysics* (Ithaca: Cornell University Press).

Scaltsas, T., D. Charles, and M. Gill 1994. *Unity, Identity, and Explanation in Aristotle's Metaphysics* (Oxford: Oxford University Press).

Sim, M. 1995. *The Crossroads of Norm and Nature* (Lanham, Md.: Rowman & Littlefield).

Wians, N. 1996. *Aristotle's Philosophical Development* (Lanham, Md.: Rowman & Littlefield).

Witt, C. 1989. *Substance and Essence in Aristotle* (Ithaca: Cornell University Press).

Woods, M. 1967. "Problems in *Metaphysics* Z, Chapter 13" in Moravscik 1967.

Chapter 10

Aristotle: Ethics and Politics

Fred D. Miller, Jr.

Aristotle's Relevance

Aristotle is still an influential voice in moral and political philosophy, alongside modern greats such as Hobbes, Hume, Kant, Bentham, and Mill. In addition to shedding light on important topics, for example, the theory of justice and its application to political constitutions, he defended theories – concerning value, moral obligation, and politics – which continue to attract adherents.

Concerning value, Aristotle defended a robust version of *moral realism*, the view that there is an objective good for human beings. That is, we can investigate moral truths through a process of analysis and proof which results in an objectively defensible theory. This contrasts with currently dominant metaethical views, for example, that concepts of good or bad must be explicated in terms of subjective preferences or expressions of attitude, or that standards of value are "constructed" by human agreement, convention, or custom, and hence that judgments of good or bad are ultimately subjective and relative to different individuals or groups.

Concerning moral obligation, Aristotle advocated *virtue ethics*, the view that a moral agent ought to act from moral virtues, that is, good settled dispositions of character such as courage, generosity, temperance, and justice. This contrasts with two other approaches popular among moral philosophers nowadays, both of which focus on the rightness or wrongness of action. According to the first, consequentialism, consequences alone should be taken into account in determining whether an act is right or wrong. On Bentham's utilitarian version of this theory, an act is right if, and only if, it tends to maximize a greater surplus of pleasure over pain for all persons concerned. According to the second approach, deontology, one is obligated to abide by moral rules or duties, for example, to tell the truth or keep one's promises, regardless of consequences. Virtue ethics, which focuses on the character of the agent, has been revived recently and is now defended as an alternative to both these approaches.

Concerning politics, Aristotle was a forerunner of *communitarianism*, which holds that political states, and communities generally, should promote shared moral values. On this view there is a tight connection between ethics and politics, and individuals are properly subject to the moral authority of the community. Further, participation in social and political activities is intrinsically good for individuals. Aristotle would reject the currently popular view that the state should take a neutral stance regarding ultimate moral values, and confine itself to guaranteeing individuals the necessities of living as they see fit.

Despite his relevance to such modern theories, Aristotle was, of course, examining moral and political issues as a Greek philosopher in the fourth century BC, and it is necessary to understand his own standpoint in order to interpret and assess his writings.

General View of Ethics and Politics

Modern ethics and politics, taken together, correspond to a special sort of Aristotelian science. Aristotle distinguishes three main kinds of science: contemplative, productive, and practical (*Top.* VI.6.145a15–16; *Met.* VI.1.1025b25, XI.7.1064a16–19). Each has a distinctive aim. The end of contemplative thought (e.g., physics, mathematics, and theology) is knowledge or truth for its own sake; the end of productive thought (e.g., poetry, medicine, or architecture) is the creation of an object distinct from the productive activity; and the end of practical thought is good action. "Practical" thought is so called because it aims at action (*praxis*), and it has three subtypes: practical wisdom concerned with the individual, economics (*oikonomikē*) concerned with the household (*oikos*), and politics concerned with the city-state. "Practical wisdom" (*phronēsis*, also translated "prudence") is a rational practical activity issuing in true judgments about actions that are good or bad for a human being (cf. *EN* VI.5.1140b4–6), and it corresponds roughly to ethics as understood today. Politics includes legislative science (*nomothetikē*) and politics in a more pedestrian sense, involving everyday political activities. The latter is subdivided into parts concerned with deliberation and legal judgment (see *EN* VI.8.1141b29–33; *EE* I.8.1218b12–14).

Ethics and politics are closely related, and together they comprise what Aristotle calls "the philosophy of human affairs" (*EN* X.9.1181b15). At various crucial junctures his *Politics* appeals for support to his "ethical discussions" (*ēthikoi logoi*) (*Pol.* VII.13.1332a22). Yet his *Nicomachean Ethics* and *Eudemian Ethics* also represent themselves as concerned with "politics" (*politikē*), short for political science (*politikē epistēmē*) (*EN* I.2.1094a27, b10–11, 15–16; *EE* I.6.1216b37, VII.1.1234b22). The term "political" derives from the Greek terms *polis* (city-state) and *politēs* (citizen). City-states like Athens and Sparta were relatively compact and cohesive units, in which political, religious, and cultural concerns were intertwined. The importance of the city-state is underscored by Aristotle's characterization of politics as the supreme science. It prescribes which sciences are to be studied in the city-state, and all the other disciplines – such as military science, household management, and rhetoric – fall under its authority. Since it governs the other practical sciences, their ends serve as means to the end of political science, which Aristotle identifies as nothing less than the human good.

Strictly speaking ethics (*ēthikē*) is a science of character (*ēthos*), but it is a practical science aiming at the good actions of individuals: "we are inquiring not in order to know what virtue is, but in order to become good, since our effort would have been useless otherwise" (*EN* II.2.1103b7–9; cf. X.9.1179a34–b2). Politics is likewise concerned with the good actions of the entire city-state: "politics takes the greatest care in making the citizens be of a certain sort, that is, good and capable of noble acts" (I.9.1099b30–2). The latter aim is paramount.

> Even if the end is the same for an individual and for a city-state, that of the city-state seems at any rate greater and more complete to attain and preserve. For although it is worthy to attain it for only an individual, it is nobler and more divine to do so for a nation or a city-state. (I.2.1094b7–10)

Further, to bring about this end, the statesman must have a good character. This suggests that ethics is in some sense a branch of politics (*MM* I.1.1181a24–8, b24–1182a1).

Ethics and politics are concerned with human actions, which Aristotle thinks has important implications for their methods. Good actions involve considerable variation and fluctuation, so that some people think that whether an action is noble or just is merely a matter of convention. Aristotle does not accept this, but he warns that in ethics one must be content with indicating the truth roughly and in outline, and in making moral claims that are only true for the most part, that is, which allow for exceptions. "It suits an educated person to seek precision in each class of things insofar as the nature of the subject permits" (*EN* I.3.1094b23–5). It is folly to expect ethics and politics to exhibit the deductive certainty of geometry. That an action of a specific type conforms to virtue is a contingent rather than a necessary truth: it is not something which holds necessarily all the time. For example, it is a contingent truth (capable of being otherwise) that it is virtuous to forgive a loan to an indigent person to purchase a meal, but it is a necessary, eternal truth (according to Aristotle) that the moon travels around the earth in a circular orbit. Hence, since practical wisdom is concerned with contingent moral truths, it is a capacity of forming justified true opinions (VI.5.1140b25–8). This explains why Aristotle frequently begins his discussions in ethics and politics with reputable opinions. He is explicit about this method when he examines the problem of moral weakness (or incontinence):

> We must, as in all other cases, set the appearances before us and, after first discussing the difficulties, go on to prove if possible, the truth of all the reputable opinions about these affections or, failing this, of the greater number and the most authoritative; for if we both solve the troubles and leave the reputable opinions undisturbed, we shall have proved the case sufficiently. (VII.1.1145b2–7)

He first canvasses the reputable opinions. These are not any opinions whatsoever, but those with some credibility: they are "the opinions of everyone or of the majority or of the wise persons, and of the latter all of them or most or the most notable and reputable" (*Top.* I.1.100b21–3). The body of opinions to which Aristotle appeals in ethical and political contexts are evidently those which would seem credible to educated citizens, rather than theories defended in his technical treatises on natural science and metaphysics (see *EN* I.13.1102a26–7). A difficulty (*aporia*) arises if these opinions conflict: for example, Socrates' judgment that passion cannot drag reason around like a slave, conflicts with the belief of most that persons sometimes fail to do what they know they ought to do, as a result of desire, fear, or anger. Aristotle resolves the conflict if possible, for example, by clarifying the sense in which one "knows" what to do. Failing this, he tries to preserve the beliefs that are most defensible and can provide a reliable basis for further inquiry. In the case of incontinence he makes a number of observations and distinctions and concludes that, in a sense, "the conclusion Socrates sought actually seems to result" (*EN* VII.3.1147b14–15). Aristotle's method is called "aporetic" in so far as it starts with a difficulty (*aporia*) and "endoxic" in so far as it relies on reputable opinions (*endoxa*). This method, which resembles the Socratic method of elenchus, is frequently employed throughout Aristotle's writings (see also *Top.* I.2.101a36–b4 and *EE* I.6, VII.2.1235b13–18).

Ethics

The traditional Aristotelian corpus includes four ethical treatises: *Nicomachean Ethics* (attributed to Aristotle by scholars), *Eudemian Ethics* (there has been controversy over its authorship, but it is now widely accepted), *Magna Moralia* (questioned by many scholars, though with some defenders, it offers valuable insights in any case), and *On Virtues and Vices* (universally rejected as spurious). The *Nicomachean Ethics* is generally regarded as the most important work, but the *Eudemian Ethics* also offers an extended discussion of many of the same topics. (An added complication is that the missing books IV–VI of the *Eudemian Ethics* are reportedly identical with books V–VII of the *Nicomachean Ethics*. Commentators often call these "the common books.") These two works often agree, but one work frequently makes an important point missing from the other, and there are also occasional disagreements. It is therefore often very illuminating to compare how the same problem is treated in these two different treatises. The following discussion will generally follow the treatment of the *Nicomachean Ethics* but sometimes refer to the *Eudemian Ethics*, and occasionally to the *Magna Moralia*. Aristotle's treatises contain important discussions of topics which cannot be examined in detail here: voluntariness and moral responsibility, moral incontinence, pleasure, and friendship. The rest of this discussion focuses on some central themes of Aristotle's ethics. Table 10.1 provides an overview.

Happiness

Aristotle's initial task is to establish that political science has a subject matter, namely, the ultimate human good. He begins with a reputable opinion: "Every art and every

Table 10.1   *Contents of Aristotle's ethical works*

Topic	Nicomachean Ethics	Eudemian Ethics	Magna Moralia
Introduction to ethics			I.1.1–8
Highest good	I.1–2	I.1–2	I.1.9–11
Methods of ethics	I.3	I.6	
Happiness	I.4–5	I.3–5, 7	
Critique of Plato	I.6	I.8	I.1.12–27
Theory of happiness	I.7–12	II.1	I.2–3
Psychology and virtue	I.13	II.1.15–18	I.4.7–5.2
Moral virtue	II	II.2–5	I.5.3–9.6; 19
Voluntariness	III.1–5	II.6–11	I.9.7–18
Particular virtues	III.6–IV	III	I.20–32
Justice	V	= IV	I.33; II.1–3
Intellectual virtues	VI	= V	I.34
Incontinence	VII.1–10	= VI.1–10	II.4–6
Pleasure	VII.11–14	= VI.11–14	II.7
Friendship	VIII–IX	VII	II.11–17
Pleasure continued	X.1–5		
Best life	X.6–8	VIII.1–3	II.8–10
Education and politics	X.9		

inquiry, and similarly every action and choice, is believed to aim at some good; and therefore it has been finely declared that the good is what all things aim at" (*EN* I.1.1094a1–3). But these goods are not on a par. For example, a bridle is a good because it is the aim of the bridle maker, but the bridle serves a higher good, namely, horse riding, which in turn serves the end of military strategy, and so forth. The highest end belongs to the master science.

In the *Eudemian Ethics* Aristotle argues that, in order to lead a good life, an individual ought to have a particular aim (for example, honor, reputation, wealth, or education) with reference to which he will act, since it is a sign of foolishness not to organize one's life in relation to an end (*EE* I.2.1214b6–11). In the *Nicomachean Ethics* he argues that we must have such an end if we are to act successfully:

> If, then, there is some end of the things we do, which we desire for itself (and the other things are for the sake of this), and if we do not choose everything for the sake of something else (for at that rate the choosing would go on to infinity, so that our desire would be empty and vain), clearly this would be the good and the best. (*EN* I.2.1094a18–22)

Aristotle has been accused of faulty logic for leaping to the conclusion that every agent must have a common ultimate good: even if every dancer must have a partner, it does not follow that every dancer must have one and the same partner. But in his defense it is not clear that he intends to establish here any more than that there must be at least one intrinsically valuable end. Similarly, if you wanted to prove that there was a common partner, a logical place to start would be first to ask each dancer: "Did you dance with someone?" and then "Who was it?" (Note that Aristotle suggests a little later, at 7.1097a28–30, that he has left it open so far whether there is one or more intrinsically valuable end.)

Aristotle remarks that there is a vague consensus that the ultimate end is happiness:

> In respect to name there is nearly general agreement. For both the many and refined persons say that it is happiness (*eudaimonia*), and they assume that living well and acting well are the same as being happy. But they dispute over what happiness is and the many do not give the same answer as wise persons. (4.1095a17–22)

Aristotle finds many of these answers wanting. The many (*hoi polloi*, an expression Aristotle often uses for the poorly educated majority of persons) equate it with pleasure, but this is a slavish or bestial end. More refined persons identify happiness with honor, but this view is also ruled out: "honor is believed to depend more on those who bestow honor than on the recipients, but we divine that the good must be something firmly in our possession" (5.1095b24–6). Further, people seem to pursue honor because this will assure them that they are meritorious, which implies that virtue or excellence (*aretē*) is what they really value. But even this is an incomplete answer, because one can be inactive or miserable even though one is virtuous. Again, happiness does not consist in wealth, because wealth is merely a means to something else. He defers discussion of the theory that happiness consists in rational activity.

Aristotle next considers the view of his teacher and friend Plato, that happiness is defined in terms of the theory of Forms. He objects that Plato's theory cannot account for the meaning of the term "good." Things are called good in many ways, when they fall into different categories (e.g., good reason, a good habit, a good amount, a good time, a good place, etc.), but Plato's theory implies that things will always be good in the same sense – just as things are white in the same sense, for example, white paper and white snow. He also objects that even if we concede the existence of Forms, they would be useless for ethics: "it is clear that it could not be achieved or attained by a human being; but we are now seeking something of this sort" (6.1096b33–5). Nor does Aristotle see how knowing the Form of the Good as an abstract pattern would provide any guidance in practical pursuits. Knowing in a general way what health is will not by itself assist a doctor confronted with a particular patient suffering from a particular disease. Similarly, abstract knowledge of the good will provide a moral agent little guidance in doing the right thing in particular circumstances.

Aristotle then begins his own positive account of happiness: it is a final end in that it is chosen always for itself and never for the sake of anything else (7.1097b1). It is also self-sufficient in the sense that when it is taken by itself it makes life worth choosing and lacking in nothing (1097b14–15). To be happy is to be blessed (*makarios*), a condition which cannot be improved. It follows that happiness is incommensurable with other goods, because otherwise a happy person could be made better off by the most trivial good. What, then, *is* happiness? Aristotle's answer takes the form of his famous *function argument* (1097b24–1098a20). The basic idea is that happiness consists in "living well," and to understand what it is for anyone to do something "well" (for example, play a flute, or make a statue), one must know his function. The argument is summarized as follows:

1. Human beings have a proper function, which is a rational life of action. (It is not growth which is shared with plants, or perception which is shared with other animals.)
2. The good of a thing seems to lie in its proper function.
3. Actually doing F is more important than merely being able to F.
4. Hence, a rational life of action consists in the soul's rational activity.
5. Therefore, the function of human beings is the soul's rational activity.
6. If the function of X is doing F, then the function of an excellent X is doing F well.
7. A function is exercised well when it is exercised according to its proper virtue.
8. Therefore, the function of an excellent human being consists in his soul's rational activity according to virtue.
9. Therefore, the human good consists in the soul's rational activity according to virtue.

Aristotle adds that if there is more than one virtue, happiness will be the exercise of the most complete (or perfect) virtue, and that it must be found in a complete life.

The function argument has been criticized from different angles. The first two premises especially have come under fire. Some critics object that premiss 1 is ambiguous. Even if the function of X determines what it is to be a good X, it does not follow that this is good *for* the X. A worm dangling on a hook would not agree that it is good for the bait to be good bait. Nor is it good for the hostage to be a good hostage. Aristotle's critics object that the most that his argument could establish is that a good human being is rationally active, not that such an activity is the ultimate good *for* human beings. But the *Eudemian Ethics* (which presents the function argument in a somewhat different way from the *Nicomachean Ethics*), tries to fill this very gap, stating, "The function of each is its end," and "the end is best, as an end; for it is assumed that the best and ultimate thing is the end, that for the sake of which all else exists" (II.1.1219b8–11). It is noteworthy that Aristotle makes similar points when he offers teleological explanations in his scientific writings. For example, regarding the cause of sleep, he states that "nature acts for the sake of something, and this is a good." Sleep is necessary and beneficial for animals, because they are unable to survive in a perpetually active condition. "But the waking state is the end, for perceiving or thinking is the end for all animals to which either of these belongs. For these are the best, and the end is best" (*Somn.* 2.455b13–25; cf. *Phys.* II.3.195a24–5; *Cael.* II.3.286a8–9, 12.292b17–19; *PA* IV.12.694b13–14; *GA* II.1.731b24–732a11; *Met.* IX.8.1050a21).

Premiss 2 has also been criticized. Why should we agree that a human has a proper function at all? Granted that Spinoza has a function qua philosopher or qua lens grinder, but does it follow that he has a function qua human being? Here again it may be helpful to consult Aristotle's natural scientific writings, where he argues that "everything is defined by its function" (*Meteor.* IV.12.390a10–13). But even if we accept that a human has a proper function, must it be rationality? The mere fact that some activity is performed only by humans does not by itself show that the action in question is part of the human function. After all, in the animal kingdom prostitution occurs only among human beings. It is unlikely that Aristotle would accept this as a good argument for including prostitution in the human function. Nor does it seem necessary: would we have to rule out rationality as the human function, if we discovered a rational species on another planet? Defenders of Aristotle maintain that we must turn to his *De Anima* and other works on psychology and biology to understand why he regards reason as paramount.

This discussion however reveals a serious problem of interpretation, which arises because Aristotle frequently advances important premises without much defense. One apparent reason for this is that, as noted above, ethics and politics can be studied by educated persons who have not been trained in the more technical branches of philosophy. Modern interpreters of the function argument face a dilemma. We can try to understand Aristotle as relying merely on common sense or ordinary language. But then his arguments often seem weak. Alternatively, we can try to support premises or fill in gaps in his ethical arguments by importing theories culled from his metaphysics and natural science. But some commentators question whether Aristotle himself intended his ethics to depend so heavily on his natural philosophy. They also worry about saddling his ethics with a "metaphysical biology" that is criticized by many modern philosophers. Nonetheless Aristotle's ethics still has considerable appeal. Those inclined to defend his argument will need to respond to the challenges posed to these crucial premises.

Moral psychology

Having argued that happiness consists in virtuous activity of the soul, Aristotle turns to a study of virtue or excellence (*aretē*). He prefaces this with a brief overview of psychology, based on external (*exōterikoi*) or nontechnical discussions (*EN* I.13.1102a26–1103a10; *EE* II.1.1219b26–1220a13). (This "exoteric" psychology resembles Plato's in dividing the soul into parts. The extent of agreement with Aristotle's own theoretical psychology in *De Anima* is a matter of scholarly debate.) The following is a simplified overview of this account.

The soul has two parts: rational and nonrational. The nonrational is further subdivided: the vegetative subpart, involved in nutrition and growth, shared with plants and other animals, that has no share in reason; and the appetitive subpart, involved in desire and passion, that at least responds to reason, for example, when we resist a desire to eat a sweet thing because our reason tells us that it is fattening. The rational part, our capacity to reason, naturally rules over the soul. The appetitive part is able to obey or disobey it. There are two main kinds of virtue: moral virtue (excellence of character), which belongs to a person when the rational part has full control over the appetitive; and intellectual virtue (excellence of thought), which belongs to the purely rational part of the soul.

Aristotle later divides the rational faculty itself: one part attains knowledge about things whose principles cannot be otherwise, and another part forms true beliefs about things whose principles are variable. The latter, believing part must be used to deliberate about what action to perform, because individual actions are variable things (*EN* VI.1.1139a6–12, 5.1140b25–8; *MM* I.34.1196b15–34; cf. *DA* III.10.433a14–15). These parts have distinctive intellectual virtues: theoretical wisdom (*sophia*) is a virtue of scientific reason, and practical wisdom or prudence (*phronēsis*) is a virtue of calculative reason. Most of Aristotle's *Nicomachean* and *Eudemian Ethics* are concerned with these virtues.

Moral virtue

Moral virtue results from habituation. This, Aristotle remarks, is suggested by the fact that the Greek word *ēthikē*, "moral" or "ethical," is derived from the word *ethos*, "habit." Therefore, moral virtues do not arise in us by nature. By "nature" Aristotle understands an internal principle of change or rest (see *Phys.* II.1.192a13–14, 20–3). For example, a stone persists falling downward and cannot be habituated to rise even if it is thrown into the air repeatedly. According to Aristotle this is due to the stone's nature: it is composed of the element earth and thus has an intrinsic tendency to move downward to its "natural place." Again, we possess the powers of sight and hearing by nature: we are born with them and can exercise them whenever a color or sound is present. But the moral virtues are not innate but acquired through practice: "we learn by doing, for example, people become builders by building and lyre-players by playing the lyre; so too we become just by doing just acts, temperate by doing temperate acts, brave by doing brave acts." Legislators provide further evidence, because they make the citizens good by instilling habits in them. In a good constitution this is accomplished. "It does not make a small difference, then, whether we form habits of one kind or another from our very youth; it makes a very great difference, or rather all the difference" (*EN* II.1.1003a14–b25).

Aristotle considers a difficulty (*aporia*) for the thesis that we learn virtues by acting virtuously: it takes a good flute player to play well; similarly, someone can perform just acts only if he is already a just person. Although Aristotle frequently follows Socrates in treating the virtues as analogous to arts and crafts, he argues that in this respect they are dissimilar. What we care about in the case of arts and crafts is whether their products are good. But in the case of virtue, we care not only about the action itself but also about why the agent did it. Consider a case in which soldiers fight side by side to defend the city-state. The seasoned veteran might risk his life because he is already courageous. His inexperienced comrade is not yet courageous, but imitates the older warrior in an effort to acquire this virtue. We can thus distinguish two senses of "virtuous" acts: (1) those resulting from a virtuous character, and (2) those resembling virtuous acts in sense 1. Aristotle spells out sense 1 more precisely: "The agent acts while he is in a certain condition: in the first place he must have knowledge, secondly he must choose the acts, and choose them for their own sakes, and thirdly his action must proceed from a firm and unchangeable condition" (5.1105a30–3). This distinction solves the difficulty and establishes an important principle of moral education: it is by doing virtuous acts in sense 2 that we learn to do virtuous acts in sense 1. So, the inexperienced soldier comes to be as courageous as his experienced comrade, at least in part by acting like him in situations calling for courage.

Aristotle now turns to the question: What is virtue? He tries to define an item such as virtue by asking, first, what sort of thing it is (genus) and, then, what distinguishes it from others of the same kind (differentia). Regarding the genus, virtue and its opposite vice could be one of three sorts: a feeling (e.g., fear or confidence), a capacity (ability to feel afraid or confident), or a state (the disposition to feel fear and confidence in a certain way). Virtue and vice cannot be feelings, because we are praised or blamed for our courage or cowardice but not simply for feeling fearful or confident. Also, courage involves deliberate choice to respond to a situation, whereas feeling fear or confidence as such do not. Virtue and vice cannot be capacities either, for similar reasons. In addition, we have capacities by nature, but as seen earlier we acquire virtue and vice by habituation. Hence, by elimination, virtue and vice must be states or dispositions (EN II.5).

Regarding the differentia of virtue, he recalls the definition of happiness: "virtue is the state by which a human being becomes good and performs his own function well" (II.7.1106a22–4). But how does moral virtue, specifically, accomplish this? Aristotle here employs a method similar to that of De Anima, where he distinguishes capacities of the soul such as sight and hearing in terms of their respective proper objects, colors, and sounds. In the case of a virtue such as courage its objects are feelings (fear or confidence) and actions (running various sorts of risks). Aristotle's key idea is that these feelings and actions involve a continuum of greater or lesser: we can feel more or less afraid in a given situation, and we can perform more or less dangerous actions. It is possible to choose an amount that is more, or less, or intermediate, when compared with other alternatives. But the "intermediate" can be understood in two ways: an absolute or arithmetical mean; or the mean relative to us, which may vary from person to person. If ten pounds of food is too much for someone to eat, and two pounds too little, six pounds will be the arithmetical mean. But this may be too little for the powerful weightlifter Milo, and too much for a beginner. The gymnastics instructor must find the appropriate mean for each athlete. The same principle applies to moral virtue:

> For example, it is possible to feel fear and confidence and appetite and anger and pity and in general pleasure and pain both too much and too little, and in both cases not well; but to feel them at the right times, with reference to the right objects, toward the right people, with the right aim, and in the right way, is what is both intermediate and best, and this is characteristic of virtue. Similarly with regard to actions also there is excess, defect, and the intermediate. (6.1106b18–24)

Aristotle then defines virtue as "a state involving deliberate choice, which lies in a mean relative to us and which is determined by reason." He adds that "reason" here means the reason which a practically wise person (*phronimos*) would use to determine the mean (1106b36–1107a2). He elsewhere describes this as "correct reason" (*orthos logos*) (II.2.1103b32, III.5.1139b29). The importance of this addition will soon be evident.

Aristotle distinguishes a number of virtues and vices, which concern different sorts of feelings and passions. He sets out a table of these in *Eudemian Ethics* II.3:

Excess	Deficiency	Mean
irascibility	unfeelingness	gentleness
foolhardiness	cowardice	courage
shamelessness	shyness	modesty
intemperance	insensibility	temperance
envy	[indifference]	righteous indignation
gain	loss	justice
lavishness	stinginess	liberality
boastfulness	self-depreciation	self-esteem
obsequiousness	surliness	friendliness
servility	stubbornness	dignity
vanity	false humility	greatness of soul
vulgar extravagance	pettiness	magnificence

In each case Aristotle views as virtuous the disposition (*hexis*) to avoid the extremes of excess or deficiency. In his detailed study of these dispositions, Aristotle argues that the excellent person (*spoudaios*) performs virtuous actions for the sake of their sheer nobility (*to kalon*) and not from ulterior motives, for example, make money, advance one's reputation, obtain pleasure, or avoid bodily injury (*EN* III.7.1115b14–15, 12.1119b16, IV.1.1120a23–4, 2.1122b6–7; *EE* III.1.1229a4; *MM* I.19.1190a28–30). An agent is noble and good (*kalos k'agathos*) because he practices noble acts for their own sake (*EE* VIII.3.1248b34–6). For such a person, good action (*eupraxia*) is an end in itself (cf. VI.5.1140b7).

Justice

The virtue of justice is especially important for Aristotle's political philosophy, and it involves special complications (*Nicomachean Ethics* V). Justice, for example, does not seem to conform to Aristotle's general analysis in terms of a mean between two opposed vices, because it has only one opposite: injustice. Aristotle begins by remarking that justice is spoken of homonymously (i.e., ambiguously), as we can see more clearly from its opposite injustice. Sometimes a person is unjust in the sense of "lawless," and sometimes in the sense of being "unfair" or "taking too much." Likewise, "just" has a broad or universal sense of "lawful," as well as a narrow sense of "fair." The universal sense of "justice" presupposes a theory of legislation:

> The laws in their enactments on all subjects aim at the advantage either of everyone in common or of the best persons or of those who have authority according to virtue, or something of the sort; so that in one sense we call those acts just that tend to produce and preserve happiness and its components for the political community. (V.1.1129b14–19)

Justice in this universal sense is not a particular virtue like courage. Instead it is the same as complete virtue, not in itself but in relation to other persons. It is complete excellence in the fullest sense, because its possessor can exercise his virtue in relation to other persons and not merely in relation to himself. Similarly, its opposite, universal injustice, is identical with the totality of vice. (This explains why universal justice has just one opposite, universal vice.)

Particular justice is, however, a special virtue like courage, and its opposite (*pleonexia*, having too much) is a special vice, involving an excessive desire for gain. There are in fact two kinds of particular justice: distributive justice, which is concerned with the distributions of honor, money, or other things that are divided among the citizens; and corrective justice, which is concerned with rectifying transactions, whether voluntary (e.g., loans or sales) or involuntary (e.g., adultery, fraud, murder, or robbery).

Distributive justice is especially important for Aristotle's political theory, since it applies to the distribution of offices. It implies that people should be treated equally in terms of their merit or desert. Distributive justice is analyzed in terms of a geometrical proportion, which is an equality of ratios, for example:

$$\frac{1}{2} = \frac{2}{4}$$

A distribution is just provided the recipients get shares proportionate to their merit. For example, in the case of individuals X and Y:

$$\frac{\text{Merit of } X}{\text{Merit of } Y} = \frac{\text{Share of } X}{\text{Share of } Y}$$

For example, if individual X invested twice as much as Y to their common business venture, then it is only just for X to receive twice as much earnings as Y.

Aristotle suggests that distributive justice is a mean: the person who acts unjustly takes too many goods, and the person who is treated unjustly has too little; in the case of evils, conversely, the unjust person takes too much, and the person treated unjustly receives too little. This seems implausible. The person who gets too little seems to be a victim rather than vicious. Being disposed to take less than one's share does not seem to be a vice. Aristotle might have done better to argue that a ruler is vicious who assigns shares that are too great or too little.

Moral knowledge

It is hard to take issue with "nothing in excess" as an abstract ideal. But a common criticism of Aristotle's virtue theory is that "the mean relative to us" is indeterminate in practice. (Aristotle seems to invite the same criticism which he directed against Plato's Form of the Good.) In the case of liberality or generosity, for example, if you are solicited by a charity after already giving to several others, how helpful is it to hear, "Give a moderate amount, neither too much nor too little"? A problem also arises regarding moral dilemmas, when the virtues seem to collide. In commenting on others' looks or performances, should you be truthful or considerate of their feelings? Aristotle's virtuous person opts for candor:

> He must be open in his hate and love, for to conceal one's feelings is characteristic of fearfulness. He must care more for truth than for what people will think. He must speak and act openly, for he speaks freely because he is contemptuous. And he is prone to tell the truth, except when he speaks ironically to the many. (IV.3.1124b26–31)

Aristotle's great-souled man may impress a modern reader as insensitive and a bit pompous. But the main philosophical difficulty is that "the mean relative to us" seems open to different interpretations, and what someone sees as "intermediate" may reflect personal subjectivity and cultural bias. For example, Aristotle emphasizes masculine traits in his catalogue of virtues. He sometimes acknowledges this, contending that the temperance, courage, or justice of a man is not the same as that of a woman: "the courage of a man is shown in commanding, in a woman in obeying." The implication is clearly that female virtue is subordinate to male virtue. Aristotle contrasts his own view with that of Socrates, who maintains that virtue is the same for all human beings (*Pol.* I.13.1260a20–4). A modern critic might complain that Aristotle (unlike Socrates) has mistakenly identified the virtue of a man or male with the virtue of a human being. (The Greek word *anēr* means "man" in the sense of "male," whereas the word *anthrōpos*, translated as "human being" or "man" in the generic sense, applies to both females and males.)

This shows the importance of the addition which Aristotle made to his definition of the virtuous mean: it is determined by correct reason, that is, "reason employed by a practically wise person to determine the mean" (II.6.1106b36–1107a2). Aristotle's virtue ethics must include a theory of practical wisdom, and this is the burden of *Nicomachean Ethics* Book VI. This compares and contrasts practical wisdom (*phronēsis*) with other intellectual virtues, including theoretical wisdom (*sophia*) and craft-knowledge (*technē*). It is possible here to mention only a few highlights of Aristotle's complex and difficult discussion. As we have seen, theoretical wisdom is concerned with invariable necessary truths (e.g., general principles of physics or mathematics), whereas practical wisdom like craft-knowledge is concerned with variable contingent facts. Practical wisdom and craft-knowledge also differ in how they value their distinctive activities: An expert in a craft like medicine engages in medical activities for the sake of a further end such as health, whereas the practically wise person engages in virtuous action as an end in itself (5.1140b6–7).

Still, practical wisdom also resembles craft-knowledge in an important way: An expert in a craft like medicine is skilled at deliberating about how to promote a specific end such as health. Similarly, a practically wise person seems to be "able to deliberate finely about what is good and advantageous for himself, not in some particular respect, e.g., about what sorts of thing promote health or strength, but about what sorts of thing promote the good life generally" (5.1140a25–8). Practical wisdom is defined as "a true state involving reason capable of action concerning what is good or bad for a human being" (1140b4–6).

Further, craft-knowledge requires both knowledge of universal truths and experience of particulars, for example, when a doctor prescribes a diet:

> If someone knew that light meats are easily digestible and healthful, but did not know which sorts of meat are light, he would not produce health, but someone who knows that bird meats are healthful will produce health better. And practical wisdom is concerned with action. So it must have both [universal and particular knowledge], or especially the latter. (7.1141b18–21)

In addition to having universal knowledge, for example, "Light meats are healthful," the doctor must be able to pick out a particular thing, for example, bird meat, which falls under this universal principle. Similarly, the practically wise person must be able to pick out a particular action which falls under the universal principle, for example, "The mean between fear and boldness is courage."

Because it concerns particulars, practical wisdom involves perception – not perception in the strict sense of a color or sound, but, presumably, the perception that a particular action is virtuous (8.1142a25–30). Aristotle remarks that practical wisdom is related to another intellectual virtue, called *nous* (which defies translation, although attempts include "comprehension," "intuition," and "understanding"). *Nous*, in short, consists in our ability to grasp the ultimate premises on which reasoned argument is based. In the theoretical realm, it apprehends the first universal principles of a demonstrative science such as physics or geometry.

> In the practical realm, it grasps the ultimate and contingent fact, that is the other premiss; for these are the starting points of that-for-the-sake-of-which, since the universals [come to be] from the particulars. Of these then one must be perception, and this is *nous*. (11.1143b2–5)

The role of practical *nous* in grasping the last particular premiss is intensely debated by commentators.

This leaves a major problem: How does one apprehend the first premiss, which defines the ultimate end? In the case of a craft such as medicine or architecture, the end is some external good which we need or want, that is, health or a house. But a basic task of ethics is to define what our ultimate end or good is. Aristotle states (in *EN* III.4) that our end is the object of wish (*boulēsis*), but how do we know what we should wish for? Is this the role of practical wisdom also? Aristotle's answer may come as a surprise: "Our function is fulfilled in accordance with practical wisdom and moral virtue. For virtue makes our aim correct, and practical wisdom makes the means to the end correct" (VI.12.1144a6–9, 13.1145a4–5). Critics object that this does not solve the problem. Even if it is true that morally virtuous persons pursue the correct end, Aristotle has not explained how they *know* that they have the correct end. Perhaps they have been brought up to have certain sorts of desires, which happen to be desires for the good. But then they are simply lucky, since they could have acquired desires for the bad instead. And this is no help at all to those of us who would like to be virtuous, but have not had the benefit of such an upbringing – or who are uncertain whether we have had the right upbringing. Defenders of Aristotle try to show that he has further resources, for example, by extending the application of practical *nous*, but this is clearly a serious difficulty for his moral epistemology.

The best life

After his intricate discussions of virtue and moral knowledge, Aristotle at last completes his account of happiness. He previously defined it as rational activity of the soul according to virtue. But he subsequently found that the rational faculty was divided into two parts, the scientific (concerned with immutable and necessary principles) and the calculative (concerned with variable and contingent facts). Scientific reason has a distinctive virtue, theoretical wisdom (*sophia*), and activity, contemplation (*theōria*). Calculative reason also has its virtue, practical wisdom (*phronēsis*), and activity, good deliberation (*euboulia*) culminating in noble acts. Given the earlier definition of happiness, should we conclude that it consists in the activity of *both* rational faculties, or in the activity of one of them to the exclusion of the other?

Aristotle's earlier remarks suggested different answers to this question. He said that theoretical wisdom is a part of complete virtue, so that "by being possessed and being actualized it makes a person happy" (VI.12.1144a3–6). He also stated that practical wisdom does not have authority over theoretical wisdom, any more than medicine has authority over health: "it does not use it but considers how it may come to be; it gives orders for its sake but not to it" (13.1145a6–9; cf. *EE* VIII.3.1249b13–15; *MM* I.34.1198b8–20). Just as health is the end for medicine, theoretical wisdom is a higher end for practical wisdom. This suggests that complete happiness consists exclusively in the activity of contemplation (*strict intellectualism*).

But other comments suggest a more inclusive view of happiness. Aristotle said that both forms of wisdom are choiceworthy in themselves, because each of them is a virtue of one of the rational parts (12.1144a1–2), and, as noted above, he has observed that virtuous actions are done for the sake of their nobility, that is, for their own sakes. This suggests the view that complete happiness consists of the activity of both forms of wisdom, with practical wisdom playing a subordinate role (*moderate intellectualism*).

Aristotle's discussion of the best life thus presents problems: Does he favor strict intellectualism or moderate intellectualism? And do his arguments hold up on either interpretation? In support of the strict interpretation, Aristotle explicitly says that contemplative activity is complete happiness (X.7.1177a17). He offers several reasons for this conclusion. (Note that these frequently appeal to what seems or is believed to be the case.) (1) Contemplation belongs to our supreme faculty, and its objects are the supreme objects of knowledge. (2) It is more continuous than any other action. (3) It is agreed that this activity is the most pleasant of activities. "At any rate it seems to have marvelously pure and firm pleasures." (4) Happiness was called self-sufficient, and this is found most of all in contemplation. The morally virtuous person needs external equipment in order to practice virtues such as justice, temperance, or courage, whereas the wise person is able to contemplate even by himself. Granted that he contemplates better in the company of others, he is more self-sufficient than the morally virtuous person. (5) Contemplation would seem to be valued for itself alone. For nothing else results from contemplating, whereas morally virtuous actions produce other benefits. (6) Happiness seems to involve leisure, which is found especially in contemplation. The moral virtues are typically exercised in spheres like politics or war, and seem the antithesis of leisure. "We make war in order to be at peace," and we engage in politics in order to make the citizens, ourselves and others, happy. For all these reasons, then, "the contemplative activity of the intellect . . . will be the complete happiness of a human being" (1177a12–b26).

But (as is so often the case) Aristotle immediately qualifies this conclusion. "This sort of life is superior to the human way. For one will not live this way insofar as he is a human being, but insofar as something divine is present in him" (1177b27–8). The contemplative life is the closest humans can come to God, who, according to Aristotle, is solely engaged in contemplative activity (8.1178b21–2). Therefore, we should strive to live in accordance with the best thing within us, thought (*nous*), which is most of all what a human being is (7.1177b26–1178a8).

Aristotle then makes a major concession: "The life according to the other kind of virtue is happy in a secondary way, for the activities according to it are appropriate for humans." Practical wisdom and moral virtue are bound up with our passions and bodily nature, whereas the virtue of thought (*nous*) is separated from these. (See the discussion of Aristotle's psychology for discussion of the separability of *nous*.) Practical wisdom and moral virtue also require external goods such as money or political office, whereas contemplation has no need of them. "But insofar as he is a human being, and lives together with numerous persons, he chooses to act according to virtue. So he will need these sorts of [external goods] for leading a human life" (8.1178a9–b7).

Does Aristotle mean that morally virtuous activity is happiness in merely a secondary or inferior degree, or does he mean that it is, in the final analysis, a secondary component of the best life for a human being (as contrasted with the purely contemplative happiness of God)? Commentators are deeply divided over this question, but in debating it, they have painstakingly clarified and criticized every step of Aristotle's argument.

Postscript on education

The last chapter of the *Nicomachean Ethics* X.9 argues that the aim of ethics – to become good persons leading virtuous lives – depends on politics. In order to respond to moral reasoning, we must have been reared properly: "the soul of the student must first have been cultivated by means of habits for noble joy and hatred, like earth which is to nourish the seed" (1179b24–6). But it is hard for young persons to be trained for virtue unless they have been brought up under the laws. By responding to legal punishments and rewards, they acquire the habit of acting like a virtuous person. This is accordingly a major task of political legislation. Aristotle finally remarks that "the philosophy of human affairs" should be completed with a general study of constitutions, which is the central topic of his *Politics*.

Politics

Aristotle's work which has come down to us under the title *Politics* looks less like an integrated treatise than a collection of essays on various topics in political philosophy, which may have been compiled by a later editor rather than by Aristotle. The following topics are discussed in the eight books:

I	Naturalness of the city-state and household
II	Critique of ostensibly best constitutions
III	General theory of constitutions
IV	Inferior constitutions
V	Preservation and destruction of constitutions
VI	Further discussion of democracy and oligarchy
VII–VIII	Blueprint of the best constitution

In addition Aristotle in collaboration with his pupils described the constitutions of 158 city-states (including that of Athens), and classified them (Diogenes Laertius V.22–7; cf. *EN* X.9.1181b6–12). Although the constitutions perished in antiquity, they were frequently quoted by ancient authorities, and a large portion of the *Constitution of Athens* was rediscovered by archeologists in the late nineteenth century. This work may be written by an early member of Aristotle's school, but it provides valuable historical information.

The task of politics

The principal task of the statesman (*politikos*) or legislator (*nomothetēs*) is to frame the appropriate constitution for the city-state. This involves creating enduring laws, customs, and institutions (including a system of moral education) for the citizens. Once the constitution is in place, the statesman needs to take the appropriate measures to maintain it, to introduce any necessary reforms, and to prevent subversive developments.

Aristotle compares the statesman to a craftsman (II.12.1273b32–3, VII.4.1325b40–1365a5). The analogy is imperfect, but valid to the extent that the statesman produces a legal system according to universal principles (*EN* VI.8 and X.9). A craftsman (e.g., a potter) produces an artifact (a vase), which can be explained in terms of Aristotle's four causes: the material, formal, efficient, and final causes (*Phys.* II.3 and *Met.* 2). For example, clay (material cause) is molded into a vase shape (formal cause) by the potter (efficient or moving cause) so that it can contain liquid (final cause).

One can also explain the existence of the city-state in terms of the four causes. It is a kind of community (*koinōnia*), that is, a collection of parts having something in common (*Pol.* II.1.1261a18, III.1.1275b20). Hence, it is made up of parts, which Aristotle describes in various ways in different contexts: as households, or economic classes (e.g., the rich and the poor), or demes (i.e., local political units). But, ultimately, the city-state is composed of individual citizens (see III.1.1274a38–41), who, along with natural resources, are the "material" cause or "equipment" out of which the city-state is fashioned (see VII.14.1325b38–41).

The formal cause of the city-state is its constitution (*politeia*). Aristotle defines the constitution as "a certain ordering of the inhabitants of the city-state" (III.1.1274b32–41). He also speaks of the constitution of a community as "the form of the compound" and argues that whether the community is the same over time depends on whether it has the same constitution (III.3.1276b1–11). The constitution is not a written document, but an immanent organizing principle, analogous to the soul of an organism. Hence, the constitution is also "the way of life" of the citizens (IV.11.1295a40–b1, VII.8.1328b1–2).

The existence of the city-state also requires an efficient cause. On Aristotle's view, a community of any sort can possess order only if it has a ruling element or authority. If the city-state is a going concern, this element is its ruling class or governing body (*politeuma*). This ruling principle is defined by the constitution, which sets criteria for political offices, particularly the sovereign office (III.6.1278b8–10; cf. IV.1.1289a15–18). However, on a deeper level, there must be an efficient cause to explain why a city-state acquires its constitution in the first place. Aristotle states that "the person who first established [the city-state] is the cause of very great benefits" (I.2.1253a30–1). This person was evidently the legislator (*nomothetēs*), someone like Lycurgus who founded the constitution of Sparta, or Solon who reformed that of Athens. The term "statesman" (*politikos*) is bestowed on anyone capable of performing the role of founding or leading a city-state.

The notion of final cause dominates Aristotle's *Politics* from the opening lines:

> Since we see that every city-state is a sort of community and that every community is established for the sake of some good (for everyone does everything for the sake of what they believe to be good), it is clear that every community aims at some good, and the community which has the most authority of all and includes all the others aims highest, that is, at the good with the most authority. This is what is called the city-state or political community. (I.1.1252a1–7)

Soon after, he states that the city-state comes into existence for the sake of life but exists for the sake of the good life (2.1252b29–30). The theme that the good life or happiness is the proper end of the city-state recurs throughout the *Politics* (III.6.1278b17–24, 9.1280b39; VII.2.1325a7–10).

To sum up, the city-state is a hylomorphic (i.e., matter-form) compound of a particular population in a given territory (material cause) and a constitution (formal cause). The constitution itself is fashioned by the legislator and is governed by statesmen, who are like craftsmen (efficient cause), and the constitution defines the aim of the city-state (final cause, IV.1.1289a17–18).

The comparison between city-state and artifact requires an important qualification. The population is not in Aristotle's view merely passive and plastic material like clay. He argues that "a human being is by nature a political animal" (I.2.1252b30–1253a1), and that everyone naturally has the impulse to live in a political community (1253a29–30, III.6.19–30). He argues also that the city-state exists by nature, because it arises out of natural human impulses and serves human natural ends (1252b30–1253a1). This view of the city-state (*political naturalism*) has been criticized by modern political philosophers, especially its "teleological" assumption that humans have natural ends or potentials, including the innate tendency for political life. Further, even if we accept Aristotelian teleology, his claim that the city-state exists by nature is puzzling. An acorn exists by nature because it has an essentially intrinsic moving principle, an innate tendency to grow into an oak tree. A vase exists not by nature but by art, because its moving principle is in the potter who fashions it out of clay. If the statesman is like a craftsman, then the city-state would seem more like a vase than an acorn. The city-state, as Aristotle understands it, looks like a kind of "natural artifact," since it owes its existence to nature as well as a human efficient cause. Is this a coherent idea? It might be suggested that the city-state is analogous to a beehive or a bird's nest. On Aristotle's view these things come to be and exist by nature although they do not possess internal principles of change as do living things (*Phys.* II.8.199a7–8, 29–30). Might the city-state be somehow the product of nature and human reason working together?

It is in the framework of the four causes that Aristotle understands the fundamental practical problem of politics: What constitutional form should the legislator and statesman establish and preserve in what material for the sake of what end?

Citizenship and constitutions

Aristotle states that "the statesman and legislator is wholly occupied with the city-state, and the constitution is a certain way of organizing those who inhabit the city-state" (III.1.1274b36–8). His general theory of constitutions proceeds from a definition of the citizen (*politēs*), since the city-state is by nature a collective entity, a multitude of citizens. Citizens are distinguished from other inhabitants, such as resident aliens and slaves, and even children and seniors are not unqualified citizens. After further analysis he defines the citizen as a person who has the liberty (*exousia*) to participate in deliberative or judicial office (1275b18–21). In a democratic city-state such as Athens, for example, citizens had the right to attend the assembly, the council, and other bodies, and to sit on juries. The Athenian system differed from a modern representative democracy in that the citizens were more directly involved in governing. But full citizenship tended to be restricted even in democratic city-states like Athens, with women, slaves, resident aliens, and some others excluded. Aristotle further states that the city-state (in the unqualified sense) is a multitude of such citizens which is adequate for a self-sufficient life (1275b20–1), and he characterizes the constitution as the form and principle of identity of the city-state (3.1276b1–11).

Aristotle defines the constitution more precisely as a way of organizing the offices of the city-state, particularly the sovereign office (III.6.1278b8–10; cf. IV.1.1289a15–18). The constitution thus defines the governing body, which takes different forms: for example, in a democracy it is the people, and in an oligarchy it is a select few (the wealthy or well born). Before attempting to distinguish and evaluate various constitutions Aristotle considers two questions. First, why does a city-state come into being? He recalls the thesis, defended in *Politics* I.2, that human beings are by nature political animals, who naturally want to live together. He then adds that "the common advantage also brings them together insofar as they each attain the noble life. This is above all the end for all both in common and separately" (III.6.1278b19–24). Second, what are the different forms of rule by which one individual or group can rule over another? Aristotle distinguishes several types. He first considers *despotic rule*, which is exemplified in the master–slave relationship. Aristotle thinks that this form of rule is justified in the case of individuals who lack a deliberative faculty and thus are "natural slaves" requiring a natural master to direct them (I.13.1260a12; slavery is defended at length in *Pol.* I.4–8). Although a natural slave allegedly benefits from having a master, despotic rule is still primarily for the sake of the master and only incidentally for the slave (III.6.1278b32–7).

Aristotle's discussion of slavery presents many difficulties. He asserts without evidence that there are many such "natural slaves" (especially among barbarian, non-Greek populations). Further, it might be objected, even if some persons are congenitally incapable of self-governance, why should they not be ruled primarily for their own benefit, rather than that of their masters? He next considers *paternal and marital rule*, which he also views as defensible: "the male is by nature more capable of leadership than the female, unless he is constituted in some way contrary to nature, and the elder and perfect [is by nature more capable of leadership] than the younger and imperfect" (I.12.1259a39–b4). Aristotle is persuasive when he argues that children need adult supervision because their rationality is "incomplete" (*ateles*) or immature. But he also alleges (again without substantiation) that, although women have a deliberative faculty, it is "without authority" (*akyron*), so that females require male leadership (I.13.1260a13–14). (Aristotle's arguments about slaves and women appear so weak that some commentators take them to be ironic. But what is obvious to a modern reader need not have been so to an ancient Greek philosopher. Could Aristotle have been persuaded that his treatment of slaves and women runs afoul of his own more defensible principles?) It is noteworthy, however, that paternal and marital rule are properly practiced for the sake of the ruled (for the sake of the child and of the wife, respectively), just as arts like medicine are practiced for the sake of the patient (III.6.1278b37–1279a1). In this respect they resemble *political rule*, which involves equal and similar citizens taking turns in ruling for the subjects' advantage (1279a8–13). This sets the stage for the fundamental claim of Aristotle's constitutional theory: "constitutions which aim at the common advantage are correct and just without qualification, whereas those which aim only at the advantage of the rulers are deviant and unjust, because they involve despotic rule which is inappropriate for a community of free persons" (1279a17–21).

The distinction between correct and deviant constitutions is combined with the observation that the government may consist of one person, a few, or a multitude. Hence, there are six possible constitutional forms (*Politics* III.7):

	Correct	Deviant
One ruler	Kingship	Tyranny
Few rulers	Aristocracy	Oligarchy
Many rulers	Polity	Democracy

This sixfold classification (which is adapted from Plato's *Statesman*) is the starting point for Aristotle's inquiry into the best constitution, although it is modified in various ways throughout the *Politics*. For example, he observes that the dominant class in oligarchy (literally rule of the *oligoi*, i.e., few) is typically the wealthy, whereas in democracy (literally rule of the *dēmos*, i.e., people) it is the poor, so that these economic classes should be included in the definition of these forms (see *Pol.* III.8, IV.4, and VI.2 for alternative accounts). Also, polity is later characterized as a kind of "mixed" constitution typified by rule of the "middle" group of citizens, a moderately wealthy class between the rich and poor (*Pol.* IV.11).

Aristotle turns to arguments for and against the different constitutions, which he views as different applications of the principle of distributive justice (III.9.1280a7–22). Everyone agrees, he says, that justice involves treating equal persons equally, and treating unequal persons unequally, but they do not agree on the standard by which individuals are deemed to be equally (or unequally) meritorious or deserving. He assumes the aforementioned analysis of distributive justice in *Nicomachean Ethics* V.3: Justice requires that benefits be distributed to individuals in proportion to their merit or desert. Thus in a political context:

$$\frac{\text{Merit of } X}{\text{Merit of } Y} = \frac{\text{Rights of } X}{\text{Rights of } Y}$$

The oligarchs argue that the wealthy property owners are more meritorious and thus should have greater political rights than the poor, whereas the democrats contend that all free-born citizens are equally meritorious and thus should each possess equal political rights. Aristotle thinks that both of these views of political justice are mistaken, because they assume a false standard of political merit and, ultimately, an erroneous view of the ultimate end of the city-state. The city-state is neither a business association to maximize wealth (as the oligarchs suppose) nor an agency to promote liberty and equality (as the democrats maintain). Instead, Aristotle argues, "the good life is the end of the city-state," that is, a life consisting of noble actions (1280b39–1281a4). Hence, the correct conception of justice is aristocratic, assigning political rights to those who make a full contribution to the political community, that is, to those with virtue as well as property and freedom (1281a4–8). This is what Aristotle understands by an "aristocratic" constitution: literally, the rule of the *aristoi*, that is, best persons. Aristotle explores the implications of this argument in the remainder of *Politics* III, considering the rival claims of the rule of law and the rule of a supremely virtuous individual. Here absolute kingship is a limiting case of aristocracy. Again, in books VII–VIII, Aristotle describes the ideal constitution which is best in the sense that "anyone whatsoever can act in the best way and live happily" (VII.2.1324a23–5). Happiness is here defined as "the actualization and complete employment of virtue" (*Pol.* VII.13.1332a7–9), with a cross-reference to *Eudemian Ethics* II.1.1219a38–b2 (cf. *EN* I.7.1098a16–18, 10.1101a14–16).

Ideal and attainable constitutions

The purpose of political science is to guide "the good legislator and the true statesman" (IV.1.1288b27). Like any complete science or craft, it must study a range of issues concerning its subject matter. For example, gymnastics (physical training) studies what sort of training is advantageous for what sort of body, what sort of training is best or adapted to the body that is naturally the best, what sort of training is best for most bodies, and what capacity is appropriate for someone who does not want the condition or knowledge appropriate for athletic contests. Political science studies a comparable range of constitutions (1288b21–35): first, the constitution which is best without qualification, that is, "most according to our prayers with no external impediment"; second, the constitution that is best under the circumstances "for it is probably impossible for many persons to attain the best constitution"; third, the constitution which serves the aim a given city-state population happens to have [that is best], based on a hypothesis:

> for [the political scientist] ought to be able to study a given constitution, both how it might originally come to be, and, when it has come to be, in what manner it might be preserved for the longest time; I mean, for example, if a particular city happens neither to be governed by the best constitution, nor to be equipped even with necessary things, nor to be the [best] possible under existing circumstances, but to be a baser sort.

Hence, Aristotelian political science is not confined to the ideal system, but also investigates the second-best constitution, the one which is the best that most city-states are capable of supporting. This is the closest approximation to full political justice which the legislator can attain under ordinary circumstances. Although

Aristotle's political views were influenced by his teacher Plato, he is very critical of the ideal city-state set forth in Plato's *Republic* on the grounds that it overvalues political unity, it embraces a system of communism that is impractical and inimical to human nature, and it neglects the happiness of the individual citizens (*Pol.* II.1–5). In contrast, in Aristotle's own "best constitution" (described in *Politics* VII–VIII) each and every citizen will possess moral virtue and the equipment to carry it out in practice, and thereby attain a life of excellence and complete happiness (see VII.13.1332a32–8). Commentators disagree over whether Aristotle viewed the individual citizens as bearers of political rights. But it is clear that his theory of political justice implies that in a just constitution, all of the citizens will hold political office and possess private property, because "one should call the city-state happy by looking not at a part of it but at all the citizens" (VII.9.1329a22–3). Moreover, there will be a common system of education for all the citizens, because they share the same end (*Pol.* VIII.1). This is in keeping with Aristotle's concerns about moral education in the *Nicomachean Ethics*. But if (as is the case with most city-states) the population lacks the capacities and resources for complete happiness, the legislator must be content with fashioning a suitable constitution (*Pol.* IV.11). The second-best system typically takes the form of a polity (in which citizens possess an inferior, more common grade of virtue) or mixed constitution (combining features of democracy, oligarchy, and aristocracy, so that no group of citizens is in a position to abuse its rights).

In addition, the political scientist must understand existing constitutions even when they are bad. He adds that "to reform a constitution is no less a task [of politics] than it is to establish one from the beginning," and in this way "the statesman should also help existing constitutions" (IV.1.1289a1–7). *Politics* Books IV–VI are mainly concerned with actual constitutions. As noted earlier Aristotle and his pupils also collected the constitutions of 158 city-states, and arranged them by type: democratic, oligarchical, tyrannical, aristocratic. The political scientist should also be cognizant of forces of political change which can undermine an existing regime. Aristotle criticizes his predecessors for excessive utopianism and neglect of the practical duties of a political theorist. His emphasis on practical politics, including his controversial "advice to the tyrant" (*Pol.* V.11), has led some commentators to indict him as a Machiavellian. But there is also some evidence that his best constitution serves as a regulative ideal by which to evaluate existing systems. For example, in *Politics* IV.11 his recommended "middle constitution" seems to be modeled after the ideal state, and in V.9 he prescribes educational systems for democracies and oligarchies. The political scientist must evidently combine ideal theory and practical politics. Whether Aristotle succeeded in reconciling these two agendas is a matter of continuing controversy.

These topics occupy the remainder of the *Politics*. Books IV–VI are concerned with the existing constitutions, that is, the three deviant constitutions, as well as polity or the mixed constitution, the best attainable (IV.2.1289a26–38). The whole of Book V investigates political change and revolution. Books VII–VIII are devoted to the ideal constitution. Aristotle's attempt to carry out this program predictably involves many difficulties, and scholars disagree about how the two series of books

(IV–VI and VII–VIII) are related to each other: for example, which were written first, which were intended to be read first, and whether they are ultimately consistent with each other. Some modern scholars even recommend renumbering the books, so that the books conventionally numbered VII–VIII become IV–V and the three "middle" books IV–VI become VI–VIII.

Conclusion

Aristotle continues to influence contemporary ethics and political philosophy because his writings contain deep and thought-provoking discussions of perennial concerns: What is the nature of happiness and well-being? Does virtue have a place in a moral life? Are ethical standards based on human nature or convention? What is the proper relation of the individual to the state? Should morality have a role in politics? What principles of justice should govern our political system? Is democracy or some other system the most just? Should a just system observe "the rule of law"? What are the causes and proper cures for political conflict and revolution? Even now, as they ponder these questions, ethical and political thinkers of all stripes can come together in endorsing Aristotle's call for a morally educated citizenry.

Acknowledgments

I received very helpful criticisms of an earlier draft of this chapter from Lawrence Jost and David Keyt. I am also grateful to several graduate students for commenting on earlier versions: Mahesh Ananth, Jason Gatliff, Carrie-Ann and Khalil Khan, Pamela Phillips, and Anton Tupa. The discussion of Aristotle's politics includes material which originally appeared in F. Miller, "Aristotle's Political Philosophy," in the *Stanford Encyclopedia of Philosophy* (winter 2000) <http://plato.stanford.edu/archives/win2000/entries/aristotle-politics> and is reused here in revised form with permission.

References and Recommended Reading

Translations

There are many fine English translations of Aristotle's works on ethics and politics, but readers are advised to compare different versions, because translators must make controversial decisions of interpretation. A convenient source is vol. 2 of *The Complete Works of Aristotle: The Revised Oxford Translation* edited by Jonathan Barnes (Princeton, N.J.: Princeton University Press, 1984). The translations often have generally informative introductions, notes, and bibliographies. The editions are listed alphabetically by last name of translator.

Translations of Aristotle, Nicomachean Ethics

Apostle, Hippocrates G. (Grinnell, Ia.: Peripatetic Press, 1984).

Crisp, Roger (Cambridge: Cambridge University Press, 2000).

Irwin, Terence. 2nd ed. (Indianapolis: Hackett Press, 2000).

Ostwald, Martin (Totowa, N.J.: Prentice-Hall, 1962).

Pakaluk, Michael. Books VII and IX (Oxford: Oxford University Press, Clarendon Aristotle Series, 1999).

Rackham, Harris (Cambridge, Mass.: Harvard University Press, Loeb Library, 1934); also with introduction by Stephen Watt (Ware, UK: Wordsworth Classics, 1997).

Ross, W. D. Revised J. L. Ackrill and J. O. Urmson (Oxford University Press, Oxford World's Classics, 1998); also in Barnes, *Complete Works of Aristotle.*

Rowe, Christopher. With philosophical introduction and commentary by Sarah Broadie (Oxford: Oxford University Press, 2002).

Thomson, J. A. K. Revised Hugh Tredennick with introduction and bibliography by Jonathan Barnes (Harmondsworth, UK: Penguin Books 1976).

Translations of Aristotle, Eudemian Ethics

Rackham, H. Bound with *Athenian Constitution* and *Virtues and Vices* (Cambridge, Mass.: Harvard University Press, Loeb Library, 1952).

Solomon, J. In Barnes, *Complete Works of Aristotle.*

Woods, Michael. Books I, II, and VIII (Oxford: Oxford University Press, Clarendon Aristotle Series, 2nd ed., 1992).

Translations of Aristotle, Magna Moralia

Armstrong, G. Cyril. Bound with H. Tredennick translation of *Metaphysics*, vol. 2 (Cambridge, Mass.: Harvard University Press, 1935).

Stock, St. G. In Barnes, *Complete Works of Aristotle.*

Translations of Aristotle, Politics

Apostle, H. G. and Gerson, L. P. (Grinnell: Peripatetic Press, 1986).

Barker, Ernest. Revised R. F. Stalley (Oxford: Oxford University Press, Oxford World's Classics, 1998).

Jowett, Benjamin. Edited by Stephen Everson and bound with *The Constitution of Athens* (Cambridge: Cambridge University Press, 1996). Also in Barnes, *Complete Works of Aristotle.*

Keyt, David, Books V and VI (Oxford: Oxford University Press, Clarendon Aristotle Series, 1999).

Kraut, Richard. Books VII and VIII (Oxford: Oxford University Press, Clarendon Aristotle Series, 1998).

Lord, Carnes (Chicago: University of Chicago Press, 1985).

Rackham, Harris. English translation and Greek text (Cambridge, Mass: Harvard University Press, Loeb Library Edition, 1932).

Reeve, C. D. C. (Indianapolis: Hackett Publishing, 1998).

Robinson, R. Books III and IV. Revised ed. with supplementary interpretive essay by David Keyt (Oxford: Oxford University Press, Clarendon Aristotle Series, 1996).

Saunders, Trevor J. Books I and II (Oxford: Oxford University Press, Clarendon Aristotle Series, 1996).

Simpson, Peter L. Phillips (Chapel Hill: University of North Carolina Press, 1997).

Sinclair, T. A. Revised by Trevor J. Saunders (Harmondsworth, UK: Penguin Books, 1992).

Commentaries on Aristotle's Ethics

Anton, J. and Preus, A., *Essays in Ancient Greek Philosophy*, vol. 4: *Aristotle's Ethics* (Albany: SUNY, 1991). Essays on Aristotle's methodology, the function argument, virtue and character, moral reasoning, and moral issues involving persons and property.

Barnes, Jonathan; Sorabji, Richard; and Schofield, Malcolm, *Articles on Aristotle*, vol. 2: *Ethics and Politics* (London: Duckworth, 1975). Essays on happiness, virtue, theory of action, moral epistemology, moral weakness, pleasure, political naturalism, slavery, economics, political conflict, peace, and history. Extensive bibliography.

Bosley, Richard; Shiner, Roger A.; and Sisson, Janet D., *Aristotle, Virtue, and the Mean* (Edmonton, Canada: Academic Printing, 1995). Critical studies of Aristotle's analysis of virtue as a mean between two extremes, and the relation of his theory to modern virtue ethics.

Broadie, Sarah, *Ethics with Aristotle* (Oxford: Oxford University Press, 1991). Comprehensive study covering happiness, virtues and parts of the soul, voluntariness, practical wisdom, incontinence, pleasure, and the place of contemplation in the good life, with bibliography.

Cooper, John M., *Reason and Human Good in Aristotle* (Cambridge, Mass.: Harvard University Press, 1975). Influential interpretation of Aristotle's account of moral reasoning, and defense of an intellectualist interpretation of Aristotle's theory of happiness.

——, *Reason and Emotion* (Princeton: Princeton University Press, 1999). Several valuable essays on Aristotle's ethics and politics, including "Contemplation and Happiness in Aristotle: A Reconsideration," which revises Cooper's intellectualist interpretation in *Reason and Human Good in Aristotle*.

Dahl, Norman O., *Practical Reason, Aristotle, and Weakness of Will* (Minneapolis: University of Minnesota Press, 1984). Clear overview of Aristotle's views on practical reason and of the problem of incontinence.

Hardie, W. F. R., *Aristotle's Ethical Theory*, 2nd ed. (Oxford: Oxford University Press, 1980). Commentary on the *Nicomachean Ethics*. Although beginners may find it sometimes demanding and technical, it contains helpful discussion of difficult passages in Aristotle.

Heinaman, Robert (ed.), *Aristotle and Moral Realism* (Boulder, Colo.: Westview Press, 1995). Critical essays discussing Aristotle's moral epistemology, including its relation to modern moral realism.

Kenny, Anthony, *The Aristotelian Ethics* (Oxford: Oxford University Press, 1978) and *Aristotle on the Perfect Life* (Oxford: Oxford University Press, 1992). These works emphasize the *Eudemian Ethics* as a source for Aristotle's mature moral philosophy.

Kraut, Richard, *Aristotle on the Human Good* (Princeton: University of Princeton Press, 1989). Comprehensive discussion of Aristotle's views on happiness and moral obligation.

Reeve, C. D. C., *Practices of Reason: Aristotle's Nicomachean Ethics* (Oxford: Oxford University Press, 1992). Emphasis on the place of reason in Aristotle's ethics, arguing that Aristotle viewed ethics as a science.

Sherman, Nancy, *Aristotle's Ethics: Critical Essays* (Lanham, Md.: Rowman & Littlefield, 1999). Illuminating essays on happiness, virtue, reason, incontinence, friendship, and feminism.

Rorty, A. O., *Essays on Aristotle's Ethics* (Berkeley: University of California Press, 1980). Important collection of essays covering the major topics of Aristotle's ethics.

Stewart, J. A., *Notes on the Nicomachean Ethics of Aristotle* (Oxford: Oxford University Press, 1892). Although many notes deal with textual issues and are studded with quotations in Greek and other languages, the careful reader can glean many valuable philosophical insights.

Commentaries on Aristotle's Politics

Keyt, David, and Miller, Fred D., Jr. (eds.), *A Companion to Aristotle's Politics* (Oxford: Blackwell, 1991). Important collection of essays on the major topics of Aristotle's political philosophy.

Kraut, Richard, *Aristotle's Political Philosophy* (Oxford: Oxford University Press, 2002). Interpretation and critical examination of the modern relevance of Aristotle's political thought, discussing justice, political idealism, practical politics, and other themes.

Mayhew, Robert, *Aristotle's Criticism of Plato's Republic* (Lanham, Md.: Rowman & Littlefield, 1997). Sympathetic exposition of Aristotle's criticisms of Plato's communistic regime.

Miller, Fred D., Jr., *Nature, Justice, and Rights in Aristotle's Politics* (Oxford: Oxford University Press, 1995). Comprehensive discussion of Aristotle's *Politics*, including his political naturalism and his theory of justice and rights.

Mulgan, R. G., *Aristotle's Political Theory* (Oxford: Oxford University Press, 1997). Concise, clear introduction for students of political theory.

Newman, W. L., *The Politics of Aristotle* (Oxford: Oxford University Press, 1887–1902). An erudite discussion, still indispensable to students of Aristotle at all levels. Vol. 1 is a general discussion; vols. 2–4 contain Greek text, notes, and detailed commentary.

Simpson, Peter, *A Philosophical Commentary on the Politics of Aristotle* (Chapel Hill: University of North Carolina Press, 1988). Helpful guide to Aristotle's arguments.

Susemihl, F. and Hicks, R. D., *The Politics of Aristotle* (London: Macmillan, 1894). Introduction, Greek text, and notes. Still contains valuable discussion.

Chapter 11

Aristotle: Psychology

Gareth Matthews

Introduction

It may come as a surprise to readers to be told that there is such a thing as "Aristotle's psychology." After all, psychology was not generally recognized as a distinct discipline in our modern universities until late in the nineteenth century. Yet Aristotle did write a short, but trenchant, treatise called "On the Psyche" (*Peri psychē*, or *De anima*, "On the Soul"). And we can say, quite appropriately, that this is indeed a treatise on psychology. It includes interesting and important discussions of perception, thinking, and cognition, which are certainly topics that belong to what we think of today as psychology. Moreover, other works of Aristotle take up matters that belong to psychology. For example, his *De motu* ("On Movement") sketches his understanding of action as the integration of desires with beliefs and perceptions. This conception lies at the center of what is sometimes disparagingly referred to these days as "folk psychology." Yet despite recent advances in cognitive science and the common disparagement of folk psychology, Aristotle's conception remains basic to the way we understand human (and nonhuman animal) action today.

So there is such a thing as Aristotle's psychology. Does Aristotle also have what we could appropriately call a "philosophy of mind"? That question is much more difficult to answer. Even if, in the end, we agree with commentators who say that Aristotle's *De anima* is also a treatise on the philosophy of mind, we need to be clear that Aristotle was quite innocent of the modern concept of mind, which owes so much to the philosophy of Descartes. Modern accounts of mind and the mental, even if they are anti-Cartesian accounts, take their shape against the background of Descartes. Being innocent even of the idea of Cartesian dualism, Aristotle neither embraced it nor rejected it. The principal options he knew, and rejected, were the soul–body dualism of Plato and materialism, both the materialism of the ancient atomists, especially Democritus, and also that of the ancient pluralists, especially Empedocles. Between Platonic dualism and ancient materialism he found a middle way. Although what we think of as our main options are somewhat different today, Aristotle's "third way" remains instructive to us, partly because it suggests a somewhat unfamiliar perspective on familiar issues in the philosophy of mind. Aristotle's pre-Cartesian point of view thus challenges us to consider whether the options we consider exhaustive really are so, or whether they leave out some viable alternative.

Psychē and Life

The *psychē*, Aristotle tells us at the very beginning of his *De anima* is, as it were, "the principle of living things" (*archē tōn zōōn*) (402a6–7). That claim may strike us today as a very odd starting point for what is supposed to be a treatise on psychology. For one thing, it means that plants, too, have a psyche, and therefore, in some sense, a psychology. Despite recent efforts to make plants grow by affecting their "mood" or "attitude" through, for example, playing music to them, the idea that plants actually have what could appropriately be called a psychology is not widely accepted today. Even more eccentric to us moderns is the idea that all life functions in animals, including, of course, human animals, should be considered, in some appropriate sense, psychological. That strikes many of us as simply absurd.

It was Descartes who first taught us that it is absurd to suppose that thinking, the activity he took to be essential to mind, has anything to do with life. According to him, *anima*, the Latin word for *psychē*, is equivocal. In one sense it does indeed mean the principle by which we are nourished, grow, and reproduce. We say, drawing on this sense of *anima*, that a frozen organism is in a state of "suspended animation," provided, of course, that thawing it would reinvigorate it. But, in the other sense, Descartes insisted, *anima* means the mind, that is, the thing that thinks; and, in that sense, he says, the *anima* or *psychē* has nothing to do with life.[1]

Although psychologists today may not agree with Descartes in supposing that the mind is an independent thing in its own right, a substance distinct from the body, many would indeed agree with him that the mind, whatever exactly it is, has nothing directly, or essentially, to do with life functions. For this reason it can be an open question for them, as it could not have been for Aristotle, whether a very sophisticated nonliving thing, say, a highly developed robot, might nevertheless think, that it might, for example, have the thought that water is wet or that the thunder is now making a very loud noise.[2]

Still, Aristotle's notion that thinking is a life function has some support even today. Thus John Searle, in his 1984 Reith Lectures, says that "mental states are biological phenomena. Consciousness, intentionality, subjectivity and mental causation are all a part of our biological life history, along with growth, reproduction, the secretion of bile, and digestion."[3]

In Aristotle's Greek, an *empschyon*, an ensouled entity, is a living thing. Thus it is, for Aristotle, a verbal truth that all living things have souls. Beyond that, Aristotle supposes that the life functions are "nested" in such a way that the higher functions depend in some very important way on lower ones. Some organisms, he tells us, take nourishment, grow, and reproduce, but do not move themselves or perceive. These are plants; they have only a vegetative *psychē*. Other organisms, namely, the animals, move themselves and perceive as well as nourishing and reproducing themselves. Among mortal animals, the human ones, and only they, also think. It has been argued that what, for Aristotle, makes it appropriate to recognize thinking, along with nourishment, movement, and perception, as life functions, is that each of these capacities, in the particular organisms that have them, enable individuals to function so as to preserve the species to which they belong.[4]

Hylomorphism and the Problem of Body

As we have already noted, the most important options familiar to Aristotle for thinking about what a psyche is are (1) soul–body dualism and (2) materialism. Aristotle's great predecessor and teacher, Plato, thought of the soul as a distinct entity that is quite independent of whatever body it may currently inhabit. In fact, Plato, like Pythagoras before him, suggests that a human soul that fails to live a morally good life, may be assigned to a lower animal in its next incarnation as a form of punishment (*Phaedo* 81e–82a). On the way back to a human incarnation, souls that have practiced social virtue may temporarily ensoul bees or ants (82ab).[5]

Aristotle found the idea of transmigration of souls preposterous. He derides theorists who ignore the character of the body that receives the soul, "as if it were possible, as in the Pythagorean myths, that any soul could be clothed in any body – an absurd view, for each body seems to have a species and form of its own [*eidos kai morphēn*]" (407b21–4).

In contrast to Plato, with his soul–body dualism, the ancient atomists took the position that the soul is a collection of very fine atoms that suffuses the body to make it alive and sensitive, and to coordinate its actions. Among Aristotle's criticisms of the atomists and the other materialists is his complaint that they cannot explain the unity of an individual soul. "Some hold," Aristotle writes,

> that the soul is divisible, and that we think with one part and desire with another. If, then, its nature admits of its being divided, what can it be that holds the parts together? Surely not the body; on the contrary it seems rather to be the soul that holds the body together; at any rate when the soul departs, the body disintegrates and decays. If, then, there is something else which makes the soul one, this would be most properly the soul. (411b5–10)

A natural response to this Aristotelian insistence on the unity of the soul would be to add that, to do their collective job as soul, the elements that suffuse the living body would have to organize and structure the functional parts of the body in some determinate way. This organization might be thought to be like the harmony of an instrument. Now what makes a guitar an instrument tuned in a certain key is its having its parts related to one another in some determinately specifiable way. The thought is then natural that in the same fashion the "harmony" of the bodily parts would just be what we think of as the soul: what organizes the various bodily elements into a living being is the soul, the harmony of the living and functioning body.

Aristotle had, however, already discredited this suggestion, to be found, for example, in Plato's *Phaedo* at 85e–86d, that the soul is a harmony. "The power of originating movement," Aristotle had written in the previous chapter of the *De anima*, "cannot belong to a harmony, while all concur in regarding this pretty well as a principal attribute of soul" (407b34–8a1).

The idea of the soul as a "harmony" may strike the modern reader as rather quaint. Nevertheless, this idea is quite closely related to recent suggestions that consciousness may be only an "epiphenomenon." An epiphenomenon is said to be something like the whistle an old-fashioned steam locomotive would make. That sound obviously has no effect on making the steam pass through the small slit that produces it, let alone on making the wheels of the locomotive go around. The question is now whether the deliverances of consciousness – thoughts, emotions, desires – though they have (physical) causes, are themselves without causal efficacy.[6]

Aristotle's alternative to both materialism and soul–body dualism rejects the options (1) just another thing additional to the body, and (2) nothing but a certain kind of body. It also finds (3) the idea that the soul is a kind of harmony too weak precisely because it fails to account for the causal efficacy of the soul. What he proposes instead is the idea of the soul as form (*eidos*), where form for him is not just shape or even organization, but also the actual ability to function as a plant or animal. This ability Aristotle calls a "first" actuality, as contrasted with a "second" actuality (which is the exercise of that ability to function, as, say, when one is alert and thinking rather than unconscious).

Thus Aristotle tells us in the first chapter of Book II of the *De anima* that the soul is "the first actuality of a natural organic body" (412b5–6). Earlier he had written that the soul is "a substance as form of a natural body which has life potentially" (412a20–1). In a third formulation, he had said that the soul is "the first actuality of a natural body which has life potentially" (412a27–8).

Scholars have found various difficulties in understanding these statements, even in understanding how they can be alternative formulations of the same view. But perhaps the difficulty that has received the most attention in recent literature is what has come to be called "Ackrill's problem," after J. L. Ackrill, who identified it and effectively urged its importance.[7] The problem is that we cannot, it seems, pick out the body of a human being as something distinct from the human being whose matter the body is supposed to be.

To understand the force of Ackrill's problem one must realize that, according to Aristotle, a human corpse is a human body in name only. Once a human body, say, the body of Socrates, ceases to function in any of the ways that count as making something alive, then not only does Socrates himself cease to exist, so does his body. Socrates' body is replaced by his corpse. Thus what Socrates leaves behind, after his death, is only something that resembles his body. And so we can't say that Socrates' body is something distinct from Socrates by being something that may survive Socrates' death. But if Socrates' body is not something that survives Socrates' death, how can it be something distinct from Socrates himself?

Various solutions have been offered to Ackrill's problem. Marc Cohen, like several other commentators, suggests disambiguating the term "body." Echoing a move in Bernard Williams,[8] Cohen tells us that there is

> something that looks, acts, and functions very much like the body, although it cannot, strictly speaking *be* the body, since it will continue to exist after death, when the body no longer exists. Nor is this something the corpse, which only begins to exist at death. It is this continuing something (which non-Aristotelians are inclined to call the "body") that Aristotle needs to refer. Well, then, let him refer to it in some other way – say, as the BODY. The BODY has accidentally those properties the body has essentially, and in virtue of which the animal is alive. When the BODY functions, the body is alive; when the BODY ceases to function, the body, but not the BODY, ceases to exist.[9]

On the Cohen–Williams reworking of Aristotle's terminology, it is the BODY, which is the body of a living human being before death and also the corpse just after that human being's demise. And thus it is the BODY that has the actual ability to function before the human being's death and continues to exist for a time after death, even without that ability to perform any life functions. If this move solves Ackrill's problem, one has to say, it does so by supplementing what Aristotle actually says, rather than simply elucidating it.

Perception

So far we have talked about what Aristotle thinks a soul is and how souls are related to bodies. But Aristotle actually focuses much of his attention on the individual capacities of the soul. Prominent among these is, of course, perception. It is perception, along with self-motion, that Aristotle thinks marks off animals from other living things, that is, from plants.

Aristotle, like Plato before him, recognizes that each of the five sense modalities has objects peculiar to it. Thus sight, and only sight, perceives color, whereas hearing, and only hearing, perceives sound, and so on for the other sense modalities. In addition, and here he goes beyond Plato, Aristotle recognizes common objects of perception, such as movement, rest, number, figure, and size, which may be perceived by more than one sense modality. Finally, Aristotle considers the people, animals, and physical objects we can perceive through our senses as what he calls "incidental" or "accidental" [*kata symbebēkos*] objects of perception (*De anima* 2.6).

"With regard to all sense perception," Aristotle tells us, "we must take it that a sense is that which can receive perceptible forms without their matter, as wax receives the imprint of the ring without the iron or gold" (424a17–20). What exactly Aristotle had in mind when he talked of receiving perceptible forms without their matter has been much debated, especially in recent decades. Richard Sorabji's interpretation is perhaps the most direct and straightforward. "In vision, for example," Sorabji tells us, "the eye-jelly (*korē*) does not receive particles or other bits of *matter* from the scene observed. It simply takes on colour patches (perceptible *forms*) to match it."[10]

Thus, according to Sorabji's reading of Aristotle,[11] the eye-jelly itself actually becomes red when the subject sees a red ball. In fact, Sorabji thinks, sizes and shapes are taken on in the same way. So what the eye-jelly would receive when the red ball is seen is a red, round patch, shaded, perhaps to look spherical.

Other commentators disagree. According to Myles Burnyeat, who allies himself on this question with John Philoponus, Aquinas, and Franz Brentano, "the eye's taking on a colour is just one's becoming aware of some colour."[12] As Burnyeat makes abundantly clear, this position, if it is indeed Aristotle's own view, is so far from our present-day thinking about the physiological basis of perception, that Aristotle, so understood, would really have nothing to say to us moderns. As Burnyeat puts the point, "all we can do with the Aristotelian philosophy of mind and its theory of perception as the receiving of sensible forms without matter is what the seventeenth century did: Junk it."[13]

The interpretation of Aristotle offered by Sorabji and, before him, Slakey, has come to be called, for obvious reasons, "literalist," and the position interpretation offered by Burnyeat, for equally obvious reasons, is called "spiritualist." There is clearly room for intermediate positions between these two extremes. One of the most interesting and well developed is Stephen Everson's, in Everson (1997). According to that position "material alterations which will be cited in the material explanation of perception are such as to determine perceptual changes and are not merely necessary conditions for perceptual activity" (1997, 230). Nevertheless the finger's becoming warm at touching the hot pot is not identical with the perception of heat. Thus, Aristotle's idea of taking on the form without the matter is much more sophisticated and nuanced than initially seems to be the case. The payoff, according to Everson, is this:

> By allowing that at least perceptual events are determined by material alterations to the sense organs, [Aristotle] is able to do what none of his predecessors were able to – and that is to show why organs which possess the capacities they do have the material constitutions they do. (288)

Mental Events and Physical Events

In keeping with his hylomorphism, Aristotle understands what we might take to be mental events as physical events in a certain form. Thus he tells us that being angry is a boiling of blood or hot stuff around the heart in the way that a house is stones, bricks and timber. But just as the house materials are an actual house by being in a certain form, so the boiling blood or hot stuff is anger by being in an appropriate form. The form that makes the materials a house, he says, is the principle of covering to prevent destruction by winds, rain, and heat. And the form by which the boiling stuff around the heart is anger is the desire for retaliation, or something of the sort (403a29–b7).

The idea that a mental event, for example, an episode of feeling anger toward someone, is a physical event in a certain form, say, in the form of a desire for retaliation, seems to leave open three different styles of causal explanation. One might suppose that (1) the physical event, say the boiling of stuff around the heart in such-and-such a way, is the cause of the mental event, the episode of anger. Or one might suppose that (2) the mental event, the anger as desire for retaliation, causes the boiling of stuff around the heart. Or one might suppose that (3) the cause of the episode of anger is a joint product of stuff boiling around the heart in a context in which one desires retaliation. The third suggestion would make the existence of an episode of anger like the existence of a threshold, which Aristotle tells us is a stone or a piece of wood (matter) in a certain position (form), namely, at the foot of an opening in a house (*Metaphysics* VIII.2.1043a7–8).

Aristotle seems to suggest, however, that, in modern parlance, the mental event supervenes on the physical event.[14] If that is right, then a certain kind of boiling of stuff around the heart will take the form of a desire for retaliation, even when there has been no provocation or when there is really no one to retaliate against. Thus Aristotle tells us this:

> sometimes when violent and obvious sufferings occur, we do not feel resentment or fear, while at other times we are affected by slight and trivial things, when the body is stimulated and is in the same condition as it is when one is angry. Here is still a clearer case: one can undergo the affections of the person who is frightened, even when there is no object of fear. (403a19–24)

According to Victor Caston, "Aristotle believes that bodily states provide nontrivial sufficient conditions for the generation, persistence, and demise of individual souls."[15] And David Charles attributes to Aristotle a "nonreductive materialism" that he calls "ontological materialism" and explains this way:

> For any true psychological description of the world . . . there is some state of affairs characterisable employing only physical vocabulary such that: the obtaining of the physical state of affairs is sufficient (but not causally sufficient) for the truth of the psychological description.[16]

According to Charles, Aristotle's view is that "the occurrence of physical states 'makes true' psychological descriptions without (efficiently) causing the psychological events, states or properties, thus described, to exist."[17]

Just as some commentators, like Charles, argue for understanding Aristotle to be a qualified materialist, so others argue for understanding him to be a qualified dualist. Thus Christopher Shields offers an array of considerations for classifying him as a "supervenient dualist."[18] And Robert Heinaman, who also argues that Aristotle's hylomorphism is really a sort of dualism, tells us that, according to Aristotle, "the soul is a *dynamis* [i.e., a power or capacity] that supervenes (*epigignetai*) on the body when the organization of matter has reached a certain level."[19]

Functionalism

The discussion of anger as boiling blood in the form of desire for retaliation should make clear that what Aristotle means by "form" is much broader and richer than we might at first have thought. In particular, when Aristotle speaks of the soul as the form of a certain sort of body, he does not mean just the shape of the body, except as that shape may be important to its function. The form is really the function, indeed, the functioning of that body. A soul, as Aristotle conceives it, is a complex and highly integrated collection of capacities.

This notion of form as function, or capacity, coupled with Aristotle's desire to find an intermediate position between Plato's soul–body dualism and the atomists' materialist monism, has suggested to some recent commentators that Aristotle's position should be linked with contemporary functionalist accounts of the mind. Functionalism in the philosophy of mind is the theory that mental states are individuated by their relations to causal inputs, behavioral outputs, as well as to other mental states. Functionalists often make use of the computer analogy to try to understand what a mind is and how mental events are related to the physical events they realize. Just as a computer program is "realizable" in different physical forms, say, hard-drives of different material make-up, so mental states are realizable by different physical states. Hilary Putnam, in a paper that initiated the discussion of functionalism as a philosophy of mind, put the point this way:

> our mental states, e.g. *thinking about next summer's vacation*, cannot be *identical* with any physical or chemical states. For it is clear from what we already know about computers, etc., that whatever the program of the brain may be, it must be physically possible, though not necessarily feasible, to produce something with that same program but quite a different physical or chemical constitution. Then to identify the state in question with that realization is in a sense quite accidental, from the point of view of psychology, anyway (which is the relevant science). It is as if we met Martians and discovered that they were in all functional respects isomorphic to us, but we refused to admit that they could feel pain because their C fibers were different.[20]

Near the end of the famous paper from which this quotation is taken Putnam remarks that what we are interested in when we talk about our mental life is form and not matter. In a footnote to this remark he quotes this passage from Aristotle:

> we can wholly dismiss as unnecessary the question whether the soul and the body are one: it is as meaningless to ask whether the wax and the shape given to it by the stamp are one, or generally the matter of a thing and that of which it is the matter. (*De anima* 412a6–b9)[21]

In making this allusion to Aristotle, Putnam was, of course, prepared to understand Aristotelian form to be, not just something static like the stamp shape in the wax block, but also, and even especially, the function that a living body, or an organ of that body, performs.

Whether Aristotle should be thought to be a functionalist in the philosophy of mind, or soul, has been one of the most hotly debated topics in recent Aristotelian scholarship. Martha Nussbaum has joined Hilary Putnam in espousing a functionalist interpretation.[22] M. F. Burnyeat, in the much discussed article already referred to, "Is an Aristotelian Philosophy of Mind Still Credible?"[23] has mounted a powerful attack. And the debate continues.[24]

Belief–Desire Psychology

Whether or not Aristotle was a functionalist, there can be no serious doubt that he was the first philosopher to set out the structure of what is sometimes derided these days as "folk psychology." The central tenet of folk psychology is the principle that human and other animal actions arise from the integration of belief and desire. Aristotle gave canonical form to this idea with his notion of what has come to be called the practical syllogism. He writes:

> I want to drink, says appetite; this is drink, says sense or imagination or thought. Straightaway I drink. In this way living creatures are impelled to move and to act, and desire is the last cause of movement, and desire arises through perception or through imagination and thought. (*De motu* 701a32–6)

One premise of the practical syllogism expresses a desire (e.g., "I want to drink"). A second premise expresses a belief, or, perhaps in the case of a nonhuman animal, simply a perception (e.g., "This is drink"). And the conclusion is an action ("Straightaway I drink.")[25]

As Aristotle saw clearly, if beliefs and desires really do explain human actions, something similar must also explain the purposeful actions of dogs, birds, and other nonhuman animals.[26] But, as recent critics have pointed out, serious difficulties stand in the way of attributing beliefs to nonlinguistic animals (including prelinguistic human babies!).[27] Still, no one is now in position to dispense with Aristotelian "folk psychology" and still make sense of clearly purposive actions in human and nonhuman animals.

The practical syllogism also figures in what Aristotle has to say about *akrasia* or weakness of will, that is, doing what one knows one ought not to be doing. Socrates, Aristotle reports in Book VII of his *Nicomachean Ethics*, thought *akrasia* impossible. Although there is no scholarly consensus on what exactly Aristotle's solution is, here is one reading. When I reach for a cooling drink, I act on the premises "I want refreshment" and "This is refreshment," and somehow push aside the reasoning that I, as the "designated driver," should have followed: "I want to avoid intoxicants" and "This is an intoxicant."[28]

Problem of Consciousness

Notoriously, the notion of consciousness is central to Descartes's philosophy. Yet, by understanding thinking to be the essential attribute of mind, and by supposing the mind is a substance that is quite independent of the body, Descartes seems to leave consciousness inaccessible to scientific understanding and investigation. The resulting "problem of consciousness" is widely thought to be one of the most difficult and important problems in science and philosophy today.

Given the attention currently lavished on the problem of consciousness, it may come as a surprise to be told that, according to some commentators, the idea of consciousness plays no role at all in Aristotle's account of the soul, even of the human soul. D. W. Hamlyn deplores this lacuna. Having found that "concepts like that of consciousness do not figure in [Aristotle's] conceptual scheme at all," Hamlyn adds this comment: "It is perhaps this that gives his definition of the soul itself a certain inadequacy for the modern reader."[29] By contrast, Kathleen Wilkes applauds the absence. She thinks he does "not need any such notion as consciousness."[30]

Perhaps the truth lies in a somewhat more nuanced reading of Aristotle. Thus Richard Sorabji links the notion of consciousness in Descartes with self-awareness and reports simply that "Aristotle's remarks on self-awareness are brief, sporadic, and by no means centrally placed."[31] The topic, Sorabji adds, does not have the same interest for Aristotle that it has for Descartes, or perhaps for us.

Some of Aristotle's discussions of self-awareness are likely to be overlooked, or underappreciated. Charles Kahn, in a seminal article "Sensation and Consciousness in Aristotle's Psychology,"[32] calls our attention to this passage from Aristotle's *Nicomachean Ethics*:

> If the one who is seeing perceives that he is seeing and the one who is hearing that he is hearing, and the one who walks that he walks, and similarly for other activities, there is something which perceives that we are acting, so that if we are perceiving [it perceives] that we are perceiving, and if we are thinking [it perceives] that we are thinking. But [to perceive] that we are perceiving or thinking is [to perceive] that we exist – for our life and being has been defined as perceiving or thinking; and to perceive that one is alive is a thing which is intrinsically pleasant. (1170a29–b1)[33]

Yet even Kahn warns us against expecting too much from Aristotle on this subject. "On the side of subjective awareness," Kahn writes in a more recent article,

> where post-Cartesian philosophy and psychology have constructed a realm of mental states and mental events, Aristotle has only the barest outline of a theory. . . . From a few scattered comments, however, we can safely conclude that personal self-awareness is conceived as a function of the *aisthētikon*. There seems to be no corresponding notion of personal or individual subjectivity in the self-awareness of *nous* as such, no place for a noetic ego, no personal "I" as the proper subject of *noēsis* [intellection].[34]

Perhaps Aristotle's lack of interest in what Kahn calls "a noetic ego" is connected with his refusal to take seriously the problem of how I can know whether I am now dreaming. This problem is mentioned and discussed briefly, without resolution, in Plato's *Theaetetus* at 158be. Aristotle, surprisingly to a modern reader of Descartes, puts this problem in a bag of irresolvable perplexities and seems to suggest that their very irresolvability reveals that they are not genuine difficulties, but rest on the mistaken assumption that everything can be demonstrated (*Metaphysics* 4, 1011a3–13). Aristotle's idea seems to be that my passing an awakeness test could never demonstrate successfully that I am really awake, since it might be, for all I know, that I am only dreaming that I am passing the test.

If, like Descartes, Aristotle had found the philosophical dream problem philosophically gripping, he might have been interested in reconstructing his knowledge from a first-person perspective. If he had done that, or even tried to do it, he might have paid philosophical attention to thought's ego and made a place for a "personal 'I' as the proper subject of *noēsis*." But he did not.

Active and Passive Intellects

In chapters 4 and 5 of Book III of the *De anima* Aristotle sketches an account of the intellect (*nous*) that was very influential in the Middle Ages, but has become something of an embarrassment to many admirers of Aristotle today. According to this account, the intellect can be divided into an active part and a passive part. The passive part he seems to conceive as ideal matter – something that can take on any form whatsoever. The active part he thinks of as analogous to an artisan – something that can give any form whatsoever to the passive intellect.

Since the passive intellect can become anything one can think about, it cannot, Aristotle tells us at 429a18–29, be "mixed with the body." The idea seems to be that if the passive intellect were, say, a mass of ganglion cells in the cerebral cortex, then the active intellect could not make itself into ganglion cells, so as to enable the thinker to think about ganglion cells in the cerebral cortex. Nor, of course, could it make ganglion cells into stem cells, let alone into dump trucks or heavenly bodies, so as to be able to think about them. But that seems to mean that the intellect is not the form of the brain, in the sense of being the capacity of the brain (or any other physical organ), to think about dump trucks or mathematics or the upcoming holiday.[35] And such a conclusion is certainly one any modern-day functionalist interpreter of Aristotle should sternly resist.

On the other hand, those philosophers who hope to find in Aristotle a way to undergird a belief in human afterlife have, many of them, welcomed Aristotle's rather puzzling claims about the active and passive intellects. Aquinas, in particular, uses the Aristotelian idea that the human intellect has an operation "in which the body does not share" as a reason for saying that the individual human soul "subsists in itself" and therefore survives a human being's bodily death to await a sort of "recompletion" at the time of the resurrection.[36] Thus, on Aquinas's use of Aristotle, although an individual human soul is indeed the form of an individual human body, and not an independent entity, it is nevertheless a "subsistent thing," something that can survive death and await union with a resurrection body.

It is not at all clear that Aristotle himself had any such thoughts about the possibility that an individual person might survive death. In any case, he denies of the agent intellect "that it sometimes thinks and at other times not." And he adds, "In separation it is just what it is, and this alone is immortal and eternal" (430a22–3). The great medieval Islamic philosopher Averroes (1126–98) made such comments of Aristotle the basis of a doctrine, according to which human immortality is general, not individual.

Charles Kahn has recently suggested that, although Aristotle certainly rejects the idea of transmigration of souls, his doctrine of the immateriality of intellect serves a function similar to at least one use Plato makes of the transmigration idea. Kahn writes:

> The Platonic myth of the *Phaedrus* claims that a soul which is to enter a human body must previously have had a prenatal glimpse of the Forms, since a human being "must be able to understand what is said in language by reference to some form, passing through many sense perceptions to a unity gathered together and grasped by reason (*logismos*)." (249b)[37]

Kahn continues:

> The incorporeality of *nous* is Aristotle's prosaic substitute for the doctrine of recollection. Both doctrines, recollection and incorporeality, may be understood as metaphors for something about the human intellect we do not fully understand – and perhaps inevitably so, since it is by means of the intellect that we understand everything else.[38]

In any case, one thing we have to say about chapters 4 and 5 of *De anima* III is that there is no generally shared understanding among scholars today as to what Aristotle may have had in mind in writing them.

Conclusion

Perhaps Aristotle's most enduring contribution to psychology is his idea that human and animal action is the logically structured integration of desire and belief (or perception). Aristotle thinks the logical structure of this integration can be captured in what he calls "practical reasoning," specifically in the "practical syllogism." Many people who have never read a word of Aristotle make common use of his idea that when one does something, A, one's doing A expresses both some desire that one has and also the belief that doing A will satisfy that desire.

Aristotle's most intriguing (and elusive!) suggestion in psychology is his idea that the human mind or soul is the form of the human body. Whatever exactly "form" is taken to mean in this context, it clearly rules out thinking of the mind as either the body itself, or as an independent substance only temporarily and accidentally "housed" in some human body. That there should be some such third alternative to both materialism and mind–body dualism is very attractive to many thoughtful people today.

As I have indicated above, some philosophers today see Aristotle as a functionalist, indeed, as the first functionalist in the history of philosophy.[39] They note that, when Aristotle identifies the psyche, not as an independent substance in its own right, but rather as the form of a living body, he means the form to be the functional realization of that living body. Other philosophers today[40] argue that Aristotle's conception of matter is so different from ours that he cannot count as a functionalist in our modern sense.

Some philosophers today,[41] find in Aristotle something like a modern theory of property supervenience, according to which psychological properties supervene on physical ones. According to property supervenience theories, any given psychological property, C, will be paired with some physical property, F, such that, necessarily, anything with F will have C. But the supervenience idea seems to run afoul of Aristotle's insistence that *nous* (intellect) has no bodily organ.

One might suppose that John Searle's idea that human consciousness is an emergent property of the human brain[42] parallels Aristotle's view of the psyche as the form of the body (perhaps especially, Aristotle suggests, of the heart or brain[43]) and that Aristotle is therefore an emergentist. Yet since Searle[44] seems to deny that emergent mental states have any causal powers except those that result from the relevant lower-level physical states, his version of emergentism, anyway, does not seem to fit Aristotle.[45]

Of course, scholars differ among themselves on how best to understand Aristotle. Similarly, philosophers of mind differ seriously among themselves on how best to understand minds and the mental. The most we can say at this point is that several important controversies in Aristotelian scholarship bear in interesting and important ways on several important controversies in the philosophy of mind, and vice versa. Even if Aristotle is not an up-to-date philosopher of mind or philosophical psychologist, there is good reason to think one will become a better philosopher of mind and philosophical psychologist, as well as a better student of Aristotle, if one can become clear about why we can and should, or cannot, or should not, return to Aristotle for enlightenment in psychology and the philosophy of mind.

Notes

1   Descartes (1984), 246.
2   See Putnam (1975b).
3   Searle (1984), 41.
4   Matthews (1992).
5   See also Plato's *Phaedrus* at 249ff.

6   For a full discussion of epiphenomenalism, as well as the harmony idea, see Caston (1997).
7   Ackrill (1972–3).
8   Williams (1986), 192.
9   Cohen (1987), 119. Cf. Whiting (1992) and Shields (1999), ch. 5.
10 Sorabji (1992), 209, Sorabji (1974), 74.
11 In recent scholarship it is Thomas J. Slakey who first staked out this interpretation of Aristotle. See Slakey (1961).
12 Burnyeat (1992), 18.
13 Ibid., 26.
14 For a fully nuanced discussion of this claim see Caston (1993) and Caston (1997), esp. pp. 332–9.
15 Caston (1997), 335.
16 Charles (1984), 214.
17 Ibid.
18 Shields (1988).
19 Heinaman (1990), 90.
20 Putnam (1975a), 293.
21 Ibid., 302.
22 See Nussbaum (1978), Essay 1.
23 Burnyeat (1992).
24 For the Nussbaum–Putnam response to Burnyeat, see Nussbaum and Putnam (1992). For other functionalist interpreters, see Cohen (1987, 1992), Irwin (1991), Shields (1990), and Wedin (1988). For other critical responses to functionalist readings of Aristotle see Robinson (1978), Modrak (1987), esp. pp. 28–9, Granger (1990), Heinaman (1990), Code (1991), and Miller (1999).
25 See Anscombe (1957), 57–66.
26 See Nussbaum (1978), xvii–xx.
27 Davidson (1982).
28 For further discussion of this issue see, e.g., Davidson (1970).
29 Hamlyn (1993), xiii.
30 Wilkes (1992), 122.
31 Sorabji (1974), 71.
32 Kahn (1966).
33 See Kahn (1966), p. 78, fn. 82, for a discussion of the textual difficulties in this passage.
34 Kahn (1992), 375.
35 For an alternative way of reading Aristotle on these issues see Shields (1997).
36 *Summa theologiae* 1a q.75 a.2.
37 Kahn (1992), 378.
38 Ibid., 378–9.
39 See, e.g., Shields (1990).
40 See, e.g., Code (1991), Burnyeat (1992), and Miller (1999).
41 See, e.g., Everson (1997), but again, Caston (1993, 1997).
42 Searle (1992), 14.
43 See *Metaphysics* Z 10 at 1035b26–7.
44 Searle (1992), 112.
45 See Code (1991) and Miller (1999).

References and Recommended Reading

Ackrill, J. L. (1972–3), "Aristotle's Definitions of *Psuchē*," *Proceedings of the Aristotelian Society*, 73, 119–33.

Anscombe, G. E. M. (1957), *Intention*, Ithaca, N.Y.: Cornell University Press.

Barnes, J. (1971–2), "Aristotle's Concept of Mind," *Proceedings of the Aristotelian Society*, 75, 101–14.

Bolton, Robert (1978), "Aristotle's Definitions of the Soul: *de Anima* II 1–3," *Phronesis* 23, 258–78.

Brentano, Franz (1977), *The Psychology of Aristotle*, R. George, trans., Berkeley: University of California Press.

—— (1992), "*Nous Poiētikos*: Survey of Earlier Interpretations," in Nussbaum and Rorty (1992), 313–41.

Burnyeat, M. F. (1992), "Is an Aristotelian Philosophy of Mine Still Credible? A Draft," in Nussbaum and Rorty (1992), 15–26.

Caston, Victor (1993), "Aristotle and Supervenience," *Southern Journal of Philosophy*, 31 suppl., Spindel Conference 1992: "Ancient Minds," J. Ellis, ed., 107–35.

—— (1997), "Epiphenomenalisms, Ancient and Modern," *Philosophical Review* 106, 309–63.

Charles, David (1984), *Aristotle's Philosophy of Action*, Ithaca, N.Y.: Cornell University Press.

Charlton, W. (1980), "Aristotle's Definition of Soul," *Phronesis* 25, 170–86.

Code, Alan (1991), "Aristotle, Searle, and the Mind–Body Problem," in Ernest Lepore and Robert Van Gulick, *John Searle and His Critics*, Cambridge, Mass.: Blackwell, 105–113.

Cohen, S. Marc (1987), "The Credibility of Aristotle's Philosophy of Mind," in M. Matthen, ed., *Aristotle Today*, Edmonton: University of Alberta.

—— (1992), "Hylomorphism and Functionalism," in Nussbaum and Rorty (1992), 57–73.

Davidson, Donald (1970), "How Is Weakness of Will Possible?" reprinted in Davidson, *Essays on Actions and Events*, Oxford: Oxford University Press, 1982, 21–42.

—— (1982), "Rational Animals," *Dialectica* 36, reprinted in E. LePore and B. McLaughlin, eds., *Actions and Events*, Oxford: Blackwell, 1985, 473–80.

Descartes, René (1970), *Philosophical Letters*, Anthony Kenny, trans. and ed., Oxford: Clarendon Press.

—— (1984), *The Philosophical Writings of Descartes*, vol. 2, J. Cottingham, R. Stoothoff, and D. Murdoch, trans., Cambridge: Cambridge University Press.

Everson, Stephen (1995), "Psychology," in *The Cambridge Companion to Aristotle*, J. Barnes, ed., Cambridge: Cambridge University Press, 168–94.

—— (1997), *Aristotle on Perception*, Oxford: Clarendon Press.

Granger Herbert (1990), "Aristotle and the Functionalism Debate," *Apeiron* 23, 27–49.

Hamlyn, D. W. (1993), *Aristotle's De Anima: Books II and III*, Oxford: Clarendon Press.

Hardie, W. F. R. (1976), "Concepts of Consciousness in Aristotle," *Mind* 85, 388–411.

Hartman, Edwin (1977), *Substance, Body and Soul* (Princeton: Princeton University Press.

Heinaman, Robert (1990), "Aristotle and the Mind–Body Problem," *Phronesis* 35, 83–104.

Irwin, T. H. (1991), "Aristotle's Philosophy of Mind," in S. Everson, ed., *Companions to Ancient Thought*, vol. 2: *Psychology*, Cambridge University Press.

Kahn, Charles H. (1966), "Sensation and Consciousness in Aristotle's Psychology," *Archiv für Geschichte der Philosophie* 48, 43–81.

—— (1992), "Aristotle on Thinking," in Nussbaum and Rorty (1992), 359–79.

Kosman, L. A. (1975), "Perceiving that We Perceive: *On the Soul* III,2," *Philosophical Review* 84, 499–519.

—— (1992), "What Does the Maker Mind Make?" in Nussbaum and Rorty (1992), 343–58.

Matthews, Gareth B. (1992), "*De Anima* 2:2–4 and the Meaning of *Life*," in Nussbaum and Rorty (1992), 185–93.

Miller, Fred D., Jr. (1999), "Aristotle's Philosophy of Soul," *Review of Metaphysics* 53, 310–37.

Modrak, Deborah K. W. (1981), "An Aristotelian Theory of Consciousness?" *Ancient Philosophy* 1, 160–70.

—— (1987), *Aristotle: the Power of Perception*, Chicago: University of Chicago Press.

Nussbaum, Martha C. (1978), *Aristotle's De Motu Animalium*, Princeton: Princeton University Press.

Nussbaum, Martha C. and Rorty, Amelie Oksenberg (1992), *Essays on Aristotle's De Anima*," Oxford: Clarendon Press.

Nussbaum, Martha C. and Putnam, Hilary (1992), "Changing Aristotle's Mind," in Nussbaum and Rorty (1992), 27–56.

Putnam, Hilary (1975a), "Philosophy and our Mental Life," *Mind, Language and Reality: Philosophical Papers*, vol. 2, Cambridge: Cambridge University Press, 291–303.

—— (1975b), "Robots: Machines or Artificially Created Life," *Mind, Language and Reality: Philosophical Papers*, vol. 2, Cambridge, Cambridge University Press, 386–407.

Robinson, H. M. (1978), "Mind and Body in Aristotle," *Classical Quarterly*, NS 28: 105–24.

—— (1983), "Aristotelian Dualism," *Oxford Studies in Ancient Philosophy* 1, 123–44.

Searle, John (1984), *Minds, Brains and Science*, Cambridge: Harvard University Press.

—— (1992), *The Rediscovery of the Mind*, Cambridge, Mass.: MIT Press.

Shields, Christopher (1988), "Body and Soul in Aristotle," *Oxford Studies in Ancient Philosophy* 6, 103–38.

—— (1990), "The First Functionalist," in J. C. Smith, ed., *Essays on the Historical Foundations of Cognitive Science*, Dordrecht: Kluwer, 19–33.

—— (1993), "Some Recent Approaches to Aristotle's *De Anima*," in Hamlyn (1993), 157–87.

—— (1995), "Intentionality and Isomorphism in Aristotle," in John J. Cleary and William Wians, eds., *Proceedings of the Boston Area Colloquium in Ancient Philosophy*, vol. 11, 307–30.

—— (1999), *Order in Multiplicity: Homonymy in the Philosophy of Aristotle*, Oxford: Oxford University Press.

Slakey, Thomas J. (1961), "Aristotle on Sense-Perception," *Philosophical Review* 70, 470–84.

Sorabji, Richard (1974), "Body and Soul in Aristotle," *Philosophy* 49, 63–89.

—— (1992), "Intentionality and Physiological Processes: Aristotle's Theory of Sense-Perception," in Nussbaum and Rorty (1992), 195–225.

Wedin, Michael V. (1988), *Mind and Imagination in Aristotle*, New Haven: Yale University Press.

—— (1989), "Aristotle on the Mechanics of Thought," *Ancient Philosophy* 9, 67–86.

—— (1993), "Tracking Aristotle's *NOUS*," in Michael Durrant, ed., *Aristotle's* De Anima," London: Routledge, 128–61.

Whiting, Jennifer (1992), "Living Bodies," in Nussbaum and Rorty (1992), 75–91.

Williams, Bernard (1986), "Hylomorphism," *Oxford Studies in Ancient Philosophy* 4, 189–99.

Wilkes, K. V. (1992), "Psychē versus the Mind," in Nussbaum and Rorty (1992), 109–27.

Part V

Hellenistic Philosophy: Introduction

After the death of Aristotle in 322 BC, Greek Philosophy underwent some surprising transformations and developments. Fueled in part by the expansion of Greek influence east into Asia Minor and south into Egypt following Alexander's conquests, Greek Philosophy came to acquire a new and cosmopolitan significance throughout the Mediterranean region. In view of its illustrious history, Athens remained the center of philosophical gravity, though other broader intellectual pursuits migrated to Alexandria, a city in North Africa founded by Alexander and lavishly patronized by its rulers, the Ptolemies. The schools of Plato and Aristotle remained in Athens, headed now by their followers, some of them impressive and original thinkers in their own rights and others rather less so. They were joined in Athens by two new schools, equally if differently systematic, Stoicism and Epicureanism, which came to eclipse both the Academy and the Lyceum in prestige and influence. Stoicism in particular quickly rose to prominence, numbering many of the leading philosophical minds of the day among its adherents and so in some ways setting the agenda for the philosophical discourse of the era. Against these two schools, both regarded as "dogmatic" by their detractors, there arose varieties of skepticism disposed to dispute and deflate the positive theories promulgated by the Stoics and Epicureans. Eventually, even Plato's own Academy took a skeptical turn, though some of its adherents denied any such reorientation; as far as they were concerned, Plato, like Socrates before him, had been a skeptic all along.

The result of these developments by the mid-third century would have been striking to anyone familiar with the philosophical milieu of Athens during the time of Plato and Aristotle. No Socrates wandered through the *agora* posing uncomfortable questions; the Academy was now more interested in debunking the theories of others than in developing, refining or defending any Platonic theory of Forms; and the Lyceum had drawn in its philosophical horns, having become increasingly concerned with empirical research, narrowly construed. The intra- and interscholastic dialectic of the now dominant schools was extremely lively, even palpable: Stoics advanced theories, received skeptical challenges of all stripes, responded and revised their views in light of them, and then reissued the improved versions for the next round of scrutiny and confrontation. Within the schools themselves, little was received as orthodox, even though there came to be core propositions broadly definitive of each movement.

At its most general level, Hellenistic Philosophy (conventionally dated from about the time of Aristotle's death down to 31 BC) became highly – and self-consciously – systematic in its aims and expressions. Its two principal constructive schools, Stoicism and Epicureanism, put forth doctrines whose overarching ambitions were all-encompassing. Each advanced a complete analysis of human nature in order to reveal its proper place in the broader cosmos. They shared too a common conception of the point of doing philosophy: philosophy, however technical and theoretical it may become, serves the interests of human happiness. If we understand the universe and its workings, they urged, we may more easily find a way to live in accordance with nature. Living in accordance with nature is the closest we can come to a guarantee of our own happiness; and human happiness remains for the Hellenistic philosophers, as it had been for Socrates, Plato, and Aristotle before them, something we can and should seek. Even many of the skeptics who taunted the "dogmatists" shared this goal. It is just that they derided as laughably pretentious the grand task of understanding humanity's place in the great cosmos of the universe. That realization by itself, though, they suggest, affords the possibility of happiness in a different way: acquiescence in our own limitations carries equanimity in its wake; and equanimity in its turn begets human happiness, since unhappiness results from thwarted ambition, whether practical or theoretical. So, by ridding ourselves of misplaced ambition – either by understanding the world and our place in it or by understanding that such understanding is forever bound to elude us – we may discover our path to happiness. In these different ways, then, all of the primary Hellenistic movements share the common goal of securing such happiness as life affords. At least to this extent, then, they all embrace a broadly practical orientation.

Though correct as far as it goes, this characterization obscures some deeper differences between the schools; and it also may be taken to suggest that Hellenistic Philosophy was practically *rather than* theoretically oriented. That would be a serious distortion. On the contrary, Hellenistic Philosophy, especially because of the driving influence of Stoicism, witnessed highly technical developments in logic, philosophy of language, metaphysics, causation, and philosophical psychology. The truth is that Hellenistic Philosophy was practical *by* being theoretical. A brief introduction to the principal schools shows how this is so.

First, though, the notion of "schools" or "movements" requires a brief clarification. When the authors of the following chapters speak of the Hellenistic "schools" of philosophy, they are not meaning to refer to organized institutions with set curricula or determinate courses of study. Rather, the Hellenistic philosophers formed schools closer to the sense in which naturalism in fiction or neorealism in painting are called schools. The Hellenistic philosophers grouped themselves together under very broad credos, fundamental postulates, and methodological proclivities. Even then it is possible to see disagreement and development within the schools, sometimes in response to external pressures, sometimes simply in terms of their own internal dynamics. Importantly, especially for the Epicureans, the Hellenistic schools defined themselves primarily by their loyalty to a founder: the Stoics followed Zeno, the Epicureans were devoted to Epicurus, and the Academics looked to Socrates and Plato as their progenitors. Of course, as may be seen especially in the case of the Academics, the members of the various schools could assume a fair bit of latitude in determining precisely how loyalty to their founder was to be understood. Although every naturalized American swears an oath of loyalty to the American Constitution, legitimate divergences of opinion – regarding fundamental assumptions as well as points of detail – invariably, and appropriately, arise concerning how that oath is to be understood and implemented. So too with the Hellenistic schools. Every Stoic is a follower of Zeno; but Stoics will differ about how best to manifest their allegiance to his teachings. In terms of settled doctrine, the Epicureans appear to have been the most cohesive, both because of the highly articulated character of Epicurus' teachings and because of his evident and uncommon personal magnetism.

Stoicism

Zeno of Citium (b. 333 BC) came to Athens from Cyprus while still a young man in order to pursue philosophy. He emerged as the leading figure in a group which met to discuss philosophical topics in a painted colonnade or porch (*stoa* in Greek), which eventually lent its name to his group. Having associated at first with some Academics and Socratics, Zeno broke way and instituted his own sect, along with his most devoted pupil and eventual successor Cleanthes (331–232 BC), who led the school from the time of Zeno's death in 262 until 232 BC, when he was in turn succeeded by early Stoicism's most powerful philosophical mind, Chrysippus (280– 207 BC). Zeno instituted a framework of physical theory, metaphysics and logic which was later augmented by Cleanthes, mainly in the areas of theology and cosmology, and which was made complete and rendered precise by Chrysippus.

As Mitsis shows, some central features of the Stoic system are strikingly modern – at least in the sense that many modern sensibilities find them congenial. The Stoics are materialists: to exist is to be causally efficacious and only bodies can cause things to happen. Everything which occurs does so within a perfectly determined causal nexus; nothing is random, nothing happens by chance or by the intrusive agency of a meddlesome divinity. Still, the universe is not itself blind in its direction. It is instead a highly rational expression of an intelligence; or, in a way, the universe is itself, for the Stoics, a divine intelligence which the wisest of humans, the sage, understands and accepts. The sage alone is happy, because the sage alone conforms completely to the divine structure of the universe. He is indifferent to conventional goods, including honor and wealth, and even to health, except insofar as these things may conduce to living in accordance with nature. Since happiness requires an understanding of the structure of the universe, the sage will be a philosopher, highly skilled in dialectic and with a complete grasp of the nature of human cognition. The sage is, then, both wise and a practitioner of philosophy, where "wisdom is the precise knowledge of the divine and the human" and "philosophy is the practice of expertise in utility."[1] The sage, that is, knows what is true and uses this knowledge to govern his every deed.

Epicureanism

Of all the Hellenistic schools, Epicureanism is most completely dominated by its founder, Epicurus (341–271 BC). Born in Samos and reportedly exposed in his youth to the atomism of Democritus, Epicurus came to found philosophical circles in Mytilene and Lampsacus before coming to Athens in 306 to do the same. In antiquity his sect was known as "the Garden", a name given it, as with the Stoics, by their meeting place. The garden in question was adjacent to Epicurus' house outside of Athens, a geographical fact which already has some ramifications for our understanding of Epicureanism. Epicurus was little concerned with public affairs. He was not interested, as the Stoics evidently were, in conducting philosophy in a publicly overt way or in having public impact or influence. Rather, his was an inward-looking community, devoted with affectionate regard to Epicurus as their leader and teacher and to one another as dear friends. So too was Epicurus indifferent to public reputation or standing. His community reportedly admitted members of low social standing, including women and slaves, who would have been systematically excluded from other more socially conscious outfits. They evidently lived austerely though not ascetically, a practice which renders inapt but explicable the contemporary meaning of "Epicurean" as applied to a person keen to pursue sensuous or luxurious pleasures. It is inapt since the Epicureans lived no such lives; still, it is explicable insofar as Epicurus was a committed hedonist. Although his hedonism involves a simple commitment to the view that pleasure is the highest good, Epicurus differs sharply in his conception of pleasure from someone who seeks pleasure in lavish indulgence.

In fact, as Konstan makes clear, Epicurean hedonism is a narrowly circumscribed affair. Epicurus urged his attendants to study physics, in part because he thought that doing so would have notably salutary practical results. Physics teaches us that atomism is true: the world is made of tiny spherical atoms, just as the Presocratic Democritus had taught many years before. The thesis of atomism carries with it a commitment to materialism. The entire world – including all of humanity, together with its thoughts, feelings, hopes, and desires – is made up of atoms swirling in the void. When we die, the atoms which constitute us scatter to the winds. So, when we die, we end. It follows, then, that physics teaches us that we have no reason to fear death: when we are, death is not; and when death is, we are no more. This realization, contends Epicurus, helps to cure us of one of our most basic fears, as well as of our gnawing irrational hopes for immortality. We desire so much because we are afraid of death; when we no longer have this fear, the desires to which it gives rise dissipate. Since pleasure consists in desire satisfaction, and pleasure is our ultimate good, it follows that the study of physics is key to our own individual happiness. This simple recommendation, it turns out, yields some unexpected directives. The

Epicureans sought to live in terms of these directives, with no regard for how others might come to view them.

Skepticism

Epicureans and Stoics are *dogmatists*: they think that they know all sorts of things. The Epicureans think atomism, and so materialism, is true; and they act accordingly. The Stoics think that they know not only logic, but all manner of facts about the material universe and its internal causal connections. They too find directives for life in their philosophy. Given that they know so much, and given that knowledge governs action, the Stoics and Epicureans develop elaborate ethical theories in whose terms they conduct all of their affairs.

How did the Epicureans and Stoics come to know so much? The Skeptics thought that they never did. Dogmatic pretense to knowledge needs to be exposed for what it is, and the Skeptics accepted this as their mission. Given that their primary interest lay in refuting others, the Skeptics did not form a school, not even in the sense in which the Stoics and Epicureans did. Even so, it is possible to discern common patterns of inference and standard tropes of refutation in their various responses to the views of others. And it is even possible to uncover regulative theses accepted by many Skeptics. That is, a Skeptic might develop an argument to show that knowledge is impossible. When asked whether the conclusion of this argument is itself known, the Skeptic need not be tripped up, at least not immediately. Instead, the Skeptic need only note that the conclusion *seems* to be true, where that does not implicate him in any claim to knowledge, even though it does suffice to cast doubt on all the claims to knowledge advanced by the dogmatist.

Questions regarding skeptical methods and commitments become rather tricky rather quickly. As Hankinson shows, ancient Skeptics devised a variety of nimble strategies for advancing their cause without succumbing themselves to any form of dogmatism. In fact, skepticism admits of degrees and embraces several different strands of antidogmatism. Two principal movements dominated the Hellenistic intellectual landscape, the Academics and the Pyrrhonists. Of these, the most prominent were the Academics, so named because they grew out of Plato's school, the Academy. After Plato's death in 347, his school continued along a consistent, unremarkable path for over a century until it was vigorously transformed by Arcesilaus, who took over its headship in 272. As Cicero reports, Arcesilaus was primarily concerned to refute Zeno, the founder of Stoicism.[2] If Cicero reports his intentions correctly, Arcesilaus was not interested in victory for victory's sake. Rather, he looked to Socrates as a model. If we are honest, he thought, just as Socrates was honest, we will admit that there is a deep obscurity in the world around us, and we will conclude that our ignorance too is deep and permanent, just as Socrates himself concluded.[3] So, when we find someone claiming to know things with certainty, we will be motivated to show them the error of their way. This we do by refuting them.

This picture paints the Academic Skeptics as largely reactive and dialectical. A dogmatist asserts something; the Skeptic goes on the attack. While it is certainly true that a pattern of Stoic assertion followed by Skeptic rejoinder followed by Stoic refinement characterizes much of the interscholastic dialectic of the period, it remains possible that Arcesilaus also mounted broader positive attacks of his own invention. So too with another prominent Academic Skeptic, Carneades (213–129 BC), who was the fourth head of the Academy after the change in direction brought about by Arcesilaus. Carneades famously argued one day, on an embassy to Rome in 155 BC, that justice is a virtue, something to be prized and cultivated by every human. The next day he argued the opposite case, that justice is not a virtue, but merely the product of a local agreement arrived at for narrow purposes of self-promotion. This form of argument, providing compelling reasons on opposite sides of a case, was a favorite technique among the Skeptics. After all, if I am now convinced that justice is a virtue and now convinced that it is no such thing, how can I claim to know anything about justice at all? Better, say the Academics, simply to admit our ignorance and live with it.

This form of argumentation found a distinct realm of application in the second skeptical movement, Pyrrhonism, named for its founder Pyrhho (c. 360–270 BC). Most noteworthy is the use to which this pattern of argumentation was put by Sextus Empiricus, a second-century AD compiler and Pyrrhonist skeptic, and also our best source for earlier Pyrrhonist views. Sextus retails ten "modes" of skepticism, ten set patterns of argumentation which all share a common pattern: for any given x, x appears in incompatible ways relative to different contexts or different perceivers (this wine appears sweet to one person and not sweet to another; killing an innocent human seems never justified, but then again justifiable in some extreme contexts); there is no "criterion of truth" to settle the matter decisively; so, we should suspend judgment with regard to x. The best we can say with respect to x is that it seems a certain way, and then again that it seems a different and incompatible way as well.

The Pyrrhonists are distinctive among the Skeptics in hearkening back, in terms of their ultimate recommendations, to the Epicureans, and to a lesser extent, to the Stoics. Of course, no Pyrrhonist is a dogmatist. Still, Pyrrhonists agree with the other schools that we should seek to live unranked by discord or strife. The dogmatists had wanted to achieve that goal by discovering the truth and then conforming to it. The Pyrrhonists deny that such discovery is possible. Even so, in the face of conflicting appearances, we should simply suspend judgment. With suspension, however, comes tranquility and quietude. If we give up striving to know what we cannot know, peace and calmness will soon overtake us, and our lives will become blessedly free from disappointment. Surely, the Skeptics suggest, a life lived thus unperturbed is a life worth pursuing.

Notes

1　Aetius I, Preface 2 (*SVF* 2.35 = LS 26A). In citing the often fragmentary sources for the views of the Hellenistic philosophers, whose works have not come down to us as Plato's or Aristotle's have, scholars typically cite the original source of the quotation (here Aetius, a Greek doxographer of the first century AD), followed by the location in the canonical collection of Stoic fragments (*SVF, Stoicorum Veterum Fragmenta* (2.35), and finally by a citation to the superb English language source book of Long and Sedley (LS) 1987 (26 A). For practical purposes, students wanting to explore an issue or quotation more fully will want to turn first to Long and Sedley.

2 Cicero, *Academica* 1.43–5 (= LS 68A).

3 It is debatable whether we should accept Arcesilaus' characterization of Socrates. On Socratic ignorance, see the section "Socrates' 'Method' and Moral Viewpoints" in chapter 3 of this volume.

–––––––– Chapter 12 ––––––––

Epicureanism

David Konstan

Introduction

In the latter half of the fifth century BC or the first half of the fourth, Democritus (his precise dates are uncertain) developed a theory, perhaps inspired by an earlier contemporary named Leucippus, according to which all of nature consisted of atomic particles of matter moving in a void. Democritus also maintained that the ideal of life was "good cheer" or contentment (most recent edition: Taylor 1999; critically reviewed in Konstan 2000). Plato never mentions Democritus explicitly, but his hypothesis of existing but nonmaterial ideas or forms which include ethical abstractions such as virtue or the good is manifestly incompatible with Democritean materialism. It was Aristotle, however, who subjected the notions of minimal particles and empty space to the most searching criticism, and who developed as well a complex account of human motivation that went far beyond anything that we can detect in the ethical fragments, many of dubious authenticity, ascribed to Democritus. Undeterred, or rather, it would appear, incited by Aristotle's analysis, Epicurus, writing two or three decades later (his dates are 341–271 or 270 BC), refined the atomic theory in subtle but important ways, elaborated an ethical vision that denominated pleasure as the highest good, and evolved an epistemology that dispensed entirely with nonmaterial entities.

The basis of Epicurus' philosophy is his physical theory, to the extent that it can be reconstructed from the surviving evidence: some of the gaps may be filled in through plausible inferences from the known facts. Epicurean ethics or moral psychology is in many ways a function of the materialist view implicit in the atomic hypothesis (the Epicureans argued that happiness depends on the conviction that there is no afterlife – see below). So too, in turn, is Epicurus' explanation of knowledge and perception. Here again, it is productive to pose questions to the theory that go beyond what Epicurus' ancient critics – and they were many – raised, and to suggest answers that are compatible with the surviving texts and fragments. Before beginning, however, it is well to review the sources on which our knowledge of ancient Epicureanism is based.

Sources

The most reliable and extensive material is contained in three letters written by Epicurus to disciples, in which he summarizes the basic principles of his physical and ethical theories, along with two collections of brief sayings or quotations extracted from his writings. The letters, and one set of sayings, are recorded by Diogenes Laertius in his essay on Epicurus, which forms the tenth and final book of his *Lives of the Philosophers* (the other set survives in an independent tradition). Diogenes also surveys in his own words other doctrines advanced by Epicurus. In addition to these texts, there is an assortment of papyrus rolls recovered from the library of Philodemus, an Epicurean who lived in Rome in the first century BC and worked in the city of Herculaneum, on the slopes of Mount Vesuvius; Herculaneum was buried when the volcano erupted in AD 79. Many of these rolls, which are of course badly charred, report controversies between Epicureans and other schools, or arguments within Epicureanism itself, that are subsequent to the founder's ideas.

There are also remains of Epicurus' own works, most notably his long treatise *On Nature*, which was the major exposition of his views. Around the same time that Philodemus was writing, the Roman poet Lucretius composed his *De rerum natura* (a Latin version of Epicurus' title *On Nature*), a didactic poem in which he expounded more or less faithfully the physical and epistemological theories of Epicurus (for his fidelity to the master, see Clay 1983; Sedley 1998). From a hostile point of view, Cicero rehearsed and criticized Epicurus' ideas in several of his philosophical works, such as *On the Ends of Good and Evil* and the *Tusculan Disputations*. Still later, in the second century AD, another Diogenes erected a large inscription, only partially excavated, in the city of Oenoanda in what is now southwestern Turkey, in which he had carved the basic tenets of Epicureanism. In addition to these sources, there are many references to Epicurean doctrines in a wide variety of philosophical treatises, often from antagonistic parties, such as Plutarch, the skeptic Sextus Empiricus, and the ancient Greek commentators on Aristotle, which sometimes fill in important lacunae.

Physical Theory

Democritus had held that the atoms are particles of varying shape and size, infinite in number, which move freely in the endless void until they are caught up in vortical currents produced when large numbers of atoms congregate in one region. Such vortices generate a local universe or cosmos, contained within a membrane of tangled atoms, wherein the now regular motions produce the familiar effects of gravity and the displacement of lighter items by heavier. In this condensed environment, there arise complex combinations of atoms, linked by protruding hooks and cavities, that are the basis of all the perceptible objects in the our world. Such objects are susceptible, of course, to change and disintegration, and any compound entity can in theory be pulverized right down to its atomic constituents, but no further. For the atoms themselves are uncuttable, as the Greek name signifies (a- = "not"; the root *tom-* means "cut").

Aristotle, in his *Physics*, challenged the notion that an object could be composed of minimal or partless items, pointing out that when any two minima came into contact, they would have to overlap entirely – since they could have no edges distinct from the rest of themselves and still be partless – and thus could not generate an extended magnitude. Hence, a line could not be said to be composed of points; points inhere in a line, but they have no independent existence and cannot be assembled into a linear stretch. Now, it is not known for certain that this critique is addressed specifically to Democritus' atomic theory; after all, we have seen that Democritus' atoms had hooks and other features, and so can hardly have been partless. Be that as it may, it appears that Epicurus was moved by Aristotle's arguments to distinguish between the atoms, which are unsplittable, and true minima, which obey the Aristotelian constraints of not existing separately – hence Lucretius' term, *minimae partes* or "minimal parts," which makes it clear that they are always embedded in some larger entity – and, a fortiori, of not entering into combinations to form atomic particles. Like Aristotle's points, Epicurus' minima could only be said to move incidentally, as parts of the atoms in which they had their existence.

All very well – but why did Epicurus think that he needed minima at all, as opposed to physically indivisible particles which were of small but finite, rather than infinitesimal, size? Why not simply allow that these corporeal bodies were dense matter unmixed with void – physically uncuttable (*atomos*) in the sense that they are made of the hardest material in the universe – without positing further constituents that had the curious property of being absolutely partless? It is not possible to answer this question with confidence, but one of Epicurus' motives may have had to do with the paradoxes posed by Zeno (whether these had an influence on Democritus' thinking must remain moot). Zeno had argued that for Achilles, swiftest of the Greeks, to catch a tortoise that has a head start on him, he has to make an infinite number of moves: for each time he reaches the place where the tortoise was, the tortoise will have advanced by a certain amount – less than the distance Achilles covered, but still greater than zero. There is no way of stopping this progression: hence, Achilles cannot overtake the tortoise, since it is impossible to make an infinite number of moves in a finite interval of time. While there are various ways to respond to this conundrum, Epicurus may have reasoned that there is an absolute minimum span, below which it is impossible to go. Thus, when the gap between Achilles and the tortoise was reduced to this tiny but nonzero magnitude, he crossed it in a single bound, and caught up with the beast.

How long does it take Achilles to traverse this least space? If it is a finite interval of time, then he would have to dawdle a while before making the final move (the jump itself cannot be subdivided); but why should that be the case? Aristotle (*Physics* Book 6) had argued that for a minimalist answer to Zeno's paradoxes to be effective, it was not enough to posit partless entities, whether separable or not, nor even to assume that space was divided into quantum units; one had also to suppose that time itself was granular, that is, formed out of a sequence of instants that were themselves partless and hence inseparable from the temporal continuum. And if both time and space are quantized in this manner, that is, composed of tiny but finite bits which have no parts and cannot be subdivided, then, Aristotle argued, motion too must be saltatory, that is, occur by leaps, with each particle crossing one minimum of space in one least fraction of time. This view further entailed the disturbing consequence that all atoms move at a uniform speed. This was the price one had to pay in order to resolve Zeno's puzzles in this way.

It is not clear that one must accept all the consequences drawn by Aristotle, who had his own answer to Zeno; why, for example, must atoms move at the rate of one spatial minimum per minimum of time? If they could tarry for two or more temporal units in the same place, then they could move at varying speeds. Whatever objections we may raise to Aristotle's reasoning, however, Epicurus seems to have taken his arguments wholly on board, with the result that his atoms do indeed all move at the same velocity, and they do so by crossing a least spatial interval in a single instant, that is, the minimum unit of time. Hence, as Simplicius, who wrote a commentary on Aristotle's *Physics* in the sixth century AD, puts it (p. 934.23–30, Diels; translation in Konstan 1989): it is incorrect to say that an atom moves over a smallest interval; rather, one should say that it has moved. On the atomic level, space, time and motion are discontinuous.

Whatever the reason why Epicurus developed his theory of quantized space and time, whether in response to Zeno or under the influence of Aristotle or perhaps even from Democritus himself, once it was part of his system, he, or his followers, had to face the difficulties to which such a view was exposed. Sextus Empiricus posed the problem most cunningly (*Against the Mathematicians* 10.144–8). Imagine, he wrote, that two atoms are nine minima apart, and are approaching each other at a uniform speed, as Epicurean theory required. After one interval of time, they will be seven minima from one another; after two instants, five spatial minima; two more instants, and they will be separated by a distance of one minimum. Now what? asked Sextus. If one atom crosses the interval before the other, it violates the hypothesis of uniform velocity; they cannot meet halfway across, since a minimum is by definition partless. But neither is there any reason for them to change direction, since they have not been deflected by an obstacle. Epicurean theory seems to have created an impasse for itself.

One can imagine solutions to this dilemma, but it is hard to know whether the Epicureans thought of them. Perhaps the mathematics of minima is different from macromathematics, and talking of an interval composed of an odd or even number of minima is nonsense – like asking whether a line is composed of an odd or even number of points. We know that the Epicureans posited an order of magnitude that is incomprehensibly large but "not strictly infinite"; atoms, they held, come in an incomprehensibly large variety of shapes, though the number of atoms of each kind was infinite. There was a reason for this arithmetic category: if atoms came in infinite varieties, they must ultimately reach perceptible size (as all the possible arrangements of any given number of minima are exhausted), and this is contradicted by experience, since nothing is indivisible at that level. Minima have some size, and can be summed to finite magnitudes. How many are required? It is tempting to say: an incomprehensibly large number, in which case the minimum would be the inverse of this curious order of magnitude. As quasi-infinitesimals, the minima might have properties that are different from those of strictly finite entities. Perhaps, again, motion at the quantum level was governed by special rules that prohibited certain states. At this stage, we do not know the Epicureans' answer, if indeed they had one.

Epicurean atoms were, as we have seen, univelocitous. But why did they move at all? Why not just stand still? It is unclear whether Democritus' atoms had to be in motion (it seems their speeds could vary), but Epicurus added a property to the atom that, among other things, required them to move: namely, weight. The motive for this innovation is not entirely clear. Democritus had assumed that gravitational effects were produced when atoms entered a swirl or vortex; in intercosmic space, they were presumably weightless. By Aristotle's time, the vortex had fallen out of favor as an all-purpose cosmological mechanism, and Epicurus may have felt he needed a different kind of principle. He thus ascribed to atoms a universal tendency to fall at a uniform rate – fast, but not infinitely so (they cross an incomprehensibly large interval in a finite amount of time). But what could falling mean in an infinite, globally homogeneous universe? As Aristotle had already inquired, which direction in such a system would be down, and why was it so favored?

Again, we can provide possible answers, and again, it is not possible to be certain that the Epicureans came up with them. We know that atoms normally change direction only when they encounter another atom in their path: the Epicureans call this collision, but encounter is a more neutral term. (Atoms may also veer from their path by one minimum – apparently a shift of track, rather than of angle – at random moments, but this does not affect macrophenomena, except perhaps insofar as it serves to explain freedom of will: see below.) Two atoms meet – let us skip the problem of how they cross a final spatial minimum lying between them – and must now move off in another direction. Which? There is no evidence that they did so according to a geometrical rule, like angle of incidence equaling angle of reflection. Suppose, then, that as atoms emerge from encounters, there is a statistical tendency, however small, to favor a particular direction over others. Call that direction down. This is a perfectly coherent thesis, in principle not unlike the challenge to the so-called parity principle in modern physics, which proposed that the universe had an innate right–left orientation on the basis of the fact that particles behave differently depending on which side they emerge from certain atomic interactions. "Down," for the Epicureans, is thus a vector rather than a place. Local gravitation, as on our planet, can be explained on this principle as follows. When atoms collect in locally dense concentrations, they are frequently deflected by one another, with the result that they move in all directions (though down is still statistically favored, however slightly). The cosmic medium, then, is falling relatively slowly. Imagine that the earth is a broad, flat disk, as the Epicureans maintained. It will float like a leaf, retarded, thanks to its shape, in its downward motion by the resistance of the circumambient atomic fluid or atmosphere. Smaller, narrower objects on top of the planet will fall faster, since they penetrate the medium more easily: hence, gravity. On the bottom, of course, anything not rooted to the surface will drop off it, as indeed the Epicureans believed.

Once more, there are problems with this account. Around the time of Epicurus, astronomers were demonstrating that the earth was spherical, and calculating its circumference with a fair degree of accuracy, in part by showing that noon at one latitude, when the sun was directly overhead, was a different hour at another latitude – the absolute times being synchronized by celestial phenomena such as eclipses. How could the Epicureans, with their flat-earth hypothesis, account for the variable inclination of shadows at the same moment? One way would be to suppose that the sun is both quite small and very near the earth; it would thus cast angular shadows at the extremes when it was directly over the center of the disk (see Furley 1993). In fact, the Epicureans did maintain just such a view of the sun's size and position, and also insisted on a radical agnosticism concerning the causes of other heavenly phenomena such as eclipses. But whether they did so to counter the round-earthers, or for some other reason (they claimed, for example, that fires at a distance, unlike other objects, are roughly the size they seem), is uncertain.

If Epicurean physics confronted these and other predicaments on the atomic and subatomic level, still other difficulties lay in wait at what we may call the level of molecular chemistry. It was a premise of atomism that the atoms have no secondary properties, such as color, taste, or the like, whether because atoms are inalterable while qualities such as color are subject to change, or because perceptible qualities are conventional (they may appear one way to one person and another way to another), whereas atoms and the void, as intelligible entities, are "true" (see Democritus A49, B9, Diels–Kranz). Perceptible qualities are a consequence of atomic combinations, whereas atoms themselves have no other attributes than size, shape, and, in Epicurus' if not Democritus' system, weight. The features of the atoms that enter into stable compounds can indeed affect their attributes: for example, the presence of jagged atoms may explain why certain foods taste bitter. But jagged atoms as such have no flavor; it is only the compound that does. The reason for denying secondary qualities to atoms is that such qualities are perceived to change, while atoms are ex hypothesi inalterable (if they could disintegrate, the universe would crumble into nothing). The Epicureans seem to have believed that if atoms had intrinsic properties, such as taste, then it would be impossible to explain how sweet substances can be rendered bitter, or green leaves turn yellow, without supposing a transformation in the atoms themselves. This is not an inexorable conclusion, and a case can be made for Anaxagorean elements, which share at least some characteristics of the substances they form. For the Epicureans, however, such a theory entailed more problems than their own.

The advantage of a complex theory of causation such as Aristotle's is that it can explain how highly elaborated organisms such as plants or human beings are formed out of a material substratum. Such natural entities have, according to Aristotle, an innate form that acts as their final cause: the end product is an active principle, and is operative in the process of reproduction. The Epicureans posited a purely material universe, composed exclusively of atoms and void, and hence admitted only mechanical causes resulting from the interactions of atoms. Explaining how biological creatures emerged from such processes was not easy, given that their conception of atomic physics was quite impoverished: it did not include, for example, a notion of force, or attraction and repulsion. The Epicureans were obliged, accordingly, to depend on nothing more than snarled and tangled atoms, which vibrated at their uniformly rapid velocities within the confines of the clasped-together compound. Not every combination was possible, as they knew: monstrous forms such as centaurs did not exist, and the reason was that such amalgams were unstable. Had atoms come in infinite varieties, it would be difficult to see why this should be so: here was another reason for holding that the number of atomic shapes was incomprehensibly large but not strictly limitless. A more precise account of species formation was unavailable to the Epicureans, and their theory at this level was largely speculative.

Just as individual creatures come into being and perish, so too does the local cosmos – though not, of course, the infinite expanse of the universe as a whole, with its infinite atomic particles. Planets are formed and evolve, and give rise to different life forms, subject to the limitations inherent in the noninfinite variety of atomic shapes and sizes, and all this occurs solely as a result of random combinations of particles in space, unguided by any ulterior or final purpose. Epicurus did indeed recognize the existence of gods, who somehow managed to endure forever (the details of this part of his theory are very obscure), but he insisted that they had no role whatever in determining the course of natural events. In the early epoch of the world, when the planet was more fertile, it produced various creatures through spontaneous generation, some of which were unadapted to their environment and perished, while those fit to survive and reproduce were the ancestors of present life forms. This is not precisely a Darwinian account, since the Epicureans seem not to have recognized the role of mutation in the formation of new species, but it does constitute an elementary principle of natural selection.

Ethics

Human society also developed from primitive beginnings to its present degree of sophistication, with no divine plan directing its evolution. Originally, humans were hardy and solitary creatures, presumably emerging readymade from the earth in this condition. But in time the species softened, in part as a consequence of reproduction and the affections aroused by offspring and by sexual intimacy, and this change permitted people to unite for mutual protection against wild beasts and other perils. In due course, people discovered new proficiencies: how to build houses, sow crops, and – extremely important in the progress of human society – language, which developed out of instinctive cries but subsequently achieved the stage at which the meanings of most words were conventional rather than natural.

In the early phase of society, life was relatively simple, and wants were limited by the general scarcity of goods. Later, however, as life became more secure and resources more abundant, people began to compete for the available surplus, and some individuals emerged with greater power than the rest, leading to tyrannies and other unequal relations among classes. It is reasonable to suppose that the invention of language helped to enable these new ambitions: without the ability to form abstract concepts, it is difficult to imagine that a creature, endowed merely with sense perception, would seek to acquire symbols of wealth or status, such as gold or purple garments. We shall return to this point when we come to consider Epicurean psychology. However that may be, human society advanced to the technical sophistication of Epicurus' own day, which in principle could assure prosperity for all the citizens of a typical city-state, as Lucretius observes in the proem to the sixth book of his poem. But although a good life might now be within the reach of all, it remains as remote as ever from being realized, because people pursue goals that are contrary to what their nature requires, thereby causing themselves and their fellow human beings even greater misery than that to which humankind was exposed in the primal stages of social evolution.

The remedy for this paradoxical state of affairs, in which suffering increases with material prosperity, is provided precisely by Epicureanism, which affords an account of what happiness consists in, explains why human beings have failed to attain it even though external or material conditions are supremely favorable, and offers a set of practices designed to help individuals achieve the ideal state to which their nature summons them. Epicureanism thus furnishes an ethical goal, a psychology of what we may call abnormal behavior, and a therapy. We shall examine these three components of Epicurus' philosophy of man in order.

Epicurus posits as the natural aim of human life a state of freedom from distress, or, in Greek, *ataraxia*. Ataraxy has two aspects, one physical, the other mental. On the one hand, one ought, to the extent possible, render the body free from pain; on the other hand, the mind must be liberated from irrational fears and desires, which leave it prey to every kind of discontent and cause it to engage in self-destructive behavior, even to the point of suicide. Epicurean psychology addresses the latter problem, but Epicurus had first to establish what the pain or perturbations of body and soul consist in, and why liberation from them should be tantamount to human fulfillment. This part of the system involves the Epicurean doctrine of pleasure.

Pleasure is not precisely the goal of the individual; that is better described as nonperturbation. But nonperturbation or ataraxy is the only true form of pleasure, according to Epicurus, and the one cannot exist without the other. Epicurus defines pleasure as freedom from pain. But this freedom has two aspects: first, it is pleasurable to be freed from pain; second, it is pleasurable to be free of pain. The former of these is what Epicurus calls kinetic or mobile pleasure; the latter he calls static pleasure. An example of mobile pleasure is eating when one is hungry. Hunger is painful, because the body lacks what it requires to sustain itself; the lack must be replenished, and the process of replenishment is enjoyable. But clearly, as the body's need is met and the hunger appeased, the pleasure that is achieved by eating diminishes: one does not normally enjoy eating when entirely full. To continue to enjoy oneself in terms of kinetic pleasure alone, one must be continually in need and desirous of what can satisfy the need, whether it is hunger, sleep, warmth, sex, or whatever want human nature is subject to or human ingenuity can devise. Such was the view of the philosophical school known as the Cyrenaics, and they took the argument to its logical conclusion: one must increase one's desires and seek new ways of gratifying them.

The difficulty with this view is twofold, according to Epicurus. First, on such a view, pleasure is always accompanied by distress, for when the painful deficiency that gives rise to appetite departs or dissipates, the pleasure too is terminated. Kinetic gratifications, then, are mixed, since they are compounded of pleasure and pain. Plato had long since demonstrated the unsatisfying nature of this kind of enjoyment (*Gorgias* 496C–497A; cf. *Philebus* 31E–32D, 46A–50C). What is more, such mobile pleasures drive one continually to seek more intense satisfactions, and thus have the effect of increasing rather than reducing the mental agitation that Epicurean philosophy was concerned to eliminate. The ever restless pursuit of satiation is the antithesis to Epicurus' ideal of tranquillity.

Epicurus accordingly posited an alternative kind of pleasure, which is not a process but a state: it is the pleasure that derives from well-being as such, not fulfillment of a need but being without need. For the Cyrenaics, and certain other ancient schools of thought, such a condition was regarded not as pleasurable but rather as neutral, between pain and pleasure. Criticism was directed also at the relationship between the two types of pleasure: did static pleasure kick in only when mobile pleasure had terminated, or did it gradually increase as the need was met, thus rising as mobile pleasure declined? But if static pleasure varies with satiation in this way, does it not partake of process too, and so is it not simply a stable condition? Once again, it is difficult to be certain just how the Epicureans responded to these objections, given the fragmentary state of the evidence, although various possibilities suggest themselves.

So far, the two kinds of pleasure have been discussed solely in terms of the body. Are there pleasures of the mind as well? In one sense, yes: pleasure is perceived, and perception resides in the soul, not the inanimate body. But are there pleasures and pains specific to the mind and independent of one's corporeal condition? This is harder to determine. Certainly, mobile pleasures would seem to pertain exclusively to the body: the mind does not experience lack in the sense of depletion, which can then be recharged. But perhaps there is a pleasure associated with the reduction of painful psychological states, such as fear. Static pleasure, correspondingly, would consist in the absence of fear and similar mental perturbations. One kind of disturbance, according to Epicurean doctrine, involves precisely the opposite state to fear, namely, desire, which is a reflex of a lack or want, and hence a sign of pain. Some desires, of course, are normal and inevitable, just as some fears are: the desires for food and shelter, for example, are classified by Epicurus as being both natural and necessary. Other desires are natural but not necessary: these include, one supposes, the desire to listen to music, enjoy the odor of perfume or flowers or the taste of a particular food, and so forth. Finally, there are desires that are neither natural nor necessary: such is greed – the desire for limitless wealth – or ambition, the desire for power and reputation. These last desires are detached from basic needs, and tend, for reasons to be discussed below, to drive people to limitless accumulation, distracting them from the contentment that lies easily available to all.

Where do such irrational desires come from? Ultimately, from false beliefs about what the good of humankind consists in, but more immediately from irrational fears.

These fears are not of something harmful, such as fire, which can induce pain and which one naturally seeks to avoid. Rather, they are fears of unreal things, or things which do not affect us, and thus are more like anxieties than fears. The distinction is captured in a portion of the inscription mounted by Diogenes of Oenoanda:

> As a matter of fact this fear is sometimes clear, sometimes not clear – clear when we avoid something manifestly harmful like fire through fear that we shall meet death by it, not clear when, while the mind is occupied with something else, it (fear) has insinuated itself into our nature and [lurks] . . . (35.II, trans. Smith 1993: 385).

The last word ("lurks") is based on a possible but by no means certain restoration of the Greek text, and after this the inscription breaks off.

I expect that the unclear fear to which Diogenes refers pertains to the fear of death, the principal irrational fear, according to the Epicureans, whether it is the fear of nonexistence as such or of punishment in an afterlife. It is to compensate for or protect ourselves against this irrational terror that we set out to acquire rulership and riches, as though poverty and weakness were, in Lucretius' words, the antechamber to hell (*On Nature* 3.59–67). It is at this point, moreover, that Epicurean psychology and ethics intersect with Epicurean physical theory: for the surest way to abolish the fear of death is to understand that there is no afterlife, nor any possibility of surviving the dissolution of the body. There is no such thing as spiritual substance; the soul, like the body and everything else in the universe, is compounded of atoms and void, and when a person dies and the body decomposes, the tenuous, highly mobile atoms of which the soul is made escape into the ambient air to scatter irrecoverably. How do we know that the soul is material? In part, because it interacts with the body. When you feel fear, your flesh trembles, your heart beats faster; correspondingly, a wound to the body produces effects in the mind. But a nonmaterial substance could not affect, or be affected by, matter (cf. Lucretius 3.161–76). The Epicureans had no time for fictitious transmitters between spirit and matter such as Descartes's pituitary gland.

Nor is death painful (although dying may be): for where death is, we – as sentient human beings – are no longer; hence "death is nothing to us." The atomic theory, on Epicurus' view, demonstrates irrefutably that the soul has no existence separate from the body; once that fact is securely grasped, the anxieties that death motivates will evanesce, and with them the irrational desires that they generate. Human beings will at last be free to enjoy lives free of mental perturbation, their bodily wants met by the simple and easily accessible things it takes to eliminate hunger, thirst, and the other basic needs. Pleasure and ataraxy lie that close at hand.

But if this is all it requires to be as happy as is humanly possible – and Epicurus describes this state as blessed and equal to the joy of the very gods despite their immortality, since duration does not augment or diminish happiness – then what prevents us from acknowledging the truth of his doctrine and enjoying the bliss that comes with it? Clearly, resistance to accepting Epicureanism is deep-seated, and it is incumbent on Epicurus both to explain why and to propose ways of overcoming it. Social conditioning is obviously one factor. In the beginning, Lucretius assures us, human beings were not superstitious; such irrational beliefs arose only with developed civilization. Here, the invention of language may play a role, as suggested above: "I fear death" sounds like a well-formed sentence, on the analogy of "I fear this flame," but it is not. For death is nothing, and hence not a proper object of fear. It is an illusion of language, or what Epicurus calls "empty belief." A second factor may be the pervasive regime, in advanced societies, of punishment, which arose in order to contain transgressive behavior and then, to make it the more effective and ineluctable, was projected onto the gods as judges in the afterlife. For Epicurus, any concern for the well-being or sins of humankind was incompatible with the perfect happiness and tranquillity that the gods must, on his view of them, perpetually enjoy. But transgressive desire is motivated, as we have seen, by this very principle of terror, which is thus counterproductive, albeit perhaps inescapable under current conditions, as a means of eradicating wrongdoing.

Irrational desires themselves, in turn, may play a part in producing anxiety. Lucretius, at all events, describes the traditional torments of the underworld, such as Tantalus' forever unsatisfied hunger and thirst and the Danaids' hopeless task of carrying water in perforated jugs, as projections onto the afterlife of the unhappy state of human beings here on earth, who strive endlessly to fill cravings that are insatiable because their objects meet no genuine need (3.978–9). It may be, then, that irrational fears and desires form a closed loop, each reinforcing the other; that too would explain in part why they are so difficult to eliminate.

Knowledge and Perception

The above account is speculative. What is certain is that false or empty opinion is inveterate among human beings, and must be counteracted by steady instruction in materialist physics if one is to transcend the ancient fears of divine retribution which such philosophies as Platonism and Pythagoreanism promoted in their turn. One method is to attack all belief in divine causation, since if gods are responsible for such natural disasters as volcanoes and earthquakes, it is only a short step to supposing that the purpose of these disasters is to chastise human sin. Hence, Epicurus and his followers sought to explain all natural events by causes based on the atomic theory, without introducing any unnecessary hypotheses. Only those causes were admitted whose operations were plainly perceivable; where phenomena were not open to inspection up close, one had then to confess ignorance and accept the possibility of a variety of explanations, no one of which could be safely eliminated. This was the case with most celestial phenomena, such as eclipses, for example: they might be caused by an object passing in front of the sun or moon, or by a winking out of these bodies themselves, or by some other means, and it was superstition rather than science that inclined a person to opt for one cause rather than another in this case. The basic principles guiding the interpretation of physical events, according to Epicurus, are confirmation, as by a closer look (thus proving, e.g., that the stick in the water is not really bent), and the absence of disconfirmation, that is, that nothing in what we perceive tells against such and such an explanation, but does so against all others.

What, then, of the atomic theory itself, which is certainly not open to direct confirmation by the senses – the ultimate source of all our information about the world? This is a case of proof by the absence of disconfirmation, along with arguments based on conceivability. By the latter we arrive at the belief in void or empty space: if it did not exist, there could be no motion, since solid matter would occupy the entire universe. Aristotle and the Stoics did not share this view: for them, motion was possible in a plenum, in which objects could slide past each other, as in water, without either of them backing into a vacuum. For Epicurus, such a process was wholly counterintuitive: at the microscopic level, it was necessary for the constituent particles of one or the other object to recede before the other could advance, and this could not happen if the way were blocked by other atoms lined up behind them. If the material universe were a plenum, then, motion would be impossible. But this possibility is disconfirmed by the evidence of our senses, which shows that motion occurs. Hence, there is void.

Epicurus, evidently following the lead of Democritus, explained sense perception, like everything else, in terms of atoms. In the case of vision, for example, all visible objects continually emit thin atomic films or laminas – Epicurus called them *eidōla* or "images," while Lucretius used the Latin term *simulacra*. These films conform to the shape of the object that ejects them, and preserve certain other features encoded in its molecular pattern, such as color. They flit through the air, and when they encounter an eye, which is the organ that is suited to receive and process them, they yield the sensation of sight in a living creature. A number of problems with this account suggest themselves. Would not such films be distorted as they pass through the air? Indeed they are, which explains why a square tower in the distance looks round, for example: the edges of the laminas are worn away in transmission. In some fashion or other, moreover, air that is pushed ahead of the films produces the perception of depth or remoteness. But if these membranes, however thin, conform to the object both in shape and in size (let's say, of a mountain), how do they enter the eye? Perhaps bits of multiple laminas are admitted and then reassembled in some manner inside the organ. Conceivably, the membranes shrink for some reason before they reach the eye, although there is no good evidence for either of these hypotheses. Clearly, the films must be exceedingly thin, since the mass of the object that discharges them is not perceptibly reduced over time: might they be just one atom deep? Yet they are tough enough to travel great distances without tearing apart. Mathematical theories of optics in antiquity provided simpler explanations, but they were not concerned to reduce all phenomena to atomic motions and combinations.

Not just sight, but all the senses (apart from touch) were explained by way of such laminas, with the details modified to suit the case in point, for instance, the capacity of sounds to penetrate walls – although they emerge muffled, thanks to atomic interferences in the denser medium. But the most extraordinary aspect of the theory of films or *eidōla* is that the Epicureans used them to explain not just perception but imagination as well. When we think of an object, we are really just attending at that moment to exceedingly fine laminas that are perpetually drifting through the atmosphere, having been given off by the object – or a similar one, perhaps – at some earlier time. We may leave aside the question of how long such films endure: since the Epicureans accounted for dreams we have of dead people by this mechanism, presumably they lasted a substantial period of time. Since we can summon all sorts of thoughts to the imagination at a given moment, there must be a huge number of *simulacra* speeding by in our immediate neighborhood, somehow preserving their fragile integrity. It seems, moreover, that a single lamina is not sufficient to produce sensation or imagination; rather, a series is required (note that individual atoms are thus imperceptible by nature, and not merely because they are very small). The picture here is quite cluttered – although no more so than that which modern physics evinces.

Still missing from the Epicurean account of imagining, however, is how or why we attend to some laminas and not others – unless, of course, we are wholly at the mercy of the environment, as we are in the case of sensation, where we see or hear what is there, not what we choose. For Epicurus, however, our freedom to imagine what we wish was a primary datum of experience. Accordingly, he supposed that human beings can direct their attention to one thing rather than another – at least, this is a plausible interpretation of what he calls "casting the mind." Just how free an act this is remains unclear, since our thoughts are presumably conditioned by our prior experience, including mental associations. Epicurus is clear, nevertheless, that human behavior is not wholly predetermined by the mechanical interaction of atoms. For a completely predictable universe, which, in Epicurus' view, would entail ethical or psychological fatalism, is disrupted by the action of the swerve, that slight deviation from the true, mentioned above, which occurs spontaneously in the course of atomic motion. It is here that the perfect chain of causality is broken.

How the swerve supports the doctrine of free will is not entirely clear from our sources. Is there a swerve every time we make a choice? If so, are we really free to choose if our choice is nothing more than a symptom or effect of such a swerve, which, despite the fact that it is random, is just as much a physical event as ordinary atomic motions and collisions? In any case, why are human beings, on this account, any freer than rocks or water? Perhaps a swerve generates greater effects among soul atoms, which are small, round, and highly mobile, than it does in more tightly bound compounds made of larger and more irregular particles. If nothing else, the swerve means that one cannot foresee or calculate every action that a human being will take, and that may have been enough to secure, for Epicurus, freedom from fate and a sense of responsibility for one's acts – including the decision to adopt the philosophy of Epicureanism and thus lead a happy and unperturbed life.

We have so far been discussing thought in the sense of imagination, but clearly there are reasoning processes that are not reducible to mere images, or attention to films of objects. The Epicureans pondered the question of how we make inferences from signs, though whether the sophisticated arguments presented by Philodemus in his treatise *On Signs* (trans. De Lacy and De Lacy 1978) represent the thought of Epicurus himself or are later developments is uncertain. What does go back to Epicurus is the idea that error derives from the addition of opinion or belief to the evidence of the senses; for the senses themselves do not deceive, but simply report what is there. Such opinion, then, must depend on some kind of mistaken inference. False beliefs are transmitted from generation to generation by education or socialization, which in turn depends heavily on language, in the case of human beings. There are also certain basic concepts that are either innate or acquired – the evidence is not decisive on this score – by which we form judgments. In any case, stripping away irrelevant associations from the basic meanings of terms is one of the procedures that Epicurus recommends for returning to an accurate view of nature and of the best life for humankind.

Practice

Such are the kinds of arguments that the Epicureans deployed against their opponents, whether Platonists, Aristotelians, or (later) Stoics, in order to undermine the belief in divine interference in the universe, the ultimate purpose of which was to eradicate the fear of death and punishment in the afterlife. Instruction in materialist doctrine was not all, however. Given the ubiquitous pressure to gain wealth and power at the expense of psychological tranquillity and physical comfort, all but the most exceptional individuals require strong support from a like-minded community in order to make progress toward understanding and accepting the tenets of Epicureanism, and modifying their behavior accordingly. Thus, the Epicureans encouraged the formation of local groups of friends, who met regularly to celebrate the creed of the master and deepen their grasp of its principles. The letters that Epicurus wrote to his disciples, and the collections of important maxims, were intended to serve as aids to memory, encapsulating in brief the fundamental precepts of the school. In addition, the Epicureans sought to determine the best ways in which more advanced members might promote the progress of the rest, achieving the right blend of healthy criticism with supportive encouragement. Epicurean pedagogy, which we know about chiefly from the papyrus rolls preserved from Philodemus' library (e.g., the treatise *On Frank Criticism*; translation in Konstan et al. 1998), may well have served as a model of instruction for other ancient sects, up to and including Christian communities.

Correspondingly, the Epicureans discouraged participation in political life, since such activity was normally incompatible with peace of mind; besides, a life in politics was usually motivated by just the kinds of ambition that Epicureanism was intended to cure. This does not mean that Epicurus was hostile to social order as such. Epicureans were prepared to offer advice to kings, for example – one recalls that Epicurus was eighteen years old at the death of Alexander the Great, and although he spent his adult life in Athens, real power now lay in the hands of Hellenistic monarchs rather than with democratic institutions. He allowed a place for praise and blame in education, and also for chastisement, although he was more concerned with well-being than with virtue, a stance that caused Cicero to deny that Epicureanism counted as a philosophy at all.

Nor did Epicurus approve of a radical break with the style of life led by ordinary people, as the Cynics did, for example. He recommended that one observe traditional ritual practices, such as sacrifices and other forms of worship (that we imagine gods was, for Epicurus, evidence that they exist as the source of the films that impinge on us), but that one do so in a proper spirit of piety: this means contemplating the gods' perfect contentment and ataraxy, which can serve as a model and ideal for ourselves. In this sense, the Epicureans had no revolutionary program of political change. Their approach was to spread the word by example and instruction. But they did not hesitate to include in their fellowship women, slaves, and other marginalized elements in the ancient Greek cities, thereby provoking the scorn of some of their rivals – the women members, for example, were derided as courtesans, although some rose to positions of leadership within the far-flung communities that had already come into existence in Epicurus' own time. Despite the quietism of the school, then, its mode of life and ideals had, or might have, radical social implications.

This, then, is the outline of Epicurean doctrine. Of course, many details have been omitted, and there is not space to examine the many controversies to which the theory has given rise. The intention is to suggest the overall coherence and power of the theory, and to point to places in which further research or speculation may be profitable. The fragmentary texts are as tantalizing as any task in Hades, but much more fun. And the ultimate goal of Epicureanism, which is a tranquil life free of superstitious terror, remains today as valid and urgent as it was two thousand years ago.

References and Recommended Reading

The basic collections of Epicurean writings in English translation:

Long, A. A. and David Sedley. 1987. *The Hellenistic Philosophers.* 2 vols. Cambridge: Cambridge University Press.

Inwood, Brad, and L. P. Gerson. 1997. *Hellenistic Philosophy: Introductory Readings.* 2nd ed. Indianapolis: Hackett. (The Epicurean part is also published separately.)

Long and Sedley organize materials by topic (atomic theory, ethics, etc.) and subtopics, bringing together brief selections from various sources followed by detailed commentary. Greek and Latin texts are in vol. 2. Inwood and Gerson translate complete texts or sets of excerpts, where possible. Thus, you will find Epicurus' "Letter to Herodotus" translated as one continuous text in Inwood and Gerson (this is how Diogenes of Laertius quotes it); in Long and Sedly it is divided up, and the bits are assembled with related fragments from other sources.

Other works cited in this chapter:

Clay, Diskin. 1983. *Lucretius and Epicurus.* Ithaca, N.Y.: Cornell University Press.

De Lacy, P. H., and E. A. De Lacy. 1978. *Philodemus: On Methods of Inference,* edited with translation and commentary. Rev. ed. with the collaboration of Marcello Gigante, Francesca Longo Auricchio, Adele Tepedino Guerra. Naples, Italy: Bibliopolis. *Philodemus on Signs.* 2nd ed. Naples, Italy: Bibliopolis.

Furley, David. 1996. "The Earth in Epicurean and Contemporary Astronomy." In Gabriele Giannantoni and Marcello Gigante, eds., *Epicureismo greco e romano: Atti del congresso internazionale, Napoli, 19–26 maggio 1993*. Naples, Italy: Bibliopolis, vol. 1: 119–25.

Konstan, David. 2000. "Democritus the Physicist" (review of Taylor 1999). *Apeiron* 33: 125–44.

——, trans. 1989. *Simplicius on Aristotle's Physics 6*. Ithaca, N.Y.: Cornell University Press.

Konstan, David, Diskin Clay, Clarence Glad, Johan Thom, and James Ware. 1998. *Philodemus on Frank Criticism: Introduction, Translation and Notes*. Atlanta: Society of Biblical Literature Texts and Translations (Greco-Roman Religion).

Sedley, David. 1998. *Lucretius and the Transformation of Greek Wisdom*. Cambridge: Cambridge University Press.

Smith, Martin Ferguson, ed. 1993. *Diogenes of Oenoanda: The Epicurean Inscription*. Naples, Italy: Bibliopolis.

Taylor, C. C. W., ed. 1999. *The Atomists: Leucippus and Democritus: A Text and Translation with a Commentary*. The Phoenix Presocratics 5 = Phoenix Supplementary Volume 36. Toronto: The University of Toronto Press.

Chapter 13

Stoicism

Phillip Mitsis

Introduction

Of all the philosophical schools of antiquity, Stoicism arguably has had the greatest influence on both the form and content of modern philosophy. Many of the questions we now take to be obvious and many of the arguments that now appear to be fairly standard are found for the first time in Stoic texts. For example, questions about the connection between free will and determinism – questions that scholars have trouble finding articulated explicitly in Plato or Aristotle – are formulated by the Stoics crisply, and in a way that contemporary philosophers find readily comprehensible. Problems about the relation between language and the world and about the way that we mentally represent the world to ourselves are posed in Stoicism in a manner so recognizably modern that it often can make the epistemologies of Plato and Aristotle seem puzzlingly archaic in comparison. In ethics, too, the Stoics seem distinctly modern. Indeed, they have been deemed by no less a figure than Henry Sidgwick, the great Victorian ethicist, to have actually effected the transition from ancient to modern conceptions of ethics by arguing that morality is structured by a divine code of natural law – a moral law apprehended by human reason and valid for all human beings everywhere at all times. Again, the contrast with the *polis*-bound political thought and strictly agent-centered moral theories of Plato and Aristotle is striking.

Stoic Approach to Philosophy: Importance of Systematicity

That we often find Stoic, rather than Platonic or Aristotelian, ways of looking at issues more smoothly compatible with our own is no mere coincidence. It has its roots, to a great extent, in the historical fact that the Stoics, as opposed to Plato or Aristotle, loomed largest for the early modern philosophers who gave shape to modern philosophical thought. One hardly can read, for instance, Spinoza on free will and determinism, Locke on mental representation, or Kant on the structure of morality without noticing specific Stoic philosophical preoccupations in the background. For better or worse, then, Stoic problems often have become our problems. At the same time, though, however much we may discern Stoic formulations underlying the types of questions we now ask, we are likely to be taken aback or even repelled by the kinds of answers that they themselves actually offer. Take, for instance, the following example related in Cicero's *Tusculan Disputations* (3.30). Anaxagoras, on receiving the news of his son's death, was reported to have calmly observed, "I was already aware that I had begotten a mortal." This attitude and comment, cited approvingly by Stoics as paradigmatic of the proper way of responding to the world, captures a feature of Stoicism that is perhaps most familiarly associated with them, that is, a certain "stoical" detachment and lack of emotion when facing the vicissitudes of the world.

We might find Anaxagoras' stoic response somehow emotionally deficient and lacking in appropriate human feeling or we might be inclined to see something admirable and courageous in his composure and in his being "philosophical" when confronted by personal misfortune. Or we might feel the tug of both these attitudes at the same time and be uncertain about what to say. Whatever our initial inclinations here, however, the Stoics think that we will not really be in a position to make a coherent judgment about Anaxagoras' response until we understand something more – and that something more, we might be surprised to learn, is the entire organization of the universe. At first sight, such a claim might appear not only rather unlikely, but also unhelpful. We might think it unlikely because it is hard to see what immediate relevance the entire organization of the cosmos has to a particular individual's attitudes about something like the death of a son. Some people might, for example, be wowed by the fact that there are black holes in the universe or others might be rather indifferent; still others might just be ignorant of their existence. But whatever the case, it seems odd to claim that facts about black holes or our attitudes to them should have any direct relevance in assessing the appropriateness of an individual's reactions to the death of a child. Indeed, we might suspect that we would do better to consign explanations of this type to the province of astrologers or to other such charlatans. By the same token, we might justifiably suspect that such a view ultimately will prove unhelpful to us, since even few charlatans have ever had the chutzpah to claim that they have knowledge of the entire organization of the universe. Who, after all, could hope to know that? Thus, even if such knowledge turned out to be relevant, how could we hope to acquire it and bring it to bear in assessing the appropriateness of any of our emotional responses to particular events? If the bar is set so high that no one can hope to approach it, it is not clear of what use it is to us.

The Stoics, therefore, seem vulnerable to challenges not only about the relevance but also about the possibility of actually achieving the kind of knowledge they claim is necessary for guiding our responses to the world. Not surprisingly, their ancient opponents attacked them vigorously on both these scores. At first glance, one might indeed suppose that these particular Stoic claims provide such easy targets that we might do better to pass over them quickly. But this would be a mistake, since in making their claims, the Stoics, among other things, are explicitly relying on a powerful view about the nature of philosophy and philosophical argument that are not dismissed so easily. This view of philosophy is worth considering, moreover, not only because historically it has had important adherents – to name but a few, Kant, Hegel, Marx, and Derrida – but because it draws together some central intuitions about the nature of language, knowledge, belief, and action.

For the Stoics, philosophy and philosophical argument form a coherent system in which various elements and modes of inquiry – for example, metaphysical, epistemological, psychological, physical, ethical, and so on – form a mutually supporting and harmonious whole. Unlike Socrates, who claimed that he could inquire into the nature of virtue without having knowledge about the cosmos, or indeed, perhaps without even having a theory about what counts as knowledge, the Stoics think that any particular philosophical view is tied to a host of other philosophical assumptions and decisions that we neglect at our peril. Many scholars now believe that the Stoics were innovators in this regard as well and essentially invented the notion of systematic philosophy. But whatever the truth here, it certainly is the case that the Stoics made much of the coherence and unity of their philosophical system. They expended great effort, moreover, in setting out and arranging the topics from what, in their view, comprise philosophy's three main divisions: logic, physics, and ethics.

Still, we might wonder, what does all this rather technical sounding philosophical apparatus have to do with our initial question? My son dies. How am I to respond? Just as Anaxagoras, I certainly might be aware that my dead son was mortal – how could I not? Yet, I surely might also believe that his death is something bad and a source of grief to me. The Stoics, however, argue that such a judgment would be premature and that it depends, among other things, on a series of (mistaken) views about what is valuable, about my son's place in nature, about the relation of his death to other events surrounding it, and about the propositions I have used in representing his death to myself. We will have to decide how far we are willing to follow the Stoics in this particular line of argument, but we should notice a formal element in their claim that is not without some plausibility: our beliefs are often connected and they rely on each other in ways that more systematic examination and exposition can help to bring out. When we begin to discover the nature of these connections, moreover, we may come to revise our initial beliefs about things as well as our reactions to them.

For instance, I may think that abortion is wrong. But my moral views about its wrongness are likely to be connected to my views about what makes someone a human being and at what point a fetus meets these criteria (a metaphysical question). So too, my ethical and metaphysical views here are likely to be connected to my conception of what psychological functions characterize human persons and at what point a fetus begins to manifests such functions (a psychological question). Of course, it is still a large step from this point about connections among our ethical, metaphysical, and psychological beliefs to the claim that we must understand the entire organization of the cosmos in order to answer our question about Anaxagoras. But at least we are in a better position to understand the Stoics' drive to explore questions systematically and their attempt to make explicit the connections and mutual implications among our various beliefs.

According to the Stoics, then, we need to follow out the connections among all of our beliefs, and our beliefs about the death of a son are no exception. Indeed, they insist that if we consider the death of anyone, including ourselves, only in isolation, we are likely to come to some very wrong conclusions both emotionally and intellectually. Why am I grieved by the death of my son? Well, minimally, in the first instance, it must be because I think that there was something deeply important about my son being alive. The Stoics will be quick to point out that I am relying quite obviously on a particular ethical judgment about what is valuable. They also will argue, more controversially to say the least, that the conception of value I am using to make such a judgment is badly mistaken. But before stopping to examine any of their individual claims and arguments in any one area, it may be helpful to continue following out the general contours of their system. Now, apart from thinking that my son's death is something bad, I might also have such related thoughts as "If only he had not died now, when he was still so young and had so much more life and happiness awaiting him" or "How unlucky he was to be killed in a freak car accident." Again, the Stoics will point out here that such thoughts rely on a particular view of causality, of time, and of the nature of events and the connections we see among them. In saying that my son was unlucky and the victim of a freak accident, I am assuming a particular view of the nature of causes and events – in their opinion, mistaken, since they think that all events in our lives are determined by an all-encompassing causal nexus or network. For the Stoics, events can be neither accidental nor freak, since they are part of a providentially designed whole in which all individual events are for the benefit both of the parts and of the whole. The timing and the nature of the events that make up our lives and the event that is our death are all predetermined as parts of a plan which is the expression of a divine *logos* that is both provident and perfectly rational. Again, we may disagree with the Stoics' claim here, but we can begin to see why the Stoics think that more global questions about the nature of the cosmos – for example, "Are events in it ordered and connected or are they random?" "Is the world structured in a way to benefit its individual parts?" – affect our judgments about more local events such as the death of a son.

Our views about causality, in turn, raise questions about the nature of causal interactions. What enables things to interact causally? What must they be made of and what properties do they display? When someone dies, what exactly happens? Does something of one's personality, as many have believed, continue to survive, perhaps in the form of an incorporeal soul? Some might perhaps find consolation in such a notion of an incorporeal soul, but how does something incorporeal act in the world and how is it acted upon? What is the nature of the constituents of the world? In addition to such fundamental questions about the nature of the physical world, inquiry into the constituents of the world involves, for the Stoics, further questions about language, since to predicate any property of the world or to describe the qualities of any object involves linguistic propositions. What are these and how are they related to the world? When I form the proposition "My son's death is bad," what am I predicating about the world and how am I representing the event to myself? Moreover, all of these questions are related, for the Stoics, to several further epistemological ones. How can I know and justify any of the assumptions and beliefs that I am relying on? Is knowledge possible? What is its connection to language? How do we understand causal explanations, and so on? And finally, to bring us full circle to our original question, what role does know-ledge play in human action? What is its scope and what role does it play in human emotions?

I have touched on a few of the connections that Stoics see between our various beliefs – they see many more – and it is clear that we might disagree with many, if not all, of their individual conclusions about particular philosophical questions. But we will miss something important, and something that they thought was especially important, about their philosophical thinking if we underestimate the systematic considerations underlying their thought on particular topics. With this in mind, we are now in a better position to turn to more detailed consideration of these. I will follow the particular trajectory of argument sketched above, beginning with ethics, moving through psychology and its underlying physics, and concluding with logic. This does not necessarily reflect a particular Stoic procedure that we have any evidence for, since in principle they take no individual branch of inquiry to be foundational or prior to the others. They do not, for instance, insist that inquiry depends on finding some one unimpeachable, certain starting point in the manner of Descartes. They believe that there are many points of entry into their system. One might therefore, in their view, just as soon begin from a different starting point and proceed in a different way, for example, from logic to ethics to physics (as some Stoics did) or from physics to logic to ethics (as did others). But they are convinced, of course, that regardless of where one starts, all roads eventually lead to the Stoa and to the same system overall.

Stoic Sources

It is perhaps especially ironic, in light of the Stoics' many ringing endorsements of the unity of their system, that nothing approaching a unified account actually survives. Indeed, from its traditional founding in Athens by Zeno of Citium in 300 BCE, we have just two bits of direct evidence from the first two hundred years of Stoicism: less than forty lines of a hymn to Zeus by Cleanthes (?331–230 BCE), Zeno's friend and successor as head of the school, and a few fragments of the *Logical Investigations* of Chrysippus (?280–208/4 BCE), the third head of the Stoa and its most brilliant and prolific early exponent. This is the equivalent of barely a couple of stray pages from the hundreds of works written by early Stoics. To make matters more complicated, what evidence there is from later writers, even for individual areas of Stoic philosophy, comes from a bewilderingly wide variety of historical periods, social contexts, and individuals – most with aims other than systematic, textbook-style exposition and from several who are vehemently hostile. Among avowed Stoics themselves, these include, for instance, Epictetus (50–130 CE) a Phrygian slave who wrote nothing, but whose lectures were written down in Greek by the historian Arrian; Seneca (1 BCE–65 CE) an immensely rich tutor and advisor to the emperor Nero, who wrote in a highly polished and rhetorical Latin style for public consumption; Marcus Aurelius (121–80 CE) Roman emperor from 161–80, whose spiritual diary in Greek (which has come to be called *Meditations*, though he entitled it merely *To Himself*) was not intended for publication and saw the light some two hundred years after the emperor's death. When one reflects for a minute on the variety of personages, circumstances, and possible aims of just these three sources for later Stoicism – an emperor writing a diary, a slave lecturing, and a politician writing in a highly charged and dangerous political situation – one sees the potential difficulties that loom for anyone trying to explore and understand Stoic doctrines. Moreover, many of our most detailed sources are critical, such as Galen (129–210/15 CE), personal physician to Marcus Aurelius, or even overtly hostile, such as Plutarch (45–125 CE), a dogmatic Platonist who wrote a number of polemical treatises against the Stoics. Given how difficult it is to give an account of the philosophy even of an author such as Plato, whose work we have in abundance, it is easy to understand how the fragmentary glimpses we have of Stoicism refracted through our many sources often make precision difficult. Moreover, when scholars debate over possible developments in Platonic doctrines, they at least have a substantial body of work to analyze from one writer. Debates over developments in Stoicism must try to bring coherence to fragmentary or hostile accounts occurring in different languages and historical contexts over the course of several hundred years – and in the context of a philosophical tradition that encouraged continual debate about its major tenets.

Stoic Ethics

Yet for all this, it is possible to begin with at least one general ethical claim that Stoics of every stripe would endorse, even if they gave expression to it somewhat differently, as the following important passage makes clear:

> Therefore Zeno in his book *On the nature of man* was the first to say that living in agreement with nature is the end (*telos*) which is living in accordance with virtue. For nature leads us to virtue. So too Cleanthes in his book *On pleasure*, and Posidonius and Hecato in their books *On ends*. Further, living in accordance with virtue is equivalent to living in accordance with experience of what happens by nature, as Chrysippus says in *On ends* book I: for our natures are parts of the nature of the whole. Therefore, living in agreement with nature comes to be the end, which is in accordance with the nature of oneself and that of the whole, engaging in no activity wont to be forbidden by the universal law, which is the right reason pervading everything and identical to Zeus, who is the director of the administration of existing things. And the virtue of the happy man and his good flow of life are just this: always doing everything on the basis of the concordance of each man's guardian spirit with the will of the administrator of the whole. (Diogenes Laertius 7.87–8)

This passage is from Diogenes Laertius' *Compendium of the Lives and Opinions of Philosophers* (250 CE), which is a collection of excerpts from a wide variety of sources, and is what might be called, somewhat charitably, the closest thing we have to a History of Ancient Philosophy surviving from antiquity. The quality of Diogenes' evidence is often uneven, but in many ways, his is the most comprehensive account of the history of Stoicism that we have from any ancient source (see Diogenes Laertius 7.38–160). This passage is especially valuable moreover, since it indicates that there was a basic agreement during the initial two hundred years of Stoicism about what the goal or end (*telos*) of human life is. Moreover, in a sense, it gives a capsule summary of many of the central ethical claims that Stoics of every era would espouse.

The question of the *telos* of human life is the basic ethical question for Hellenistic philosophers generally, and we might be variously unimpressed or amused by Zeno's initial claim that our goal in life is to live in agreement with nature. We might be amused if we recall the long tradition in Greek thought of invoking nature to justify all manner of behavior. There are characters in Aristophanes' *Clouds*, for instance, who argue that it is natural for sons to beat up their fathers and sleep with their mothers, just as the chickens do, while the Cynics argued that it was in accordance with nature to masturbate in public and in general to live as unconstrained as dogs among the artificial conventions of human societies. On the other hand, others claimed that living in accordance with nature entailed very different kinds of behavior. Aristotle, for example, thought that living in a *polis* with one's fellow citizens, perfecting a range of intellectual and practical virtues, and becoming as godlike as possible was in accordance with nature. Clearly, one moral that we might draw from this is that the notion of acting in accordance with nature is exceedingly elastic and it can include mandates for us to live either like beasts or like gods. Some scholars have seen both these tendencies alive and in conflict throughout the history of Stoicism, while others have seen a historical progression in Stoicism from a more Cynic to a more Aristotelian view of what it means to live in accordance with nature. Given the elasticity in the concept of nature, it is easy to see why very different conclusions might be drawn about the Stoics' injunction to live in accordance with it. At the same time, it would be hard to find a Greek thinker who does not invoke nature in defense of his views. So, apart from its potential for furnishing amusement, trying to cite facts about nature in order to justify moral claims might appear to be one of those exercises that is so flexible that its conclusions are doomed to be either inconsistent or inconsequential. More important, though, we might well wonder whether this is the right way to think about moral claims in the first place. We might plausibly suppose, for instance, that nature is something about which facts can be observed and described. Morality, on the other hand, has to do with values and prescriptive claims that tell us what we ought to do. Attempting to mix these two types of explanations, either by deriving moral claims from nature or reducing value claims to natural ones might seem to involve one in a series of fundamental mistakes that go beyond charges of excessive flexibility.

To see what sense can be made of the Stoics' appeal to nature and how they thought nature and morality are related, we would do best to turn to their doctrine of *oikeiōsis*. This is a word that is difficult to translate adequately and I will follow the lead of many scholars who leave it transliterated. Derived from the Greek word for household (*oikos*), *oikeiōsis* has strong connotations of possession, belonging, appropriateness, and affection. It also includes a cognitive dimension that is captured by one scholar's apt paraphrase of it as the "recognition and appreciation of something as belonging to one."[1]

> They [The Stoics] say that an animal has self-preservation as the object of its first impulse, since nature from the beginning appropriates it, as Chrysippus says in his *On ends* book 1. The first thing appropriate to every animal, he says, is its own constitution and the consciousness of this. For nature was not likely either to alienate the animal itself, or to make it and then neither alienate it not appropriate it. So it remains to say that in constituting the animal, nature appropriated it to itself. This is why the animal rejects what is harmful and accepts what is appropriate (Diogenes Laertius 7.85).

Trying to figure out what is natural in human behavior can be difficult, especially given the fact that much of human behavior is learned, often in very artificial or corrupt circumstances. When watching someone go into paroxysms of pleasure while sniffing a fine burgundy or tasting a complex sauce, it might be difficult to say out of hand whether such behavior counts as natural. The Stoics therefore appeal to the untutored behavior of animals and children as an initial test for what is natural. Such so-called cradle arguments, that is, arguments based on infant behavior, do not exhaust their view of nature and natural behavior – far from it – but one might still wonder what relevance this evidence has for their claim that living in accordance with nature is the same as living in accordance with virtue. Clearly, we do not think animals or children capable of virtue in the required sense. Indeed, if we remember Aristophanes, their behavior can be appealed to in order to justify just the opposite. So it is certainly fair to demand from the Stoics an explanation of how animal behavior and virtuous behavior are related and how Zeno can claim "nature leads us to virtue."

The Stoics' argument begins from the empirical claim that all animal behavior, from the outset, can be observed to have self-preservation as its goal. They treat this as a given of nature and think that they can cite abundant evidence in support of their claim that animals as well as human beings are endowed with a primary "impulse" toward their self-preservation. The notion that organisms are organized and manifest an innate drive for their own preservation is, in their view, a datum of the best contemporary science. However plausible this claim about the goal of our primary instincts, it still seems very far from issuing in any genuine prescriptions relating to moral virtue, however. The demands of self-preservation do not of themselves preclude what might ordinarily be taken as immoral behavior. The Stoics continue their argument, however, by noticing that as humans develop they are attracted to things that are appropriate for their survival and repelled by those that are not. They also argue that unless we possessed self-consciousness and felt affection for ourselves, we would not desire things conducive to our health and reject the things that are the opposite. Cicero gives the following account of the various stages that develop out of our initial self-love:

> the first appropriate act is to preserve oneself in one's natural constitution; the next is to retain those things which are in accordance with nature and to repel those that are contrary; then when this principle of choice and also rejection has been discovered, there follows next in order choice conditioned by appropriate action; then, such choices become a fixed habit; and finally, choice fully rationalized and in harmony with nature. It is at this final stage that Good properly so called first emerges and comes to be understood in its true nature (*De finibus* iii 5–6).

The Stoics argue that as we continue to pursue those things appropriate to our self-preservation, we begin to discover ourselves as agents with a capacity for making choices. The principle of *oikeiōsis*, therefore, underlies not only our development of a settled disposition for choosing things that are appropriate – such things as health, life, pleasure, reputation – but also a growing recognition and appreciation of our capacity for rational choice as something that belongs to us and is our own. We might compare John Rawls's so-called Aristotelian principle in this context: "Other things being equal, human beings enjoy the exercise of their realized capacities . . . and this enjoyment increases the more the capacity is realized, or the greater its complexity."[2] The Stoics claim that in the course of our psychological development, the capacity that we come to appreciate and value most is our capacity for making rational choices. This is a key step in the Stoics' argument that licenses, among other things, their claim that as we begin to value our own rational faculty, we begin to value others as rational beings as well, since we come to recognize the unique value of rationality per se, wherever it is manifested. Such recognition serves, for instance, as a foundation for justice, which is grounded in a respect for the rationality of others. So too, rationality is a defining feature of nature which we begin to see as something that shares this uniquely valuable trait with us, but in a more perfect form. This more perfect form of rationality turns out to be the rationality of nature which itself is a divinely provident *logos*.

The final stage of *oikeiōsis* is our realization and appreciation that rationality is the *only* thing that can be called good, both the rationality that is manifested in our capacity for choice and in the rational order of the universe writ large. It is our reason alone, moreover, that is to be identified with our virtue and our happiness, and hence functions as our natural *telos*. This radical claim goes far beyond the kind of intuition captured by Rawls's Aristotelian principle and is at the heart of many of the Stoics' most distinctive and controversial claims. First, it sets up a stark and unbridgeable division in our psychological and moral lives. On the one side are the things that were the objects of our initial natural impulses, things ordinarily taken to be goods such as health, life, wealth, and reputation. On the other are our reason, virtue, and happiness. Like Christianity's subsequent conception of a triune God, this Stoic trinity is a source of great power in their system, but also of many practical and logical mysteries.

One can quickly feel its power, since it offers us a vision of a life in which our ethical lives and happiness are entirely under our own control and in no way dependent on external conditions or events. If our happiness or virtue were somehow dependent on circumstances external to our selves, the Stoics believe, our lives would be prey to instability and fears of loss:

> Yet no one can be happy without a good which is secure, stable and lasting . . . The man who would fear losing any of these things cannot be happy. We want the happy man to be safe, impregnable, fenced, and fortified, so that he is not just largely unafraid, but completely. (Cicero, *Tusculan Disputations* 5.41 = LS 65L).

The wise man is completely unafraid, no matter what sorts of external threats he may face, since everything important to him is internal and under his own control. It is by giving his full and abiding attention to what is in his own power – his inner mental disposition and his power of rational choice – that he achieves happiness and virtue. External circumstances are not under our control and can make no difference to our happiness or ethical lives. Later Stoics, such as Epictetus, were to make this radical separation between inner resources and external adversity the central focus of their discussion, and they offer many vivid illustrations of how Stoicism can provide us with an invulnerable inner freedom in the face of even the most horrendous external conditions. Indeed, this has been one of the most compelling legacies of Stoicism and it is not uncommon to hear stories of prisoners of war or victims of torture relying on Stoic insights to maintain their moral resolve and dignity in the face of terrible adversity.

At the same time, however, this exclusive emphasis on the inner elements of our moral lives comes with a certain cost, a cost that many think is too high. According to the Stoics, what we have control over and what we can be held responsible for are our inner moral impulses and resolve. Our happiness, too, is to be strictly identified only with these inner states. The way that our moral choices play themselves out in the world will typically be dependent on external conditions and have external consequences, however. The Stoics are obviously aware of this, but they insist, nonetheless, that we should display complete indifference to the external results of our moral choices, since all things external are an occasion for indifference. This idea that we should be indifferent to the actual results of our choices strikes many as both psychologically implausible and morally problematic, however, and for the following reasons. Let us suppose, for example, that Anaxagoras sees his son in danger on the battlefield and courageously attempts to save him, but ultimately fails. We might agree that a crucially important element in assessing Anaxagoras' action is the moral quality of his inner intention. We might judge his action very differently if we were to find out, say, that his sole intention in attempting to save his son was to make sure that the valuable family armor he had given him was not lost to the enemy. But the Stoics make the stronger claim that the only thing that matters, both from a moral point of view and from the point of view of one's own happiness, is that one makes the right moral choice. External results are of no consequence. Thus, Anaxagoras' failure to save his son, provided that his attempt reflects the right moral choice in the situation, should occasion him no regret since his son's death, being something external, is a matter of indifference both from the moral point of view and from the perspective of his own happiness. It is this stronger claim that many will balk at. The idea that our moral choices can be unhinged from their consequences in this way and assessed utterly independently seems to offer, at best, a recipe for moral priggishness and at worse, a license for personal and political disaster.

One can easily imagine circumstances either in the small occurrences of daily life or in the context of grander political decisions where an absolute indifference to the external results of one's choices might seem deeply culpable. Moreover, that one's external failures in the world are entirely unconnected to one's happiness seems psychologically implausible as well.

Stoic Psychology and Physics

The Stoics think they can meet such objections, however, and their response draws, in part, both upon their psychological theories and on their theory of the underlying causes of external events. They argue that once we understand the true nature of these, we will come to see that there is nothing morally problematic or psychologically strange about showing utter indifference to external failures that are not in our control. Even if such external failures include failing to save one's son.

The Stoics argue that very few humans ever reach the final stage of *oikeiōsis* in which one comes to perfect one's rationality and to view rationality as the only good in the universe. As we have seen, such sages, "as rare as the phoenix," will treat things that are naturally appropriate to life – health, reputation, pleasure, and the desire to preserve life itself – with indifference, since they realize that perfected rationality is the only good. A sage will understand that it is not such naturally appropriate things in themselves that are valuable, but only and uniquely his rational selection among them. This will account for his indifference to the death of a son, since he understands that life in itself is not a good. It also will account for his lack of grief or any other variety of strong emotion in the face of death, since he will realize that death has not taken away anything valuable either from his son or from him. But even if a sage understands all this, we might object that he still might be prey to strong emotions. I might rationally understand, for instance, that garden snakes offer me no threat, yet be terrified when I accidentally come across one resting under one of my tomato plants. What gives the Stoics confidence that rational understanding alone is sufficient to guarantee tranquility and happiness, and that when we have perfected our reason our tranquility will not be disturbed by troubling fears, passions, and desires?

Unlike Plato, who thought that one might achieve a rational understanding of something, yet still might fall prey to irrational emotions that issue from separate parts of one's psyche and overcome one's reason, the Stoics deny any such division in our psychological make-up. They think that our psyches are unitary, or more precisely, that a human soul is a unitary rational substance (*pneuma*) and that passions are movements of this rational substance. Passions, they insist, are best described as instances of weak or perverse reason. "Some people [i.e. the Stoics] say that passion is no different from reason, and that there is no dissension and conflict between the two, but a turning of the single reason in both directions, which we do not notice owing to the sharpness and speed of the change" (Plutarch, *On Moral Virtue* 446f = LS 65G). Let us go back for a moment to my reaction to the snake. On a Platonist construal, I may be convinced rationally that the snake is harmless, but some other nonrational part of me overcomes this conviction and makes me react with irrational fear when confronted by the snake. The Stoics on the other hand, in a sense reviving Socrates' view about the relation between knowledge and the good, think that if I show any fear, it must be a failure of understanding. That is, if I really understood that the snake presents no threat, I would not fear it. The fact that I react with fear shows that I do not really understand that it cannot harm me. What a Platonist describes as my reason being overcome by an irrational fear is actually better described as a rapid alternation between two beliefs – my belief that the snake presents no threat and my belief that it actually does.

In characterizing our reactions in this way, the Stoics are relying on a distinctive, and in some ways idiosyncratic understanding of our emotional lives. What typically pass as emotions are really just wrong beliefs and not the movements of other discrete parts of our psyches. The Stoics, thus, offer a very powerful challenge to psychologies that view emotions as the result of a psychic conflict or as a product of free-standing irrational forces in our mental lives. Moreover, they believe that we are entirely responsible for our emotions, because emotions are merely mistaken beliefs that we are free to acquire or rid ourselves of. They thus deny that there are any ingrained emotional patterns or behaviors that are not amenable to rational control and that might pose a threat to our happiness or virtue.

The Stoics think, therefore, that they can offer strong psychological backing for their claim that Anaxagoras has no reason to be disturbed by the loss of his son, if his death can be shown to be in accordance with reason. But how can they hope to show that? It is here that the Stoics must appeal to their account of causality and the wider rationality of nature:

> It is the peculiar characteristic of the wise man that he does nothing which he could regret, nothing against his will, but does everything honorably, consistently, seriously, and rightly, that he anticipates nothing as if it were bound to happen, is shocked by nothing when it does happen under the impression that its happening is unexpected and strange, refers everything to his own judgment, stands by his own decisions. I can conceive nothing which is happier than this. It is an easy conclusion for the Stoics, since they have perceived the final good to be in agreement with nature and living consistently with nature, which is not only the wise man's proper function, but also in his power. It necessarily follows that the happy life is in the power of the man who has the final good in his power. So the wise man's life is always happy. (Cicero, *Tusculan Disputations* 5.81–2 = LS 63M)

Nature has its causes and effects. If we appreciate that we are ourselves completely enmeshed in the causal nexus of the universe and come to understand its rational directionality, we will not be caught unawares by its workings. Still less will we surprise ourselves by engaging in actions we later come to regret. Instead, if we follow the path of the sage, we will mold our beliefs to the rational structure of the universe and will thereby avoid the tendency of lesser minds to rail against what is and must be the case.

Stoic Logic

We best mold our beliefs to nature in the required way if we master logic and dialectic. Indeed, "the sage is always a dialectician" (DL 7.83; *SVF* 2.130). The centrality of logic to the Stoic outlook is easy to appreciate once its role in the right ordering of action and attitude is fully apprehended. We have seen that the sage achieves an equanimity that is uncommon for the vast majority of human beings. Presumably, no such achievement is possible without the logical acumen required both for parrying the false and pernicious views promulgated by the confused, and for constructing positive theories moored to the true structure of the rational universe. In the first instance, in the course of daily affairs it often becomes necessary to refute those who would compel us down the wrong path in life with false and meretricious theories about the emotions, about the appropriate sphere of action, or about the direction of the rational universe itself. At the same time, the sage will be expected to be in a position to advance positive doctrines, and to do so in compact, even pithy language. So renowned was Chrysippus in this regard, in fact, that the general opinion was that "if the gods had dialectic, it would be no different from that of Chrysippus" (DL 7.180; *SVF* 2.1).

When Stoics practice dialectic, they perforce demonstrate dexterity with language, and understand themselves to appreciate not just the rhetorical features of linguistic usage, but the deep semantic structure of natural language as well. This particular Stoic concern with language led to one of their most intriguing and distinctive contributions: their doctrine that significant speech involves more than merely phonetic features of natural language. They rightly point out that it is entirely possible to hear the sounds of some spoken speech without grasping, even vaguely, the meanings associated with the utterances heard. If we do not understand Chinese, for instance, then we apprehend nothing semantic when in the presence of Chinese speakers. Language must therefore be significant in virtue of something beyond its merely phonetic features. According to the Stoics, language is significant in virtue of its expressing what they call *lekta*, language-independent bearers of semantic value akin to *propositions*, conceived as abstract entities that are expressed and grasped by language users in successful episodes of communication. Some *lekta* are true or false; others encode commands, prayers, imperatives, all of which are meaningful, though not truth-evaluable (DL 7.66–7).

Among *lekta*, according the Stoics, we find both the simple and the complex. Of special interest to the Stoics are complex *lekta*, because of the role they play in logic: complex *lekta* permit movement from proposition to proposition in an orderly truth-preserving fashion. For included among the complex *lekta* of the Stoics are conditionals, disjunctions, and conjunctions (DL 7.71–4), all of which have key roles to play in constructive argumentation. Indeed, it is in virtue of their attending to such *lekta* and their interrelations that Stoics came to make their most significant and lasting advances in logic and logical theory. For the Stoics took a keen interest in a simple, but vexing question: What is it for one proposition to *follow* from another? If we say *if p then q*, and assert *not q*, then it *follows* that *not p*; but if we say *if p then q*, and then assert *not p*, it does *not follow* that *not q*. Why should that be? These facts do not seem to depend in any way upon what we believe or wish to obtain. On the contrary, if we fail to appreciate the nature of these connections, then we fall into error. Accordingly, the sage will need to appreciate, and master, all such connections if he is to reflect in his beliefs and actions the rational structure of the universe. Logic canonizes what is rational, by capturing valid connections that hold independently of our local beliefs; and dialectic, in its turn, represents logical relations in plain and transparent language. So, the sage will, in his complete disposition to follow the direction of the rational universe, excel in both logic and dialectic to the point of exhibiting a godlike prowess.

Conclusion

The Stoics, as we have seen, often offend against what passes as common sense, and they seem to expend special efforts in making our ordinary emotions, desires, commitments, and indeed, our ordinary lives in general appear just that: ordinary. They do so by urging us to become gods and by offering us a divine-like perch from which to view human affairs, a perch fortified by reason and a divine knowledge of the providence of nature. Many philosophers have warned that such Stoic thoughts are untimely, not only because they are dangerous to one's own humanity and one's relations to others, but because they are deeply mistaken about our relation to nature. The Stoics, in this view, are both too optimistic about the perfectibility of human beings and misguided about the nature of what such perfection would be; they therefore offer a dream that is not only impossible but also false. But such wholesale rejection of the Stoic project seems to me unwarranted, however. The urge to become divine is by no means an impulse limited to Stoicism. It can be found in almost every ancient philosopher and school of philosophy, and often just below the surface of those modern philosophers who have come under their influence. Indeed, one can hardly fail to be touched by this aspect of ancient philosophy unless one takes up a purely scholastic relation to the authors one reads. The Stoics, perhaps, give vent to this impulse for divinity in ways that can strike one as extreme, especially for those whose views about their own prospects for divinity have been conditioned by Christianity. But it is the very extremity and logical implacability of their claims for our divinity that have been and will continue to be a source of the enduring power and attraction of Stoicism.

Notes

1 Gisela Striker (1983), p. 145, offers a lucid discussion of these issues.
2 John Rawls, *A Theory of Justice*, p. 426.

References and Recommended Reading

Primary Sources

Inwood, B. and Gerson, L. P., *Hellenistic Philosophy: Introductory Readings* (Indianapolis, 1998)
Long, A. A. and Sedley, D. N., eds., *The Hellenistic Philosophers*, 2 vols. (Cambridge, various reprints)

Secondary Sources

Algra, K. et al., eds., *The Cambridge History of Hellenistic Philosophy* (Cambridge, 1999)
Annas, J. E., *Hellenistic Philosophy of Mind* (Berkeley, 1992)
——, *The Morality of Happiness* (Oxford, 1993)
Bobzien, S., *Determinism and Freedom in Stoic Philosophy* (Oxford, 1998)
Colish, M. L., *The Stoic Tradition from Antiquity to the Early Middle Ages* (Leiden, 1985)
Erskine, Andrew, *The Hellenistic Stoa, Political Thought in Action* (London, 1990)
Frede, M., *Essays in Ancient Philosophy* (Oxford, 1987)
Hahm, D. E., *The Origins of Stoic Cosmology* (Columbus, 1977)
Ierodiakonou, K., ed., *Topics in Stoic Philosophy* (Oxford, 1999)
Inwood, B., *Ethics and Action in Early Stoicism* (Oxford, 1985)
Long, A. A., *Hellenistic Philosophy* (2nd ed., Berkeley, 1986)
——, *Stoic Studies* (Cambridge, 1996)
——, *Epictetus: A Stoic and Socratic Guide to Life* (Oxford, 2002)
——, ed., *Problems in Stoicism* (London, repr. 1996)
Nussbaum, M. C., *The Therapy of Desire: Theory and Practice in Hellenistic Ethics* (Princeton, 1994)
Rawls, J., *A Theory of Justice* (Cambridge, Mass., 1971)
Rist, J. M., ed., *The Stoics* (Berkeley, 1978)
Striker, G. 1983, "The Role of Oikeiosis in Stoic Ethics," *Oxford Studies in Ancient Philosophy* 1, 145–68
——, *Essays on Hellenistic Epistemology and Ethics* (Cambridge, 1996)

Chapter 14

Academics and Pyrrhonists

R. J. Hankinson

Introduction

The Hellenistic age saw the elaboration of two distinct strands of philosophical Skepticism. One, ascribed to its eponym Pyrrho, fell into desuetude after the death of Pyrrho's poetical amanuensis Timon around 230 BC, to be revived by Aenesidemus towards the middle of the first century BC. The other originated in Plato's old Academy, and flourished vigorously for two centuries, until Aenesidemus' defection and other institutional difficulties brought about the end of the Skeptical Academy. In this chapter, I concentrate on the Academics, since they represent the dominant strand of Skepticism in the period; but I mention Pyrrhonism throughout, and towards the end offer a brief survey of those doctrines of Pyrrho and Aenesidemus which belong undisputably to the Hellenistic age.

Arcesilaus and the Skeptical Method

After Plato's death in 347 BC, control of Plato's Academy passed first to Plato's nephew Speusippus (much to Aristotle's chagrin, apparently) and then to the mathematically inclined Xenocrates, both of whom (so far as we can tell: their remains are fragmentary)[1] sought to continue the Master's work, while adding a few idiosyncratic touches of their own, notably Xenocrates' opaque contention (which infuriated Aristotle) that "the soul is a self-moving number" (Frs. 165–88 Isnardi Parente). On Xenocrates' death in 314, the leadership of the school passed to Polemo, and on his death in 275 to the shadowy Crates (not to be confused with the Cynic of the same name, renowned for his public sexual performances with Hipparchia).

When Crates died in his turn in 272, Arcesilaus took over the school (Diogenes Laertius [DL], *Lives of the Philosophers* 4.32). Later writers thought that Arcesilaus' accession was marked by a radical change of direction:

Arcesilaus founded the Middle Academy; and he was first to hold his assertions in check (*epischōn*) because of the contrariety of arguments. (1: DL 4.28 = LS 68D;[2] cf. Sextus Empiricus, *Outlines of Pyrrhonism* [*PH*] 1.232–4)

This holding in check or suspension of judgment, *epochē*, is further attested in other sources:

some say that he never wrote a book because of his *epochē* about everything. (2: DL 4.32 = LS 68E)

Sextus Empiricus, who is at pains to distinguish his brand of Skepticism from other philosophies, none the less saw him as a kindred spirit:

Arcesilaus seems to me to have much in common with the Pyrrhonian doctrines, so that his way and ours seem to be virtually identical; for he is never found asserting anything concerning whether anything obtains or not, nor does he privilege anything over anything else in terms of credibility or otherwise, but suspends judgement about everything. He also holds that the end (*telos*) is *epochē* (which is accompanied as we have said by tranquillity [*ataraxia*]). (3: *PH* 1.232 = LS 68I)

That last parenthesis intrudes Sextus' own Pyrrhonism (cf. *PH* 1.25–30); but he clearly attributes to Arcesilaus a reluctance to make positive claims about the nature of things, a refusal to consider any statement more or less epistemically privileged than any other, and a consequent suspension of judgment. This is borne out by Plutarch:

these ("the Academics of Arcesilaus's circle") were the ones who suspend judgement about everything. (4: *Against Colotes* 1120c = LS 68H)

Our most detailed source for Academic Skeptical epistemology is Cicero's *Academica*:

(1) It was with Zeno, so we are told, that Arcesilaus began his battle, not from obstinacy or desire for victory . . . but because of the obscurity of things which had brought Socrates to admit ignorance, as also previously his predecessors Democritus, Anaxagoras, Empedocles, and almost all the ancients who said that nothing could be grasped or perceived or known, that the senses were limited, the mind feeble, the course of life short, and that (to quote Democritus) "truth is submerged in an abyss" [= Fr, 68 B 117 DK][3] with everything in the grip of opinions and conventions, nothing left for truth and everything wrapped in darkness. (2) Accordingly Arcesilaus denied that anything could be known, not even that thing itself, the one thing Socrates had left for himself; so deep did he think was the obscurity in which everything was hidden that he held that nothing could be discerned or understood. (3) For these reasons no-one must assert or affirm anything, or give the approval of assent to anything, but he should curb his rashness . . . for it would be the height of rashness to accept something

either false or not certainly known; and nothing is more disgraceful than for assent and approval to outrun knowledge and perception. (5: Cicero, *Academica* 1.43–5 = LS 68A)

Cicero clearly ascribes to Arcesilaus a doctrine of suspension, in the face of the undecidability and obscurity of things. But where Socrates said that he knew only one thing, namely, that he knew nothing else, Arcesilaus apparently goes one better, claiming not only that (K1) nothing can be known, but also (K2) it cannot even be known that nothing is known (a stance already foreshadowed by the atomist Metrodorus of Chios: DL 9.58). Elsewhere, Cicero stresses Arcesilaus' adherence to (K1):

Arcesilaus first drew this particular lesson most powerfully from various books of Plato and from Socrates' talk: nothing is certain. (6: Cicero, *Orator* 3.67; cf. *On Ends* 2.2; *Nature of the Gods* [*ND*] 1.11.)

But surely, it has been argued, (K2) undercuts (K1) – Arcesilaus cannot strongly claim that nothing is known if he doesn't know that nothing is known.

This line of argument has fueled the dominant modern account of Arcesilaus' Skepticism, owed originally to Pierre Couissin (1929, 1983), which holds that Arcesilaus did not affirm that nothing could be known; indeed he did not affirm anything. Rather, his argumentative practice (and numerous ancient sources attest to his dialectical skill: cf. e.g. DL 4.37) was purely destructive – he sought merely to undermine and refute the positive doctrines of others (principally the dominant Dogmatic[4] school of his day, the Stoics), making no claims whatsoever (and hence none about the possible scope of knowledge) in his own voice. This view is supported by a first-century papyrus, "he asserted nothing, but only refuted the other schools" (*Index of Academics* 20.2–4), and it is also suggested by the polemic of the second-century AD Platonist Numenius, quoted in the Christian writer Eusebius, which portrays Arcesilaus as a mere peddler of sophistry.

Arcesilaus, then, would simply be a practitioner of refutation, following his own interpretation of Socratic procedure: give him a position, and he will reduce it to incoherence; but he says nothing on his own account.

Thus, on this Dialectical Interpretation (DI), when Arcesilaus said that nothing can be known, he means that nothing can be known *on the Stoic account of knowledge*; and when he says that one is forced to suspension, he means that the Stoic, who by his own lights should never assent to mere opinion (cf. *Academica* 2.59, 101; *M* 7.152, 155–7), ought to suspend judgment about everything; and this is indeed the conclusion reached at *M* 7.155: "it will follow even for the Stoics that the Sage will suspend judgement." To see why, we need to look briefly at the Stoic account of knowledge. We will return to a consideration of the merits of the DI later on. Suffice it to say at this stage that, while *M* 7.155 and other texts clearly do show it to be Arcesilaus' goal to reduce the Stoic position to incoherence, they neither assert nor imply that this was his *only* goal.

Criterion of Truth

The second-century AD Platonist Numenius, in his unflattering portrait of Arcesilaus preserved in Eusebius' equally polemical *Preparation for the Gospel*, says that Arcesilaus spent much of his time in philosophical combat with the Stoicism of Zeno of Citium, the school's founder:

> Arcesilaus, seeing that Zeno rivalled him in the art and could overcome him, he immediately set himself to demolish the arguments brought up by him. (7: ibid. 14.6.12; cf. 5.11 = LS 68G)

and he goes on to remark that,

> seeing that both the doctrine of the cataleptic impression (*kataleptike phantasia*)[5] and its name, which he [i.e. Zeno] had been the first to discover, were highly regarded in Athens, he [i.e. Arcesilaus] employed every means to assail it. (8: ibid. 15.6.13 = LS 68G)

Whatever we make of his motivations (and 5(1) above gives a different account of them), Arcesilaus was roused to philosophical action by Zeno's optimistic new epistemology, in which the notion of the cataleptic impression was central:

> there are two types of impression, one cataleptic, the other non-cataleptic; the cataleptic, which they hold to be the criterion of matters, is that which comes from something existent and is in accordance with the existent thing itself, and has been stamped and imprinted; the non-cataleptic either comes from something non-existent, or if from something existent then not in accordance with the existent thing; and it is neither clear, nor distinct. (9: DL 7.46 = LS 40C; cf. Sextus, *Against the Professors* [*M*] 11.183)

There are some impressions (primarily, but not exclusively, sense-impressions) which are such as to report their objects truly, clearly and distinctly, faithfully representing their contours. When we assent to these, we have the right to be certain that we are not mistaken:

> between knowledge and ignorance he [sc. Zeno] placed apprehension, numbering it neither among the good things nor the bad, but holding that it was trustworthy on its own. (10: Cicero, *Academica* 1.42 = LS 41B)

This is supported by a passage of Sextus:

> For they [sc. the Stoics] say that there are three of them interrelated to each other, knowledge, opinion, with apprehension lying between the two of them; and of these knowledge is the secure and firm apprehension unalterable by reason, opinion is weak [and false][6] assent, while apprehension is intermediate between these, being assent to a

cataleptic impression. According to these people, a cataleptic impression is one which is true and such that it could not be false. (11: *M* 7.150–2 = 41C LS [part])

Neither the impression, nor even the assent to it, amount to knowledge as such, which must be more stable and structured; but it is infinitely superior to mere opinion, which is beneath the Stoic Sage's contempt. An impression is really that,

an imprinting (*typōsis*) on the soul, the name having been appropriately borrowed from the imprints made by the seal in wax. (12: DL 7.45; cf. 9 above)

When our senses are in good order, then we can know that they give us accurate information.

But how can we know that they are in good order? The last sentence of 11 suggests an answer: when the impressions are such that they could not be false. But this simply pushes the issue a stage further back: how can we *know* that an impression is such that it could not be false? And this is where Arcesilaus inserts his Skeptical wedge. We may suppose, Cicero writes, that Arcesilaus

(1) asked Zeno what would happen if the Sage could not apprehend anything, and if it was also the mark of the Sage not to form opinions. (2) Zeno, I imagine, would reply that he [i.e. the Sage] would not form opinions because he could apprehend something. (3) What sort of thing? An impression, I suppose. (4) What sort of impression? An impression that was impressed, sealed, and moulded from something which is, just as it is. (5) Arcesilaus then asked if this held even if there were a true impression exactly the same in form as a false one. (6) Here Zeno was acute enough to see that if an impression proceeding from something existent was such that there could be an impression of something non-existent of exactly the same form, then no impression could be apprehended. (7) Arcesilaus agreed that this addition to the definition was justified, since one could not apprehend an impression if a true one were such as a false one could be. (8) However he argued forcefully in order to show that no impression of something existent was such that there could not be an impression of something non-existent of the same form. (13: *Academica* 2.77 = LS 40D)

A cataleptic impression, then, is one which is true, derives from a real object, faithfully reports that object and is also "of such a type as could not come from something non-existent" (DL 7.50).

Sextus elaborates:

(1) they added "of such a type as could not come from something non-existent" because the Academics did not suppose, as the Stoics did, that an impression could not be found in all respects similar to it. (2) For the Stoics assert that he who has the cataleptic impression fastens on the objective difference of things with the skill of a craftsman, since an impression of this kind has a special characteristic of its own compared with other impressions, like horned serpents as compared with all other serpents; (3) while the Academics hold that a false impression could be found exactly similar to the cataleptic one. (14: *M* 7.252 = LS 40E [part]; cf. ibid. 152, 163, 248, 416, 426)

The battle lines between the two philosophers are now reasonably clear. The Stoics, in order to secure the infallibility of their Sage, need certain impressions unequivocally to convey the truth. But, Arcesilaus points out (13(5)–(7), 14(3)), an impression can only do this if it is such that it is inconceivable that one exactly like it could have arisen delusively. But this simply doesn't seem to be the case (13(8)): what are these supposed internal characteristics (14(2)) which mark out the cataleptic impression, at any rate to the expert cognizer, as such? And how can we be sure we are not deluded about *them*? Cicero sums up the debate:

> there are four general premisses which conclude to the position that nothing can be known, apprehended, or comprehended, around which the whole debate centres: (i) that some false impression exists; (ii) that this cannot be apprehended; (iii) that in the case of impressions among which there is no difference it is not possible that some of them can be apprehended while others cannot; (iv) that there is no true impression deriving from the senses to which there does not correspond another impression which does not differ from it and cannot be apprehended. Of these four, everybody admits (ii) and (iii); Epicurus does not grant (i), but you [sc. the Stoics and their followers] with whom we are arguing allow this too; the whole conflict concerns (iv). (15: *Academica* 2.83 = LS 40J [part]; cf. 2.40–1)

The Academics argued that, even if you granted that some particular impression was veridical, for all of its internal characteristics it might have been false. They bring up examples of identical twins (you may correctly identify your current Castor-impression as a Castor-impression – but a Pollux-impression would have seemed no different, and hence you cannot know for sure that the impression really is of Castor: ibid. 2.20, 2.55–6, 2.57–8, 2.84–6; *M* 7.409–10), and indistinguishable eggs: is this really the egg you saw earlier?

The Stoics reply that mothers can tell their twins apart, and cite the legendarily perspicuous egg-discriminators of Delos in support of their contention (underwritten by their Leibnizian metaphysics) that no two impressions can ever be exactly alike, and hence any two distinct impressions (or perhaps rather impressions with distinct content, broadly construed)[7] are in principle discriminable.

The Academics counter that it is not enough for them to be discriminable only in principle – they must be discriminable *by us* if we are to claim certain knowledge.

This dialectical to-ing and fro-ing went on for a long time, and it is unclear which of the Academic contentions just rehearsed should be ascribed to Arcesilaus; some of them probably derive from later Academic philosophers, notably Carneades (c. 219–c. 229 BC), of whom more shortly. But so far it seems as though the Skeptics have the better of the argument. It doesn't seem good enough to suggest that an impression will be cataleptic just so long as it meets the Stoic criteria, including the all-important no-false-congeners condition (13(6)), if we cannot in principle know for certain when we have one; for it is supposed to function as a criterion, a means of discriminating, and surely it can only do that if we can recognize it as such.

However, Michael Frede, in an influential article (Frede 1983/87), has argued that, properly interpreted, for the Stoics the force of the cataleptic impression is causal – there are some veridical impressions which are, of their nature, such as to cause us (or at any rate those of us in good cognitive condition) to assent. If this is right, then there is no need to suppose that we can infallibly recognize them as such: "they play their criterial role not through our awareness of this feature [sc. their appropriately veridical quality] but through the causal effects they have on our minds in virtue of this feature" (Frede 1983/87, 168).

This is attractive, but it is bought at the cost of making most Academic argument an *ignoratio elenchi*; the Academics behave as though they suppose that the Stoic criterial cataleptic impression will be such as to be transparent (at any rate under ideal circumstances) to its recipient. Moreover, if the Stoics had indeed held the position Frede ascribes to them, one would expect the Academic attack to take the different form of pressing the Stoics on the question of how they can know that there are such impressions at all (given that what is distinctive about them is not transparent to the recipient).

But in any event, the structure of Arcesilaus' argument is clear. The Stoics define "opinion" as "assent to what is not apprehended" (*M* 7.156), and agree that an impression is cataleptic only if it could not have false congeners. Since this last condition is unrealizable (because of the twins argument and the like), any assent must be an opinion; but since the Sage never opines (13(1); Stobaeus, 2.111.18–112.8 = LS 41G), the Sage must never assent, and hence suspend judgment about everything. But it is still unclear whether this is being offered solely as a position that the Stoic Sage is forced to, willy-nilly (as the DI has it), or whether Arcesilaus thinks that it is, in some sense, the right position to adopt.

Criterion of Action

The ancients standardly distinguished between criteria of truth and criteria of action (the distinction may well originate with Arcesilaus); and the texts suggest that Arcesilaus was prepared to essay one of his own. But here too it is controversial whether his arguments should be taken at their face value, or only as indications of what the Dogmatic opposition (principally the Stoics) are committed to and could accept.

Sextus reports that

> since it was necessary to inquire into the business of living, which is not such as to be obtained without a criterion, and upon which happiness (i.e. the *telos* of life) depends for its credibility, Arcesilaus says that someone who suspends judgement about everything will regulate his choices and avoidances, and in general his actions, by what is "reasonable" (*eulogon*), and by proceeding according to this criterion he will go right (*katorthōsei*), since happiness comes to be through wisdom (*phronēsis*), and wisdom consists in right actions (*katorthōmata*), while a right action is that which having been performed has a reasonable defence (*apologia*); therefore anyone who attends to the reasonable will act rightly and be happy. (16: *M* 7.158 = LS 69B)

Arcesilaus is here answering the charge, perennially raised against Skeptics, that Skepticism makes living impossible, because it undermines any reason for action. Skeptics have no beliefs, hence a fortiori no beliefs about things choiceworthy or avoidable – but in default of such beliefs they will simply do nothing, until, as Hume put it, "the necessities of nature, unsatisfied, put an end to their miserable existence" (*Enquiry Concerning Human Understanding* XII, §II, 128).

The fact that Arcesilaus' argument is a response to this challenge is itself strong prima facie evidence against the DI: why should the Academics need to provide a criterion of action at all if their entire practice was merely destructive, and their advocacy of *epochē* simply on behalf of the Stoic? It is sometimes pointed out that the language of 16 is strongly Stoic in flavor; but against that it has been noted (by Striker 1980, among others) that as a matter of fact no argument ascribed to Arcesilaus ever proceeds solely on the basis of premises to which the Stoics would have subscribed.

Moreover, the Stoicizing language of 16 is used, deliberately one may suppose, in a non-Stoic way. For the Stoics, *katorthōmata* are right actions performed in a state of complete and infallible knowledge by the Sage; no *katorthōma*, by definition, can ever turn out wrong or be frustrated.[8] But the Arcesilaan criterion of *ex post facto* justification is clearly designed to accommodate cases where, through no fault of the agent (that is what it is for the action to have a "reasonable justification"), the action goes awry, exactly what should not happen on the Stoic account of perfect action; and indeed this is precisely how the Stoics characterize "fitting actions," *kathēkonta*, performed by those on the way to, but not having yet achieved, sagehood (Stobaeus, 2.85.13–86.4; DL 7.107). Thus "going right," for the Academic, is not, as it is for the Stoic (at least in the final stage of sagehood), a matter of always getting it right – but this is the best we can manage in this life.

All this strongly suggests that Arcesilaus means to offer the reasonable defense criterion as more than simply a way out of a difficulty that arises *for the Stoics* if the Academic arguments go through; why should he want to do such a thing in any case? I conclude[9] that the DI is mistaken, at least in its full generality. Arcesilaus' argument is designed to provide an escape route *for the Academics* faced with the Dogmatist's Humean charge that Skepticism, if genuinely accepted, would result in paralysis and hence death, which was known to the ancients as the *apraxia* (inactivity) argument. And this is borne out by Cicero:

> Arcesilaus did not attack Zeno merely for the sake of criticizing him, but because he wanted to discover the truth. No-one before him had held, or even suggested that a man could hold no beliefs, and indeed not only could but should do so if he were wise; but this seemed to Arcesilaus not only true and honourable, but worthy of the sage. (18: Cicero, *Academica* 2.76–7, LS 68O)

It remains to reconsider the case of K1 and K2 above, and along with it the question of whether Arcesilaus did himself subscribe to the view that nothing was apprehended (or apprehensible: the Greek terms are systematically ambiguous between the categorical and the modal sense). After all, you can suspend judgment without supposing, dogmatically as Sextus saw it (*PH* 1.1, 1.236), that nothing is known, as the Pyrrhonian Skeptic is supposed to: it is here that Sextus notoriously discerns the crucial difference between the Pyrrhonian and the Academic (*PH* 1.236), mistakenly, according to DI-theorists.

If K2 really undercuts K1, then Arcesilaus is not claiming that nothing can be known (or at any rate *to know* that nothing can be known). But apprehension is a special, Stoic kind of knowledge, defined as assent to a cataleptic impression that one recognizes as such. An impression of this sort reports faithfully the contours of an object. But the content of K1 itself is not itself an object, as it would have to be if it were itself to be the subject of cataleptic impression, as K2 denies it can be. But K2 now makes that denial simply on the grounds of category-mistake – you could never *apprehend* that nothing was apprehended; but that now has no tendency to undercut K1. Far from refuting K1, K2 simply turns out to be a special case of it; and hence there is no bar to supposing that Arcesilaus really did think that nothing could be apprehended.[10]

Carneades' Epistemology

Arcesilaus died in about 243 BC. About his successor, Lacydes, little is known, although Numenius tells an amusing story about his slaves turning the dialectic of Academic Skepticism against him: they had been stealing food from his cellar and then resealing the door; when Lacydes accuses them of this, they point out that the seals are indistinguishable, hence he cannot know that the door has been resealed. Although apocryphal, such stories often preserve, in distorted form, genuine information; and it appears from this one that Lacydes developed some form of memory Skepticism:

> Lacydes had decided that he should be opinion-free, and hence put no trust in memory, since memory is a form of opinion. (18: Numenius, in Eusebius, *Preparation for the Gospel* 14.7.9)

This was presumably because memory involves defeasible beliefs about what actually took place (memory can play tricks upon us); so no statement about the past should command assent.

Lacydes' successors Evander and Hegesinus are mere names to us. But with the accession of Carneades (c. 219–c. 129 BC), the Academy takes yet another turn. Ancient sources speak of Carneades' as the "New" or "Third" Academy; and his importance in the history of Skepticism is hard to overestimate. It is also, given the nature of the sources, hard to evaluate. Carneades, like Arcesilaus (and Socrates for that matter) wrote no books, and while his pupil Clitomachus wrote many, none of them survives. We must rely again on excerpts and précis in later, often hostile sources.

Moreover, even his followers did not know quite what to make of him. After his death, two conflicting interpretations arose: one, owed to Clitomachus, making him into a purely dialectical Skeptic (Cicero, *Academica* 2.139), the other, espoused by Metrodorus of Stratonicea and then by Philo of Larissa (c. 160–c. 83 BC), who was one of Cicero's teachers, ascribing to Carneades a more moderate Skepticism, along with a sophisticated fallibilist epistemology. That he did develop such an epistemology is clear form the sources; what is not clear, again, is whether he did so on his own account or merely in the course of argument (Cicero opts for the Philonian position: *Academica* 2.98–111).

Whatever the truth of that, he was famous in his time. In 155 BC he was chosen as one of the three philosophical ambassadors sent by Athens to Rome to plead the Athenians' cause (along with a Stoic and a Peripatetic). Carneades took the opportunity to deliver two public lectures on justice. In the first, he offered an unexciting defense of conventional morality; in the second he refuted the claims of the first point by point. In the resulting controversy, the elder Cato had Carneades thrown out of the city for endangering the morals of the young (Carneades no doubt reveled in wearing that particular Socratic mantle). The Christian Lactantius, no friend of Skepticism, comments:

> in his first speech [he] assembled all the arguments in favour of justice in order that he might overturn them . . . not because he thought justice ought to be disparaged, but to show that its defenders had no certain or firm arguments about it. (19: *Divine Institutes* 5.14.5 = LS 68M)

So Carneades certainly practiced dialectical, destructive argument, much of it targeted against the great Stoic Chrysippus (c. 280–c. 205 BC): "if Chrysippus had not existed, neither would I" (DL 4.62), he said, turning around the Stoic maxim "if Chrysippus had not existed, neither would the Stoa" (DL 7.183).

Eusebius reports that

> (1) Carneades took up the succession, and established a Third Academy. He applied the same method in argument as Arcesilaus, and he also adopted the practice of arguing on each side of a question, and used to upset all the arguments used by others. (2) But in the principle of *epochē* alone he differed from him, saying that it was impossible for a man to suspend judgement upon all matters, and there was a difference between "non-evident (*adēlon*)" and "non-apprehensible (*akatalēpton*)," and while everything was non-apprehensible, not everything was non-evident. (3) He was also familiar with Stoic arguments, and he grew famous by his eristic opposition to them, aiming not at the truth, but at what appeared plausible (*pithanon*) to the multitude. (20: *Preparation for the Gospel* 14.7.15)

According to 20(2), then, Carneades differed from Arcesilaus over the scope of *epochē* (which implies that both of them had positive views about the matter); while agreeing with him that all things are nonapprehensible, nonapprehensibility does not necessarily entail *epochē*, since only in cases where things are nonevident should we actually suspend judgment. Carneades follows Arcesilaus in meaning by *akatalēpsia* the unattainability of Stoic *katalēpsis*, absolutely and infallibly indefeasible knowledge. But for all that, things may be evident, as opposed to matters of obscure speculation: it is evident to me that I am now sitting at my desk, and while evidence of this sort does not guarantee veridicality (for reasons already canvassed by Arcesilaus), it is a sound basis (other things being equal) for forming the sort of inclination required for action.

If this is right, Carneades' divergence from Arcesilaus amounts to little more than a terminological clarification: whereas Arcesilaus will evade the *apraxia* argument by saying that, although we suspend judgment, we may still be inclined to act, although without belief (here construed as strong commitment to the truth of some claim), Carneades will say that we may make judgments, weakly, although they should not be construed as involving belief in this strong sense.

Sextus (*PH* 1.230) indeed claims that Carneades and Clitomachus "say that they are persuaded and take something to be plausible with a strong inclination, while we simply yield without commitment, we differ in this respect," which seems to suggest that the Academics do have some strong beliefs; but Sextus' text in fact rather suggests that, for any *p*, Carneades will incline strongly not to *p* but rather to the proposition that *p* is plausible (compare Arcesilaus' criterion of reasonable justification: above, 16(2)); and one might suggest that if one assents strongly to the claim that *p* is plausible, then one will (as a matter of psychology rather than logic) assent weakly to *p*, in other words *p* will strike one as being (defeasibly) action-guiding.

We will return to action in a moment; but let us go back to the attack on Stoic epistemology, which Carneades renewed with a vengeance. Carneades centered his contentions around the concept of plausibility (*to pithanon*). The Stoics themselves talked in such terms: they speak of "plausible conditionals" (although precisely what they meant by this is disputed), and they talk of the plausibility and implausibility of impressions (*M* 7.242–6). Moreover, prompted no doubt by Academic dialectic, they make a key concession:

> whereas the older Stoics declare that this cataleptic impression is the criterion of truth, the more recent ones added the clause "provided that there is no obstacle (*enstēma*)." For there are times when a cataleptic impression occurs, yet it is incredible (*apistos*) because of the external circumstances. (21: Sextus, *M* 7.253–4 = LS 40K [part])

Thus

> the cataleptic impression is not unconditionally the criterion of truth, but when there is no obstacle to it. For this latter, being evident and striking, takes hold of us, as they say, practically by the hair and drags us to assent. (22: *M* 7.257 = LS 40K [part])

Admetus sees his wife Alcestis brought back to life (*M* 7.254: Euripides, *Alcestis*, 1120–40): not unreasonably, he thinks that his apparently clear visual impression must be delusive (since he knows she is dead). But the impression *is* caused by her, in the appropriate way, accurately represents her, and (let us suppose) couldn't have come from anything else. All the Stoic conditions for an impression's being cataleptic are satisfied (the no-obstacle clause of 21 is *not* presented as a further such condition) and *still* Admetus refuses to accept it as such. The cataleptic impression is no longer the infallible determiner of truth.

The Stoics now hold that five things need to "concur" in order for the impression to hold good: the sense-organ, the object perceived, the environment, the manner, and the intellect (*M* 7.424). The notion of "concurrence" is vague, but it suggests that there must be agreement between the explicit content of the impression and what we know (or at the very least have good reason to believe) about the circumstances in which the impression has arisen. But this, of course, simply provokes Skeptical questioning at another level: how can we know, or even have good reasons to believe, that the conditions for impressions are favorable?

The Stoics have been pushed a long way from their original, optimistic position. Carneades begins his attack on Dogmatic epistemology by noting (in good Skeptical fashion) that different philosophers disagree about the criterion of truth: is it reason, sensation, impression, or some combination of them (*M* 7.159)? Each of these is on occasion delusive (7.159). Moreover, if there is to be such a criterion, it must be internally discernible, in other words those in possession of it must know (infallibly) that they are; the criterion must be "capable of revealing both itself and the object which produced it" (7.161). But this twofold role introduces the possibility of error: the clarity of the impression itself is a fact about it, not about its purported object. Its clarity and distinctness are logically independent of the state of affairs it supposedly represents. Hence

> we cannot allow every impression to be a criterion of truth, but only the true impression, if any. Then since there is, once again, no true impression of such a type that it could turn out to be false, but for every apparently true impression an indiscernible false one is found, the criterion will turn out to be an impression that may be either true or false. But the impression which may be either is not cataleptic, and not being cataleptic will not be a criterion. (23: *M* 7.163–4 = LS 70A)

Thus Carneades, like Arcesilaus before him, demolishes the Stoic criterion, along with every other positive attempt to found a sound epistemology on firm criteria of truth. But even so,

> since he himself too has some criterion demanded of him for the conduct of life and the attainment of happiness, he is effectively compelled to adopt a position on this by taking as a criterion the plausible (*pithanē*) impression and the one which is simultaneously convincing, unreversed, and thoroughly tested. (24: *M* 7.166 = LS 69D)

Insofar as an impression represents an object, its truth or falsity is a matter of its correspondence (or lack of it) with that object:

> however in relation to the experiencer it is only either apparently true or not apparently true; of these the apparently true is called "manifestation" by the Academics, and "plausibility" or a "plausible impression" for neither what seems immediately false, nor what is true but does not seem so to us, is of a nature to convince us. (25: *M* 7.168–9 = LS 69D)

The impression may be more or less clear, and plausibility comes in degrees; even the clearest and most convincing may yet turn out false.

In fact, the Admetus case had been used by the Academics themselves (almost certainly Carneades), for the very reasons that prompted the Stoics to introduce the no-obstacle clause, to illustrate an instance of an impression satisfying only two of the Carneades' three conditions on epistemic eligibility:

> when Alcestis had died, Heracles . . . brought her up again from Hades and showed her to Admetus, who received an impression of Alcestis that was plausible and thoroughly tested; since, however, he knew that she was dead his mind recoiled from its assent and reverted to unbelief. (26: *PH* 1.228; cf. *M* 7.180)

An impression's plausibility (a) is a function of its internal characteristics: force and vivacity, clarity and distinctness. It is thoroughly tested (b) when its content has been checked against that of other impressions and found to be consistent with them. It is unreversed (c) just in case its content is not in conflict with something else one accepts. This is clarified by another example:

> when a rope is lying coiled in a dark room, to one who enters in a hurry it presents simply the plausible appearance of being a snake; but to the man who has looked carefully around and investigated the conditions, such as its immobility, its colour, and each of its other properties, it appears as a rope according to an impression which is plausible and thoroughly tested. (27: *PH* 1.227–8)

But even after passing all the tests, the appearance is still an appearance; the possibility, however remote, still exists that something might yet turn up to disturb the smooth coherence of the impressions; we are left with plausibility, albeit highly confirmed, and not incontrovertible truth.

The Stoics took over the Admetus example from the Academics to show how, given the no-obstacle clause, it did not threaten their criterion. Conversely the Academics adopt the terminology of the plausible impression from the Stoics (*M* 7.242–6), even to the division of such impressions into those which are true, those which appear true but are in fact false, and those which are (in a sense) both true and false, since they are caused by a real object, but do not represent it (Academics: *M* 7.168–9, 174–5; Stoics: *M* 7. 243–5).

But, it may now seem, little separates the Stoics from Carneades, on the assumption that he intended the epistemology of plausibility to supply his own positive answer to the *apraxia* argument (as 24–5 suggest): pragmatically the positions are hard to distinguish.[11] But Carneades insists that no assent, at least of the type demanded in Stoic theory, is required for action. According to Clitomachus, he "accomplished a Herculean task in ridding the mind of that fierce and monstrous beast, assent, that is of opinion and rashness" (Cicero, *Academica* 2.108). Any strong assent (as opposed to a weak inclination)[12] produces opinion (i.e., unjustified commitment to truth), and that is incompatible with wisdom. The distinction is that, while the Stoics insist that a philosophically responsible account of justified human action must make reference to the way the world actually, indubitably, is, the Academics deny any such commitment.

Academic Ethics

Carneades did not confine himself to epistemological argument. On the contrary, he ranged widely in ethics (as his notorious lectures on justice attest), metaphysics, and theology.

For the Hellenistic philosophers in general, ethics was the summit of philosophy; everything else was subordinated to answering the Socratic question of how one best should live. But, as Carneades points out, here too there is endemic disagreement among the so-called experts:

> since there is disagreement on what this [i.e., the greatest good] consists in, we should draw on the Carneadean division. . . . Carneades scouted not only all opinions on the final good which philosophers have held up to now, but all the possible opinions. In this pursuit, he said that no expertise (*technē*) can originate from itself alone. There is no need to develop this point with examples; for it is evident that no expertise is concerned just with itself, but expertise and its object are distinct. Since, then, corresponding to medicine as the expertise in health and navigation as the expertise in sailing, prudence is the expertise in living, it must be the case that prudence derives its constitution from something else. (28: Cicero, *On Ends* 5.16 = LS 64E)

The ostensible target here is the Dogmatists' (here again primarily the Stoics') claim that there is some determinate expertise concerning living. The Stoics hold that the only thing worth having, the only thing choiceworthy for its own sake, is virtue itself, which they equate with prudence (DL 7.89). But, Carneades argues, they themselves define a *technē* as "a system of jointly exercised impressions directed towards some useful end" (*M* 1.75, 2.10, 7.109, etc.). But in that case virtue, if it is a *technē*, must have some object distinct from itself, in which case it is not the ultimate end.

This argument is ad hominem, and there are possible lines of defense available to the Stoics.[13] but for all that, their view of the structure of desirable and undesirable things, in which such traditional goods as health, beauty, wealth, even life itself are viewed as strictly speaking indifferent (albeit "preferred": DL 7.101–5), was clearly a tempting target.[14] And indeed Carneades also sought to trap the Stoics into admitting that these "indifferents" really were partially constitutive of the good life, and hence, since they were vulnerable to external fortunes, so too was the good life itself, contrary to the Stoics' insistence that virtue, and hence happiness, were always within our grasp, since they were purely cognitive conditions (Cicero, *Academica* 2.131). But this is all dialectical; we hear nothing about any Carneadean claims regarding the supreme goal or *telos* (contrast Arcesilaus: 3 above).

Metaphysics and Dispute

The methodology of discerning contradictions in the positions of particular Dogmatic schools, as well as pointing to the apparently endemic and undecidable dispute between them, is also applied to metaphysics. Cicero rehearses a collection of Skeptical physical and metaphysical arguments at *Academica* 2.117–28, all of which are probably owed to Carneades.

Aristotle holds the world to be eternal, the Stoics and Epicureans take it to be created (2.119); the Atomists think that everything arises as a result of random interactions, the Stoics that the world is governed by a providential fate (2.220). Equally, different schools say different and incompatible things about the gods (Cicero, *ND* 1.1–5).

As regards providence and fate, Cicero's *On Fate* is our best source for Carneadean argument, directed both against Epicureans and Stoics. The Epicureans supposed that the world must be causally indeterminate in order to allow for human freedom; the Stoics held that freedom and determinism were compatible. Against the Stoics, Carneades mounts the following argument:

> (a) if all things come about through antecedent causes, all things come about through the interconnection in a natural chain. (b) If that is so, all things are the product of necessity. (c) If that is true, nothing is in our power. (d) But there is something in our power. (e) But if all things come about through fate, all things come about through antecedent causes. (f) Therefore it is not the case that whatever happens happens through fate. (29: *On Fate* 31 = LS 70G [part])

The Stoics accept (e), and hold its antecedent to be true; but this, along with (a) and (b), entails (c), which contradicts (d), which the Stoics accept; but if (d) is not false, then (f) is true, contrary to the Stoic position. The Stoics, as compatibilists, argued that (b) does not entail (c); but Carneades' argument at least deserves notice (and there are still plenty of philosophers who take it to be sound, although there is no need to suppose that Carneades did).

The Epicureans, in effect, accept the argument of 29, denying the antecedent of (a), introducing the notorious, uncaused atomic swerve to account, among other things, for human freedom. Carneades, however

> showed that the Epicureans could defend their case without this fictitious swerve. For since they taught that a certain voluntary motion of the mind was possible, a defence of that doctrine was preferable to introducing the swerve, especially as they could not discover its cause. And by defending it they could easily stand up to Chrysippus. For by conceding that there is no motion without a cause, they would not be conceding that all events were the results of antecedent causes. For our volition has no external antecedent causes. (30: *On Fate* 23 = LS 20E)

When we say someone acts without a cause, Carneades continues, we mean without *external* cause: their volitions still cause their actions, but the volitions themselves are not caused. It is not clear how satisfactory that argument is; but it is reasonably clear that the Epicureans solve nothing with their swerve.

Carneades also argued that Stoic determinism fatally undermined the notion of responsibility: if all of our actions are determined by an ineluctable fate which is outside our control, then we cannot be legitimately held responsible for what we do, as the Stoics maintain. Again, we have no time to follow out the implications of that anticompatibilist argument, or to assess its cogency. But it has formed the core of all subsequent attempts to deny the availability of a middle way between hard determinism and libertarianism.

On the other hand, with equal perspicuity, Carneades saw that a denial of causal determinism need not entail any modifications to the semantic principle of bivalence. The Epicureans thought, perhaps following Aristotle (*On Interpretation* 9, esp. 18a6–8, b26–31), and certainly influenced by the so-called Master Argument of Diodorus Cronus,[15] that if statements about the future were true, then the future must already be settled, and hence rejected bivalence for future contingent statements: that is, they held that certain propositions about the future had no truth-value (Cicero, *On Fate* 21; *Academica* 2.97). The Stoics, equally convinced of the relation between future truth and necessity, held that all statements about the future were either necessarily true or impossible (*On Fate* 21).

Carneades replied that mere future truth was no indication that the event or state of affairs in question was now ineluctably settled (Cicero, *On Fate* 26–31):

> even if every proposition is true or false, it still doesn't follow automatically that there are immutable, eternal causes to prevent anything from occurring in any way other than that in which it will occur. The truth of statements like "Cato will enter the Senate" is effected by contingent causes, not by causes bound up in nature and the world. (31: Cicero, *On Fate* 28 = LS 70G [part])

For all that, if it is now true, it will happen – but it is not *made* to happen by the fact that it is true; indeed, it need not be made to happen by anything. Rather, some event in the future will make it now true. That event can be as contingent as you like:

> it matters greatly whether things which are going to be true are the product, from eternity, of a natural cause, or whether the truth of things which are going to be can be understood without their being eternally embodied in nature. (32: Cicero, *On Fate* 32 = LS 70G [part])

Not even Apollo could know the future unless that future was now causally settled (ibid.: this claim is also deployed against divination – see further below). Thus Carneades argued that if the future was known, it was causally determined,[16] and if causally determined then settled in truth-value – but the reverse entailments do not apply. Carneadean considerations were to be at the forefront of the long debates concerning God's foreknowledge, determinism, and human freedom (e.g., in Boethius, Ockham and Valla).

Logic and Identity

Other aspects of Stoic logic and metaphysics also drew Carneades' fire. He argued that the sorites paradox rendered Stoic logic useless (Cicero, *Academica* 2.91–4),[17] and the Liar paradox equally undermined it (ibid. 95–8), in particular because a liar-sentence (e.g., "this sentence is false")[18] is unevaluable for truth, and yet the Stoics accept bivalence.[19]

The Academics also took issue with the Stoic account of substance and identity. Here the issues are subtle. The starting point is an argument attributed to the fifth-century comic poet Epicharmus: things (paradigmatically animals) are simply composed of the matter that makes them up. But that matter is in a constant state of flux; hence nothing remains the same from one instant to the next. That argument has clear Heraclitean origins (see, e.g., Frs. 22 B 12, 49a, 91); and it will trouble only materialists committed to the view that nothing (an enduring immaterial soul, for instance) exists over and above material aggregates.

But the Stoics were materialists: and they were troubled by these arguments,[20] which were leveled at them with renewed vigor by the Academics. Their response was to say that, in Socrates, say, at any one time there are two coexisting coincident individuals, one "the material substrate," whose identity-conditions are given extensionally by the identity of the set of its material components (and hence which constantly alters its identity), the other the "peculiarly qualified individual," whose identity is determined by the persistence of identifying features (a snub nose, for instance).

This doctrine attracted Carneadean scorn (reported by Plutarch, *On Common Conceptions* 1083a–84a, 1077c–e, a work deriving directly from Clitomachus, and hence indirectly from Carneades): it means that two distinct individuals may, indeed must, occupy the same spatiotemporal region, which is awkward for philosophers like the Stoics who take all individuals to be material. But it is not clear whether this is too high a philosophical price to pay; indeed the jury is still out on the question (although that fact in itself is a testament to the force of the Academic dialectic).

Theology and Divination

Carneades' theological arguments set the terms of debate for centuries. All of them are dialectical in intent, designed merely to expose the weaknesses in opposing positions, as the structure of Cicero's Academic dialogue (which draws heavily on Carneadean argument) *Nature of the Gods* itself makes clear. First, an Epicurean spokesman lays out the case for the disengaged gods of Epicurus, which is then answered by Cotta for the Academics; then the Stoic case is made and answered in its turn.

Cotta argues that the world was not, as the Stoics claimed, providentially organized for the benefit of humankind (*ND* 3.65–93): it contains too many unpleasant and dangerous elements (vipers, for instance), which cannot plausibly be explained away, as the Stoics heroically seek to, as conferring some obscure benefit (3.65); sinners' ways prosper, and as the Stoics themselves allow, most people are foolish, but wisdom is the only good (3.66–75). If the Stoics reply that it is through our own culpable misuse of reason that we go wrong, then it would have been better not to have been made reasonable; while "if the gods cared for men, they would have made them all good" (3.76–80).

Perhaps most impressive is an elegant statement of the problem of evil:

> either God wants to remove evil but cannot, or he can but doesn't want to, or he has neither the will nor the power, or he has both will and power. If has the will but no power, he is weak, which is not proper to God. If he has the power but not the will, he is grudging, which is equally alien to God. . . . But if he does have the will and the power (as alone is fitting for God), where do evils come from, and why does God not remove them? (33: *ND* 3.65)

Carneades also attacked arguments for the gods' existence, and the coherence of our conceptions of them: if God were sentient, he must be affectable, if affectable then alterable; but if alterable, then alterable only for the worse (since God is by definition perfect), and moreover destructible (*M* 9.146–7; *ND* 3.29–34), as at any rate the later Stoics (contemporaries of Carneades) thought He was not. Moreover he offered an interesting cumulative argument designed to show that if anything is worth worshipping as a god, then everything is (*ND* 3.43–52; *M* 9.182–90).

The Stoics argued from the existence of gods to the possibility of divination – but the evidence rather suggests we should run the argument the other way, from the impossibility of divination to the nonexistence of the gods. The Stoics further argue that if the gods are providential, they will provide us with signs to predict the future. But firstly there is no reason to think the gods providential: and even if they were, it is not clear that it is in our interest to know the future.

Philo and the End of the Academy

Cicero reports, in his *Academica*, the bare outlines of a dispute within the Academy that took place in his own time, in the 90s or 80s BC, between the two leading Academics of the time, Philo and Antiochus, a dispute which led to the end of the Academy as an institution (later writers such as Sextus, exhibiting the doxographer's mania for classification, describe Philo and Antiochus as the founders of the "Fourth" and "Fifth" Academies respectively: *PH* 1.220, 235). Antiochus in particular had profoundly Dogmatic leanings: Sextus says he "introduced the Stoa into the Academy" (*PH* 1.235), and Cicero portrays him in the *Academica* as steadfastly supporting the Stoic criterion of the cataleptic impression (e.g. 2.18–39; 2.50; 2.111), as well as developing a detailed, positive, syncretistic ethics and physics (1.15–42).

Philo, an adherent of the view that Carneades did propose his practical epistemology of plausibility in his own voice, apparently went further:

> Philo and his associates say that, as far as the Stoic criterion [i.e. the cataleptic impression] is concerned, things are unapprehended, but as far as their own natures are concerned they are apprehended. (34: Sextus, *PH* 1.235 = LS 68T)

That is admittedly obscure; but it seems that he claimed that some things could actually be known (*Academica* 2.18). Antiochus replies that, by rejecting the Stoic condition of the discernibility of cataleptic presentations from any false sibling (14(1); 15(iv)), Philo undercuts his own position:

> when Philo weakens and abolishes this, he abolishes the criterion of the unknown and the known, which leads to the inference that nothing can be apprehended – so he is brought round by carelessness to the position he most wants to avoid.[21] (35: *Academica* 2.18 = LS 68U [part]; cf. 2.43–4).

Antiochus further accuses him of abolishing the distinction between true and false (by rejecting the cataleptic impression), none the less he still wants to maintain that some impressions are true, and some false "than which nothing could be more inconsistent (2.111)."

Carneades, in not making any pronouncements about truth in his own voice, can evade these charges;[22] Philo is, at first sight, in a tougher position, since he wants to hold that some things are true, but that they are not securely distinguishable from what is false. On what basis could he make such a claim? Antiochus said, according to Cicero, that Philo found this objection particularly worrying (*Academica* 2.111); and perhaps with good reason. But Cicero replies on his behalf:

> that would be the case if indeed we abolished truth altogether; but we do not: for we distinguish true impressions from false ones. The type (*species*) is <the source> of our acceptance; we have no mark of apprehension. (36: 2.111)

That too is obscure;[23] I take it to mean that we can distinguish the notions of truth and falsity in regard to impressions without knowing (for certain) which of our impressions are true. In other words, we know *what it would be* for them to be true, even if we can never know that those conditions have been satisfied. What we go on is the general nature of the impression (its vividness and plausibilty) which it can share, in the event of its being true, with an indistinguishable false congener. This is the meaning of "type" here: the "types" are determined by their phenomenal contours, and those include no particular, determining sign of their being true, "no mark of apprehension."

But the question, exploited by Antiochus, still remains: why should Philo suppose any impressions to be true (in the sense of accurately reporting the world) if he cannot tell of any particular impression that *it* is true? The standard way of knowing, for some domain, that there is an *F* in it is by knowing of some specific denizen of the domain that it is F – but this is what Philo bars himself from doing. Numenius writes:

> but as time went by and his *epochē* began to fade as a result of ordinary life he no longer remained firm in his convictions about these things, but the clarity (*enargeia*) and agreement (*homologia*) of his experiences turned him around. (37: in Eusebius, *Preparation for the Gospel* 14.9.2)

Discounting for the hostility, Numenius suggests that Philo began to think that the very fact that his experience was as stable and mutually confirmatory as it was was a good reason for supposing that it accurately reflected the world; the very success of the Carneadean fallibilist picture invites us to suppose some metaphysical underpinning for it; the best explanation of the *enargeia* and *homologia* of my experiences is that the vast majority of them tell the truth, in a straightforwardly realist fashion.[24]

Philo supposes that there are indefinitely many things he knows, although none of them (at least those with empirical content)[25] are such that he knows (for sure) that he knows them. In this, he interestingly anticipates contemporary reliabilist accounts of knowledge and justification. But he has moved far from the original Academic position, even as modified by Carneades. It is not difficult to see how Aenesidemus (fl. c. 80 BC) could denounce the Academy in disgust as "Stoics fighting with Stoics" (Photius, *Library* 170a16–17), and decamp to revive the Skepticism of Pyrrho.

Outline of Pyrrhonism

About Pyrrho himself (c. 360–c. 270 BC), relatively little is known for certain. He wrote nothing, but his reputation was celebrated by his disciple Timon, in a mock-epic poem called the *Silloi*, extensive fragments of which survive. But the *Silloi* is more concerned to mock the pretensions of other philosophers than it is to record the thought of its hero:

> verily, no other mortal could rival Pyrrho. (38: Eusebius, *Preparation* 14.18.17 = LS 2A = DC 57)[26]

> such was the man I saw, unproud and unsubdued by everything which has subdued both unknown and known alike, volatile crowds of people, weighed down this way and that with passions, opinion, and vain lawmaking. (39: ibid. 14.18.19 = LS 2B = DC 58)

> Old man, how and whence did you find escape from the bondage of opinions and the empty wisdom of the Sophists? How did you break the chains of all deception and persuasion? You did not concern yourself with discovering what winds pass over Greece, and from and to what each thing passes. (40: DL 9.65 = LS 2C = DC 60)

Diogenes Laertius' *Life* is based on a relatively early account by Antigonus of Carystus – but as usual it is longer on anecdote than it is on doctrine. Thus we learn that he avoided nothing and took no precautions, but withstood everything as it occurred, carts, precipices, dogs, etc., placing no trust in the senses (41: DL 9.62 = LS 1A [part] = DC 6)

and that he relied upon the good offices of friends to prevent him from coming to harm. Although these stories, like those which assert that he showed his indifference by washing pigs, remained calm during a terrifying storm at sea, but was ashamed of having been frightened by a dog (DL 9.66, 68), are obviously apocryphal, they are testimony to his reputation for philosophical indifference; however

> Aenesidemus says that it was only his philosophy that was based on suspension of judgement, and that he did not act carelessly. (42: DL 9.62 = LS 1A [part] = DC 7)

Moreover,

> Aenesidemus says in the first book of his *Pyrrhonian Arguments* that Pyrrho determined nothing dogmatically as a result of opposing argument (*antilogia*), but adhered to the appearances. (43: DL 9.106 = LS 71A = DC 8)

Evidently, there were some points of contact between the Academics and the attitudes and practices attributed to Pyrrho. The Stoic Ariston described Arcesilaus, in a witty parody of Homer's description of the chimera, as "Plato in front, Pyrrho behind, Diodorus in the middle" (DL 4.33); and at the very least, Pyrrho's example of a life of indifference will presumably have appealed to the Academics.

But it is unclear to what extent, if at all, Pyrrho was a genuine epistemological Skeptic. Prior to the Aenesidemean revival, Pyrrho was seen as a dusty cul-de-sac in Greek philosophy. Cicero refers to him a few times, but always as the purveyor of a superannuated moral theory. Modern commentators are divided as to whether he really was a Skeptic, or rather a certain sort of Heraclitean Dogmatist.[27] The only real evidence that has survived is a fragment of one of Timon's prose works, reported by Aristocles and preserved in Eusebius:

> it is supremely important to investigate our own capacity for knowledge, since if we are so constituted that we know nothing, there is no need to continue enquiry into other things. . . . Pyrrho of Elis was also a powerful spokesman of such a position. He himself has left nothing in writing, but his pupil Timon says that whoever wants to be happy must consider these three questions: (i) how are things by nature? (ii) What attitude should we adopt towards them? (iii) What will be the outcome for those who have this attitude? According to Timon, Pyrrho declared that things are equally indifferent (*adiaphora*: perhaps "undifferentiable"), unmeasurable (*astathmēta*), and undecidable (*anepikritos*); for this reason[28] neither our sensations nor our judgements tell us truths or falsehoods. Consequently we should not put our trust in them but should be unopinionated (*adoxastoi*), uncommitted (*aklineis*) and unwavering (*akradantoi*), saying concerning each thing that it no more is than is not, or that it both is and is not, or that it neither is nor is not. For those disposed thus the consequence will be first non-assertion (*aphasia*) then tranquillity (*ataraxia*) says Timon; Aenesidemus says pleasure. (44: Aristocles, in Eusebius *Preparation* 14.18.1–5 = LS 1F = DC 53)

The text is unclear in several places (see n. 27); and the interpretation disputed even where it is not. On the interpretation I favor, Pyrrho ascribes the impossibility of arriving at any firm judgment of things to the Heraclitean indeterminacy of the world; he is not, then, strictly speaking a Skeptic, but rather adheres to a metaphysical position that makes clear determination of things an impossibility (and hence renders unambiguous ascriptions of properties to things neither strictly true nor strictly false); the upshot is "nonassertion" (i.e., a refusal dogmatically to predicate properties of things), from which follows *ataraxia* (later, Sextus would describe *ataraxia* as supervening upon *epochē* as a welcome but unintended consequence: *PH* 1.25–30; cf. 3 above).

If this is right, Pyrrho will have provided primarily a model of a life lived without commitment to later Skeptics (including Academics, who rarely mention him), rather than a genuinely Skeptical epistemology. Sextus, our best source for later Pyrrhonism, mentions him only a handful of times, and then generally on such terms: we call ourselves Pyrrhonists, he says, "from the fact that Pyrrho seems to us to have adopted a Skeptical attitude more consistently and clearly than any of his predecessors" (*PH* 1.7).

Aenesidemus

After Timon's death around 230 BC, Pyrrhonism fell into decay. Diogenes tries to construct a "succession" of Pyrrhonists, carrying the torch from one generation to another, as doxographers were wont to do: but he evidently finds the task more than usually difficult. At all events, we know next to nothing about Pyrrhonism in the 150 years that separate Timon from Aenesidemus.

Aenesidemus is also an enigmatic figure, in part becuase it is unclear just how much of his argumentation lies behind Sextus' presentation of Pyrrhonism. Some scholars have supposed Sextus to be in large part merely a dummy for Aenesidemean ventriloquism – but I am inclined to reject that suggestion, in part because Sextus rarely mentions his great predecessor, and when he does he often appears in a puzzlingly Dogmatic light.

On a number of occasions, Sextus talks of "Aenesidemus, in agreement with Heraclitus,"[29] hardly a Skeptical turn of phrase. Moreover

> Aenesidemus and his followers say that there is a difference in things apparent, and says that of these some appear in common to all, while others appear privately to individuals, and of these those which appear in common to all are true, while those which do not are false. (45: *M* 8.8)

And that does not seem Skeptical at first sight either. However, the point of Aenesidemus' argument may precisely have been that, since nothing appears the same to everybody, nothing is unrestrictedly true (but cf. 47 below).

Our best, albeit compressed, source for Aenesidemus' own writings is an entry in the library catalogue of the ninth-century Byzantine patriarch Photius recording the contents of Aenesidemus' *Pyrrhonian Arguments* (cf. 43):

> the whole aim of the book is to ground the view that there is no ground for *katalēpsis*, whether through perception or thought. Consequently, he says, neither the Pyrrhonists nor the rest know the truth in things; but the philosophers of the other schools, as well as being ignorant in general, and wearing themselves out uselessly and expending themselves in ceaseless torments, are also ignorant of the very fact that they apprehend none of the things of which they think that they have gained apprehension. But he who philosophizes after the fashion of Pyrrho is happy not only in general but also, and especially, in the wisdom of knowing that nothing is firmly grasped by him. And even with regard to what he knows, he has the propriety to assent no more to its affirmation than to its denial. (46: Photius, *Bibliotheca* 212, 169b18–30 = LS 71C [part])

Thus Aenesidemus explicitly adopted Pyrrho as a model; but again it is not clear precisely how. The last two sentences suggest that the limit of his knowledge is that he has no firm apprehension – and even that he will not positively assert. This bears comparison with the position of Arcesilaus (above, §3); and yet

> (1) in the first book he distinguishes the Pyrrhonists from the Academics in almost precisely the following words. He says that the Academics are Dogmatists: they lay down some things with confidence and unambiguously, while the Pyrrhonists are aporetics and free from all dogma. (2) Not one of them has said either that all things are apprehensible or that they are non-apprehensible, but that they are no more of this kind than that, or that they are sometimes of this kind and sometimes not, or that for one person they are of this kind, for another person not of this kind, and for another not even existent at all. (3) Nor do they say that all things in general, or some things, are accessible to us, or not accessible to us, but that they are no more accessible than not, or that they are sometimes accessible to us and sometimes not, or that they are accessible to one person but not to another. (4) Nor indeed do they say that there is true or false, convincing or unconvincing, existent or non-existent. But the same thing is, as it might be said, no more true than false, convincing than unconvincing, existent than non-existent; or sometimes the one, and sometimes the other; or of such a kind for one person, but not for another. (5) For the Pyrrhonist determines absolutely nothing, not even the claim that nothing can be determined (we put it like this, he says, for want of a better way to express the thought). (47: ibid. 212, 169b36–170a14 = LS 71C [part])

The charge that the Academics were negative Dogmatists is also echoed by Sextus (*PH* 1.1–4, 1.226–31), although its veracity is disputed by adherents of the DI. Modes of expression are distinguished by 47(2)–(4) that are disallowed for the Pyrrhonist from those which are acceptable; and the implication is that the Academics breach the rules of Skeptical speech, by affirming that nothing is apprehensible, by denying that anything is accessible, and so on. By contrast the Pyrrhonist will say of everything that it is no more thus and so than not, or that it is sometimes, and sometimes not, or that it is to one person and not to another. That is, Aenesidemus appears to allow relativized propositions, while disallowing absolute ones. Thus, in default of universal agreement as to the apparent properties things have, we are unable to say how they really are (cf. 45); which in Sextus' hands is to become the paradigm Skeptical argument.

The rest of Photius' summary bears this out. Book 2 sought to derive contradictions and incompatibilities concerning "principles, causes, affections, motion, generation and destruction, and their opposites" (Photius, *Bibliotheca*, 212, 170b4–8) with a view to establishing the impossibility of grasping them; equally, the third book dealt with "intellect"[30] and perception and their properties: working through an elaborate set of contradictions, he puts them too beyond our access and apprehension. Book 4 impugned physics, cosmology and theology, and also attacked indicative sign-inference while Book 5 dealt with the causal explanations (see §14); finally books 6–8 dealt with ethical topics – choice and avoidance, good and bad, the virtues, happiness and the end of life.

Much of this no doubt mirrored, indeed it surely made use of, arguments owed to Carneades of the sort we have already examined. Crucially, though, it appears that, while Aenesidemus does say that nothing is apprehended (sc. by the Stoic criterion), since if it were so apprehended we would *know* it to be so – but we don't, and so it isn't, he does not assert that nothing is apprehensible (sc. in its own nature) – we know nothing of natures, and hence we do not know whether things are naturally inapprehensible. Thus the conclusions of his arguments in the later books of *Pyrrhonian Arguments* are compatible with his methodological strictures in 47(2)–(4); and 47(5) on makes perfectly good sense.

Modes of Skepticism

Sextus (*PH* 1.36–163) discusses ten "modes," or basic argument-patterns, which he says "were handed down by the older skeptics" (36), although he does not elaborate on the latters' identity. It is usually assumed that he means Aenesidemus, and Diogenes discusses the same ten modes in the course of his account of Aenesidemus, although again without clearly attributing them to him (DL 9.79). Aristocles speaks of "nine modes of Aenesidemus," although his presentation is confused and deficient, while Philo of Alexandria (c. 30 BC–c. AD 45), our earliest source, details eight of the ten, although again without referring to Aenesidemus. Sextus once (*M* 7.345) speaks of "the ten modes of Aenesidemus," although only in passing, and the reference is unclear.

At all events, it seems likely that Aenesidemus did make use of the material we now know as the Ten Modes (even though there is no trace of them as such in Photius' summary of the *Pyrrhonian Arguments*); and perhaps it was he who first systematized them. In any event they clearly belong, at least in some formulation, to the relatively early history of Pyrrhonism. The Modes all share a general structure:[31]

(1)   *x* appears *F* relative to *a*;
(2)   *x* appears *F** relative to *b*;
(3)   at most one of *F* and *F** can objectively hold of *x*;

but

(4)   no criterion is available to favor either of them;

so

(5)   we should suspend judgment as to what *x* is like in its real nature.

That clearly recalls some of the material dealt with earlier; and it coheres with the reports that Aenesidemus made *epochē*, with *ataraxia* supervening upon it, the end of Skepticism (DL 9.107; cf. Photius, 212, 170b30–5; and see 3 above).

Ataraxia, freedom from disturbance, was a common aim of the Hellenistic schools, endorsed by the Epicureans and (to a limited extent) by the Stoics. But it does not figure prominently, if at all, in Acacemic Skepticism (Cicero has Carneades make the end "enjoying the primary things in accordance with nature," but only for dialectical purposes: *On Ends* 5.19). We achieve tranquillity as a result of suspending judgment, although without intending to do so; it follows "like a shadow following a body," in a phrase Diogenes attributes to "Timon and Aenesidemus and their followers" (DL 9.107). Thus the Pyrrhonists sought to evade the obvious objection that, by setting something up as a goal, they were *ipso facto* dogmatizing. This defense is prominent and subtly carried out in Sextus (PH 1.1–30); but if Diogenes is right, it at least originated earlier.

Sextus is in general careful too to make *epochē* a causal rather than a logical consequence of the "anomaly in things," again to avoid charges of self-refutation: the Pyrrhonist places no trust in logic, and hence should not rely on it (*PH* 1.144–92). The evidence, fragile though it is, suggests that this is a later, perhaps Sextan development, and that Aenesidemus at any rate was happy to allow that *epochē* followed (in some sense) from the disagreements.

The different modes differ in their range of fillers for *a* and *b*: thus the first collects (alleged) differences in the way different animals perceive things, the second differences between different human beings, the third differences between different sense-modalities, and the fourth disagreements in the reports of the same sense-modality at different times, and so on.

Sextus' presentation betrays an overlay of later concerns; in particular he seeks to make *epochē* simply a cuasal consequence of the disputes, rather than something rationally to be inferred from them (and hence shows himself to be highly sensitve to the various charges of the Dogmatists that Skeptical practice fatally presupposed Dogmatic assumptions). Aenesidemus, it seems, belonged to a more innocent time, and was happy to represent *epochē* as the end (something Sextus rejects) and as something rationally arrived at.

None the less, the basic features of Aenesideman practice anticipate that of Sextus:

> Pyrrhonist discourse is a kind of recollection of appearances, or of ideas of any kind, on the basis of which they are all brought into confrontation with each other, and, when compared, are found to present much disparity and confusion. This is what Aenesidemus says in the summary of his *Pyrrhonics*.[32] (48: DL 9.78 = LS 71B)

And this too has much in common with the method of the Academics. The fundamental idea is that, unless we can find a case of absolute consensus (and perhaps not even then, since the consensus may be temporary: *PH* 1.34), we are not entitled to assert anything as an unqualified truth (45–7); but no such consensuses are to be found in any domain, be it one of perception or intellection, of sensory judgment or ethics; hence we must suspend judgment about the real nature of things. Evidently essential to the plausibility of that inference is the claim of proposition (4), that no nonquestion-begging criterion is available to decide between the conflicting appearances; and much of later anti-Skeptical argument is devoted to confuting that. The Lockean move to secondary qualities is a Skeptically inspired empirical response to such challenge, and may be judged at the very least to weaken the force of the Skeptical considerations in favour of *epochē*. But for all that, the challenge remains real enough.

Signs and Causes

Books 4 and 5 of the *Pyrrhonian Arguments* were concerned with signs and causes; and these topics were to become a crucial battleground between later Skeptics like Sextus and their opponents:

> in the fourth book he says that signs, in the sense in which we call apparent things the sign of the non-apparent, do not exist at all, and that those who believe they do are deceived by an empty enthusiasm. (49: Photius, *Bibliotheca* 212, 170b12–14)

This type of sign, called by Sextus "indicative" (*PH* 2.99), was central to Stoic methodology. By deploying such signs, they sought to arrive at unassailable understanding of the hidden structures of things in virtue of which they exhibited their particular phenomenal appearances. They defined it as "an antecedent proposition in a sound conditional, which is revelatory of the consequent" (*PH* 2.101), and a favorite example was that the fact of sweating showed that the skin must be perforated by invisible pores.

Such powerful claims provide obvious targets for Skepticism; and here much of the debate probably originated in the disputes between the various medical schools of the Hellenistic period:[33] should medicine seek to determine the nature of the hidden conditions of the body on the basis of inferences of this type (which the

Dogmatic doctors called "indications"); or should they simply rest content, as the Empiricist school urged, with compiling data about what phenomena tend to go along with what (which Sextus later calls "commemorative signs": the sight of smoke prompts one to suppose that there must be a fire, even if it is currently invisible – but of course fires themselves, unlike the subjects of Stoic-type indicative signs, are not *in principle* unobservable: *PH* 2.97–9).

In the context of discussing medical sign-disputes, Sextus writes:

> Aenesidemus in the 4th book of *Pyrrhonian Arguments* argues . . . as follows: "if apparent things appear alike to all in a similar condition, and signs are apparent things, then signs appear alike to all in a similar condition. But signs do not appear alike to all in a similar condition; and apparent things appear alike to all in a similar condition; therefore signs are not apparent things." (50: *M* 8.215; cf. 234)

That argument is one of the very few genuine fragments of Aenesidemus we possess, and as such is of great value. The Stoics suppose that sign-inference can take us from something uncontroversially evident to a hidden conclusion; Aenesidemus demurs. What functions as the sign (e.g., the sweating) may be evident; but it is far from evident what it is a sign *of.* Sextus gives a medical example at *M* 8.219–20, where different doctors draw radically different conclusions from the same apparent signs. Phenomena on their own do not determine their causes.

That latter contention, which anticipates the modern thesis of the underdetermination of theory by evidence, forms the cornerstone of his Eight Modes against the Aetiologists, summarized by Sextus (*PH* 1.180–6), and mentioned by Photius (212, 170b17–22) as occurring in the fifth book of *Pyrrhonian Arguments*:

> the first is the mode according to which, he says, aetiology in general, being concerned with non-apparent things, has no consistent confirmation from the appearances. (51: *PH* 1.181 = LS 72M [part])

But if there is (as he supposes that there always is) more than one way of accounting for the phenomena

> the Second Mode shows that frequently when there is an abundance of ways of assigning an explanation to what is under investigation, some of them account for it in one way only. (52: *PH* 1 181 = LS 72M [part])

The point is reinforced by the Fourth Mode,

> according to which, having seen how the appearances come to be, they imagine that they have also got a grip on the way things non-apparent come to be; and while perhaps the non-apparent are brought about in the same way as what is apparent, perhaps on the other hand they are not, but come to be in their own peculiar fashion. (53: *PH* 1 182 = LS 72M [part])

And by the Sixth, according to which

> they frequently allow only such facts as are consistent with their hypotheses, while passing over those which conflict with them, even though they possess an equal persuasiveness. (54: *PH* 1 183 = LS 72M [part])

Moroever, theorists prefer to make causal claims on the basis of their own preferred elemental theories (the Fifth Mode), and often give piecemeal accounts of processes that occur in a regular and stable fashion (the third Mode: here as elsewhere the Epicureans seem to be particularly the targets). Finally,

> the Seventh is that according to which they often give causes which are not only in conflict with the appearances but also with their own theories. The Eighth is that according to which, when things are frequently equally doubtful in regard to both those things which seem to be apparent and those under investigation, they construct their exposition concerning things equally doubtful from things equally doubtful. (55: *PH* 1 184 = LS 72M [part])

The Seventh is an extension of the Sixth, while the Eighth may be interpreted in the light of the Stoic sweating inference, and 50. Things which only "seem to be apparent" are interpretations of phenomena which are already loaded in favor of a certain type of explanation, in the case of sweating that the moisture has an origin internal to the body (and also that liquid cannot pass through a solid body): but these things are themselves theoretical and doubtful.

In sum, Aenesidemus' reflections on the fragility of sign-inference and causal hypothesis are well directed, and a salutary corrective to the overconfidence of much Greek theorizing. It is a pity that they survive only in Sextus' terse summaries.

Conclusions

Much more could be said about both Academic and Pyrrhonian Skepticism. Both schools continued to flourish, albeit not institutionally. As late as the fourth century, Augustine still thought it worthwhile to combat what he saw as the pernicious arguments of the Academics; and he also thought, falsely, as many others have done, that he had a knockdown refutation of them (*Against the Academics* 3.43–5; cf. 3.2–26, and n. 10 above). Another roughly contemporary Christian saint, Gegory of Nazianzus, rails against Sextus and Pyrrho as responsible for "the vile and malignant disease" of arguing contrary positions which had infected the church (*Orations* 21.12; cf. 32.25). The Christians of course saw a threat to their own emerging forms of dogma; but it is as a corrective against a more general Dogmatism that the achievements of the Skeptical philosophers can best be appreciated; and while few if any nowadays would embrace Skepticism as a way of life, the influence of the

Academic method and example has survived, sometimes in a subterranean form, and sometimes distorted (notably by Hume), until our own day, where we can see its descendants flourishing in the vigorous dialectic of the schools of analytical philosophy.

Notes

1   Collected in Isnardi Parente 1980, 1982.
2   References of this form refer to texts collected in Long and Sedley 1987.
3   "DK" refers to the fragments of Presocratic philosophy collected in Diels and Kranz 1952.
4   From the Greek *dogmatikos*: a dogmatist in this sense is simply someone committed to the truth of certain beliefs, preeminently beliefs of a theoretical cast (e.g., about the ultimate nature of matter, the structure of the world, the nature and existence of the gods); it was the manifold disagreements among the various dogmatist schools that provided the major impetus for Greek skepticism in its various varieties: see Sextus, *PH* 1.12–15.
5   Sometimes Englished as "apprehensive impression," or "cognitive impression," or "graspable impression" – but all translations are somewhat misleading, and since it is a technical term I have thought it better simply to transliterate it (as others do), and let its meaning emerge from the account given by the Stoics themselves.
6   Maconi (1988, 240 n. 26) secludes "and false," probably correctly.
7   For more on the notion of content involved here, see Hankinson 1997.
8   However, Ioppolo (1981, 147–51) argues that *katorthōma* did not become a specific technical term for the Stoics until rather later.
9   With Ioppolo 1984; Maconi 1988.
10 Similar considerations will dispose of Augustine's ingenious argument to the effect that Arcesilaus must either accept or reject Zeno's definition. If he accepts it, then there is something he apprehends (namely, the definition); if he rejects it, then for all his arguments establish (since they are based on the definition), there may well still be apprehension (*Against the Academics* 3.18–21).
11 So Galen, writing in the second century AD, thought (*On the Doctrines of Hippocrates and Plato* 5.778, Kühn 1965): see Hankinson 1992, 1997.
12 On the Skeptics' "two kinds of assent," see Frede 1984, and Bett 1990.
13 See Hankinson 1998, 98–9.
14 The Stoic position is not, however, hopeless: see Striker 1986 for a subtle defense.
15 Diodorus was a near contemporary of Aristotle's who sought to show that two Aristotelian premises ("the past is necessary"; "an impossibility cannot follow from a possibility") are incompatible with the claim "there is something possible which neither is nor will be true": Epictetus 2.19.1–5.
16 This is a mistake: one might know the future without its now being causally determined if one could simply see it laid out in a four-dimensional map – but Carneades' arguments are acute for all that.
17 On the sorites ("if 1 grain of sand isn't a heap, then neither are 2 grains; if 2 are not, neither are 3 . . . if n are not, neither are $n + 1$"), see Barnes 1982, 1997.

18 This is a typical modern case: the ancient examples are more convoluted, and involve the notions of lying and truth-telling rather than dealing directly with truth and falsity. The original "Cretan liar" case is that of the Cretan who asserts "all Cretans are liars" (i.e., everything uttered by a Cretan is false). Cicero gives the following: "if you say that you are lying, and say it truly, then you lie" (*Academica* 2.95–6): for the paradox to be properly drawn, this needs to by supplemented by "if you say that you are lying, and you are lying, then you speak truly"; i.e., "I am lying" is if true, false, and if false, true.

19 Of course much could be, and indeed is still being, said on this issue; for the ancient debate, see Barnes 1997.

20 There is a family of them; I couched the argument generally in terms of change. In the ancient world it was generally known as the "growing argument," presumably since growth is an evident fact and obviously involves material discontinuity, whereas the doctrine of a constant turnover of material components is, although plausible, more obviously theoretical: see Plutarch, *On Common Conceptions* 1038a; Chrysippus wrote a treatise (now lost) *On the Growing Argument*; Philo, *On the Indestructibility of the World* 48.

21 This passage is controversial, and admits of different interpretations which I have not the space to discuss here: see Hankinson 1997, 166–8, esp. n. 16.

22 Although critics attempted to saddle him with them: Augustine, *Against the Academics* 2.16, 2.24, 2.27.

23 See Hankinson, 1997, 183–7, esp. n. 15; Striker 1997.

24 In spite of what is sometimes maintained, there is no genuine anticipation in the ancient world of any of the modern varieties of antirealism: truth is always correspondence with facts. This is precisely why Carneades has no theory of truth.

25 It is not clear how far the Academics were prepared to extend their doubts into the realm of the a priori (although it is clear that they would have been less sanguine about the possibility of a priori knowledge than the dogmatists). But Galen at least portrays Carneades as having refused to accept the Euclidian axiom of equality: *On the Best Method of Teaching* 1.42, Kühn.

26 This fragment closely parodies *Iliad* 3.223 (about Odysseus). "DC" refers to the fragments and testimonia collected in Decleva Caizzi 1981.

27 See Bett 1994; Brunschwig 1994, 1999; Hankinson 1998, ch. 4.

28 Or, adopting a conjecture of Hirzel, "since": this suggestion has the effect of reversing the order of logical dependence between the clauses. The interpretation of this, and of much of the rest of the passage, is controversial: see Hankinson 1998, ch. 4; Brunschwig 1999.

29 *M* 7.349, 9.337, 10.216: the phrase might mean "in relation to," and hence not enroll Aenesidemus as a Heraclitean – but on balance that seems less likely, and in any case is of no help in other contexts (*PH* 3.138, *M* 7.350, 10.38) where Sextus presents us with a dogmatic-sounding Aenesidemus: see Hankinson 1998, 129–31.

30 Reading *noēsis* for the barely intelligible *kinēsis* of the MSS.

31 For a clear discussion of the Ten Modes, both in general and case-by-case, see Annas and Barnes 1985.

32 Perhaps identical with *Pyrrhonian Arguments*; perhaps not.

33 For these, see Hankinson 1998, ch. 13.

References and Recommended Reading

Algra, K., Barnes, J., Mansfeld, J., and Schofield, M. (eds.) (1999) *The Cambridge History of Hellenistic Philosophy* (Cambridge: Cambridge University Press)

Allen, J. (1994) "Academic Probablism and and Stoic Epistemology," *Classical Quarterly* 44, 85–113

Annas, J. and Barnes, J. (1985) *The Modes of Scepticism* (Cambridge: Cambridge University Press)

—— (1997) "Carneadean Argument," in Inwood and Mansfeld 1997

Barnes, J. (1982) "Medicine, Experience and Logic," in Barnes et al. 1982

—— (1989) "Antiochus of Ascalon," in Barnes and Griffin 1989

—— (1997), *Logic and the Imperial Stoa* (Leiden: E. J. Brill)

Barnes, J., Brunschwig, J., Burnyeat, M. F., Schofield, M. (eds.) (1982) *Science and Speculation* (Cambridge: Cambridge University Press)

Barnes, J., and Griffin, M. T. (eds.) (1989) *Philosophia Togata* (Oxford: Oxford University Press)

Barnes, J., et al. (eds.) (1980) *Doubt and Dogmatism: Studies in Hellenistic Epistemology* (Oxford: Oxford University Press)

Bett, R. (1990) "Carneades' Distinction Between Assent and Approval," *Monist* 73, 3–21

—— (1994) "Aristocles on Timon on Pyrrho: The Text, its Logic, and its Credibility," *Oxford Studies in Ancient Philosophy* 12, 137–81

Brunschwig, J. (1994) *Papers in Hellenistic Philosophy* (Cambridge: Cambridge University Press)

—— (1999) "The Beginnings of Hellenistic Epistemology," in Algra et al. 1999

Burnyeat, M. F. (ed.) (1983) *The Skeptical Tradition* (California: University of California Press)

Bury, R. G. (trans.) (1933) *Sextus Empiricus: Outlines of Pyrrhonism*, 4 vols. (London: W. Heinemann; New York: Putnam, 1933–1949)

Couissin, P. (1929) "L'origine et l'évolution de l'*epochē*," *Revue des Etudes Grecques* 42, 373–97

—— (1983) "The Stoicism of the New Academy," in Burnyeat 1983 (originally published as "Le Stoïcisme de la Nouvelle Académie" in *Revue d'histoire de la Philosophie* 3 (1929), 241–76)

Decleva Caizzi, F. (1981) *Pirrone: Testimonianze* (Naples, Italy: Bibliopolis) (= DC)

Diels, Hermann (1952) *Die Fragmente der Vorsokratiker*, 6th ed., revised by Walter Kranz (Berlin: Weidmann)

Everson, S. (ed.) (1990) *Epistemology*, Companions to Ancient Thought 1 (Cambridge: Cambridge University Press)

Frede, M. (1983) "Stoics and Skeptics on Clear and Distinct Impressions," in Burnyeat 1983 (repr. in Frede 1987)

—— (1984) "The Skeptic's Two Types of Assent and the Possibility of Knowledge, in Rorty et al. 1984 (repr. in Frede 1987)

—— (1987) *Essays in Ancient Philosophy* (Oxford: Oxford University Press)

Giannantoni, G. (ed.) (1981) *Lo Scetticismo Antico*, 2 vols. (Naples, Italy: Bibliopolis)

Glucker, J. (1978) *Antiochus and the Late Academy: Hypomnemata* 56 (Göttingen: Vandenhoeck & Ruprecht)

Hankinson, R. J. (1992) "A Purely Verbal Dispute? Galen on Stoic and Academic Epistemology," *Revue de Philosophie Internationale*, 45 3, 267–300

—— (1997) "Natural Criteria and the Transparency of Judgement: Philo, Antiochus and Galen on Epistemological Justification," in Inwood and Mansfeld 1997

—— (1998) *The Sceptics*, 2nd ed. (London: Routledge)

Ioppolo, A. M. (1981) "Il concetto di 'eulogon' nella filosofia di Arcesilao," in Giannantoni 1981

—— (1984) "Doxa ed epoché in Arcesilao," *Elenchos* 5, 317–63

—— (1986) *Opinione e Scienza* (Naples, Italy: Bibliopolis)

—— (1993) "The Academic Position of Favorinus of Arelate," *Phronesis* 38.2, 183–213

Inwood, B. and J. Mansfeld (eds.), *Assent and Argument: Studies in Cicero's Academic Books* (Leiden: E. J. Brill, 1997)

Isnardi Parente, M. (1980) *Speusippo: Frammenti* (Naples, Italy: Bibliopolis)

—— (1982) *Senocrate, Ermodoro: Frammenti* (Naples, Italy: Bibliopolis)

Kühn, C. G. (ed.) (1965) *Galeni Opera Omnia*, 20 vols. (originally published at Leipzig, 1821–33; repr. Hildesheim: Georg Olms)

Long, A. A., and Sedley, D. N. (eds.) (1987) *The Hellenistic Philosophers*, 2 vols. (Cambridge: Cambridge University Press) (= LS)

Maconi, H. (1988) "*Nova non philosophandi philosophia*: A Review of Anna Maria Ioppolo, *Opinione e Scienza*," in *Oxford Studies in Ancient Philosophy* 6, 231–53.

Rorty, R., Schneewind, J., and Skinner Q. (eds.) (1984) *Philosophy in History* (Cambridge: Cambridge University Press)

Schofield, M. (1999) "Academic Epistemology," in Algra et al. 1999

Schofield, M., and Striker, G. (eds.) (1986) *The Norms of Nature* (Cambridge: Cambridge University Press)

Striker, G. (1980) "Sceptical Strategies," in Barnes et al. 1980

—— (1981) "Über den Unterschied zwischen den Pyrrhoneern und den Akademikern," *Phronesis* 26, 353–69 (English version in Striker 1996)

—— (1986) "Antipater: Or the Art of Living," in Schofield and Striker 1986

—— (1990) "The Problem of the Criterion," in Everson 1990

—— (1996) *Essays on Hellenistic Epistemology and Ethics* (Cambridge: Cambridge University Press)

—— (1997) "Academics Fighting Academics," in Inwood and Mansfeld 1997

Part VI

Late Antique Philosophy: Introduction

In AD 529, as part of an effort to restore the failing Roman empire by codifying legal doctrine and enforcing Christian orthodoxy, the Roman emperor at Constantinople, Justinian, ordered the pagan schools of philosophy in Athens closed. Although hardly a political threat, the most prominent of the schools, Neoplatonism, did promulgate a non-Christian form of theism regarded as inimical to Justinian's overarching aims. The Neoplatonists could claim an ancient lineage, insofar as they were linked historically and, they maintained, doctrinally, to the Academy instituted by Plato almost a millennium before, in the early fourth century BC. Although they took their Platonic pedigree seriously, the Neoplatonists did not regard themselves as slavishly devoted to Plato alone. On the contrary, it was a hallmark of Neoplatonism to synthesize disparate and seemingly incompatible bits of Pythagoras, Aristotle, and the Stoics into the philosophy of Plato, whom they regarded as the preeminent expounder of philosophical truth.

Partly in virtue of their synthesizing tendencies, the writings of many of the Neoplatonists present as difficult and obscure. There are other sources of obscurity as well: many features of Neoplatonism are tinged with mysticism; some of it is influenced by occult preoccupations, including assays into demonology; and, most importantly, a number of their core philosophical doctrines are simply initially hard to fathom. Consequently, a fair bit of Neoplatonism has gone unexplored by historians of philosophy. In fact, many of those writing after the time of Plotinus (c. AD 205–70), who is regarded as the founder of Neoplatonism, have yet even to be translated into any modern language.

As Gerson makes clear, this neglect is unfortunate and unwarranted. Plotinus is himself perfectly aware that some of his views will sound peculiar to common sense. This is of little concern to him. Indeed, he is prepared to fault common sense on the grounds that it is implicated in incoherent positions regarding any number of central philosophical topics, including the reality of the material world, the nature of soul and its relation to the body, and the activities of thought and sense perception. To this extent, at least, Plotinus embraces a kind of philosophical reasoning extending back at least as far as Parmenides: where common sense and philosophy diverge, philosophy prevails while common sense yields. Moreover, when he considers some central Platonic commitments, Plotinus accepts consequences which seem to him to follow from them, even when Plato himself was less than definite. For example, he insists that if the soul is something immaterial, as per the picture of Plato's *Phaedo*, then it is difficult to see how it can be *in* the body, as a prisoner shackled in a prison. After all, wonders Plotinus, how can something immaterial be located in space at all? This leads him to postulate a second soul, a shadow soul, which is implicated in the material world in ways impossible for the pure individual soul, which is separate and immortal.[1] So, in a way Plato is right to think that the soul is *in* the body; and in a way, Aristotle is right too to treat the soul as an inseparable form of the body. So, concludes Plotinus, in speaking of there being many souls neither Plato nor Aristotle is focused on the one true soul which transcends the degradations resulting from all association with matter.

These doctrines are bound to sound peculiar; but, as so often with Plotinus, they are rendered explicable, and are to some degree motivated, by problems not too far below the surface in the writings of Plato, Aristotle, and the Hellenistic philosophers. To this extent, Neoplatonism serves as a study-aid to all of the most significant philosophy which preceded it.

Heading in the other direction, Neoplatonism provides an important link between pagan and Christian philosophy. For though central Neoplatonists, including especially Plotinus' student Porphyry, were decidedly anti-Christian, some early Christians understandably found the otherworldly tendencies in their thought congenial. Direct influences can be discerned in the seminal writings of the Christian Augustine (AD 354–430), who knew both Plotinus and Porphyry in Latin translation, and Boethius (AD 475–524), whose translation of Porphyry's commentary on Aristotle's *Categories* spurred interest in Aristotle's logic and ontology for hundreds of years after the final closure of the Athenian schools of philosophy. In these ways, Neoplatonism helped mold Christian thought through the Medieval period and beyond.

Note

1 For Plotinus' views on the soul and body, see the *Enneads* IV 4 and IV 7. The *Enneads* is a collection of the views of Plotinus compiled and arranged by his leading student, Porphyry, into six groups of nine subsections each (*ennea* = "nine" in Greek). The *Enneads* have a somewhat discombobulated feel to them, perhaps because they were transcriptions of oral presentations given by Plotinus, who, evidently partly blind, left them unedited.

Chapter 15

Neoplatonism

Lloyd P. Gerson

Introduction

The term "Neoplatonism" was coined by an eighteenth-century German scholar who wanted to carve up the relatively new field of the history of ancient philosophy in a perspicuous fashion. He intended the term to refer to a group of philosophers beginning with Plotinus (204/5–70 CE) and ending more or less with the last of the pagan Greek philosophers, for example, Proclus (412–85 CE), Damascius (c. 462 to after 538 CE), and his pupil Simplicius (c. 490–560 CE). Later, the term came to embrace certain Christian philosophers as well, such as Boethius (c. 480–524/6 CE) whose theories bear some affinity to those of the above-mentioned. These philosophers in no way regarded themselves as "Neo" Platonists, that is, as introducing innovations into Platonic philosophy. Rather, they thought of themselves as faithful disciples and exacting interpreters of Plato. There is, however, a certain tension between the roles of philosopher and scholar. As philosophers, the so-called Neoplatonists were not as much interested in accurately representing what Plato thought as they were in expounding the truths that they believed, as a matter of fact, Plato had most splendidly (but not exclusively) discovered. But since Plato communicated these truths in his writings and in his oral teachings, it was nevertheless essential to try to grasp their meaning, especially where this was not explicit. Hence, the primary commitment to philosophical truth necessitated scholarship with all its attendant problems. The unity of Neoplatonism, such as it is, consisted in fidelity to Plato as chief expounder of philosophical wisdom. The diversity within Neoplatonism – in some cases very considerable – is traceable in large part to the almost inevitable disputes arising from attempts to interpret Plato.

Neoplatonic Interpretations of Plato

Beginning with Plato's most famous disciple Aristotle and his contemporaries, conflicts arose about how to understand what Plato was teaching. It is worth trying to understand exactly why this should be so. Plato wrote dialogues, not treatises, and in these dialogues it is often far from evident exactly what conclusion their author wished the readers to draw. Sometimes, it is not even evident what "side" of a debate the author favored. Nevertheless, when one learns that Aristotle spent almost twenty years as an intimate of Plato, one naturally supposes that if there was any doubt in Aristotle's mind about what Plato meant in any of his writings, he could simply have asked him. For some matters, this was undoubtedly exactly what happened. But for many others, it was apparently not so straightforward. For one thing, Plato was at the center of a lively, intense, and highly sophisticated circle of thinkers, located in and around the "groves of Academe." His own thinking shaped and probably was shaped by the discussion that occurred there. Therefore, it would be risky to assume that whatever Plato thought when writing a particular dialogue (assuming we can know this unambiguously) reflected the course of his thinking afterward. In addition, Plato himself seems to hint in one dialogue, *Phaedrus*, and perhaps in one of his own letters, known as the seventh, that his writings do not reveal the entirety or the depths of his thinking about certain important matters.[1] So, it is not too difficult to see that, though Aristotle had available to him all Plato's writings and Plato himself as interlocutor, his accounts of *the* Platonic position were bound to be not entirely straightforward and unambiguous. Indeed, like the Neoplatonists themselves, Aristotle was first of all a philosopher. Therefore, he was not primarily interested in "getting Plato right" so much as he was in showing why *a*, if not *the*, Platonic position was mistaken.

Among Plato's associates were, besides Aristotle, many who called themselves disciples of Plato. Immediately after Plato's death in 347 BCE, the inherent difficulties in accurately representing Plato's views were inevitably exacerbated by the conflicts among those who wished to be known as Plato's most authentic inheritors. Both of Plato's immediate successors as "heads" of the Academy, Speusippus (c. 410–339 BCE) and Xenocrates (396/5–314/13 BCE), were, so far as we can tell from the very scanty evidence, independent thinkers, although later philosophers, including Neoplatonists, were tempted to use what they knew about these disciples of Plato as interpretative keys to understanding the master himself.

The subsequent history of Plato's Academy, from the perspective of the student of Neoplatonism, includes developments that further complicated direct access to "pristine" Platonism. Most important are the so-called "Middle Platonists," those philosophers and interpreters of Plato who, during the period of approximately 80 BCE–250 CE sought both to expound Plato's own thought as they understood it and to incorporate into Platonism various ideas arising from Platonism's nominal opponents, especially Stoics and Peripatetics. Though at first it seems surprising that self-declared Platonists would be receptive to the ideas of schools that were apparently quite hostile to Plato's distinctive doctrines, a closer look reveals some important insights into basic Neoplatonic assumptions.

What ancients generally took to be at the heart of Platonism was its commitment to an intelligible realm separated from the sensible world and to the immortality of the soul. The former commitment alone seems to leave open the possibility of various theories about how things work "here below." In fact, Plato in his extremely influential dialogue, *Timaeus* (29B–D), appeared to offer what he himself acknowledged was nothing more than a "likely story" about the structure of the sensible world. Accordingly, many later philosophers, though otherwise Platonically inclined, were prepared to accept Aristotelian or more generally Peripatetic accounts of the sensible world. They held that there was no contradiction in being a Platonist when it came to intelligible reality and an Aristotelian when it came to sensible reality. Thus, the seeds of one kind of syncretism – the blending of disparate theories – were sown in the period of the Middle Platonists.

In ethics, scholars have fairly consistently recognized in Plato's dialogues an element of rigorism or extremism, encapsulated in the claim that virtue is sufficient for happiness. Some scholars attribute this rigorism to Socrates or to a Socratic phase of Plato's philosophy. Indeed, the early Stoics took themselves to be following Socrates in their interpretation of the claim for the sufficiency of virtue for happiness. The Middle Platonists were more inclined to hold that whatever the historical Socrates believed, the dialogues of Plato represented Plato's own view. So, this ethical rigorism was naturally attributable to Plato and it was therefore rather easy to conclude that in basic ethical outlook Stoics and Platonists were in fundamental agreement.

Middle Platonists were neither naïve nor unsophisticated readers of Plato. They realized that a commitment to the existence of an immaterial or intelligible realm did for Plato have important implications for one's view of the sensible world. And they recognized that a commitment by Plato to the personal immortality of the soul, a doctrine rejected by both Stoics and Peripatetics, ought to have implications for ethics, implications that ought to be incompatible with Stoicism. A good deal of the history of Platonic interpretation in the period that includes the Middle Platonists can be told as the struggle to reinterpret either Plato, on the one hand, or Peripatetics and Stoics, on the other, in order to "harmonize" them. And here it should be added that I am not using the word "harmonize" pejoratively. Their efforts were in fact aimed at the construction of a philosophy that, though it be Platonic at the core, must be able to accommodate or incorporate truth discovered elsewhere.

Those who looked back to Plato for inspiration never supposed that Plato himself did not have his own sources. Socrates is the obvious one, but as Platonism developed in the early part of the Christian era, some philosophers began to focus on what they took to be the Pythagorean source for Plato's postulation of an intelligible world separate from the sensible world and for the derivation of the intelligible world of Forms itself from ultimate principles. In this, they were relying in part on Aristotle's own testimony which explicitly tells us that Plato was essentially a Pythagorean.[2] What came to be called "Neopythagoreanism" was both an independent revival of supposed Pythagorean ideas and a distinctive Middle Platonic approach to the interpretation of Plato. The two Middle Platonic figures who are of most importance to understanding Neoplatonism are Moderatus of Gades (c. 50–100 CE) and Numenius of Apamea (fl. mid-second century CE). In the extant fragments of Numenius' work "On the Good" two features of his interpretation of Plato are especially noteworthy. First, Numenius claimed that "Platonic" wisdom was just one version of a "perennial philosophy" that is found also in the Pythagoreans, Indian,

Egyptian, Jewish, and Persian writings.[3] This claim alone was of enormous importance in justifying for some efforts to interpret Plato by using sources of dubious
historical relevance. Second, Numenius apparently relying in part on a version of
Pythagoreanism, and in part relying on Plato's dialogues, his letters (including those
today regarded as spurious), and Aristotle's testimony about Plato's "unwritten
doctrines," argued for Plato's adherence to the derivation of the world from a triad
of fundamental principles or gods, the Good or the One, the Demiurge or creator
of the cosmos, and "the lower aspect of the Demiurge" a principle immanent in
nature.[4] As we shall see, the most important feature of this approach to "systematiz-
ing" Plato was its focus on the derivation of the sensible realm from the intelligible
and the subsequent elaboration of a hierarchical metaphysics.

Finally, mention should be made of the *Handbook of Platonism* by the mid-second
century CE Platonist Alcinous (previously identified with a philosopher named Albinus).
It is a concise but fairly comprehensive statement of how Platonism was understood
in the period before Plotinus. Notable in the *Handbook* is the identification of Forms
with thoughts in a divine mind and acceptance of the Aristotelian identification of
the Receptacle or "the nurse of becoming" of Plato's *Timaeus* (48E–49A) with
matter.[5] Alcinous apparently found it entirely natural to interpret Plato according to
Peripatetic and Stoic principles. Since, Alcinous was not a particularly original thinker
it is very likely that in his exposition of Platonism he was following well-established
practices.

Plotinus

We are unusually well informed about the life of Plotinus (204/5–270 CE) owing
to an extant biography of him by his pupil, the philosopher Porphyry (c. 232–
c. 305 CE). Briefly, Porphyry tells us that Plotinus was born in Egypt, probably to
a Greek family, but just possibly to a Hellenized Egyptian family. At the age of
twenty-eight, his passion for philosophy led him to Alexandria and to the feet of the
mysterious figure Ammonius Saccas. It may have been Ammonius who introduced
Plotinus to Platonic philosophy. Certainly, in later years Plotinus acknowledges the
considerable influence of Ammonius on his own philosophy. After about ten years
with his teacher, Plotinus conceived a plan to study Indian and Persian philosophy
by attaching himself to a military expedition of the emperor Gordian III. The
expedition self-destructed and his plan failed when Gordian was assassinated by his
troops. Reconsidering his options, Plotinus decided to move to Rome, where he
arrived in 245. There he remained until his death.

Porphyry informs us that for the first ten years of his life in Rome Plotinus
lectured exclusively on the philosophy of Ammonius, producing no personal writings. By the time Porphyry himself had arrived in Rome in 263, Plotinus, he tells us,
had written twenty-one of the works that were later to be collected by Porphyry in
the *Enneads*. The remainder of his works were written in the last seven or eight years
of his life.

The word "ennead" which Porphyry gave to his edition of Plotinus' writings is derived from the Greek word for the number "nine" and indicates the division of the writings into groups of nine. There are six of these groups, making fifty-four works in all, although the numbering and the total is artificial, since Porphyry divided certain works in order to arrive at the desired division. Although the division is not that of Plotinus himself, it is reasonable and clear. The first *Ennead* concerns ethical matters; while *Enneads* II and III include treatises in natural philosophy or physics broadly construed. The last three *Enneads* are metaphysical or focused on matters of first principles: *Ennead* IV collects the treatises on the soul; *Ennead* V is devoted to epistemological topics; and *Ennead* VI concerns matters relating to numbers, being, and the One. According to Porphyry, the treatises ascend from the earthly to the heavenly, from what is closer to mundane reality up to that which transcends this. Fortunately, Porphyry also gives us the chronological ordering of the works, but though this provides a great temptation to construct a developmental story about Plotinus' philosophy, in fact no one has made a case for development that has achieved anything like a consensus among scholars. I shall accordingly treat Plotinus' philosophy in the traditional manner as a unity.

We have already seen that Plotinus regarded himself unequivocally as a disciple of Plato. We have also seen some of the reasons why disputes arose over what constituted Platonic discipleship. Plotinus himself ruefully admits that Plato sometimes speaks "obscurely" and needs to be interpreted. In addition, by the middle of the third century of the Christian era, there had developed a long tradition of Stoic opposition to Platonic philosophy and a growing revival of Peripatetic opposition as well. Porphyry tells us that the *Enneads* are filled with "concealed" Peripatetic and Stoic doctrines.[6] These are not so much concealed as not explicitly attributed. In fact, the *Enneads* generally are soaked in the entire history of ancient Greek philosophy as Plotinus knew it. Part of the difficulty in understanding Plotinus is undoubtedly that he and his immediate readers were right in the middle of the discussion of familiar issues that we can sometimes only grasp obscurely. In any case, even a cursory reading of one of the *Enneads* shows that Plotinus regarded one of his principal tasks as defending Plato and Platonism against all opposition, especially that of the Stoics and Peripatetics. In facing this opposition, Plotinus took the important step of accepting Aristotle's testimony about Plato at face value. Nowhere does he challenge Aristotle's view of what Plato believed. Second, Plotinus was resolved to meet both the Peripatetics and Stoics head on. That is, he was prepared to defend the Platonism they rejected, in contrast to those whose defense of Plato seeks to show that his opponents have misunderstood him. Third, Plotinus was prepared to accept Peripatetic and Stoic doctrines wherever he thought they were not just not in contradiction to Plato but where they actually provided fresh insights into matters ignored or obscurely addressed by Plato himself. But the acceptance of Peripatetic and Stoic doctrines was in part a strategic move, for it enabled him to say that given the truth of what they say about this or that, other things they say, especially those things that directly contradict Plato, cannot be true.

For example, Aristotle in his *Metaphysics* offers as one reason for rejecting Plato's Forms that if Plato is right in separating Forms, then the essence of things will be separate from the things themselves.[7] This, says Aristotle, is absurd because the essence of something is what identifies it as the thing it is. Plotinus replies to this argument that it is correct to draw the inference from the separation of Forms that the essences of things are separate from the things themselves.[8] But what is absurd is not the implication that an essence should be so separated but that an individual sensible thing should be identical with an essence. Consequently, Plotinus infers that it is Aristotle, not Plato, who is wrong: sensible things are not identical with their essences, but only participate in them, and can even change their identities by exchanging essences. In short, Plotinus is prepared to accept the implications for the sensible world of making the intelligible world the real world.

The starting point for understanding Plotinus' interpretation of Plato or, if one likes, for understanding the foundation of Neoplatonism, are the reasons for the postulation of a first principle of all. In the first place, Plotinus is confident that, on the basis of the *Republic*'s postulation of a superordinate Form of the Good and on the corroboration provided by the second *Epistle*'s oblique reference to a triad of first, second, and third gods, and a traditional interpretation of *Parmenides*, especially its second part, Plato himself was committed to such a principle. In addition, and in opposition to Aristotle, Plotinus believed that he could show that, though Aristotle agreed that there must be a first principle of all, namely, his Unmoved Mover, he was wrong in thinking that an Unmoved Mover could be an absolutely first principle of all.[9] Plotinus' reason for rejecting Aristotle's version of the first principle is the best entrée to Plotinus' independent argument.

The first principle of all must be unqualifiedly simple, not merely unique. Aristotle's god is unique. It must be utterly simple because if it is not, then its parts, whatever these might be, would be ontologically prior to it and hence it would not be a first principle. The simplicity of the first principle requires an identity between *what* the first principle is and the fact *that* it is. If this were not so, then there could exist two first principles. That is, there could be two absolutely simple things that differed only in being two. But in order to be different, there would have to be some feature or attribute that would make them different and then they would not be absolutely simple. Analogous to Plato's reason in *Republic* X (597C–D) for claiming that a Form must be unique, if there were two putative first principles, what they had in common must really be the first.

Why, though, must there be *any* first principle of all? The answer to this excellent question requires an understanding that for Plotinus, as well as for virtually the entire Greek philosophical tradition, an ontological principle is a principle of explanation and as such, a cause. In short, Plotinus accepts as legitimate the questions "What explains the orderly existing world?" or "Why is there anything at all rather than nothing?" If there is no first principle of all, these are illegitimate questions. The acceptance or rejection of the legitimacy of these questions constitutes a dispute at a very deep level, but it is worth pointing out that Plotinus' position is actually made stronger by the fact that all he needs to insist on is the *possibility* of an explanation and what his opponents need to insist on is the *impossibility*. It is not even clear how the latter claim could be made good, whereas Plotinus' entire metaphysics is in effect a working out of the possibility.

The first principle of all is variously named by Plotinus. It can be called "the One" but he is quick to add that this is an illegitimate name, a name that supposes that "oneness" is the essence of the first principle.[10] In fact, the first principle is "beyond essence" in the sense that it is not a kind of thing. It can also be called "the Good" or "god" or given all sorts of honorifics, so long as it is understood that these are taken to indicate that the first principle is the ultimate cause of essence, goodness, and so on. The difficulty of describing or in general talking about the first principle of all, a difficulty Plotinus reflects upon at some length, is the origin of what later in the tradition came to be called "negative theology," a way of talking about the divine by "saying what it is not." The difficulty of referring to the first principle is also the origin of disputes within the Neoplatonic tradition, disputes centering largely on whether even the positing of a first principle undercuts its simplicity and so requires a more ultimate principle that cannot even be referred to. Henceforth, I am going to refer to the first principle of Plotinus as "the One" in line with Plotinus' own usage and most of the commentators.

The way the later Neoplatonic tradition generally came to formulate the problem that arises once one has posited an absolutely first principle of all is, unfortunately, not especially edifying. Typically, the question was "How does one derive a many from the One?" The answers usually given were not as odd as the question itself, which might reasonably be answered by saying that in fact we cannot "derive" a many from an absolutely simple One anymore than we can really make a rabbit appear in a hat where it was nowhere before. The most common metaphor used by the Neoplatonists themselves for the derivation was "emanation." But this metaphor has caused no end of confusion both within and outside the tradition.

Plotinus and the other Neoplatonists did not understand their question as one about generation in time or about how something comes from nothing. They did not understand emanation in this way. Plotinus, like *all* his predecessors and successors within the pagan Greek philosophical tradition accepted as an axiom Parmenides' claim that deriving something from nothing was not just impossible but literally inconceivable.[11] The derivation of the many, or of anything not absolutely simple, from the first principle of all, was a derivation according to atemporal ontological dependence. Sometimes this derivation is compared to the way a line is derived from a point or a solid figure is derived from a plane figure, that is, by projection. Perhaps less misleading is a comparison with the way a mathematical formula is related to all the instantiations of it, for example, the way $x = 2y$ is related to $4 = 2 \times 2$, $6 = 2 \times 3$, $8 = 2 \times 4$, etc. The key point here is that the derivation is *not* the unfolding or emptying of an ultimate ontological closet somehow belonging to the One. To suppose otherwise would be to deny the unqualified simplicity of the One. Neither is the derivation to be understood as somehow the development of something which existed – though only potentially – in the first principle. This is absurd both because even the complexity sufficient to make any meaningful claim that many things were potentially in the One would import a complexity into it and because a potency is prior to an actuality *only* in a temporal ordering. So, when Plotinus says, "the One is the *dynamis* of all" he does not mean it is potentially all things but that it is *virtually* all things, that is, it has the power to (atemporally) cause them to be or, what amounts to the same thing, sustain them in existence.[12] The idea of virtuality is fairly precise. For example, the premises of a valid deductive argument contain together virtually their conclusion. A properly functioning calculator contains virtually all the answers to the mathematical questions that its rules allow it to be asked. White light is virtually all the colors of the rainbow. An omniscient simple deity may be said to know virtually all that is knowable.

The first thing that is derived from the One, or, as Plotinus puts it, that which is closest to the One in virtue of its relative simplicity, is the second principle of all, the locus of the intelligible realm. This is the realm of Plato's Forms and an eternal Intellect. Two basic questions immediately arise. First, why do the Forms need a first principle to sustain them and second, why is an eternal Intellect insinuated in the second principle. Both questions have relatively straightforward answers according to Plotinus. Historically, Plotinus would rely on the account of the Demiurge and the evidently all-inclusive Form of the Intelligible Animal in the *Timaeus* (30C) as evidence for the coexistence of Intellect and Forms. A crucial passage in the *Sophist* (248E–249B) is also adduced by Neoplatonists generally to buttress the claim of the inseparability of Intellect from Forms. In addition, Plotinus accepts Aristotle's reasoning toward his first principle of all, though as we have seen, he denies that it is first. And this reasoning leads to an Intellect which, as Plotinus interprets it, contains all intelligible reality within it.

Philosophically, Plotinus' reply to the first question is that unless the first principle of all virtually unites all the Forms, the necessary complexity of eternal truth is left unexplained. It is not sufficient, for Plotinus, merely to hold that, say, threeness and oddness are necessarily connected such that any group of three is necessarily odd. There must be some eternal fact that explains all real or *possible* instances or examples of necessary truth. This eternal fact is of course not that three and odd are the same thing, but that there is one "thing" that is virtually both of them and of which they are parts or aspects. An apt analogy is the necessary connectedness of three-dimensionality and solidity. These are necessarily connected because there is one thing, call it a "body" that is virtually all its necessary attributes, including three-dimensionality and solidity. Part of what it is to be a body is to be three-dimensional and another part is to be solid. The virtual identity of all the Forms in the One is made more plausible by Plotinus' assumption of their *reductive* identity. That is, it is not part of the theory of Forms, whether in Plato or Plotinus, to hold that there must be Forms corresponding to every word in the language. Scientists, both ancient and modern, typically reduce the referents of ordinary language terms to more basic scientific or mathematical terms. When a scientist says that what is ordinarily taken to be X is *really* Y, he is offering a reduction. The reduction of a plethora of hypothetical Forms to mathematical or at least more basic units was evidently an intra-Academic project, as reported by Aristotle.[13]

Plotinus' reply to the question about the insinuation of an Intellect into the intelligible realm is essentially that without an eternal knower there could be no eternal truth such as is expressed in necessary propositions. It is not enough that the One be virtually all the Forms. Without an eternal knower or intellect, the diversity of that which the One is virtually would not be actual. Stated otherwise, without an eternal knower, the question "What is the ontological basis for the truth that, say, the number 3 is odd?" could only be the One. But the One is absolutely simple and the complexity of the eternal truth would only be virtually grounded, so to speak, not actually grounded.

If, then, an eternal knower is required to be eternally contemplating all eternal truth, who is this knower? Plotinus posits as second principle of all what he calls *Nous* or Intellect which is naturally if not explicitly in the texts, identifiable with the Demiurge of Plato's *Timaeus* (29Dff) and the eternal *Nous* of *Philebus* (22C3).[14] But Plotinus also holds, controversially even among later Neoplatonists, that the intellects of each person are "undescended," that is, eternally engaged in contemplation of truth and that we can "access" these incarnately when we grasp images or concepts of these truths.

Intellect is the principle of essence or whatness or intelligibility in the world as the One is the principle of being. Intellect is an eternal instrument of the One's ultimate causality. That is, the dependence of any kind of thing is an ultimate dependence on the One through Intellect which explains, paradigmatically or by exemplary causality, what that thing is. Thus, it is basically the same thing if we say that Helen is beautiful owing to the Form of Beauty or owing to Intellect. However, we must add that without the One, an image or copy of the Form or of Intellect could not exist. So, Intellect needs the One for its paradigmatic causality to produce anything at all and the One needs Intellect as instrument of its power to make anything to be. Insofar as our intellects are doing eternally what Intellect is doing, we are in a sense united with it.

The third of the three fundamental principles of reality is Soul.[15] The principle Soul is introduced not exactly to explain life, for the activity of Intellect is the highest form of life, but to explain something slightly different. For Plotinus, all life involves desire, but the desire of Intellect for union with intelligible reality is eternally satisfied. Indeed, Intellect achieves union with the One in the only way it can, by eternally contemplating all that the One is virtually. But fundamentally different is the desire that is not satisfiable except by "going outside" of oneself. The principle of Soul is what accounts for the desire of anything that can have desires for objects or goals that require those things to "go outside" themselves. Every desire other than the desire of Intellect (or our intellects) has an object something other than itself. I mean that whereas Intellect is eternally identical with its objects and so its objects are parts of what it is, all other desires, including cognitive have as objects something other than the subject of desire. For example, desiring to acquire a true belief is a desire to have an image or array of concepts in the soul. But the desire is satisfied by an identity with the concept that is only an image of the identity of Intellect with Forms. Even more clearly, a desire for food or sex or friendship when satisfied results in the subject of desire being identified by a psychic state that is only an image of an eternal ideal. The seeking that arises from desire and the being content or satisfied that arises from achievement of what is desired could not be explained by Intellect because there is a fundamental difference between the "static" state of Intellect and its images and the "dynamic" state of desire for externals.

Intellect *could* explain my being in some cognitive state but it could not explain my desiring to be in that state.

Just as Intellect is an instrument of the One so Soul is an instrument of Intellect and the One. It is owing to Intellect that, say, a plant has the nature it has, but it is owing to Soul that we can account for the plant's desiring activity, that is, its desire to grow and flourish. It should thus be clear that Soul is not a principle of self-conscious desire or even of what we would understand as intelligent desire. It is the principle of all living activity apart from the intellectual.

It is not easy to answer the question whose soul is the principle of Soul. It is certainly not the soul of the divine Intellect, which is beyond the desiring that Soul explains. It does not seem to be personal at all. In fact, it is difficult to see any difference between the principle of Soul and a Form of Soul, though it must be admitted that Plotinus is frustratingly vague when discussing this principle. There is nothing against the principle Soul not being *a* soul just as there is nothing against the Form of Tallness not being tall.

The three principles or, as Plotinus sometimes called them, *hypostases*, are the starting points for addressing the entire array of philosophical issues that he inherited from what was by then something like an 800 year long tradition. The term *hypostasis* means roughly "extra-mental existence" or "existents" in the plural. When Plotinus raises a question about the *hypostasis* of X, he is usually not in doubt that X exists in some way, but he is intent on arguing that a Platonic account of X's existence, as opposed to the account of some other philosopher, is to be affirmed. Whether Plotinus is addressing ethical, epistemological, or cosmological questions, the three principles or hypostases provide the basic explanatory categories within which answers are to be expressed. There is, however, a further principle which is not an entity of some sort like the One, Intellect, and Soul but more like a fundamental rule of operation. This rule is that the One naturally and inevitably produces (with the instrumentality of Intellect and Soul), but that all things that are produced naturally and inevitably strive to reunite with the One. This rhythm of production and return suffuses all Neoplatonism and provides the fundamental value criteria. That is, goodness and badness generally can be identified with relative proximity to union with the One, according to the ability of things to achieve such union.

All of human existence can be viewed as a drama about separation and return. Human beings are souls or persons in bodies. In Plotinus' hierarchical universe, incarnate human beings are like prodigal children, struggling to recover their birthright. As Plotinus puts it at the beginning of his famous treatise V.1 "On the Three Primary Hypostases," "What is it, then, which has made the souls forget their father, god, and be ignorant of themselves and him, even though they are parts which come from his higher world and altogether belong to it?" It will be recalled that souls "belong to" the higher world in the sense that their intellects are "undescended." Forgetfulness and ignorance characterize the incarnate human from the beginning. Even more strikingly, human beings suffer from two delusions which on the surface appear contradictory but which for Plotinus are really the same thing. They have "contempt for themselves" owing to which they are ignorant of the divine and yet they "wish to belong to themselves." The two human defects are really misperceptions of one's true identity.

Plotinus says that humans have contempt for themselves because one has contempt for that which one regards as inferior. But humans in seeking or desiring things "outside themselves," essentially material goods, implicitly declare themselves inferior to these things or to the states they would be in when they had them. Their wish to belong to themselves is based on the mistaken belief about autonomy, a mistaken belief that leads to self-contempt. Humans habitually believe that their good or happiness is achieved by satisfying their idiosyncratic desires. But if the true person is the immortal intellect, its good is the opposite of the idiosyncratic, for its good is cognitive identification with eternal truth which is the same for everyone. If humans wished to belong to their *true* selves, their orientation would not be "downward" towards the objects of desire, but "upward" in the direction of their undescended intellects.

It should be evident that self-identity is a fundamental moral as well as psychological theme for Plotinus. Consider the biblical woman Ruth who, widowed and childless, abandons her own country and faith to accompany her mother-in-law, Naomi, to Bethlehem. She says to Naomi, "Your people shall be my people and your God shall be my God." Just so, Plotinus says humans must abandon their pseudo-identities and self-consciously embrace their true identities as intellects. Obviously, the recognition Plotinus urges one to have is or is based upon philosophical argument. In this way, we can see precisely what a philosophical religion means for Neoplatonism generally. This is not to say of course that Neoplatonists, including Plotinus and especially Proclus were not very receptive to more traditional religious practices. Still, for them these must be viewed in the light of the philosophical conversion they thought was essential to ultimate happiness.

All actions are considered by Plotinus according to whether they contribute to the necessary reorientation or whether they inure one further to disorientation. Viewed thus, it seems less paradoxical to hear Plotinus say that virtue is not the most important thing in life, though in saying this he is not of course commending the opposite.[16] Rather, he is making the point that the classical virtues are molded around incarnate life and its betterment, something towards which the Stoics were more or less indifferent. Plotinus notes, rather wryly, that it would be strange to wish that a child would fall off a boat so that we could practice virtue in saving it. Would it not be better if we did not have to practice the virtue at all? This is naturally a rather tendentious example and once again Plotinus is not suggesting that refraining from saving the child would be right. He is, rather, looking to something which he characterizes as beyond virtue, or at least beyond moral virtue.

Plotinus does three things that may be thought to have turned his Platonism into Neoplatonism. First, he made explicit what he took to be the clear implications of things said, sometimes *en passant*, in Plato's dialogues. Second, he tried to defend Plato against his opponents with arguments and distinctions drawn from the opponents themselves. Third, he tried to incorporate into his Platonism the truths he thought Peripatetics and Stoics and others had revealed.

Neoplatonism after Plotinus

Porphyry and Iamblichus

When we move from Plotinus to his successors within the Neoplatonic tradition, the terrain shifts in many significant ways. First, we have very few complete works of the philosophers after Plotinus and before Proclus, and for none of Plotinus' successors do we possess the entirety of their prodigious outputs. So, frequently we are dealing with fragments or worse, indirect testimony from other, sometimes hostile witnesses. Second, the tendency to incorporate Aristotelianism into Platonism became more pronounced adding immeasurably to the complications in understanding the Neoplatonic authors. Third, a different sort of shift in terrain is occasioned by the growth of Christianity, culminating in this period in the conversion of Constantine the Great and the establishment of the Eastern or Byzantine empire. This social and political circumstance is reflected in various efforts to consolidate and defend a philosophical form of pagan theology. What this means is that although Neoplatonists generally were not interested in politics or in ethics as a locus of philosophical problems, they were intensely interested in philosophical theology and religious practices. This is deeply evident in their writings. For these reasons, the differences between Plotinus on the one hand, and Porphyry (234 to c. 305 CE) and Iamblichus (c. 245–325 CE) on the other need to be stressed within a survey of Neoplatonism. In fact, many of the doctrines and interests that are typically recognized as Neoplatonic are in fact more correctly traceable to Porphyry and Iamblichus than to Plotinus himself.

What we know about the life of Porphyry can be very briefly stated. He was a Phoenician by birth, educated first in Athens by the Platonist Longinus. He came to Rome in 263 where he met Plotinus and joined his circle of pupils. During the last three years of Plotinus' life, Porphyry was in Sicily. We do not know whether he returned to Rome and if so, when. In about 300 he produced the edition of the works of Plotinus which we use today. He died about 305.

Porphyry was a remarkably erudite man, wide-ranging in his interests and multilingual. He wrote commentaries on various works of both Plato and Aristotle and a work that is extant, *Isagoge* or "Introduction" to Aristotle's *Organon*. This last-mentioned work was immensely influential in the West owing especially to Boethius' translation and commentary on it and on the growing interest in Aristotle's logical treatises. He also wrote a treatise *On Abstinence* arguing for vegetarianism, a *Life of Pythagoras* which was part of a larger history of philosophy, an extant letter of moral instruction to his wife, *To Marcella*, an allegorical exegesis of part of Homer, *On the Cave of the Nymphs*, an epitome of Plotinian metaphysics called *Sentences Leading to the Intelligible World*, a very influential work *Against the Christians*, and three other major works dealing with religion: *On the Return of the Soul*, *Philosophy from Oracles*, and *Letter to Anebo*. There are also fragments of many other works.

Porphyry's *Isagoge* is emblematic of the tendency that grew over the next 300 years within Neoplatonism to "assign" to Aristotle philosophical mastery over the sensible world and to Plato philosophical mastery over the intelligible world. Accordingly, among the Neoplatonists the course of study leading to what was regarded as an authentically Platonic mystical union with the divine began with a study of Aristotle's *Organon*. The ascent to the divine properly began with logic. Although Porphyry did not intend his *Isagoge* to be more than an occasional work illuminating some basic concepts found especially in Aristotle's *Topics*, it became a keystone to the amalgamation of Aristotelianism and Platonism that became later Neoplatonism. At the beginning of the work, Porphyry says that understanding the nature of genus, differentia, species, property, and accident seems useful both for scientific demonstration and for (Platonic) division, thereby nicely avoiding what is clear to us, namely, that Aristotle rejected Platonic division as a method for doing science, in part because Plato did not have the necessary concepts of genus, species, and so on. Most portentously, Porphyry distinguishes a metaphysical treatment of genus, species, and so on, from their logical treatment, implying that the former would be or should be Platonic in orientation, not Aristotelian. In making this distinction, he provided the beginning of a justification for a division between Platonic and Aristototelian preeminence somewhat more sophisticated than that between the sensible and intelligible worlds, namely, between the metaphysical and the logical. In his *Sentences* and in his lost commentaries on Aristotle, Porphyry displays this strategy for harmonizing Plato and Aristotle with Plotinian categories.

Porphyry seems to have regarded himself as an "orthodox" Plotinian, hence as an "orthodox" Platonist, but it is hardly surprising that he found himself in need of interpreting Plotinus in order to defend him. In so doing he takes up positions which later Neoplatonists including Iamblichus and *his* disciples, regarded as indefensible or insufficiently nuanced. Scholars have frequently noted Iamblichus' complaint that Porphyry tended to collapse Plotinus' fundamental three hypostases, that is, that he did not sufficiently distinguish the real difference between One, Intellect, and Soul. Since much of later Neoplatonism revolves around such distinctions and their obliteration or multiplication, it is worth getting clear what the underlying issue was.

We can talk about something from different perspectives. We can say that this man is a father or brother or that he is an American or a mammal, and so on. But we are talking about one thing all the same. Or we can talk about two really different things, like this man and that man. Or, we can talk about really different or irreducible parts or aspects of one thing, like the man's shape and his weight or the man himself and his color. The first way of talking involves a mental or conceptual distinction, the second a real distinction among entities and the third, a real distinction within one entity. The threefold division of distinctions is relatively unproblematic within the sensible world. Within the intelligible world, it is an entirely different story.

Are Forms really distinct as separate entities or are they really distinct parts of one entity, say, Intellect? Is Intellect really distinct in either way from Soul or even from a soul? Is the One itself really distinct from Intellect and from everything else? This is an issue we saw broached in trying to understand emanation. Again, if, say,

Intellect and Forms are really distinct, are further real distinctions mandated, such as between the act of thinking Forms and the thoughts themselves? Is there a difference within the intelligible realm between a distinction *between* entities and a distinction *within* an entity? In order to begin to see the scope of this issue, one might reflect on the fact that Christian Trinitarian theology, Neoplatonic in origin, must struggle with the same questions. Indeed, the diversity of opinions on this matter reflects the diversity of opinions on the real complexity of the intelligible world within Neoplatonism.

Porphyry was criticized by Iamblichus for, as A. C. Lloyd put it, "telescoping" the hypostases, that is, treating Soul and Intellect as really one thing, though conceptually distinct. More significantly, if a fragment of a commentary on Plato's *Parmenides* is corrected attributed to Porphyry, he telescoped One and Intellect. The fragments do seem to make clear that One and Intellect are distinct, but the above discussion should make us ask whether the distinction is conceptual or real. Porphyry's answer to this question is not entirely clear. He does insist that Intellect is other than the One but that the One is not other than Intellect and he does so in order to maintain the simplicity of the One. For if the One *were* other than Intellect, it would have to have the complexity to be other *and* self-existing. We can see in these reflections some of the thinking behind the separation of logic and metaphysics, for logical distinctions, such as genus and species, are all conceptual. And we can also perhaps see that a real distinction within the intelligible realm is not so easily represented as a distinction among entities.

About Iamblichus we have, really, only scraps of knowledge. He was a Syrian by birth and evidently lived most of his life there. He apparently studied under Porphyry – whether in Rome or elsewhere we do not know – but certainly knew his works very well. His extant works are *Protrepticus* (essentially a collection of passages from earlier philosophers' exhortations to philosophy, especially extensive fragments of Aristotle's work by the same name), a large part of *On the Pythagorean Life*, *On the Egyptian Mysteries* (really a reply to Porphyry's *Letter to Anebo*), and several mathematical works. We possess only fragments of his various other works, including his influential commentaries both on works of Aristotle and on some central Platonic dialogues. We must rely on the testimony of later Neoplatonists to fill in the blanks regarding many of his philosophical views.

Iamblichus is certainly the most influential figure in one aspect of Neoplatonism, namely, the religious. In his work *On the Egyptian Mysteries*, Iamblichus declares the insufficiency of philosophical thought alone for salvation.[17] Rather, theurgic practices are necessary, that is, specific religious ritual acts that can provide access to the divine, especially for those incapable of philosophy. In the development and defense of theurgy, Iamblichus relied heavily on the authority of a document known as the *Chaldean Oracles*, written some time in the second century CE. This fragmentary collection of verses, deeply imbued with an amalgam of Middle Platonic ideas, has been described as a manual of pagan sacramentalism. Iamblichus, it might be said, not only insisted on the essential harmony of Plato with Pythagoras and Aristotle, but also with Homer, Hesiod, Orpheus, and the wisdom of the *Chaldean Oracles*.

It is particularly easy to misconstrue Iamblichus in this matter. His theurgic Platonism is not fairly represented as gratuitous popularization of elitist philosophy. Indeed, he railed against what he took to be the arrogance of some Platonists. Theurgy was for him the natural progression of Platonism understood in a deeply traditional fashion. Iamblichus would have no doubt sympathized with Numenius, the forerunner of Neoplatonism, who is reported to have remarked that Plato was just Moses speaking Attic Greek.[18] Thus, Iamblichus sought to create a kind of nonparticularist or nonethnocentric set of ritual practices that completely opened the hierarchical Platonic universe to human participation. Indeed, for him his "church" was the physical universe itself. At the end of his *On the Egyptian Mysteries*, he expressly rejects a conflation of theurgy with magic saying that theurgists do not bother themselves or the gods with trivialities; rather, they are concerned solely with the purification, liberation, and salvation of individual souls.

The philosophy behind the theurgy was, so Iamblichus argued, Plato's primarily as understood by Plotinus (who himself needed to be properly understood). Porphyry, said Iamblichus, had gone astray in his interpretations. A concise statement of the basic principle of Iamblichus' metaphysics is this: conceptual distinctions legitimately applied to the intelligible world must rest on real distinctions. The principle can be illustrated from Iamblichus' understanding of a fundamental problem in Plato's theory of Forms. If, as Plato says, Forms are separate from, that is, ontologically independent of the sensible world, still, it is owing to the instrumental causality of Forms that sensibles have the similarities and differences they have. So, for example, if "Helen is beautiful" is true, this is because there is beauty in her in some way. But the Form of Beauty is not in her because it is separate. So, we must make a distinction between the nature of beauty and the Form of Beauty. Indeed, we must further distinguish between the nature of beauty as it exists in the Form and the nature of beauty as it exists in Helen. The Form is unparticipated, that is, transcendent. What is participated in by Helen is the nature of the Form, in some fashion. In general, Iamblichus would insist that within the intelligible world we must recognize real distinctions between unparticipated and participated principles and the mode of participation in the latter.

As applied to the Platonic One, we must distinguish an unparticipated, utterly transcendent One from the nature of the One that is participated in. Intellect is the result of participation in this latter One. So, as a matter of basic principle we must distinguish within each order of causality within the intelligible realm (a) a first unparticipated principle; (b) this principle insofar as it is participated in; and (c) the "reflection" of (b) in the participant. Applying the basic principle to Soul, we must say that soul participates not in unparticipated Intellect but only in the nature of Intellect and thus possesses it as a reflection of that in which it participates. Accordingly, and most importantly access to the intelligible realm for individual souls is only indirect via images or reflections of unparticipated Intellect and its contents, the Forms. On this basis, Iamblichus rejected the Plotinian claim that our true intellects, those which are contemplating the Forms, were undescended.

Alexandrian and Athenian schools

Neoplatonism after Iamblichus is generally understood to have divided into two "schools," the Alexandrian and the Athenian. We know practically nothing about philosophy in Alexandria between the time of Ammonius Saccas, the teacher of Plotinus, and the end of the fourth century CE. We are only slightly better informed about philosophy beginning at that time. We know a bit about the mathematician Theon of Smyrna and his daughter, the infamous Hypathia (c. 375–415 CE), whose evidently outspoken pagan philosophizing earned her martyrdom at the hands of local Christians. Hypatia's pupil, Synesius of Cyrene, evidently getting the message, converted to Christianity. A more definite succession of philosophical leadership can be traced within the sixth century CE, culminating in two Christian Neoplatonists, Elias and David. In 610 their successor Stephanus moved to Constantinople where he became the head of the Imperial Academy. This marks the official establishment of Christian Neoplatonism in the Eastern empire. In 641, Alexandria fell to the Muslim conquerors. That date may be said to mark the beginning of Islamic Neoplatonism. It was owing in large part to the Muslims' interest in drafting the best of pagan philosophy into the service of Islam that the Neoplatonic texts available in Alexandria at the time got translated and thus preserved. Ironically perhaps, the receptiveness of Iamblichus and others to a harmonizing of Greek and non-Greek sources of wisdom made the philosophy that Muslim thinkers found in Alexandria especially congenial to their aims. In early Islamic philosophy efforts to harmonize Platonism (i.e., Neoplatonism) with Aristotelianism are especially evident.

Since almost none of the philosophical texts of Alexandrian Neoplatonists have survived, it is exceedingly difficult to take the measure of their systematic thought, with some notable exceptions, above all John Philoponus (c. 490–570 CE) and Simplicius (c. 490–560 CE). These two immensely learned philosophers and commentators were two of the major participants in the battle between pagan, that is, essentially Neoplatonic philosophy and the ascendant Christian philosophy. Philoponus was a Christian who was prepared to accept as much of Aristotelianism as he could within the framework of his Christianized Platonism. His critical commentaries on the works of Aristotle were especially revered by Arab thinkers. Simplicius was an uncompromising defender of a sophisticated Neoplatonism that was aimed against Christianizing innovation. Typical of Simplicius' approach is his commentary on Aristotle's *De caelo* which aims both to assimilate the teaching of this work to Plato's *Timaeus* and to show the superiority of the resultant position to that of Philoponus who, as a Christian, denied the eternity of the world and the distinctive material nature of the superlunary bodies.

Athenian Neoplatonism begins for us in the fifth century CE with Plutarch of Athens (?–432 CE), his pupil Syrianus (d. c. 437 CE), and his most famous pupil Proclus (412–85 CE). All of the works of Plutarch are lost and of Syrianus we have only part of his commentary on Aristotle's *Metaphysics*. In this commentary he continues the tradition of harmonizing Aristotle with Plato, but where Aristotle explicitly diverges from Plato, as in his rejection of the theory of Forms, Syrianus defends Plato.

Unquestionably, Proclus is the major figure of the Athenian school. His immense output, of which we possess a great deal, represents a sort of *summa* of Neoplatonism. Proclus was born in Constantinople in 412 and trained in Alexandria. In 430 he came to Athens to study with Plutarch and then Syrianus where he remained for the rest of his life. He became the head of the Athenian school in 437 at the death of Syrianus. Among his works that are extant at least in some substantial part are commentaries on Plato's *Alcibiades I, Cratylus, Republic, Timaeus*, and *Parmenides*, as well as commentaries on the works of Homer, Euclid, and Ptolemy. There is a five-volume work *Platonic Theology* that constitutes the most complete statement of Proclus' philosophy; the enormously valuable handbook *Elements of Theology, Hymns*, and *Elements of Physics*, as well as monographs on providence, fate, and evil, and a treatise on the eternity of the world. There is also a defense of Plato's *Timaeus* against Aristotle's attacks on it. We also know that he wrote commentaries on many other Platonic dialogues, on the works of Aristotle, on Plotinus' *Enneads*, and the *Chaldean Oracles*, though these are all lost. It is often said that Proclus was not an original thinker and that his version of Neoplatonism was especially dependent on Iamblichus and Syrianus. It is perhaps questionable whether his manifest synthesizing skill and exegetical ingenuity are not to be counted as evidence of originality. In any case, the surviving works of Proclus have provided a significant part of our knowledge about Neoplatonism after Plotinus.

Though in most matters Proclus is generally regarded to have been working out the theories of Iamblichus and Syrianus, what is distinctive about his thought can best be understood if we begin with the issue in which he opposed Iamblichus, namely, in the postulation of an ineffable One above the first principle. Proclus took a different approach. He argued that the One itself was unparticipated in order to preserve its absolute simplicity.[19] Instead, virtuality was vested in a plethora of principles named (whether by Proclus or Iamblichus or Syrianus before him) "Henads," literally "Ones" or "Unities."[20] What exactly do these Henads explain?

Henads are the entities whose natures are participated in by anything that *has* a nature of any sort. Clearly, the fundamental distinction employed by Proclus is that which is found in the distinction between a Form and its nature, though Proclus is insistent that Henads themselves are not just Forms. If, for example, one were to posit the existence of the property of sameness in the world, the explanation for this must be the eternal existence of the nature of sameness. But in order for things really to be the same, they must share in sameness. What they share in or participate in, however, namely, the nature, must be really distinct from the entity which explains the very possibility of the participating. This is the Henad.[21]

If we go to the second principle, Intellect, we saw that for Plotinus it is analyzable into an Intellect contemplating Forms. So, a Henad is needed to explain Intellect and others are needed to explain Forms. In addition, however, Proclus represents the Athenian school as insisting that a further distinction between intellectual activity itself and the achievement of intellection or intellectual life must be made. For life, then, another Henad must be posited. The Henads thus become the "intermediaries" linking the One and the second hypostasis and, indirectly, everything else that participates in the second. The (unparticipated) One is absolutely unknowable, whereas the Henads are knowable only by their effects. In addition, the infinite complexity within the second hypostasis, namely, the complexity of Forms, must be accounted for one-to-one by Henads. Similarly, there must be Henads to account for different kinds of souls and different kinds of intellect. The Henads themselves are ordered and graded according to the "reach" of their causal power. Thus, the Henad that accounts for being is all-encompassing, but the Henad that accounts for, say, the life of nonintelligent animals is lower because it is less comprehensive.

Undoubtedly, one's initial alarm at the proliferation of Henads is exacerbated by discovering that Proclus correlates each of these with the traditional Greek gods. Or perhaps it is more accurate to say that he rationalizes traditional Greek religion by identifying the gods with metaphysical principles. His *Platonic Theology* is thus a highly elaborate attempt to show the philosophical, that is, Platonic, basis and the true rationality of traditional Greek religion. In this regard the central role of the late Neoplatonic interpretation of Plato's *Parmenides* should be mentioned. It was this dialogue especially that provided the evidence for the Neoplatonic systematization of the intelligible world. It would be a serious mistake, however, to suppose that Proclus' treatment of the gods was simply a rationalizing exercise. Both in his religious writings and in the extant accounts of his personal life, his genuine religious sentiment is manifest. His devotion to theurgy was no less intense than that of Iamblichus.

It is appropriate that we end with mention of the last so-called head of the Neoplatonic Academy in Athens, Damascius. It was he who was at least the leading figure at the time of the edict by the emperor Justinian in 529 CE to end the teaching of pagan philosophy. Damascius appears to have followed the by then well-entrenched tradition of making Aristotle the focus of teaching regarding the visible world and Plato master of the invisible. Damascius is the author of an extant very long and difficult work *On Principles* which shows that disputes among the Neoplatonists in the interpretation of Plato still existed. In particular, Damascius quarreled with Proclus' interpretation of Plato's *Parmenides* and reverted to Iamblichus' postulation of an ineffable first principle above the One. The utter conceptual and linguistic unavailability of the first principle of all led Damascius to some surprisingly modern-sounding reflections on the inadequacies of language and thought for achieving metaphysical knowledge.

Neoplatonism after Damascius and his pupil Simplicius entered a new phase based on the interaction of pagan Greek philosophy generally with the great traditions of revealed religion. Naturally enough, the available robust body of reflection on and analysis of immaterial reality provided philosophers within these religions traditions with a vast array of conceptual tools and problems.

Notes

1   See *Phaedrus* 274C; *Seventh Epistle*, 341Dff.
2   See *Metaphysics* A 6.987a30ff.
3   See fr. 1 (des Places 1973).

4 See frs. 15, 16, and 21 (des Places 1973).
5 See cc. 8, 10 (Dillon 1993).
6 See Porphyry's *Life of Plotinus*, c.14, ll. 4–6, usually printed at the beginning of editions of the *Enneads*.
7 See *Metaphysics* Z 6.1031a30–b18.
8 See *Ennead* VI 3, esp. cc.1–8.
9 See V 6.1.1–14.
10 See V 5.6.24–30.
11 See Parmenides, fr. 8.
12 See, e.g., V 3.15.33.
13 See *Metaphysics* A 9.991b10–27; M 7–9.
14 On the three fundamental principles, see generally V 1. On Intellect esp., see V 9.
15 See esp. IV 1–2.
16 See I 2.4.
17 See esp. Book I, c.2 (des Places 1966) for the distinction between philosophy and theurgy.
18 See fr. 8 (des Places, 1973).
19 See his *Elements of Theology*, Prop. 116 (Dodds 1963).
20 On Proclus' doctrine of Henads see esp. *The Elements of Theology* (Dodds 1963), Props. 113–65; *Commentary on Plato's Parmenides* (Morrow and Dillon 1987), Book VI 1043–52.
21 See *The Elements of Theology* (Dodds 1963), Prop. 23, for a particularly clear statement of the principle.

References and Recommended Reading

Much of the extant Neoplatonic material after Plotinus is not translated into English or is not translated from the Greek at all. In addition, the majority of the important secondary material is not in English. Here is a brief selection of translations and monographs primarily for the English reader.

General

Armstrong, A. H. (ed.), *The Cambridge History of Late Greek and Early Medieval Philosophy* (Cambridge, 1967). Contains extensive treatment by various scholars of the entire period and beyond.

Dillon, John, *The Middle Platonists 80 B.C. to 220 A.D.* (London, 1977). A seminal study of the most important background to Neoplatonism.

Lloyd, A. C., *The Anatomy of Neoplatonism* (Oxford, 1990). A sophisticated study of some fundamental Neoplatonic metaphysical principles. This demanding work repays careful study.

Sorabji, Richard (ed.), *Aristotle Transformed: The Ancient Commentators and Their Influence* (Ithaca, N.Y., 1990). This is a very valuable collection of essays dealing in large part with Neoplatonism as a tradition of philosophy as commentary on Aristotle.

Wallis, R. T., *Neoplatonism* (London, 2nd ed., 1995). This is a clear and comprehensive introduction to the basic themes and figures in Neoplatonism. It contains an extensive, though by no means complete, bibliography.

Plotinus and Before

Armstrong, A. H. (tr.), *The Enneads*. Seven volumes with facing Greek text (Cambridge, Mass., 1968–88)

Dillon, John, *Alcinous: The Handbook of Platonism*. Translated with Commentary (Oxford, 1993). A very useful book which ranges broadly over the history of Platonism.

des Places, Edouard, *Numénius: Fragments*. Text and Translation (Paris, 1973). An excellent French translation with many notes.

Gerson, Lloyd, *Plotinus: Arguments of the Philosophers* (London, 1994). A more advanced study that focuses mainly on the central philosophical arguments.

—— (ed.), *The Cambridge Companion to Plotinus* (Cambridge, 1996). Contains a wide range of essays on fundamental Plotinian themes.

O'Meara, Dominic, *An Introduction to the Enneads* (Oxford, 1993). A very useful introduction that follows in its exposition the order of the *Enneads* given by Porphyry.

Rist, John, *Plotinus: The Road to Reality* (Cambridge, 1967). A balanced and penetrating study.

Porphyry and Iamblichus

des Places E. (tr.), *Les mystères d'Egypt* (Paris, 1966). A French translation included here because of its major importance.

Dodds, E. R., *Pagan and Christian in an Age of Anxiety* (Oxford, 1965). This is an excellent study of the intellectual background of this period.

Warren E. (tr.), *Porphyry the Phoenician: Isagoge* (Toronto, 1975)

Proclus

Dodds E. R. (tr.), *The Elements of Theology* (Oxford, 2nd ed., 1963). A groundbreaking work with an indispensable commentary.

Morrow Glenn, and Dillon, John (tr.), *Proclus: Commentary on Plato's Parmenides* (Princeton, 1987).

Rosán, L. J., *The Philosophy of Proclus* (New York, 1949). Still a very useful introductory study.

Sorvanes, Lucas, *Proclus: Neo-Platonic Philosophy and Science* (Edinburgh, 1996). A challenging but useful work on the main ideas in Proclus.

After Proclus

Richard Sorabji is the general editor of a major effort to translate the vast corpus of Aristotelian commentaries into English. The series is published by Duckworth and Cornell University Press. Many of these are by Philoponus and Simplicius and are extremely valuable:

Sorabji Richard (ed.), *Philoponus and the Rejection of Aristotelian Science* (London, 1987). A collection of original studies especially useful for the history of science.

Bibliography

Ackrill, J. L., *Aristotle's Categories and De Interpretatione* (Oxford, 1963).

——, "Plato and False Belief: *Theaetetus* 187–200," *Monist* 50 (1966), 383–402.

——, "Aristotle's Definitions of *Psuche*," *Proceedings of the Aristotelian Society* 73 (1972–3), 119–33; and in Barnes, Schofield, and Sorabji 1979, 65–75.

——, "Aristotle on *Eudaimonia*," *Proceedings of the British Academy* 60 (1975), 339–59; and in Rorty 1980, 15–34.

——, "Aristotle's Theory of Definition," in E. Berti, ed., *Aristotle on Science: The Posterior Analytics* (Padua, 1980), 359–84.

Allan, D. J., "Causality Ancient and Modern," *Proceedings of the Aristotelian Society*, Suppl. Vol. 39 (1965), 1–18.

Allen, R. E., ed., *Studies in Plato's Metaphysics* (London, 1965).

Annas, J., "Knowledge and Language: The *Theaetetus* and the *Cratylus*," in Mansion 1961, 95–114.

——, *An Introduction to Plato's Republic* (Oxford, 1981).

——, *The Morality of Happiness* (Oxford, 1993).

Annas, J., and Barnes, J., *The Modes of Scepticism* (Cambridge, 1985).

Anton, J. P., and Preus, A., eds., *Essays in Ancient Greek Philosophy*, vol. 2 (Albany, 1983).

Armstrong, A. H., *Plotinus with an English Translation*, 7 vols. (Cambridge, Mass., 1966–89).

Austin, S., "The Paradox of Socratic Ignorance (How to Know That You Don't Know)," *Philosophical Topics* 15 (1987), 23–34.

Bailey, C., *Epicurus: The Extant Remains* (Oxford, 1926).

Balme, D. M., *Aristotle's Use of Teleological Explanation* (London, 1965).

Barnes, J., *Aristotle's Posterior Analytics* (Oxford, 1975).

——, *The Presocratics*, 2 vols. (London, 1979); revised in one volume (London, 1982).

——, *Early Greek Philosophy* (Harmondsworth, 1987).

——, ed., *The Complete Works of Aristotle* (Princeton, 1984).

——, ed., *The Cambridge Companion to Aristotle* (Cambridge, 1995).

Barnes, J., Schofield, M., and Sorabji, R., eds., *Articles on Aristotle*, vol. 1, *Science* (London, 1975).

——, *Articles on Aristotle*, vol. 2, *Ethics and Politics* (London, 1977).

——, *Articles on Aristotle*, vol. 3, *Metaphysics* (London, 1979).

——, *Articles on Aristotle*, vol. 4, *Psychology and Aesthetics* (London, 1979).

Benson, H., "The Priority of Definition and the Socratic Elenchus," *Oxford Studies in Ancient Philosophy* 8 (1990), 19–65.

——, "Misunderstanding the 'What is F-ness' Question," *Archiv für Geschichte der Philosophie* 72 (1990), 125–42.

——, "The Dissolution of the Problem of the Elenchus," *Oxford Studies in Ancient Philosophy* 13 (1995), 45–112.

——, ed., *Essays on the Philosophy of Socrates* (New York, 1992), 123–36.

Bolton, R., "Definition and Scientific Method in Aristotle's *Posterior Analytics* and *Generation of Animals*," in A. Gotthelf and J. G. Lennox, eds., *Philosophical Issues in Aristotle's Biology* (Cambridge, 1987), 120–66.

Bostock, D., "Plato on 'is not'," *Oxford Studies in Ancient Philosophy* 2 (1984), 89–120.

——, *Plato's Phaedo* (Oxford, 1986).

——, *Plato's Theaetetus* (Oxford, 1988).

Brickhouse T., and Smith, N., *Plato's Socrates* (Oxford, 1994).

Brown, L., "Being in the *Sophist*, a Syntactical Enquiry," *Oxford Studies in Ancient Philosophy* 4 (1986), 49–70.

Burnyeat, M. F., ed., *The Theaetetus of Plato* (Indianapolis, 1990).

Charlton, W., *Aristotle's Physics*, 2 vols. (Oxford, 1970).

Clark, S. R. L., *Aristotle's Man: Speculations upon Aristotelian Anthropology* (Oxford, 1975).

Cohen, S. Marc, "Socrates on the Definition of Piety," *Journal of the History of Philosophy* 9 (1971), 1–13.

——, "The Logic of the Third Man," *Philosophical Review* 80 (1971), 448–75.

Cornford, F. M., *Plato's Theory of Knowledge* (London, 1935).

Cooper, J. M., "Plato on Sense-Perception and Knowledge (*Theaetetus* 184–6)," *Phronesis* 15 (1970), 123–46.

——, *Reason and Human Good in Aristotle* (Cambridge, Mass., 1975).

——, "Plato's Theory of Human Motivation," *History of Philosophy Quarterly* 1 (1985), 3–21.

——, ed., *Plato: Complete Works* (Indianapolis, 1996).

Crombie, I. M., *An Examination of Plato's Doctrines*, 2 vols. (London, 1962, 1963).

Cross, A. C., and Woozley, A. D., *Plato's Republic: A Philosophical Commentary* (London, 1964).

Dahl, N., *Practical Reason, Aristotle, and Weakness of the Will* (Minnesota, 1984).

De Romilly, J., *The Great Sophists in Periclean Athens*, trans. by J. Lloyd (Oxford, 1992).

Devereux, D., "Aristotle on the Essence of Happiness," in O'Meara 1981, 247–60.

——, "The Unity of the Virtues in Plato's *Protagoras* and *Laches*," *Philosophical Review* 101 (1992), 765–89.

Diels, H., and Kranz, W., *Die Fragmente der Vorsokratiker*, 10th ed. (Berlin, 1960).

Everson, S., ed., *Companions to Ancient Thought*, vol. 1: *Epistemology* (Cambridge, 1990).

Everson, S., ed., *Companions to Ancient Thought*, vol. 2: *Psychology* (Cambridge, 1991).

Everson, S., ed., *Companions to Ancient Thought*, vol. 3: *Language* (Cambridge, 1994).

Everson, S., ed., *Companions to Ancient Thought*, vol. 4: *Ethics* (Cambridge, 1998).

Fine, G., "Knowledge and Belief in *Republic* V–VII," *Archiv für Gesichte der Philosophie* 60 (1978), 121–39; and in Everson 1990, 173–206.

——, "False Belief in the *Theaetetus*," *Phronesis* 24 (1979), 70–80.

——, "Knowledge and *Logos* in the *Theaetetus*," *Philosophical Review* 88 (1979), 366–97.

Gallop, D., "The Socratic Paradox in the *Protagoras*," *Phronesis* 9 (1964), 117–29.

——, "Image and Reality in Plato's *Republic*," *Archiv für Gesichte der Philosophie* 47 (1965), 113–31.

Gerson, L., and Inwood, B., eds., *Hellenistic Philosophy: Introductory Readings* (Indianapolis, 1988).

Gomez-Lóbo, A., *The Foundations of Socratic Ethics* (Indianapolis, 1994).

Gosling, J. C. B., *Plato* (London, 1973).

——, *Plato's Philebus* (Oxford, 1975).

Gotthelf, A., "Aristotle's Conception of Final Causality," *Review of Metaphysics* 30 (1976), 226–54.

——, ed., *Aristotle on Nature and Living Things: Philosophical and Historical Studies* (Pittsburgh: 1975).

Guthrie, W. K. C., *A History of Greek Philosophy*, vol. 1: *The Earlier Presocratics and the Pythagoreans* (Cambridge, 1962).

——, *A History of Greek Philosophy*, vol. 2: *The Presocratic Tradition from Parmenides to Democritus* (Cambridge, 1965).

——, *A History of Greek Philosophy*, vol. 3: *The Fifth-Century Enlightenment* (Cambridge, 1969).

——, *A History of Greek Philosophy*, vol. 4: *Plato the Man and his Dialogues: Earlier Period* (Cambridge, 1975).

——, *A History of Greek Philosophy*, vol. 5: *The Later Plato and the Academy* (Cambridge, 1978).

——, *A History of Greek Philosophy*, vol. 6: *Aristotle: An Encounter* (Cambridge, 1981).

Hamlyn, D. W., *Aristotle's De Anima Books II, III*, 2nd ed. (Oxford, 1995).

Hankinson, R. J., *Cause and Explanation in Ancient Greek Thought* (Oxford, 1998).

Hussey, E., *The Presocratics* (London, 1972).

Irwin, T. H., *Plato's Moral Theory* (Oxford, 1977).

——, "Aristotle's Discovery of Metaphysics," *Review of Metaphysics* 31 (1977–8), 210–29.

——, "The Metaphysical and Psychological Basis of Aristotle's Ethics," in Rorty 1980, 35–54.

——, trans., *The Nicomachean Ethics* (Indianapolis, 1985).

——, *Aristotle's First Principles* (Oxford, 1988).

——, *Classical Thought* (Oxford, 1989).

——, "Socratic Puzzles," *Oxford Studies in Ancient Philosophy* 10 (1992), 241–66.

——, *Plato's Ethics* (Oxford, 1995).

Irwin, T. H., and Fine, G., trans. and ed., *Aristotle: Selections* (Indianapolis, 1995).

Jaeger, W., *Aristotle: Fundamentals of the History of his Development*, trans. by R. Robinson, with author's corrections and additions (Oxford, 1948).

Joseph, H. W. B., *Knowledge and the Good in Plato's Republic* (Oxford, 1948).

Kerferd, G. B., *The Sophistic Movement* (Cambridge, 1981).

——, ed., *The Sophists and their Legacy.* Proceedings of the Fourth International Colloquium of Ancient Greek Philosophy at Bad Homburg 1979, Hermes Einzelschriften 44 (Weisbaden, 1981).

Kirk, G. S., Raven, J. E., and Schofield, M., *The Presocratic Philosophers*, 2nd ed. (Cambridge, 1983).

Kraut, R., "Reason, and Justice in the *Republic*," in Lee, Mourelatos, and Rorty 1973, 207–24.

——, "The Peculiar Function of Human Beings," *Canadian Journal of Philosophy* 9 (1979), 467–78.

——, "Two Conceptions of Happiness," *Philosophical Review* 88 (1979), 167–97.

——, *Aristotle on the Human Good* (Princeton, 1989).

——, "Introduction to the Study of Plato," in Kraut 1992, 1–50.

——, "The Defense of Justice in Plato's *Republic*," in Kraut 1992, 311–37.

——, ed., *The Cambridge Companion to Plato* (Cambridge, 1992).

Kullman, W., "Different Concepts of the Final Cause in Aristotle," in Gotthelf 1975, 169–76.

Kung, J., "Aristotle on Thises, Suches and the Third Man Argument," *Phronesis* 26 (1981), 207–47.

Lee, E. N., Mourelatos, A. P. D., and Rorty, R. M., eds., *Exegesis and Argument* (Assen, 1973).

Lewis, F. A., "Foul Play in Plato's *Aviary: Theaetetus* 195Bff." in Lee, Mourelatos, and Rorty 1973, 262–84.

Lloyd, G. E. R., and Owen, G. E. L., eds., *Aristotle on the Mind and the Senses: Proceedings of the Seventh Symposium Aristotelicum* (Cambridge, 1978).

Long, A. A., *Hellenistic Philosophy*, 2nd ed. (London, 1986).

——, "Socrates in Hellenistic Philosophy," *Classical Quarterly* 38 (1988), 150–71.

——, *Stoic Studies* (Cambridge, 1996).

Long, A. A., and Sedley, D., *The Hellenistic Philosophers*, 2 vols. (Cambridge, 1987).

Loux, M., "Form, Species and Predication," *Mind* 88 (1979), 1–23.

Mackenzie, M. M., "The Virtues of Socratic Ignorance," *Classical Quarterly* 38 (1988), 331–50.

Mansion, S., ed., *Aristotle et les problèmes de méthode* (Louvain, 1961).

McDowell, J. H., *Plato's Theaetetus* (Oxford, 1973).

McKirahan, R. D., *Philosophy Before Socrates* (Indianapolis, 1994).

Miller, F., *Nature, Justice, and Rights in Aristotle's Politics* (Oxford, 1995).

Mistis, P., *Epicurus' Ethical Theory: The Pleasures of Invulnerability* (Ithaca, 1988).

Murphy, N. R., *The Interpretation of Plato's Republic* (Oxford, 1951).

Nettleship, R. L., *Lectures on the Republic of Plato*, 2nd ed. (London, 1901).

O'Meara, D. J., ed., *Studies in Aristotle* (Washington, 1981).

Owen, G. E. L., "*Tithenai ta Phainomena*," in Mansion 1961, 83–103.

——, *Logic, Science and Dialectic: Collected Papers in Greek Philosophy* (London, 1986).

——, "Socrates in the Early Dialogues," in Kraut 1992, 121–69.

Rist, J. M., *Plotinus: The Road to Reality* (Cambridge, 1967).

——, *Stoic Philosophy* (Cambridge, 1969).

——, *Epicurus: An Introduction* (Cambridge, 1972).

Rorty, A. O., ed., *Essays on Aristotle's Ethics* (Berkeley, 1980).

Rudebusch, G., "Plato's Aporetic Style," *Southern Journal of Philosophy* (1989), 539–47.

Sachs, D., "A Fallacy in Plato's *Republic*," *Philosophical Review* 72 (1963), 141–58.

Sandbach, F. H., *The Stoics* (London, 1975).

Santas, G., "Plato's *Protagoras* and Explanations of Weakness," *Philosophical Review* 75 (1966), 3–33.

——, "The Socratic Fallacy," *Journal of the History of Philosophy* 10 (1972), 127–41.

——, *Socrates* (London, 1979).

——, "The Form of the Good in Plato's *Republic*," in Anton and Preus 1983, 232–63.

Schofield, M., Burnyeat, M., and Barnes, J., eds., *Doubt and Dogmatism: Studies in Hellenistic Epistemology*, 2nd ed. (Oxford, 1989).

Schofield, M., and Nussbaum, M. C., eds., *Language and Logos* (Cambridge, 1982).

Schofield, M., and Striker, G., eds., *The Norms of Nature: Studies in Hellenistic Ethics* (Cambridge, 1986).

Shields, C., *Order in Multiplicity: Homonymy in the Philosophy of Aristotle* (Oxford, 1999).

Sorabji, R., "Aristotle on Demarcating the Five Senses," *Philosophical Review* 80 (1971), 55–79.

Stough, C., *Greek Scepticism* (Berkeley, 1969).

——, "Forms and Explanation in Plato," *Phronesis* 21 (1976), 1–30.

Strang, C., "Plato's Analogy of the Cave," *Oxford Studies in Ancient Philosophy* 4 (1986), 19–34.

Taylor, C. C. W., *Plato: Protagoras* (Oxford, 1977).

Vlastos, G., "Socrates on Acrasia," *Phoenix* 23 (1969), 71–88.

——, "A Metaphysical Paradox," in *Platonic Studies*, 2nd ed. (Princeton, 1981), 43–57.

——, *Platonic Studies*, 2nd ed. (Princeton, 1981).

——, "Socrates' Disavowal of Knowledge," *Philosophical Quarterly* 35 (1985).

——, "Is the Socratic Fallacy Socratic?" *Ancient Philosophy* 10 (1990), 1–16.

——, *Socrates, Ironist and Moral Philosopher* (Cambridge, 1991).

——, *Socratic Studies* (Cambridge, 1994).

——, ed., *Plato*, vol. 1: *Metaphysics and Epistemology* (Garden City, 1971).

——, ed., *Plato*, vol. 2: *Ethics, Politics, and Philosophy of Art and Religion* (Garden City, 1971).

——, ed., *The Philosophy of Socrates* (Garden City, 1971).

von Arnim, H., *Stoicorum veterum fragmenta*, 3 vols. (Leipzig, 1903–5); vol. 4, indexes by M. Adler (Leipzig, 1924).

Walsh, J. J., "The Socratic Denial of Akrasia," in Bailey 1926, 235–63.

Wallis, R. T., *Neoplatonism* (London, 1972).

Whitehead, A. N., *Process and Reality: An Essay in Cosmology* (New York, 1929).

Williams, B., "The Analogy of City and Soul in Plato's *Republic*," in Lee, Mourelatos, and Rorty 1973, 196–206.

Woods, M. J., *Aristotle's Eudemian Ethics, Books I, II, and VIII*, 2nd ed. (Oxford, 1992).

Index

CPSIA information can be obtained at www.ICGtesting.com
Printed in the USA
BVOW02s2126021213

337903BV00004B/27/P